When Dreams Collide

Travels in Yugoslavia with Rebecca West

When Dreams Collide
Travels in Yugoslavia with Rebecca West

Nicholas Allan

NINE
ELMS

When Dreams Collide

First published in 2022 by
Nine Elms Books
Unit 6B
Clapham North Arts Centre
26–32 Voltaire Road
London SW4 6DH
Email: info@nineelmsbooks.co.uk
nineelmsbooks.co.uk

ISBN print: 978-1-910533-63-5
ISBN e-book: 978-1-910533-64-2

Copyright © 2022 Nicholas Allan

Protected by copyright under the terms of the International Copyright Union.
The rights of Nicholas Allan to be identified as the author of this work have been asserted by him in accordance with the Copyright, Designs and Patents Act, 1988. All rights reserved.

This book is sold under the condition that no part of it may be reproduced, copied, stored in a retrieval system or transmitted in any form or by any means electronic, mechanical, photocopying, recording or otherwise without prior permission of the author.

Every effort has been made to contact all copyright holders. The publishers will be pleased to amend in future editions any errors or omissions brought to their attention.

A CIP catalogue record of this is available from the British Library.

Cover illustration and maps: Philip Kerr
Cover design: Lyn Davies
Text design, typesetting and layout: Dominic Horsfall

Printed and bound in the UK by the CPI Group (UK) Ltd.
Set in Savoy Pro.

Picture credits: National Portrait Gallery [1]; Octopus on the Slovenian Wikipedia project [10]; *La Serbie Glorieuse* [15]; Office of the President of Kosovo [16]; Getty Images [18]; Nikolai Karaneschev [21]; Government of the United Kingdom [22]; Monastery of Sremska Ravanica-Vrdnik 23]; Darko Vijinovic/AP/Shutterstock [29]; Council.gov.ru [31]; Ministry of National Education Republic of Turkey [36]; NI Institute and Museum Bitola [40]; Helene C. Stikkel [48]; Mikhail Evstafiev [49]; Associated Press/Shutterstock [54]; Mark Reinstein/Zuma Press/Profimedia [66]; Peter Northall/EPA/Shutterstock [71]. All other photographs courtesy of the author.

Every effort was made to identify and correctly attribute the copyright holder of the images in this book. In some cases, this has not been possible and no infringement is intended.

To Sarah

Contents

Author's Note	ix
Introduction	15
MONTENEGRO	23
KOSOVO	45
SERBIA	79
NORTH MACEDONIA	161
BOSNIA AND HERZEGOVINA	203
CROATIA	259
Epilogue	323
Acknowledgements	331
List of Key Events	333
List of Selected Rulers	335
Nemanjić Dynasty	337
Petrović-Njegoš Dynasty	338
Karadjordjević Dynasty	339
Obrenović Dynasty	340
Bibliography	341
Index	347

Author's Note

I have followed Rebecca West's journeys in *Black Lamb and Grey Falcon* as thoroughly as I was able, but like her I have at times combined multiple trips to the same place into a single narrative and ordered the travels to help continuity. I also copied her decision to exclude Slovenia from my itinerary. In an effort to improve readability, any unattributed quotes, including those on the chapter title pages, are West's.

Unless otherwise indicated, I have tried to use current place names throughout, as referred to in the relevant countries.

I have chosen standard Anglicisations of local words where I feel they aid comprehension or are widely accepted international standards, such as *Yugoslavia* or *Chetnik*.

Various terms are used as shorthand, so I tend to refer to Bosnia and Herzegovina as *Bosnia*, unless trying to make specific points about their combined nature or internal differences. I often describe Bosnian Muslims as *Bosniaks*; they have also been known as Turks over the years, but that would now be considered pejorative.

Kosovan means a resident of Kosovo. *Kosovar* and *Albanian* I use interchangeably in the context of the majority Kosovan population.

Given the recent history of the name change, *Macedonia* may appear for what is now officially North Macedonia. When I refer to *Macedonian* in ethnic terms, this means Macedonian Slav.

In historical sections, I often write *Austrian*, *Austro-Hungarian* and *Hapsburg* interchangeably, as I do *Ottoman* and *Turk*. The *Sublime Porte* is commonly used as a variant on the Ottoman government in Istanbul.

I have used *Chetnik* as shorthand for the broad grouping of royalist resistance groupings in Yugoslavia in the Second World War, also known as the Ravna Gora movement.

Various towns have changed their names over history, among them Rijeka/Fiume, Dubrovnik/Ragusa, Thessaloniki/Salonika. I have tried to pick the one that makes the most sense in context and hope not to have added confusion.

I often use *The Hague* as shorthand for the International Criminal Tribunal for the former Yugoslavia.

Serbian and *Croatian* are descriptives for the nationals of those countries, while *Serb* and *Croat* refer to those who claim the relevant ethnicity, especially if they live outside the relevant country's borders, such as Croatian Serbs.

Where relevant, I have tried to render names in their most commonly accepted transliterations.

The following table should aid pronunciation in Serbo-Croat:

Serbo-Croat	English approximation	Sample English word
c	ts	po*ts*
č	ch	*ch*eck
ć	tch	(roughly) ma*tch*
dž	j	*j*am
dj	dj	(roughly) sche*du*le
j	y	*y*ear
š	sh	*sh*arp
ž	zh	televi*si*on

"Somewhere far away in the world the dice had been thrown, the battles fought, and it was there that the fate of each of the townsfolk was decided."

Ivo Andrić
The Bridge over the Drina

HUNGARY
N
ROMANIA
ZEGOVINA
SERBIA
BULGARIA
MONTENEGRO
KOSOVO
ALBANIA
NORTH MACEDONIA
GREECE
AEGEAN SEA

Introduction

In 2012, I called a halt to my 32-year career and tried to picture what the rest of my life might look like. I had a comfortable middle-class upbringing – privately educated, followed by a career in finance that included long spells in both America and Asia. There was one slight area of obscurity. My mother's family was Anglo-Saxon and my father's Jewish, a fact that I was still unaware of in my early teens when I came home from school one day and repeated an off-colour anti-Semitic joke. My mother pulled me up sharply, telling me that it was both unfunny and unacceptable, and all the worse for my being half-Jewish.

I subsequently learned that my grandfather had Anglicised his family name of Abrahams in the 1920s, and that he and his two young sons had later converted to Catholicism, to the great distress of my still Jewish grandmother. A major cause was the prevalent anti-Semitism of the time, but its continuing undercurrents meant that my father was always reluctant to discuss his family background. Sadly, both my father and uncle died young, so now, with time on my hands, I thought that I would try to learn more about my unknown paternal family with the help of a researcher. The informative report that emerged traced each line of my father's family back to the early 19th century. Some of my ancestors were from longstanding Anglo-Jewish families, but around half had come to England in the early parts of the 19th century from the Azov region of Russia, from "Russian Poland", and much the biggest concentration from villages around Posen in Prussia (now Poznan, Poland).

For as long as I could remember in my working life, my diary had been programmed for months in advance, in 30- or 60-minute chunks. I felt that, subconsciously, I had begun to measure my worth by the number of meetings that I could achieve in a day. As I looked at the yawning gaps in my diary and felt the stirrings of inadequacy, I decided that I should tackle this conditioning head-on, while also investigating my family roots. I booked a flight to Krakow, a hotel on arrival, a hire car and a flight out of Poznan two weeks later. I thought that, armed with a guidebook and a history of Poland, I would explore at my leisure and refuse to even think about the details of my trip more than a day in advance. I would also visit three of the ancestral villages to see what I could glean. This latter part of the trip proved a disappointment – there was no sign of a Jewish presence in the unremarkable villages. Any trace had been obliterated by the horrors of the Holocaust and the destruction of war and time. The great synagogue at Poznan, which had once seated 1,200 of the faithful, had been turned into a communal swimming pool during the war.

In other cities, there was more to see. In the cemeteries in the old Jewish quarter in Krakow, small stones were balanced on antique gravestones with pieces of paper rolled up and stuffed in their nooks and crannies in a way that spoke of ritual and an active connection to the past. As I wandered around the overgrown Jewish cemetery in Wrocław (formerly Breslau in eastern Prussia), I marvelled at the abilities and achievements of the dead buried there: professors, doctors, artists and civic leaders commemorated by monuments of real grandeur. It brought home to me the criminal stupidity of the Nazi regime in addition to its evil; not only determining to exterminate an entire race but wiping out so many of its most capable and educated citizens in the process. At Auschwitz, the scale of the horror became even more apparent. The size of the platform at Birkenau, where the trains pulled in bearing their death-bound cargoes, was such that it was hard to make out one end from the other. The remains of the rows of huts that housed the one-in-five arrivals selected for work – over instant extermination – stretched to the horizon. The ruins of the gas chambers were the size of factories. The industrial process of the slaughter was almost beyond comprehension.

Outside my personal quest, Poland was enlightening. The grand town squares of what had once been eastern Prussia were exquisite, and I was intrigued by the turbulent past of the region. In the 16th century, the Polish-Lithuanian Commonwealth had been one of the largest countries in Europe, ruling the present-day Baltic states, Belarus and much of Ukraine. It even briefly controlled Moscow. However, the Polish heartland is a broad plain, hard to defend and sandwiched between powerful nations. Since its peak, it had suffered repeatedly as each of the Swedes, the Russians, the Prussians, the Hapsburgs and the Germans sought at different times to control or partition it. For the last 300 years, being trapped between great or would-be empires had been a very painful place to be.

I marvelled at the beauty of the historic buildings: ruined castles on hilltops, the grandness of the heart of Wrocław around its canals and the quirky architecture (to my eyes) of the old buildings in many towns. Most of all, I found myself profoundly moved by some of the churches, with their faded frescoes and ancient icons and relics. The intensity of devotion over the years, still evident today, imparted a physical energy to these spaces and instilled in me a sense of awe as I seemed to glimpse something beyond humanity. As I gazed on the image of the Black Madonna at Częstochowa, most likely a Byzantine icon from the 6th-9th century, but ascribed by some to St Luke, I felt a real sense of peace and a spiritual connection to a greater force.

On a more mundane level, travelling through Poland was a delight. There were very few other tourists, which meant that local people with whom one fell into conversation were charming and communicative. The food was mostly simple, but fresh and delicious. I enjoyed discovering dishes like sour rye soup and *pierogi* (Polish dumplings), and occasionally found real treats like baked goat's cheese with rowanberry mousse. After a single attempt, I resolved never to eat carp again.

I found my mood improving and my anxiety about the future subsiding by the day. I returned home with a new sense of calm but also an intense curiosity about Eastern Europe. I had seen how rich and different its culture and history were to that of my upbringing, but also how that history shed new light for me on the received wisdom of my Anglo-centric education.

I also reflected on the spirituality that I had encountered in Poland and the moments when I had sensed a dimension beyond day-to-day planning and cultural exploration. If I were to evolve from the well-ordered life of my past, it felt necessary to explore further some of the new threads that I had relished on my recent travels. Reading more widely, I turned my compass south to the Balkans, with Rebecca West's magnum opus, *Black Lamb and Grey Falcon*, as my guide. First published in 1941, its 1,150 pages chronicled a history of ancient empire, the trials of domination by the great imperial powers over centuries and the almost Ruritanian manoeuvrings post-independence, all set against a background of a world moving inexorably towards war. I found it completely absorbing. Given the Slavic connection, much of it resonated with what I had learned in Poland, but there were some very different angles too, not to mention West's astonishing turn of phrase.

Six months later, I set off again, this time flying into Dubrovnik with a plan to explore the mountainous highlands of Montenegro next door. I had assumed that Cetinje (the old royal capital) would be a good starting point in terms of both convenience and interesting local colour. Little did I suspect that this tucked-away town above the Adriatic would also mark a watershed in my own personal quest. The past and present seemed to merge here in a way that made me long to know more about this tiny nation, but also its large extended family.

Serbia, like Poland, had been a great power in its time, although its peak had been in the 14th century. The Balkan peninsula sat between both the great powers and the great religions of the region. Much of its Slavic population are closely related ethnically but live on the border of East and West, divided by the schism in the Christian Church between Byzantium and Rome. In fact, Slav population migrations into the peninsula towards the end of the first millennium CE are one of the elements that helped to prompt the split by separating the two traditions geographically. Later, the rise of the Ottoman Empire added another creed to the mix.

Over time, each religion came to be associated with a great power – Catholic Austria-Hungary, Orthodox Russia and Muslim Turkey. Other outside political influences played their parts. The Venetians and Italians, and even briefly Napoleon, had interests on the Adriatic coast. Britain meddled more in the heartland, particularly from the late 19th century onwards, as it sought to balance the interests of its imperial rivals. The growth of distinct nationalisms in the 19th century and their increasing identification with specific religions created opportunities for politics of division and sowed the seeds of the tragedies of the last hundred years or more. Much of the militarisation of the broader peninsula in the early 20th century was enabled by the imperial powers, who had also set the examples that the Balkan powers sought to emulate in their own ways. The ethnically separate Muslim Albanian populations in the south added yet another layer of complexity to the whole.

Despite these divisions, the myriad religious buildings throughout the region demonstrate how closely and for how long these various faiths have cohabited. Each has its own energy. I, although a Catholic, find myself deeply moved by Orthodox frescoes. There is a power and almost savagery about the best examples that engage me in character and emotional understanding in a way that many idealised images of the Western Church do not. At the other end of the spectrum, the peace and harmony of an ancient mosque can convey an essence of pure spirituality that transcends denomination. In the atmosphere of many of the old places of worship around the region, I find something deeper imbued by the centuries of prayer and contemplation that have taken place there. The sense of competition with other faiths can add an intensity and at times a discordancy, but the spirituality rises above by and large. West's major underlying theme was the tension between the purity and strength of tradition and religion on the one hand, and their darker aspects on the other. This seems as relevant as ever.

As I made my initial foray into inland Montenegro, I was again charmed by the friendliness of the people, the absence of foreign tourists, the fresh local food and the variety of landscapes. I wanted to travel further and understand better the turns of history, not least as West's account finishes on the brink of the Second World War. I could still see much of the charm that she had described, but the ravages of that conflict, the Tito years and their bloody aftermath have since left strong footprints. I read several exceptionally interesting and well-written histories of the region and its constituent parts, but they failed to convey to me the beauty or delight of travelling in this relatively underexplored region.

I resolved to retrace West's travels to see what remained and what had changed in the 80-year interlude. The ancient traditions of the region are evident from her writing, and she brings humanity to the protagonists of her narrative, whether 14th-century monarchs, 19th-century prelates or the people whom she met along her way. As I acquired more knowledge of my own, I found myself disagreeing with her views on some key figures (most notably the regent Prince Paul, whose attempts to protect his country in the early stages of the Second World War she viewed through the blinkered eyes of one on the receiving end of the Blitz). She did, however, always add interest and often humour. She was captivated by the romance of Serbia's Nemanjić dynasty in the Middle

Ages and the legend surrounding the death of its successor, Prince Lazar. She celebrated the second coming as the royal families of Montenegro and Serbia re-established their countries' independence from the Ottomans in the 19th century. In the process, she forgave certain nationalistic behaviours that we ourselves, with decades more history under our belts, would struggle to overlook, especially as their calamitous reverberations became more apparent.

I also loved West's fascination with the deeper roots of history; she could divert into the romance of Illyria, the destructive nature of the Roman Empire or the appeal of Manichaeism, sending me off on quests for knowledge that I have tried to ration sensibly in this book. I read a couple of her novels, which I enjoyed, but she seemed to have invested herself in *Black Lamb and Grey Falcon* in a different way. After a while, I would try to anticipate West's take on a particular subject only to be left surprised, not least with her ability to define an emotion or a scene with breath-taking acuity. If I were to continue travelling alone, she would be the great companion that, given the extent of her literary friendships she must have been in real life. Indeed, along my journey, I found myself at times falling into conversation with her, often in agreement, but also pointing out things that she had missed or mistaken.

I hope that, in the process, I have managed to update the history that she told and anchored it in the landscape that now exists, while also giving some sense of the joys and occasional difficulties of travelling there. There are some startlingly beautiful parts of the former Yugoslavia: the Dalmatian coast, the great religious treasures of southern Serbia, Kosovo and North Macedonia, the Turkish bridges, the wild mountains. But the scars of history are visible too: the tumbledown streets where no one has lived for decades, countless memorials and encounters with people whose lives have been almost impossibly hard. It is still difficult to believe that countries that have shared so much of Europe's history over the centuries could have seen such shocking violence in the 1990s, a decade when so much of the continent's east was tracking more positively. Although more recent events in Ukraine suggest it may not have been quite the anomaly that one had hoped.

The series of wars that were fought as Yugoslavia disintegrated after Tito's death were unimaginable to most of the world. The confusion between the institutions of Yugoslavia and those of its constituent states meant that the world failed to condemn an aggression masquerading as an attempt to preserve the status quo. President Milošević of Serbia claimed to be a peacekeeper as he sought to establish a Serbian territory that extended not only beyond his country's existing borders but beyond even those that the broader Serb population of the Balkans inhabited. As he launched repeated offensives in Croatia, Bosnia and Kosovo, he and his henchmen frequently laid claim to the historical mantle that West had so admired.

In following West's route, I would visit many locations where I would learn more of recent history, but I expanded my itinerary to include others that would fill in obvious gaps, and one or two with particular cultural appeal. I wanted to understand better how West's version of these lands had unfolded in the late 20th-century. I also hoped to get a sense of whether peace could persist.

In a 1941 letter to American journalist Alexander Woollcott, West wrote:

> Why should I be moved in 1936 to devote the following 5 years of my life, at great financial sacrifice and to the utter exhaustion of my mind and body, to take an inventory of a country down to its last vest-button, in a form insane from any ordinary artistic or commercial point of view – a country which ceases to exist?

There are moments when I have wondered something similar. Why did I decide to visit every identifiable destination in West's book, creating an inventory of my own in the process? All I know is that, once I had started, it gained a momentum of its own. I think that the contrast between the observations of another age and those of a contemporary eye can add a perspective not just historical, but also human, aesthetic and at times spiritual. This is not a history book, although it contains much history. It is a personal journey, and I have inevitably dwelt longest on those aspects of the journey that interested or appealed to me most. Where I have expressed opinions about events or individuals, they are just that, and they are my own. Nonetheless, I hope that in the pages that follow, I can deliver an inadequate appendix of sorts to Rebecca West's magnificent original, as well as an accessible introduction to an area whose natural appeal to travellers has been tarnished by recent history.

Montenegro

*"Though it was airy as Heaven, ...
it was stony like a cell ..."*

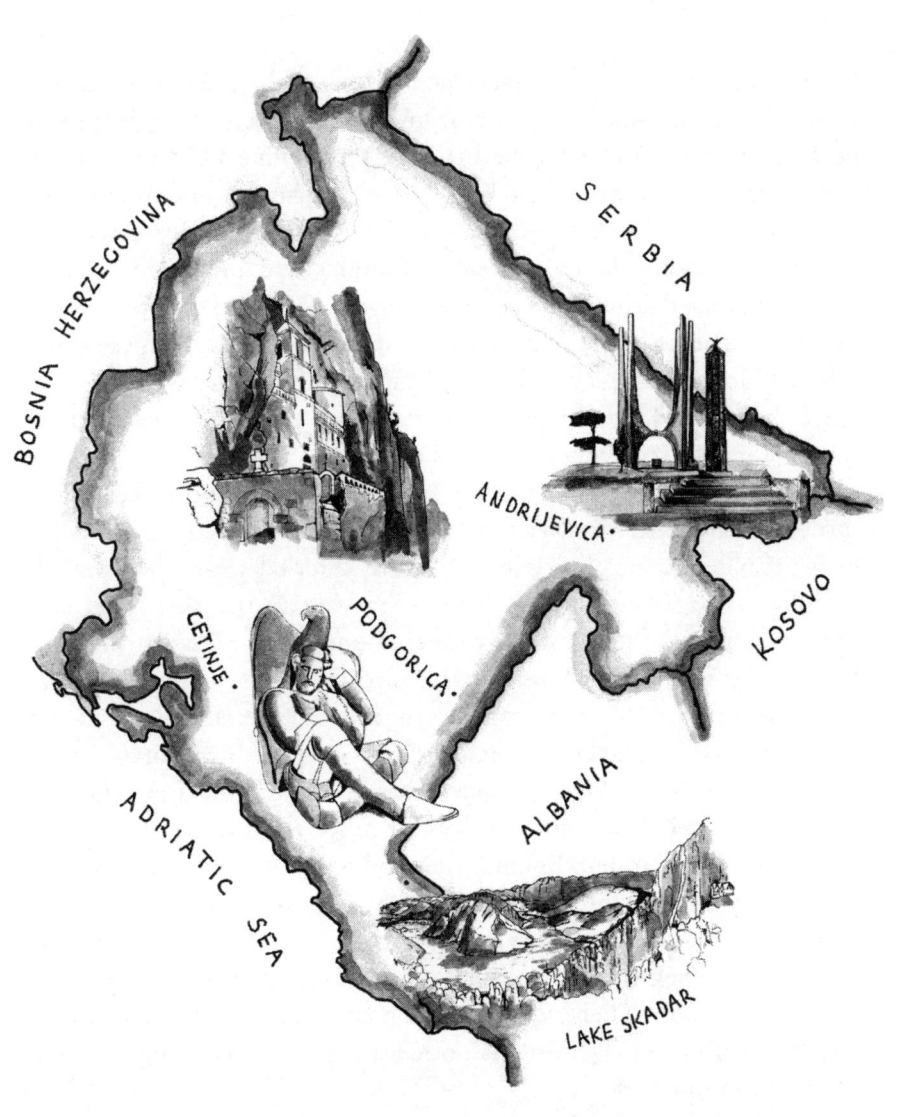

Flying into Dubrovnik, it seemed incongruous to be going in search of relics of the past when so many of my fellow passengers appeared to be embarking on a drink-fuelled tour of the southern Croatian coast. Thirty or so men wore matching red polo shirts emblazoned with "Slîppery Gîpsÿ", "Síçk Nötè" and the like. As the flight progressed and cans were cracked, the noise grew ever louder, and apparently random phrases bounced around the cabin eliciting guffaws and shouts of acclamation with each repetition. Even the middle-aged couple beside me managed to consume a gin and tonic and two small bottles of red wine apiece before we landed at 10:30 am. It seemed that I was on an entirely different mission to the rest of the plane.

Exiting the airport, most traffic turned right to Dubrovnik, while I turned south to drive down a typically Mediterranean coastal road with brilliant blue sea on the right, the shore studded with white-walled, red-tiled villages and stone churches basking in the sun. The land rose steeply to the left, initially to the mountains of Herzegovina, and before long to those of Montenegro. Already a sense emerged of one of the many divides of the former Yugoslavia (literally, "land of the southern Slavs"). The coastal belt of Dalmatia (the Illyria of ancestry) is part of the wider Mediterranean world, looking out towards Italy over the Adriatic Sea, with a history of occupation by the Venetians, Napoleon, the Ottoman Empire, Austria-Hungary, Mussolini and others. Meanwhile, in the mountains to the left, occupation had never been effective. The Ottomans had nominal control for a few centuries, but the Montenegrins had long had a reputation for independence and warlike behaviour. Their rulers had been adept at using this reputation to play great powers against each other and so preserve a high degree of self-determination.

Before long, the landscape opened up on the approach to the Bay of Kotor, shaped like an over-enthusiastically pinned butterfly. The twin islets of the Monastery of St George and the Church of Our Lady of the Rocks floated far out in the water like mirages. Time paused.

At the furthest corner of the bay is Kotor. High on the town wall was the winged lion of St Mark, signalling the earlier presence of the Venetians. Wandering through the alleys and "handkerchief-wide squares", this was still a world familiar to anyone who has been to Greece or Italy for a summer holiday. In the growing warmth of spring, the cool of the shade was welcome. In winter, Kotor has a reputation for bitter coldness, sitting as it does in the grey stone shadow of the mountain that was my destination.

Each of the twenty-five hairpin bends on the way up had been numbered by hand in paint, and with every about-turn the view broadened again. At the top, I looked out over the bay and the tree-covered coast beyond to a deep blue sea dissolving into the marginally paler blue of the sky at the horizon. It might have been the end of the world. Behind me, a much bleaker landscape awaited. Limestone ridges unevenly patched with scrubby vegetation undulated as far as the eye could see. I understood now why the Ottomans would have struggled to subdue the country, and questioned why they had even bothered, other than for the sake of completism. Occasionally, a cluster of red roofs stood out. The road passed through the small settlement of Njeguši, the ancestral village of the Petrović dynasty who dominated Montenegrin history for so long. Boards by farmhouses and cottages advertised homemade smoked ham, cheese, wine and mead in a variety of unlikely spellings.

Cetinje

At last, cresting yet another ridge, appeared Cetinje, the old capital of Montenegro, lying in a shallow green bowl. Rebecca West described the solid stone architecture of the buildings as puritanical, but on a sunny day in May there was much greater variation. It is a curious mixture of the humdrum, the rustically picturesque and the grand. The town square and tree-lined streets were full of umbrellas from competing cafes, many of the old houses were painted in pastel shades, and at odd intervals architectural curiosities held my gaze. They were evidence of the age of Nikola I, "father-in-law of Europe", who reigned here from 1860 until his forced departure to France during the First World War. Here, the great powers built embassies in their own national styles: the British red stucco "cottage" with white pilasters and windows that would look more at home in an Edwardian Channel resort; the Russian red baroque palace; the grand classical style of the Italian; the almost Art Deco French offering with mosaic-like bands of decorative tiles. The Turkish embassy was a long, low, acid-green bunkhouse with tightly boarded ground-floor windows, now the state school of drama. Grandest of all was the white Austro-Hungarian edifice with tiled roof, stone facings and chapel attached. All the key players in the late 19th century imperial waltz had a base in this small mountainous enclave.

Nikola was the last ruler from the line of prince-bishops (or *vladikas*) of Montenegro and the country's only king. As Orthodox bishops were enjoined to celibacy, the title had moved down from uncle to nephew over the generations until Nikola's uncle Danilo had renounced the episcopal role to facilitate his marriage and introduced a more traditional hereditary system for the secular aspect of his rule. Much of the early part of Nikola's reign was spent fending off the Ottoman Empire with sporadic support from each of Austria-Hungary, France, Britain and especially Russia. In 1876, Montenegro and Serbia led simultaneous attacks on their much-weakened adversary, and the Montenegrin successes (which continued long after the Serbs had been forced to agree a settlement) led to a doubling of the size of their territory and the gain of the key towns of Nikšić and Podgorica. They also finally gained access to the Adriatic at Bar, although the great powers restricted its use for any martial purposes in order to allay their fears of Russian encroachment. The secret of their remarkable success was ascribed by Stillman of *The Times* thus: "The generalship on both sides is bad, but on that of the Turks atrocious". Montenegrin troops were also notoriously bloodthirsty.

Montenegro was a *cause célèbre* in the great cities of Europe. We hear in casual Muscovite conversation in *Anna Karenina* that the Montenegrins are "born fighters". It was the subject of a speech and article by Gladstone and a sonnet by Tennyson:

> Great Tsernogora! never since thine own
> Black ridges drew the cloud and brake the storm
> Has breathed a race of mightier mountaineers.

Montenegro was also the model for Pontevedro in Franz Lehár's *The Merry Widow*, which opened in Vienna in 1905 and quickly became popular, despite Montenegrin protests at being lampooned. The first Italian performance in Trieste in 1907, conducted by Lehár himself, had to be halted for a quarter of an hour while fifty-odd members of the audience were removed for protesting that Italians should not offend Montenegro when their royal families were related.

Even F. Scott Fitzgerald referred to "little Montenegro down on the Adriatic Sea". *The Great Gatsby* shows off his "Orderi di Danilo", ostensibly bestowed on him by "Nicolas Rex" for gallantry in the First World War, although the obscure nature of the decoration was presumably designed to cast doubt on Gatsby's professed life story.

Nikola was a remarkably skilful matchmaker. Four of his daughters were educated in Russia, two marrying grand dukes. These two, spiritually inclined, became close to the tsarina and are believed to have introduced Rasputin to her. Their husbands both had important military posts and were leading figures in the pro-war camp in the run-up to 1914. Another sister married Peter Karadjordjević, subsequently King Peter l of Serbia, although he was widowed by the time of his accession. Grandest of all was the marriage of Nikola's fifth daughter, Elena, to Victor Emmanuel of Italy, over whom she towered; in pictures he would stand while she sat in an attempt to obscure the difference in height. In order to overcome the difficulty of conversion to Catholicism for a bride from a staunchly Orthodox country, she was welcomed into the Catholic Church in a ceremony on board the boat taking her from Bar to Bari.

Nikola's sixth daughter, Anna, married Franz Joseph of Battenberg, a cousin of Queen Victoria twice over by marriage. The queen appears to have found Nikola engaging company on his two visits to Windsor Castle and admired his national dress. He was clearly shrewd and educated but inclined to hide it behind a buffoonish exterior. He needed all his guile to rule over a country riven by blood feuds. Tito's Montenegrin commander, Milovan Djilas, told of the killings of his great-grandfather, both grandfathers, father, uncle and both brothers over the generations "as though a dread curse lay upon them ... The inherited fear and hatred of feuding clans was mightier than fear and hatred of the enemy, the Turks. It seems to me that I was born with blood on my eyes."

Nikola showed skill at using his countrymen's naturally warlike nature to Montenegro's – but especially his own – advantage. Relatively early in his reign, he was believed to have sold Russian wheat sent for famine relief to his starving people for personal gain. In the First Balkan War, he besieged the Albanian city of Scutari (now Shkodër), finally taking it with more difficulty than he had expected after a likely bribe to the Ottoman commander whose position had become hopeless. Nikola then withdrew his troops in the wake of protests from the great powers who felt that the balance of peace had been endangered, but only once he had secured a large foreign loan. He is also believed to have positioned aggressively on stock markets in order to profit from his imminent retreat. He had hoped to use his military successes to emerge as king of the south Slavs, but the First World War put a stop to that. He had already lost popularity given the inadequacy of his heir and his country's strained finances after so many years of war. The contrast between Nikola's unpopular surrender to Austria-Hungary in early 1916, nine days after the Austrians had attacked with Bosnian Muslim support, and the heroic withdrawal of his son-in-law, Peter of Serbia, over the mountains meant that there was only one realistic candidate in 1918 for the royal role. Recognising Nikola's self-serving behaviour, West commented on the irony that he was nonetheless "noble and romantic in appearance, and looked like the genial father of his people", postcards depicting him "with his stately Queen on his arm, walking like Jupiter and Juno through the garlanded streets". He died in exile clutching a Montenegrin stone that he had carried with him as he fled the Austrians. His son, Danilo, a chip off the old block, busied himself in exile by selling off his Montenegrin real estate, as well as some state forests, to buyers from the invading power.

Nikola and his queen, Milena, were eventually reburied in the small Court Church on the ruins of the original monastery site in Cetinje when their remains returned from Italy in 1989. The ceremony was attended by a quarter of Montenegro's population, now free to express nationalist feeling again in a more federally strained world, although not sufficiently enthused to sway elections the next year, when the Communist Party retained power with ease. A good array of regal postcards is still for sale at the Royal Mausoleum.

My quarters in Cetinje were not regal. The Hotel Grand was a Soviet-style reconstruction of an earlier hotel, badly damaged in the

1979 earthquake. The brutalist concrete exterior led to a gloomy reception area, from where I was indicated to the stairs. The stairwell was a vicious chemical yellow giving way to a series of long corridors of dark wood, down one of which I found my room. There was some compensation for the absence of hot water in the delicious Njeguški kebab that I found at a nearby restaurant, four enormous pieces of pork wrapped around smoked ham and cheese in a sensory overload of texture, smell and taste. I somehow finished it in a feeble attempt to establish my mountain credentials.

In the morning, I skirted the main town towards the monastery. It came into view across a meadow golden with buttercups and surrounded by trees full of early spring freshness. The imposing stone building ascended the base of the hill, with sturdy colonnades on each side flanking a central tower. An elaborately framed gold icon glinted from an archway high to the left. The monastery originally dates from the 15th century but was rebuilt several times as a result of the ravages of fire and war before the basis of the current building was erected in 1786.

The main gate, surmounted by a fresco of Christ and two angels, guarded a flight of stone stairs into a small sunlit courtyard. A stocky figure in a white T-shirt and jeans directed me to the chapel on one side and the shop on the other. The chapel walls were arrayed with a variety of icons and religious images of varying ages and charm. The gold-painted iconostasis, shielding the inner sanctum from the laity, soared above, displaying painted rows of saints and the blessed – examples to aspire to, carriers of one's prayers to the Almighty and possibly witnesses to one's conduct. High up, a painted crucifix of Christ was flanked by two sea serpents, representing both wisdom and evil (as personified by the snake in the Garden of Eden).

I looked around for the jewelled golden casket that contained the mummified right hand of St John the Baptist and a shard of the True Cross. I could see no sign of it, but my attention was piqued by a relatively modern wooden sarcophagus standing by the wall in the window. I resumed my study of the screen. A few minutes passed and a young monk walked in dressed in black robes, a ponytail emerging from his woollen monastic cap. He was followed by a small devout party. Walking straight to the sarcophagus, he opened it to reveal a glass cover beneath. Each of his group walked up to the box in turn, crossed themselves (right to left in the Orthodox way), gazed at the glass in deep reverence and kissed the surface at three different points. I joined the end of the line, and when my turn came, there in a jewelled container was a shrunken brown hand with the index and middle fingers extended. Beside it was a small, jewelled cross whose glass core revealed a sliver of wood. Both sat at the feet of a figure draped in gold cloth. Another mummified hand protruded from the sleeve of the left arm that lay across his chest. The monk informed me that this was St Petar of Cetinje. I looked reverently at each and kissed the glass accordingly. The idea that I might be looking at the hand of the Forerunner, the hand that had baptised Christ, and a piece of the cross on which Jesus had died struck a deep elemental note. I stood in contemplation for some time. It was only later that I reflected on the curious conjunction of the relics. St Petar, the most revered of the prince-bishops, had undoubtedly achieved much for his people; but he was also a fearsome leader of his troops in battle, who fell on their enemy "like wolves on a white flock" according to one contemporary traveller.

As I left the chapel, the monk described to me the travels of the hand of the Baptist over the years. It had been part of the treasures of the imperial court of Constantinople but was given to the Knights of Malta by Sultan Bayezid II when they were still based in Rhodes. It was moved to Russia in 1799 due to perceived threats to its safety from Napoleon, as Tsar Paul l was then Grand Master of the Order of Malta. The Dowager Empress of Russia, Maria Feodorovna, protected it again at the time of the Bolshevik revolution, depositing it in the Orthodox church in Berlin. When the church closed, the treasure was sent to Belgrade and in 1941 was left at Ostrog Monastery (a traditional refuge of safety in Montenegro) by King Peter II of Yugoslavia as he fled the Nazis. Thence it came to Cetinje.

I asked Brother Peter if it was possible to see the treasury, and he told me to wait a while. I examined the produce section of the shop, buying a gold-patterned bottle of raki infused with a bunch of herbs, and a jar of honey made from the wormwood flower that also produces absinthe. Peter reappeared mid-transaction, saying that one of his colleagues who spoke better English would give me a tour. Raffael introduced himself as the deacon priest and apologised for his poor English – "I have learned most of it from *World of Warcraft*." He said that many of the gifts came from Russia, "as we were like little brother". These included a detailed cloth embroidered by Catherine the Great and a remarkably lifelike 16th-century padded figure of Jesus on a silver cloth for use on "Great Friday". The robes of Petar II (Njegoš), St Petar's nephew and successor, and Nikola's forebear, were enormous – they must have been over six feet long and apparently hung only to his knee.

I asked how the treasures had been kept safe for so long when the old monastery had been destroyed by the Turks. Raffael told me that there had been a labyrinth of tunnels "stretching almost to the sea" in which they were concealed. Unfortunately, their complexity was such that the community had lost twelve bags of gold, which had never been found again. Many years later, at a time of flooding, a waterfall near the coast had started to produce gold coins, leading to a stampede among the amazed locals, although the government soon claimed the coins as their own. Somehow, this tale led on to a lesson about the schism between the Serbian Orthodox Church and the new government-sanctioned Montenegrin Orthodox Church, which was struggling to gain acceptance both from the local population and the broader Orthodox community. The divide was evidenced again in 2021 when Cetinje witnessed politically charged riots at the enthronement of the new Serbian Orthodox Metropolitan Joanikije, who arrived by army helicopter and was sheltered by bulletproof shields as he made his way to the monastery, while the police broke up nearby protests with tear gas.

Raffael observed that all Slavic Orthodox churches use language so similar that their adherents can understand each other's services. Across the former Yugoslavia, the language is essentially one, with only minor dialectal differences, although each country claims their own – Serbian, Croatian, Montenegrin and so on. "We have the brightest infants in the world here, all are geniuses as they can speak six languages."

He talked more of the Orthodox Church, almost unchanged for a thousand years. It had never adopted Catholic innovations like purgatory and celibacy. Orthodox priests marry and have children, and as a result there is no real vocational issue. He felt that natural instincts repressed at an early stage tend to re-emerge in middle age. As such, he felt that the Orthodox Church had avoided many of the scandals that had wracked the Western Churches. "With us, it is not sex but materialism", often closely entwined with politics.

I left, promising to return for vespers that evening. Raffael asked if I had a faith book. I queried this, wondering how I could follow along the Cyrillic script. After a brief exchange, I realised that he wanted to be friends on Facebook.

Nearby was the fortress-like residence of Njegoš, the Biljarda, named after the excitement of Montenegro's first billiards table arriving there in the mid-19th century. This had been hauled up from Kotor after the prince-bishop had become enamoured of the game on his European travels. A stone's throw away is the pocket-sized palace of King Nikola, subsequently extended by two wings. The original is a simple red box with shuttered white windows, from which an entrance hall and balcony jut out front-centre as if an afterthought stuck on for ceremonial purposes.

The displays in the museum around the corner continued the themes of ancient belief and bloodshed. The greatest treasure is *Our Lady of Philermos*, the Madonna barely discernible in her blue velvet surround, wreathed in jewels with a horseshoe headdress of diamond lilies and rubies against an ornate gold backdrop. Legend says that it too was painted by St Luke. It can be traced back to the Knights of Malta, from where it shared its travels with the sacred relics of the monastery, acquiring its elaborate setting in Russia en route. The museum also contains the death mask of Kara Mahmud Pasha, the renegade Ottoman Governor of Albania, who was decapitated following his defeat by St Petar's troops at the Battle of Krusi in 1796, helping to set the tone for future race relations at an early stage. The section on modern history evinced a guarded openness about the Montenegrin role in the regional horrors of the 1990s, including a *mea culpa* for the shelling of Dubrovnik, a recognition of complicity in atrocities against Muslims near the border areas with Bosnia and Herzegovina, but also a penance in the acceptance of 80,000 refugees from Kosovo in 1999.

A short, steep climb led to the Eagle's Crag, the mausoleum of Danilo, first of the Petrović dynasty, unifier of Montenegro's tribes and protégé of Peter the Great. He is lionised in his kinsman Njegoš's famous poem *The Mountain Wreath*, which tells the story of five brothers slaughtering the land's Muslim inhabitants on Danilo's orders, although it is now believed that this was a myth created around various incidents at the time. His early years in power were primarily focused on his battles with the Ottomans, eliciting support from both the Russians and Venetians in his ultimately successful quest for effective independence for Montenegro. His burial place watches over the town. A simple headstone surmounted by an Orthodox cross gives his dates of birth, accession and death. It is sheltered by a turquoise-lined canopy topped with another cross. It is a remarkably tranquil memorial to a monk who spent so much of his life in combat, even if his last years saw greater peace. This blend of religion, violence and power would recur throughout my wanderings.

On the small hill behind the monastery is the tower where Turkish heads used to be impaled for display. Sir John Gardner Wilkinson, visiting Cetinje in 1844,

> ... counted the heads of twenty Turks, fixed upon stakes, round the parapet ... and below, scattered upon the rock, were the fragments of other skulls, which had fallen to pieces by time; ... the face of one young man was remarkable; and the contraction of the upper lip, exposing a row of white teeth, conveyed an expression of horror, which seemed that he had suffered much, either from fright or pain, at the moment of death.

The tradition of taking the heads of one's enemies as trophies was always strong in Montenegro. St Petar had been reprimanded by Napoleon's Marshal Marmont for the practice, to whom he retorted: "It is surprising that you should find this practice shocking, since you French cut off the heads of your King and Queen." Fifty years on, Wilkinson remonstrated with the then *vladika*, Petar II (Njegoš), asking that the Montenegrins should give up their custom of decapitation and display. Njegoš agreed, but only on the condition that the Turks showed equal restraint. Wilkinson's request to the Vizier of Herzegovina met with a similar response – the Turks would stop taking heads if the Montenegrins did. In practice, both sides continued to head-hunt into the 20th century.

I returned to the monastery for vespers as promised, where Raffael explained that as a man, I should stand on the right, while women stood on the left. Almost at once, a large woman dressed in black stood directly in front of me; I wondered if she was a nun and thus above lay rules or had positioned herself deliberately to block me, an apostate, from getting too close to the sanctuary. The congregation slowly grew. Each new arrival went on a circuit of the chapel, visiting a succession of icons (worshipping *through* them, rather than them directly). All kissed a few key images, some went on an extended tour of the chapel's artefacts. Meanwhile, no action was visible for the first 15 minutes, although prayer was audible from behind the screen. After a while, priests started to emerge and sing, the congregation joined in, and exotic melodies built to create an almost physical presence inside the chapel walls. A ringing sound preceded Raffael's emergence from behind the iconostasis carrying a censer with bells suspended on its chains. Each member of the congregation and several icons were blessed with a sonorous waft of incense. Towards the end of the service, the entire congregation lined up to kiss the great treasures of the monastery, which had been exposed once more. I headed back to the hotel ruminating on the incongruous collection that I had now witnessed twice, but also on the breadth of Raffael's congregation, young and old, clearly engaged by his humanity and humour. I was sure that the traumas of recent history must have further fuelled the search for spiritual comfort.

The next morning, I drove some ten miles to the top of Mount Lovćen to see the cemetery of Njegoš, the great poet prince-bishop, described by West as having "a genius of the Miltonic sort". *The Mountain Wreath* was the touchstone of local nationalism in the 19th century. Djilas described its popularity as he read it aloud in his village as a youth; his audience "found in it the essence of their ancient and still-present struggle for survival and the honour of their name on a soil that was barren in everything but men".

Njegoš believed strongly in the independence and culture of the Slavs; he corresponded widely with intellectuals, including Ilija Garašanin, a thinker and senior minister in Serbia at the time, who promoted the recreation of the great Serbian Empire of the 14th century. The poem is dedicated to the ashes of the father of Serbia, Karadjordje. While Njegoš's nationalism was primarily focused on true independence from the Ottoman Empire, he also opposed the centralising influence of Austria-Hungary in Croatia. In the 1830s, Metternich had prevented him from obtaining a visa to travel to Paris, considered a hotbed for radical ideas. Njegoš set in train the initial modernisation of Montenegro, adopting national rather than clerical dress for himself, founding political institutions and a police force, and encouraging education. He even imported the country's first modern printing press, although soon after his death his successor, Prince Danilo, under renewed attack from the Turks, had to melt down the lead type to make shot.

Njegoš is viewed as the father of modern Montenegro, although the words of *The Mountain Wreath* have acquired an unwelcome resonance in the last few decades. While it may be unfair to look at it too literally through 21st-century eyes, it is not hard to see why recent history has led people to do so. Bishop Danilo exhorts the Montenegrins to kill the Muslims in their midst:

> *Let those who bear the honour-studded arms*
> *and those who hear the heart beat in their chest*
> *strike for the Cross and for heroic name!*
> *We should baptize with water or with blood*
> *those blasphemers of Christ's glorious name.*
> *Let's drive the plague out of our sheephouses!*
> *Let songs ring forth, songs of all these horrors.*
> *On blood-stained stones let the true altar rise.*

The report comes back after the deed:

> *As wide and long that Cetinje Plain is,*
> *not one witness was able to escape*
> *to tell his tale about what happened there.*
> *We put under our sharp sabres all those*
> *who did not want to be baptized by us.*
> *But all those who bowed to the Holy Child*
> *and crossed themselves with the sign of Christian cross,*
> *we accepted and hailed as our brothers.*
> *We set on fire all the Turkish houses,*
> *that there might be not a single trace left*
> *of our faithless domestic enemy.*

Danilo rejoices:

> *You have brought me great gladness, my falcons,*
> *great joy for me. Heroic liberty!*
> *This bright morning you've been resurrected*
> *from every tomb of our dear forefathers!*

Njegoš lies at the top of the land's eponymous black mountain (Crna Gora), sacred to Montenegrins, at a site of his own choosing "where the eagles cross in their flight". His remains were moved back to Cetinje in 1916 to make way for an unpopular monument to the Austrian Emperor Franz Joseph, but he was reinterred there in 1925 in a ceremony attended by King Alexander of the newly unified south Slav kingdom. The secular chapel that functions as the mausoleum was conceived by the Croatian sculptor Ivan Meštrović, an early 20th-century advocate of Yugoslavism, of which Njegoš was a symbol. It was finally completed in 1974, a now communist monument to Slav unity in the shape of a royal grave.

The hills were splashed with yellow broom and the road led through tunnels of silver birch. Many of these still retained their autumnal colours, although the new green growth had already emerged. With the glint of their trunks, it was as though the seasons had been telescoped into a single moment of colour contrast. The views out over the highlands of Montenegro were barely terrestrial. In the distance, Lake Skadar shone with a silvery turquoise evanescence.

The initial path is up a flight of some 500 elegant stone steps, much of it through a great arched passage cut through the mountaintop like the approach to a potentate's palace in an early cinematic fantasy. As I emerged blinking into the sunlight, the mausoleum itself became apparent another 50 or so steps on. The inner sanctum is guarded by two idealised Montenegrin women in traditional dress, carved from granite, massive and severe, bearing the entrance lintel on their heads. Inside, the great man sits cross-legged under a golden mosaic canopy. He is carved from a single block of polished dark green stone, deep in thought, fingering prayer beads, while an eagle behind him seems to stand guard. The concentration in his eyes is accentuated by his overhanging brow and prominent straight nose. His left arm props up his head, while his right is pressed to his chest as if to contain his emotions. After a while, I tiptoed out, not wanting to disturb him. Downstairs, his remains had been reinterred under a simple white marble slab adorned with a cross, a double-headed eagle and his dates. It was a shock to see that he was not even thirty-eight when he died in 1851.

Budva

So back to the coast, where in a grove near Budva, Cadmus, the founder of Thebes, and his wife Harmonia are said to have been turned into snakes. Budva itself is another walled town marked with the winged lion of St Mark, described by West as "a little white tortoise against the blue sea". It has been reassembled beautifully since the destruction wrought by the 1979 earthquake, but the outside of the town walls, where West had enjoyed seeing black-clad locals selling their produce, is now home to rows of restaurant awnings. Inside the old town, one would be pushed to find the Albanian buckles and Turkish swords that her party had bought, although a large array of beach and evening wear was certainly available. The square below the citadel drew me in. The gold-hued grey of its four churches still exuded the warmth of the midday sun as the temperature began to dip. The stones underfoot had been polished by the traffic of time. Down narrow alleys and around corners were the remains of antique columns. A palm tree grew out between massive ancient stone blocks. I was back in Dalmatia.

Breakfast the next day witnessed the almost agricultural progress of two men with shovels and wheelbarrows remodelling the beach ahead of the day's arrivals. In *Black Lamb and Grey Falcon*, as West's party left Budva, they were greeted by the sight of a cluster of expensive cars, where the representatives of various Albanian delegations had crossed the border into Montenegro to enable them to contact their governments freely. It was clear that the world was sliding to war. These days, important visitors arrive on expensive yachts.

Buoyed by the sun, I drove on down the coast. Inches before a blind corner, I was overtaken by a shiny black BMW with Belgrade plates.

Rounding the bend, I saw the same trick repeated on the car in front, but the racer had failed to notice a policeman standing on the bend beyond. We tortoises had beaten the hare. West had described Montenegro as a land "defiled by the presence on its roads of twisted and pointless wrecks of automobiles". It is not purely a Montenegrin phenomenon; through much of the Balkans, black gravestones at the side of the road mark the site of fatal accidents. The frozen photo-etched faces of the deceased stare out as you pass.

After a while, I turned to climb again towards Lake Skadar. It gleamed silver in the sunshine as first glimpsed from the mountains. I left the main road, passed over the railway line and an Ottoman bridge, and followed a winding lane along its south side towards the Albanian border. Within a mile, I seemed to have retreated a century or more. There were signs for local produce, primarily wine and raki, a glimpse of an occasional farmhouse, an absence of cars and an abundance of wildflowers on all sides. Clouds of red smoke bush stood out above the green undergrowth. Deep pink bells of wild gladioli hung over rocks and grass. The lake was now a deeper blue reflection of the sky, stretching out on all sides to uninhabited hills, themselves fading to blue as they neared the horizon. The causeway far to the left could have been an ancient bridge were it not for the occasional glints of crossing cars. A deserted monastery sat on a small island in the middle distance. A cuckoo called. When the country was suffering under sanctions in the 1990s, the lake was famous for the fleets of small boats that used to smuggle fuel across it from Albania, but today nothing broke the surface of the water. I drove on, hoping to find a view to its far end, but as the road seemed to move ever further away, I retraced my path.

Passing a farmhouse, a figure emerged and flagged me down, asking for a lift back along the lake. After brief formalities, he told me that he was a footballer returned home, tired of the corruption in Serbian football after a career with Red Star Belgrade and others. He seemed happy back in this tranquillity, a sentiment that echoed with my own joy at spending less time in a city, both at home and out here. He gave me his views on the prowess of the main teams in the English Premier League and most of Europe's national sides. He was diplomatically non-committal about England, disparaging about Serbian attitudes and had strong praise for the Bosnian team, who he thought were the best in the Balkans. I asked him if the communities around the lake were mixed. He said that his village was Orthodox, the one next door was Catholic and there was a Muslim one up the valley. Everyone got along unless politicians stirred things up. However, when asked about Kosovo, he grimaced, muttering about drugs and prostitution. I dropped him off and headed north, crossing the River Morača, just above where it flows into the lake, a violent blue-green colour. Higher up the valley, it becomes a purer bright blue as it tumbles down through endless rocky gorges, a colour celebrated in folk song.

Andrijevica

Sixty miles further on and one valley over to the east lies Andrijevica, on the banks of the River Lim not far from the Albanian border. The Lim is the longest tributary of the Drina, ultimately making its way into the Danube and the Black Sea. Driving up the Morača, the trees seemed to defy gravity, growing on vertiginous slopes and out of cracks in rocky faces. On the switchback route between the two valleys, there were more cattle and horses on the road than cars. Farmers nodded acknowledgement as I passed. A sign at a fork in the road indicated the way to Andrijevica to the left, but two black lines through the name of Peć (Peja in Kosovo) to the right showed all too graphically the post-Yugoslav divide; it had long been frontier country out here. Edith Durham wrote about the longing for Old Servia (of which Kosovo was a significant part) when she stayed in Andrijevica at the beginning of the 20th century, remarking on how her "map ceased at the Montenegrin frontier, and beyond was a blank" as she planned a trip to see the great Orthodox monasteries at Dečani and Peć, still then under Ottoman control. She wrote of life in the town as "either quiet to dullness, or it is filled with very grim realities. For the Albanians across the border are an ever-present danger". Yet they too were in danger, for the Montenegrins were inclined, at moments of stress, to go looting and killing often unarmed Muslim communities well into the 1920s.

West had visited the war memorial outside the town, where on a grassy terrace looking out at the mountains, the Vasojevići clan had built a collective church in 1887. She had studied the black marble obelisk, surmounted by an eagle with wings outstretched, on which were inscribed the names of the clan members who had died in the continuous wars here between 1912 and 1921. During that period, they had fought the Ottomans, the Albanians, the Austrians and the Serbs in turn, the latter in protest at Montenegro being incorporated into Serbia after the First World War. The names number between 700 and 800. Another monument is to the Serbian soldiers who died in the retreat to Albania in 1915. They have been joined by monuments that bear testament to subsequent episodes of troubled history. In a notorious incident in July 1944, the Skanderbeg Division of the SS massacred over 400 civilians in Andrijevica. This was a unit formed of Kosovan Albanians, with a reputation for criminal brutality, especially in Orthodox areas. A graffitied white concrete edifice, like a giant inverted table with its six legs pointing skywards, frames a black marble block, on which are inscribed the names of 666 local fighters killed during the Second World War; while a simple black tablet set below a stone cross commemorates those who died in the 1990s. Busts of national heroes on concrete plinths stare out at the scene. Over the road, I scrambled up a grassy bank to see the graves of tribesmen who had been executed by the Austrians, their deaths by hanging depicted on the stones. Other graves contain the remains of those who had been dispatched by King Nikola for "demand[ing] a liberal constitution". A young officer, who died in 1909, stared out from a gravestone, seemingly still seeking to convince a rare visitor of the rectitude of his cause. The voices of the past spoke directly of the turbulence of the last century.

Podgorica

Morača Monastery lay on the road to Montenegro's present-day capital, Podgorica. It was built in the 13th century by a grandson of Stefan Nemanja, the founder of Serbia's great Nemanjić dynasty. The earliest of the whitewashed walls of the original church date back to its founding in 1252. Inside, the frescoes typify the solemnity and ritual quality that distinguish many Orthodox frescoes from those of the Western Church. One can see the direct line to ancient Rome. The deeply grooved face of John the Baptist stares out, his torso swathed in sheepskin. St Luke paints an icon of the Virgin among other scenes from his life. Early Serbian saints and bishops in geometrically patterned copes of black and white crosses mingle with the saints of the New Testament. Always prominent among them are St Simeon (Stefan Nemanja's adopted name when he retired to Mount Athos as a monk) and St Sava, his youngest son; the identification of the Orthodox Church with constitutional power dates back long before the prince-bishops of Montenegro. Outside the church, the Virgin and Child adorned a drinking fountain where twin taps and hanging tin mugs offered refreshment to the thirsty. In the garden, multi-storeyed wooden beehives were painted vivid shades of yellow, turquoise, lime green and white, like three-dimensional pastoral Mondrians.

As I neared my car, an unkempt figure in a tracksuit appeared and asked if I was heading to Podgorica. I signalled that I would give him a lift. As he climbed into the car, the smell of tobacco and raki arrived first. We only had a few words of each other's language, but he told me as we drove along that he had been visiting his father's grave and how hard it was to visit the monastery and refuse a drink, so try as he might, he had accepted two beers and could no longer drive. The beers must have been sobering compared to the volume of spirits that had chased them down. As we descended the long valley to Podgorica, he bounced between my right arm and his car door, the ride punctuated by his occasional remarks about tiredness and the evils of raki ("bad, very bad"). He clearly felt he that he owed me some hospitality and suggested that he buy me a drink as we neared the city. I demurred and, in response to his question about my destination, gave the street name rather than the hotel itself, out of self-protection. He gestured for me to pull over by a well-to-do lady taking an evening stroll, whom he proceeded to ask for directions with surprising aggression as I murmured apologies through the window. At last, he climbed back in and told me to drive on. Two blocks later, he clambered back out, offering effusive thanks as an unlit cigarette twitched at the corner of his mouth; if I turned right at the end of the road, I would be there. After two full circuits of the city and conversations with a variety of local taxi drivers, I arrived at last. The Crna Gora Hotel had been billed in my guidebook as having an old-fashioned Edwardian charm, but it had seemingly since metamorphosed into a fully refurbished Hilton. I allowed myself a night of relative luxury.

The Montenegrin capital sits on the Morača. West was disparaging about it, saying that they "had not wasted one moment looking at the sights of [Podgorica], for too evidently it has none". The town was under Ottoman rule for 400 years, becoming part of Montenegro only after the Congress of Berlin in 1878. Prior to that, it had been largely Muslim, but two thirds of the population fled the town in the succeeding decades in an uncomfortable foreshadowing of more recent events. The town was largely destroyed in the Second World War, although some of the old Muslim quarter remains, where a minaret rises elegantly above the narrow streets. In the wake of the war, the capital of Montenegro was moved from Cetinje to Podgorica (renamed Titograd) to signal the end of the royalist era and herald the new socialist future. Much of the rebuilt town is grey and grid-like, but there are still cultivated open spaces and large gardens, an echo of the local citizen who expressed amazement to Edith Durham in 1904 that potatoes were not grown in London. The bright water of the Morača bubbling through a gorge in the main park added another rustic note, but there was little to make one linger for long.

Some 25 miles to the north-west lies the Monastery of Ostrog. Its white facade sits high in the cleft of a cliff ("a bleak pigeon-hole") its positioning inevitably lending it a defensive air. Its primary dedication is to St Basil, a local 17th-century bishop, and is a significant pilgrimage site as a result of the miracles ascribed to him. The darkened shrine had an altar screen of beaten copper and painted scenes of the Old Testament with something of the intensity of El Greco. On the far side of the chamber lay St Basil himself, richly draped in a wooden sarcophagus carved with garlands. Below the monastery is a church dedicated to the Blessed Martyr Stanko, a local shepherd boy killed by the Turks in 1712 for attesting to his Christian faith.

The monastery's remote location rendered it a place of refuge over the years. Early in the First World War, the Serbians left the remains of King Stefan (the First-Crowned) here on their long retreat to the coast. At the beginning of the Second World War, young King Peter was sent here for safety from the air raids in Belgrade, bringing with him the hand of the Baptist and the shard of the True Cross that I had seen at Cetinje. The Nazis looted the monastery's gold and arrested Serbian Patriarch Gavrilo, stripping him to his shirt and making him walk barefoot over the hills in the summer heat for 200 miles. He was later interned at Dachau.

More recently, identification of the monastery with power drew possibly unfair adverse attention from its association with Radovan Karadžić, the Bosnian Serb war criminal, who was born nearby and was a strong adherent to the Orthodox faith. He christened his daughter here and later made one of his last public appearances at the annual Ostrog pilgrimage before he vanished from sight. In a later interview, when the metropolitan was asked about Karadžić, he opined that he would be better to face justice at The Hague than "live in a hole like a hunted animal".

Outside the modern Parliament building in Podgorica stands a statue of King Nikola parading on a horse high atop a plinth of pinkish marble. Imperiously, he looks to his left while his horse inclines to the right. It was unveiled in December 2005 by Milo Djukanović shortly before the Montenegrin independence referendum. Djukanović, although only born in 1962, has been the country's dominant political figure for thirty years, serving as prime minister six times and president twice. During that period, he has tracked from ardent Yugoslav and Milošević ally to become the father of independence. The excesses of the Bosnian Serbs and Milošević saw the Podgorica government distance itself from Belgrade in the 1990s, reinforced by the desire to end the damaging international blockade imposed on their country alongside Serbia. Unveiling the statue signalled Montenegrin pride in their particular history, but the cultural, linguistic and economic ties with Serbia have always been important, becoming entrenched in the latter half of the 20th century. They were repeatedly allies on the battlefield, although neither party realised that the bloodthirsty habits of the 19th century would attract a very different reaction at the end of the millennium. Both now seek to become members of the European Union. One hopes that this can be achieved in mutual friendship and that Montenegrin pride in an often savage history can be channelled in ways more fitted to modern times.

Kosovo

*"The black lamb and the grey falcon
had worked together here."*

SERBIA
MONTENEGRO
MITROVICA
PEJA
GAZIMESTAN
PRISHTINA
PRIZREN
ALBANIA
NORTH MACEDONIA

Nemanjina, the broad street that leads down to the old railway station in Belgrade, passes the remains of the Yugoslav Ministry of Defence. It was built to evoke a canyon of the Sutjeska River, scene of the Partisans' battle with and great escape from the Germans in the summer of 1943, subsequently made into a film in which Tito was played by a suitably spruce Richard Burton. The building was badly bombed by NATO in 1999 as it tried to force the Serbian government to cease its policy of ethnic cleansing in Kosovo. Chasms gaped across the street where a bridge had formerly spanned the void. An empty concrete window frame looked up to the sky. The main building's sagging floors and drunkenly angled panels of rose-coloured stone were especially discordant in the otherwise elegant urban setting.

At the bottom of the hill, the old railway station of Belgrade stands just above the River Sava in front of a large open square criss-crossed with tramlines. It has an Austrian appearance. A pedimented arch dated 1884 in prominent Roman numerals is flanked by white pilasters. Banded stone wings create a presence of grave solidity. Once a stop on the Orient Express, it would look quite at home in a black and white film with the hiss of escaping steam, men in well-buttoned overcoats and women in seamed stockings. Beside the old building is the bus station, less distinguished in appearance but thronged with people. It was from here that I caught an airless bus to Prishtina, thinking that to drive around Kosovo in a car with Serb plates would be unwise.

The bus filled up as we made regular stops on our journey south. The driver treated us to intermittent bursts of air conditioning. A girl asked if she could sit beside me, introduced herself as Tamara and chatted on and off through the five-and-a-half-hour journey. She was a Kosovan Serb from Gračanica in her first year of high school, and had been visiting a friend in Belgrade for the weekend. Her long-range ambition was to be a lawyer, and she hoped to get into Belgrade University as it was much better than the local alternative at Mitrovica. She asked where I planned to go in Kosovo. When I said Prizren, she remarked that she could not go there as it was Albanian. Over 90% of the population of Kosovo is Albanian now and Serbs make up under 5%, although the split was around 70:30 at the end of the 19th century. I spent some time helping her with an essay on our relationship with the media, a potentially delicate subject in the context of Kosovo.

We drove south down the broad agricultural valley of the Morava River before ascending into the hills after Kruševac, Prince Lazar's capital and the base from which he led his army out against the Ottomans with such unforeseeable long-term consequences in 1389. The motorway service station boasted a Restaurant Tito with a replica of his study and library and an extensive display of photographs and medallions. Crossing the border was painless, with the bulk dual inspection of our paperwork remarkably well coordinated. Once into Kosovo, the landscape changed, notably in the scattergun approach to development. Ugly small boxes, often unfinished, seemed to have been erected on any available flattish space.

Prishtina

Geographically, Kosovo is a plain comprising two main river valleys ringed by mountains. Prishtina, the capital, sits below the hills to the east in Kosovo proper, while the plain in the west is often referred to as Metohija (from the Greek μετόχια [*metóchia*], meaning "monastic estates"), which contains some of the greatest historical and architectural treasures of the Serbian Orthodox Church. We were dropped some way from the city centre by the main north-south highway in a non-descript compound serving as the bus station.

The heart of Prishtina itself is no longer the "dull and dusty little village" of West's time, but a concrete jungle built by communist planners, latterly boosted by foreign aid. I found my hotel easily, carrying with me the engaging confirmation email that said: "Hello Dear. It's everything ok." Two of the illuminated stars on the side of the building were dark, ranking the hotel rather more accurately than its literature. However, it was clean, friendly and convenient. After a short walk, I sat nursing a beer and watched the corso. On an early summer evening, there was a happy, animated air. The Grand Hotel across the main square was a modernist block that looked unfinished; its brown external panelling resembled aging chipboard. After staying there in the early 1990s, Robert Kaplan described the stained bile-green carpet in his room and thought that the elevator resembled "a graffiti-scarred toilet stall". Its grimy, cavernous lobby did not suggest that it was much more welcoming now. Online, I came across a quote from the current President of Kosovo: "I don't think it is the worst hotel in the world, but that is because the world is very big." I turned and found some richly marinated lamb for dinner in a restaurant down a small alleyway. Prishtina's food is consistently impressive, the demand for its restaurants fuelled by the large number of foreign-funded residents.

As I headed back down the main pedestrian avenue to my bed, I passed the prominent statue of Skanderbeg. Equestrian statues are a feature of Balkan capitals, and each symbolises a national identity. Skanderbeg is the iconic Albanian national hero who led his people in revolt against the Ottoman Empire in the 15th century, but arrived too late to bolster his Hungarian allies as they were scattered in the second Battle of Kosovo in 1448. The Prishtina version is a copy of the original at Skanderbeg's capital of Kruja in Albania and was erected in the newly independent Kosovo on Albanian National Day in 2001. Another equestrian statue of Skanderbeg stands in the main square in Tirana.

The following day, I set off to walk around the old town. It was shortly before school started and young people gathered in chattering groups on corners. The girls' uniforms of tartan kilted skirts in a black and white checked pattern were worn over their normal daywear with great cross-cultural charm. Opposite their high school, the handsome stone doorway of the Fatih Mosque, built by Mehmed III in 1460-1, led to an ornate, blue-patterned interior flooded with light from tiers of arched windows rising high into the dome. By contrast, a short walk away, tucked down a side street, was the modest Pirinaz Mosque, a square white building with a simple tiled roof and a modern wooden lean-to as an entrance. It was built a hundred years after the Fatih Mosque, reputedly on the original burial site of Lazar after the first Battle of Kosovo, but this appeared unacknowledged now.

The town is mostly newly built, although there are occasional older timber-framed buildings of clay and brick, mostly in poor repair. In an old Ottoman house in a walled garden, the ethnographic museum is filled with detail about the Albanian people and their way of life and rituals. I learned that pregnant women were not allowed near foreigners to protect them from the evil eye. Brides were taken to their new husbands' homes with scarves over their faces, the idea being that, if they did not know where they had come, they could not return home should they became disenchanted with their new life. The dead were buried with a green apple and work tools, head pointed to sunrise (although later to Mecca, Rome or Constantinople, depending on religion). The wife of a deceased man would often wear her dress inside out, and the different religions wore different coloured headscarves in mourning. Condolences were expressed by saying: "Let God leave the others untouched." Tradition has long governed Albanian life, and the Kanun, often associated with the history of blood feuds and how these were regulated, covers aspects of life from punishment for criminal wrongdoing to rights of ownership of swarming bees.

Walking out into the sunlight, I saw a pair of shoes hung from an electrical cable high above the street, an informal alert to drivers of high vehicles. The shaped metal covers on a pair of chimneys resembled a pair of birds in conversation. Out in the market, stalls were selling fruit, vegetables and large bags of loose tobacco in addition to cartons of Marlboro. Many of the vendors were elderly men in suits and white Albanian egg-shaped hats made of lambswool (the *qeleshe* or *plis*). The tree-lined streets around the market gave a glimpse of West's rural backwater.

A large yellow villa still commanded attention as intended, inadvertently highlighting the refinement of the stone minaret of the neighbouring mosque. It was the Ottoman governor's house, built in 1898, and now repurposed as the National Museum. A broad white staircase arched up to the entrance from each side in theatrical style. Inside, the displays were entirely focused on the recent conflict, the history told in large part through framed copies of articles from the *New York Times*. Centre-stage was the motorbike of Adem Jashari, one of the founders of the Kosovo Liberation Army, bullet holes visible in the seat. Beside it, a picture showed him standing bushy-bearded in camouflage gear gazing into the middle distance in a quasi-messianic pose. Alongside him, two rifle-bearing companions, one in fatigues and one in national costume, stare straight at the camera with an appearance of grim purpose. Jashari's killing in 1998 alongside twenty family members at the hands of the Serbian "Special Anti-Terrorism Unit", after the latter besieged his family farm for three days, marked the escalation of the armed Kosovan uprising. He has acquired near-martyr status, and both the airport and national theatre are named after him.

I climbed in my local hired car and drove south to visit the Monastery of Gračanica. The wide avenues that ring the city revealed an assortment of undistinguished utilitarian blocks enlivened by lines of laundry drying in the sun high above street level and a density of satellite dishes that hid entire rooflines. I passed the grey concrete domes of the Serbian Orthodox church that had been in the process of construction on Milošević's orders until the world changed in 1999. Its matt curves are oddly threatening, suggesting a military rather than a religious installation. It may well metamorphose into another war memorial.

Nearby is the National Library, one of the oddest pieces of architecture I have ever seen. It looks as though a fleet of lunar buggies are indulging in an orgy. Ninety-nine white domes of varying sizes sit atop a dense cluster of well-windowed concrete boxes, possible references to the *plis* hat. The whole appears to be encased in a tailor-made security grille. It is reported that, at the inauguration ceremony, the local head of the Communist Party asked why the scaffolding had not been taken down. For nearly ten years before 1999, the Albanian faculty were not allowed to set foot in the library; during the NATO bombardment, it was used as a Yugoslav army command centre. After the Serb withdrawal, uniforms and grenades were littered through the building and the law faculty's books were found packaged up, ready to be shipped to Serbia.

Once out of the city, the roadsides were crowded with red poppies waving in the wind, and the plains stretched miles to the distant hills that bordered Kosovo to the west. West remarked on the bare surroundings of Gračanica, and the landscape around is indeed featureless. She talked of its being an island, in the sense that there was no longer any evidence around it of the civilisation that gave birth to this remarkable building. Now, of course, it is an island in a very different way. Outside the monastery gates were two pallets stacked with rolls of polythene-wrapped razor wire. Near the compound, the familiar if weathered colours of monastic beehives greeted me, but the wooden boxes were stacked unused in a long, low shelter. The main church is exquisite. Honey-coloured stone is given energy by the imaginative use of slender terracotta bricks. These space the stones and provide detailing around arches and windows while also forming geometric patterns inside arches. Arches rise above arches and are themselves surmounted by lead-capped cupolas of faded russet. It seems ideally sized for worship rather than grandeur. I walked around it again and again, marvelling at the variation and harmony of the whole. I think that I have never seen a lovelier building.

It was built as part of the great building programme of the Nemanjić king, Milutin, who expanded the Serbian-controlled lands into Macedonia around 1300, moving his capital to Skopje and marrying Simonis, daughter of the Byzantine emperor. This was his fifth marriage and clearly a source of great satisfaction to Milutin. Fortuitously, one of his earlier wives died just before the marriage was agreed. Milutin quickly claimed that that particular marriage had ended illegally; any subsequent ones had thus been invalid, leaving him free to move on, with a logic of which Henry VIII would have been proud. An earlier attempt to marry an aunt of Simonis had foundered when the emissaries sent to inspect the Serbian court had been shocked by the poverty of the country and the extreme asceticism practised at court by Milutin's mother, Helen of Anjou. To cap it all, the Byzantine party found their horses stolen when they attempted to ride out to head off the prospective bride.

Inside the church, the three naves are covered with frescoes. Milutin stands on one side of an archway facing Simonis and holding a model of the church that he has built here. The lower half of the fresco is badly damaged, but the top remains in good condition. He looks out bleakly, long-bearded in opulent gold- and pearl-decorated robes and crown. His proud stance is the only real sign of character. His wife opposite is doll-like, her tight-lipped face featureless and round, but then she had only been five when married off. Her robes and crown are even more brocaded and elaborate than those of her husband. Both of their eyes have been scratched out – this may be a result of Turkish iconoclasm, though more likely of the peasant belief in the healing (or possibly aphrodisiac) quality of the powder scraped from the eyes of frescoes. Sadly, such defacement is a common sight in this part of the world.

West makes much of the mystic qualities of the depictions on the walls. The ecstasy of Elijah in his cave, his yellow robes Italianate in style, with trees like giant thistles on either side. The baleful gaze of a stick-thin figure of St John the Baptist. The Angel Gabriel comes to tell Mary the unexpected news of her impending motherhood; she looks up shyly from beneath her eyebrows with an expression of concern and resignation, pulling her cloak around her as if to seek some comfort as she contemplates the challenges ahead. A female saint is savaged by lions. Mary is carried on her deathbed witnessed by her son (as both man and infant) and a host of grave-looking saints. The frescoes were the work of Mihailo and Evtihije, two famous painters from Salonika, and somehow capture both the fluidity of the art of the Western Church and the intensity of the Eastern. I stood contemplating the walls in silence for some time.

Leaving the monastery compound into the street, I looked back and saw that a roll of razor wire ran all the way along the top of the tile-capped stone wall that surrounded it. It brought home the isolation of the remaining Serb pockets in Kosovo. Gračanica is the heart of the Serb community in Kosovo, with many of the communities around supplying Serb quotas for the government in Prishtina; but here, and even more so in the remoter Orthodox monasteries, they are untrusting islands in an alien world.

I crossed the road to get some money from a cash machine, but it only offered Serbian dinars, of little use outside a ten-mile radius in a country that generally uses euros, so I drove on. In an indication of its symbolic importance, Gračanica is the image on the Serbian two-dinar coin.

Ten miles on are the ruins of Lazar's castle at Novo Brdo. It stands prominently on the ridge of hills to the east of Prishtina. It was quite deserted. By the late 14th century, the Nemanjić dynasty had died out. The last king, Uroš the Weak, was unable to control his network of feudal lords and died childless. The most powerful of the local rulers who filled the gap was Lazar Hrebeljanović, based out of Kruševac in central Serbia, but crucially controlling the rich mines here. He also became the leading protector of the Serbian Orthodox Church. Under the expansionist Ottoman policy of Sultan Murad I, Serbia and Bosnia and their silver mines became key targets. Lazar had already lost the town of Niš in 1386, and in 1389 Murad assembled a larger army. Lazar joined forces with a Bosnian army and forces from western Kosovo, commanded by his son-in-law, Vuk Branković. The ensuing battle on a plain north of Prishtina has fuelled Serb legend ever since. Both Lazar and Murad died that day and neither side could claim a clear victory. However, the scale of the damage sustained by the Serbs meant that they were unable to resist the Turks as they returned over the years with ever greater resources. Over time, the cult of Lazar grew, fanned by Njegoš's *The Mountain Wreath* and even more so by a song, *The Downfall of the Serbian Empire*, taken from a 19th-century anthology. In this, on the eve of the battle, Lazar is visited by the prophet Elijah in the shape of a falcon bearing a book from the Virgin Mary. He is offered the choice of an earthly kingdom or a heavenly one. He chooses the latter.

> *An earthly kingdom lasts only a little time,*
> *But a heavenly kingdom will last for eternity and its centuries.*

And so to battle and a brave and honourable end, betrayed by Vuk Branković. This latter likely embellishment to the story may well result from the help that Branković's son gave to the Turks when they faced the Hungarians at the second Battle of Kosovo some sixty years later. The legend of Kosovo Polje, the battlefield (literally, "field of blackbirds"), with its echoes of the Last Supper, could be turned in the wrong hands to justify the second coming of the Serbs and their Orthodox Church in their God-given mission against Islam.

Lazar's castle looks impressive from below but is little more than a few crumbling battlements now, with heaps of stones around them that grow as the walls gradually disintegrate. The views are spectacular, looking out over wooded hills as far as the eye can see. The proprietress of the small coffee shop by the entrance reminisced in lilting English about her visit to Guildford many years before. A small Saxon church had been converted into a mosque centuries earlier, the stump of a stone minaret standing beside it. From the castle, the remains of the mine pithead were visible, now abandoned, with a scattering of buildings around. During the 15th and 16th centuries, the mines here made Novo Brdo (also known as Neuberg due to the high concentration of German-speaking labourers) the largest town in Kosovo. I drove past the decaying shells of old mine buildings behind barbed-wire fences, gradually being reclaimed into the hillside by vegetation. The corrugated iron-clad conveyor belt from the mine to the main processing area looked like an alien presence in a landscape of fresh green trees and rocks. All was silent. The town of Novo Brdo below now consisted of only four grey-fronted peeling apartment blocks and a school. There was no trace of its prosperous past.

I returned to Prishtina in a contemplative mood. I gave a lift to a security guard, who told me that he had been an Albanian refugee in Switzerland. We conversed haltingly in pidgin German. "*Krieg Ende gut. Economy nicht sehr gut.*"

That night I had arranged to have dinner with a senior Serbian figure in the EU mission to Kosovo. We were joined by a Kosovo Albanian friend of hers visiting from London. The latter talked about his experiences living in Prishtina as the troubles escalated in the 1990s. Growing up, he had had many Serb friends. Some families took off to Belgrade as the tension increased, others just vanished. Two friends with whom he used to go hunting started wearing paramilitary uniforms one day and talked about shooting Albanians ("Did you see how he ran?"). Serb neighbours would stand outside the apartment building, pointing out to the Yugoslav military which flats were inhabited by Albanians. Then his school was shut down, and a policeman asked why he had been to a meeting two days earlier. When he asked how the policeman had known, the response was: "We know what you people are like."

At that point, the family fled to Macedonia. In one instance, he had a machine gun stuck in his mouth. At the border, families were separated, and his official papers were destroyed. He ended up in a refugee centre outside Leeds, where he said that there was open fear and hostility on the faces of local residents whenever they ventured out. Now, he was living in London and writing, though working as a waiter to supplement his income.

Hearing this man's account of the ratcheting-up of fear as the situation had worsened, and of the privations that he had suffered after leaving Kosovo, gave an immediacy to the trauma of the period that all my reading and news-watching had not managed to convey.

Both my companions chatted about how good life had been for many under Tito, with cheap holidays in Montenegro, something that I have heard echoed repeatedly as former Yugoslavs reminisce about childhood holidays on the Adriatic coast. They talked of the speed of private rebuilding in Kosovo and how little visible evidence of the war remained; very apparent when contrasted with the divided or "cleansed" towns of Bosnia, Croatia and Serbia, presumably reflecting the ethnic homogeneity of the bulk of this country. They mentioned the aftereffects of the conflict on the many Albanian victims of rape and their families, but felt that the practical nature of Albanian culture would help most work through their issues with time. We discussed the island nature of the Serbs' existence here. I was told that Serbs were all selling up their property unless located in one of the Serb enclaves. Those who remained, they suggested, were likely to stay, despite the difficulties; many had guaranteed jobs in the administration and were often on two pensions (Serbian and Kosovan).

After dinner, I walked back to my hotel trying to think of analogies with other divided countries such as Ireland or Israel, eventually settling on Nagorno-Karabakh as the closest equivalent: a country within a country of which it does not wish to be a part, faced with considerable obstacles to achieving true independence.

Peja

I set off early the next morning, heading west to the great Serb ecclesiastical treasures of Peć and Dečani. Before long, the snow-capped black mountain in front (Crna Gora or Montenegro) became visible, looming until it seemed to fill the windscreen and envelop the entire prospect. On the bilingual place name signs, the Serbian Cyrillic script had been painted over or crossed out, leaving only the Roman letters of the Albanian names visible (Peja/Deçan).

Peja suffered particularly badly in the 1999 war, and its charms seem diminished as a result. Tony Blair Street at the centre is a short, broad boulevard with aggressively undistinguished concrete blocks on either side housing uninviting restaurants at pavement level. Much of the old market area was set on fire by Serb troops in 1999 and has been rebuilt with no real eye to the past. An occasional handsome stone building stands out, and the Bajrakli Mosque in the centre of the market has been beautifully restored.

Along the River Bistrica, a long pedestrian street lined with cafes and bars proved livelier. West witnessed the corso here and talked of the "passionate faces and fantastic dresses" of the participants. As they walked past cafe tables ornamented with red Coca-Cola umbrellas, the passion was still evident, but the dress code was now the ubiquitous casualwear of any modern locale. Around the town were streets named after other international figures who had helped to bring about peace in Kosovo – Bill Clinton, General Wesley Clark and Madeline Ollbright [*sic*]. A large, bronze-painted statue showed the figure of Adrian Krasniqi, the first KLA soldier to die in uniform, looking resolute and athletic with rocket-launcher in hand. He died aged twenty-five attacking a Serb police station. Overall, Peja showed the effects of recent history as clearly as any large town in Kosovo.

Not far outside town is the Patriarchate of Peć, seat of Serbian archbishops and patriarchs since the 14th century, although the earliest part of the church building dates from the 1200s. To enter, I had to leave my passport with the armed guards at the gatehouse and drive along the banks of the river some way to the walls of the large monastery compound. The river flowed swiftly around narrow rocky bends towards the harsh mountainous landscape of Albania. Inside, the church stands some distance from the other buildings. It was described by West as having the colour of a fair woman's skin, but injudicious painting of the exterior now suggested an overlong spell in a tanning parlour. Three churches sit side by side emerging in a common porch (or narthex). Many of the paintings aggrandise the Nemanjić dynasty. The "throne of St Sava" sits in the narthex, with a depiction of him in a fresco above, although he is wearing ceremonial robes and a mitre, a piece of historical inauthenticity presumably designed to bind his authority to the office. From here, Serbian prelates have presided over assemblies through the centuries. Christ blesses the royal dynastic tree that dominates the wall to the right of the entrance. The churches contain the stone sarcophagi of patriarchs past. Serbian rulers process along the walls of the Church of the Apostles, with a regally robed Lazar included in the otherwise Nemanjić family parade.

The earliest frescoes at Peć date back to the 13th century, but some are from as late as the 17th, and there is considerable variation in quality. West talked of their merciless quality, making much in particular of the depiction in the narthex of the Virgin suckling Jesus, "the infant ... not so much a baby as a reduced adult ... sucking his mother's nipple with mature unsmiling greed, as if he meant to take the last drop". This is characteristically well observed, as is her description of a vast Virgin picking up the child in her arms, gripping him with "fingers of masonic strength, which are as ten towers ... affixed to her huge palm", with the Christ child's "glittering enraged face proclaiming revolt against this imprisoning benevolence". There are more human depictions too. In the Church of the Virgin, Joseph and Mary embrace over the newborn with the customary love and pride of new parents. Elsewhere, Joseph looks almost resentful at Mary ignoring him while bathing their baby. The spiritual atmosphere is imbued in the walls here, despite the simultaneous sense of siege. The nun who was on duty as I arrived looked at me suspiciously, relatively unused to unknown visitors. However, by the time I had bought a book, examined each fresco in turn with its assistance and bought two candles, she was almost welcoming, although I faced admonishment for lighting my candles in the Church of the Apostles, unaware of the perspex shelter outside designed for the purpose.

The Orthodox Church was so tightly wound into the state by the Nemanjić dynasty that, when the state fell, the Church provided the ongoing sense of nationhood to the Serb people. It retained close links to power through history, and the Peć Patriarchate was a key beneficiary later. In the 16th century, one of two brothers was taken as part of the *devshirme* (tribute in blood), whereby the Ottoman Empire would remove Christian boys to Istanbul to be forcibly converted to Islam and trained for service in either the military or civil service. This particular boy subsequently rose to become Sokollu Mehmed Pasha, grand vizier of the empire. The other brother, Macarius, became Archbishop of Peć and Patriarch of the Serbian Church. With the help of his brother in Istanbul, the Church's autonomy was restored and even expanded. Macarius rebuilt the narthex at Peć, along with several other monasteries, and is a great saint in the Serbian canon.

More recently, the controversial 1988 "Declaration of the Bishops of the Serbian Orthodox Church against the Genocide Inflicted by the Albanians on the Indigenous Serbian Population, together with the Sacrilege of their Cultural Monuments in their Own Country" marked a politicisation of the Orthodox Church that damaged its standing badly over the rest of the century. Issued a year after Milošević's initial grandstanding to the Kosovan Serbs, when he first played the nationalist card aggressively, and a year before his triumphal rally at Gazimestan, its language was more alarmist than spiritual. Through the bloody years of the 1990s, the Church seemed too willing to sanction the likes of Karadžić and Milošević, while still pleading for peace. There are echoes here of the behaviour of the Catholic Church in Croatia in the Second World War, where the balance was more profoundly askew. The behaviour of the Orthodox Church in the conflict helps explain, though not excuse, the damage wreaked on church buildings at the end of the conflict and in the riots of 2004. It also explains the very high level of security around the greatest monuments.

From Peć, it was a short drive to Visoki Dečani Monastery, founded by Stefan Uroš III (known as Dečanski) in the 14th century. He was the son of Milutin (the founder of Gračanica) and had been blinded by his father for participating in a failed rebellion against him, blindness being a disqualification from the kingship. However, the action was performed ineptly (if at all) and he ultimately succeeded his father, having feigned loss of sight until it was safe to reveal the truth. (The monastic version is that Dečanski was cured through the intercession of St Nicholas the Miracle-Worker.) He only reigned for nine years before he was overthrown by his son, Stefan Dušan, who had him strangled to death. His body still lies in the church at Visoki Dečani, the source of many miracles for the faithful who have prayed there. His carved wooden sarcophagus shows a cord around his neck held by two men. Both Orthodox and Muslim women have crawled beneath it through the centuries in the belief that it will allow them to conceive.

I slalomed past the red and white pyramids of a roadblock and left my passport with the jovial UN guards at the entrance to the monastery. I entered through solid metal studded gates, each decorated with a medallion in the form of the bearded and helmeted head of a guardian.

In the centre of the manicured compound sat an elegant church built of striated grey and honey-coloured stone, faintly reminiscent of Tuscany. The architect was a Franciscan friar from Kotor, so the exterior is a blend of Roman and Byzantine architectural traditions. It is decorated with the sort of stone carvings that one might find on a medieval monastery in Western Europe. A lion and a griffon surmount the entrance door and a variety of animal and human heads support the arched roof cornice. The windows have further scenes and floral decorations: St George kills the dragon above one, while St John baptises a distinctly plump Christ, thigh-deep in the Jordan, above another.

Entering the church, one is struck by its height, its soaring pillars carved with further figures top and bottom. The narthex is spacious and the windows substantial enough that one can see the frescoes covering the wall clearly. Above the main door into the church, Dečanski and Dušan (who completed the church after his father's untimely death) pray to Christ and receive scrolls from a cherub. Once inside the main body of the church, the combination of height and the subdivision of the space make study of the frescoes all but impossible.

A friend from Belgrade had told me to introduce myself to Father Sava, the abbot. He had a reputation for reaching out beyond the Serb community, as well as a facility with IT. I found him, surprisingly boyish, in the traditional black robes and high black cylindrical headpiece (*kalimavkion*) of an Orthodox monk. He was friendly but preoccupied by the imminent arrival of the bishop ahead of the feast of the Ascension the next day. He suggested that I wait to hear the greeting chant by the monks. I sat in the sun by a handsome stone fountain, water splashing out from four ancient spouts into an octagonal trough. The assembled monks chatted merrily to one another while listening out for the bishop's car. One tracked his progress on a mobile phone, grinning broadly at what he was hearing. Elderly ladies swapped cheery stories in the sun, their pastel headscarves lightening their otherwise all black attire.

After some time, a general movement signalled the arrival. The monks formed a long black line together with the devout. I stood at the end. The bishop was grey-whiskered, with a large medallion hanging from a silver chain around his neck, and walked with a handsome metal-capped stick. He hugged each member of the line one after the other and had his ring kissed in return. I prepared for the same, but he stuck out his hand and wished me good afternoon, before progressing on to the church.

Inside, the monks' chanting was reminiscent of plainsong; harmonies just askew from anticipated patterns developed into unexpected resolutions. A blind monk sang solo passages in a tenor of celestial purity. All too soon, it came to an end. I joined another line and, shuffling forward, came to kiss the perspex lid above the covered corpse and visible blackened hand of St Stefan Dečanski.

Gjakova

Outside in the sunlight, the monastic party headed for the refectory, and I collected my passport from the cheery Italians on the gate. I drove on to Gjakova, where I had booked a night in a restored house in the old part of town. Gjakova has always had a much higher proportion of Albanians than other Kosovan towns and was seen by the Serbs as a hotbed of Albanian nationalism during the troubles. It suffered badly and witnessed several massacres. The old wooden market was torched in 1999, but it has been restored well and feels authentic.

The Hotel Çarshia e Jupave was all I could have hoped for. It was an old stone building off a courtyard, fitted out in wood, clean, comfortable and friendly. For breakfast the next day, I looked out over a small river eating fresh strawberries, an omelette with sliced peppers and homemade bread served with a fiery cream cheese and pepper paste. It was one of the nicest hotels that I encountered on my travels.

Many of the town's buildings are made from simple but sizeable stone blocks. Here and there, the decaying tiled shell of a prosperous home indicated where a Serb must have lived twenty years ago. The clocktower is a partial recreation of a 1597 original, which was destroyed in the Balkan Wars in 1912, losing its belfry to Montenegro. On that occasion too, the Albanian population of the region was treated brutally. Edith Durham reports Montenegrins boasting that they had not "left a nose on an Albanian up there". The severing of noses to demonstrate prowess to one's commander was another Montenegrin tradition, reminiscent of the Japanese custom, in the late 16th-century raids on Korea, of rewarding their soldiery according to the number of noses submitted on their return; a mound in Kyoto still enshrines at least 38,000 noses from that period.

From the far side of the river, the town had an understandably defensive appearance. White-plastered overhanging first floors had fortress-like windows above solid stone walls. I appeared to be the ethnographic museum's first visitor for some time. I admired the old, white-painted stoves adorned with a riot of different pillar styles and mouldings, as if Wedgwood had indulged in a pre-Raphaelite fantasy. While examining a display on *plis* manufacture, I was buttonholed by an insistent guide. He was a burly figure of sixty or so, sporting several days' growth and dressed in a black T-shirt and jeans, with a very limited selection of popular English words at his disposal. After a whistle-stop tour of his selected highlights of the museum, primarily examples of early 20th-century machinery imports from England that he thought might resonate with me, he led me down the road for a cup of coffee. As we passed the small red wreck of a hatchback sitting forlornly on flat tyres, with the tops of exploding seats visible inside, he gestured to wait. Unlocking it, he proceeded to root around the metre-high sprawl of books that I could now see filled every corner of the car, including the boot. After a minute, he emerged triumphant, brandishing a UN High Commission for Refugees book on the humanitarian challenge in Kosovo, which I was induced to buy after minimal barter. Its pictures spoke eloquently of the trauma of displacement and the challenges of returning home that the Albanian population faced in Kosovo in 1998 and 1999. We sat drinking coffee while he complained in splintered English about the quality of modern architecture in Gjakova. I saw a plaque on the wall opposite, clearly erected to a Second World War Albanian Partisan hero. When I pointed it out to my new friend, he spat out "communeest" disdainfully. He agreed to be photographed in front of it to gales of laughter from both himself and a passing friend. We parted with a bone-crunching handshake.

The Kosovo Albanians were not great supporters of the Partisans in the Second World War, whom they perceived as Serb-dominated, and even the Kosovan Serbs were rather more drawn to the royalist Chetnik resistance than to Tito. The Albanians were more inclined to support a move towards a Greater Albania, and a few were recruited by the Nazis into the vicious and ineffective Skanderbeg SS unit. Tito's initial meeting at Jajce in 1943 to plan for his Yugoslavia did not include any Kosovo Albanian representatives, and at the end of the war the new Partisan government faced an armed revolt for six months or so before it was able to restore order. Ultimately, Kosovo was included in the Yugoslav constitution as an autonomous entity within Serbia. The dream of a Greater Albania essentially died with the mutual postwar agreement of Tito and Enver Hoxha (the new Stalinist leader of Albania). Life in Kosovo was very tough in the first half of the Tito era as the loyalties of both sections of the population were considered to be suspect. The secret police, controlled by Tito's henchman and deputy prime minister, Aleksander Ranković, enforced anti-Albanian policies with brutality. After Ranković's fall from power in 1966, Kosovo was allowed more freedom, and the Albanian population became more assertive. Those were the golden years that my dinner companions in Prishtina had remembered so fondly, although even then economic opportunities lagged well behind educational advances, causing periodic unrest.

At the Hadum Mosque, detailed geometrical patterns framed holy buildings and trees in faded orange, blues and greens. Nearby was the Bektashi Tekke. Gjakova is a well-known centre for dervish sects, and their *tekkes* (lodges) have an elegant solidity as one walks around the town. The dervishes represent the mystical side of Islam and especially revere Muhammad's son-in-law Ali, in addition to the Prophet himself. In the Balkans, they typically have at least weekly ceremonies of chanting and will drink alcohol, but do not participate in the famous whirling dances found in Turkey.

The custodian showed me pictures of the Frashëri brothers, well-born adherents of the dervish sect from southern Albania, who in the late 19th century were among the founders of the League of Prizren, the forerunner of the eventually successful fight by the local Albanian people to gain control of Kosovo. One of the brothers, Naim, considered a great national Albanian poet, looked out into the middle distance in a bowtie and winged collar with an air of purpose. Along the walls were photographs of the sect leaders from 1790 to the present day, all with bushy white beards and white cylindrical hats. Other images showed the debris-filled shell of the building after its near-total destruction on 7th May 1999 and the restored whole before the reopening ceremony eight years later. The green-robed chief dervish cut a red ribbon surrounded by beaming faces. As I left, I was shown the cool pistachio-green gallery by the entrance, light shining through its arched windows, where the bodies of past sect leaders lie at peace again. The keeper of the *tekke* bade me farewell – "God bless Tony Blair and England."

Along the main cobbled street of the market, wooden shopfronts looked much as they must have done a century ago, despite the destruction of the intervening years. There were even horses with carts tied up for loading and unloading. I experienced some childish amusement at the name of a ladies' hairdresser (*Frisere Femrash*), which turned to bemusement when I found out that it meant "lingerie coiffeuse". The Catholic cathedral had selected an unfortunate shade of pale green to detail its architectural features. Opposite was the opportunity to buy a range of violently hued bouquets. At least the Catholics and Muslims appeared to coexist well.

Further down the road behind a wired barrier were the ruins of the old barracks, a low, malevolent block turning to grey as its painted exterior gradually eroded. The darkness behind the blank window cavities was oddly disturbing. It is a daily reminder of the horrors of the past. Further on is the Taliqi Bridge, an Ottoman gem with six arches of surprisingly varied sizes supporting V-shaped humps, traversed by an old cobbled road; its beauty is oddly more evident for being sandwiched between an informal rubbish dump on one side and a communist-era concrete road bridge on the other. Back in 1999, there was a checkpoint here from which twenty Albanian citizens were rounded up and taken away.

Prizren

Nearing Prizren, one is increasingly encircled by the snow-patched mountains that separate Kosovo from Albania and cradle the town. The flat land below was disfigured by empty factories and much ill- or unplanned development. Herds of cows grazed right up to the motorway verges, their bells a constant background noise away from large towns.

The centre had much more charm. The Bistrica River flowed beside the main street between stone-clad embankments. A pedestrian walkway on one side and a broad pavement on the other gave the sense of a town designed for use by humans rather than cars. Girls in red tartan kilts chatted happily as they made their way home after school. Prizren was relatively untouched in 1998 and 1999, although it did see some destruction of Serb property by returning refugees. It suffered worse in the 2004 riots, with Orthodox sites particularly targeted.

Outside *tekkes* and mosques, water flowed. A turban-capped marble fountain was decorated with two snakes winding up staffs to crossed scimitars, beneath which an old brass duck-headed tap waited. A row of weathered spouts flowed into a series of small gullies. Beside each was a wooden seat to assist the faithful as they washed ahead of prayers. Time had slowed down. There was little sign now of Prizren's heritage as the weapons producer of the Balkans; in 1866, there had been 208 weapon shops in the town, fifty-three of them specialising in producing gun barrels and bullet chambers.

Nearby is the League of Prizren Museum, destroyed by Serbian forces in March 1999 and reconstructed and reopened with surprising speed by November of the same year. The first meeting of the League was in 1878, a gathering of representatives from a number of Albanian lands, though the majority were from the surrounding parts of Kosovo and Albania. Initially, it was formed in loyalty to the sultan, designed to protect any Albanian territory from infidel rule. This was in large part a reaction to the agreement at the Congress of Berlin for the Ottoman Empire to cede part of western Kosovo to Montenegro. The Albanians could see that the expansionist mindsets of the newly created independent states of Serbia and Montenegro alongside that of Greece would require a defence strategy. Mehmed Ali Pasha, the Ottoman official sent to persuade the local communities to accept the secession, was shouted down in Prizren and besieged when he moved on to Gjakova. In an attempt to escape, he and his party shot eight locals, before he was decapitated and his head paraded through the streets on the end of a pike. The resulting stand-off and the repulsing of Montenegrin forces in the following two years led to a revision of the congress' plan, leaving western Kosovo still part of the Ottoman Empire, while Montenegro was compensated with coastal territory.

Over time, the League's ambitions shifted from wanting a degree of autonomy within the Ottoman Empire to an ambition for something much closer to a fully-fledged Albanian state. Having achieved *de facto* control in Kosovo, the League turned its focus to Macedonia, with the intention of moving on thereafter to Shkodër (Scutari), present-day Albania. An Ottoman army was sent out and crushed the rebels with great efficiency, arresting their leaders, but dealing with them reasonably mercifully.

These events coincided with Serbia, Montenegro and Bulgaria initiating mass expulsions of Muslims from the territory that they had taken from the Ottomans in 1877 and 1878. Around 50,000 refugees may have arrived in each of Kosovo and Macedonia. There was also a migration of Serbs north, and by 1912 some 60,000 may have moved the other way, impelled by difficult conditions in Kosovo and the pull of Mother Serbia.

The movement for some sort of Albanian independence continued to appear in various guises. In 1899, the League of Peja restated a desire for more autonomy, and there was a series of tax revolts in the early 20th century, many of them regional and uncoordinated. Over the border in Macedonia, the Internal Macedonian Revolutionary Organisation (IMRO) had started mounting raids on the Ottomans with the aim of achieving autonomy for the local (largely ethnic Bulgarian) population there. The Kosovars were induced to support the Young Turk movement in Istanbul by deception; its aim of a modernised, centralised government from Turkey was almost the polar opposite of Kosovan ambitions, although they did want to be Ottoman. In 1912, the revolts against their masters finally coalesced to a scale that forced the concession of a high degree of autonomy to the Albanian population. Within months, the victory had turned to dust. The Serbs swept through Kosovo in the First Balkan War, driving out the Ottomans and reclaiming their self-perceived historical legacy with multiple references to Lazar and 1389. A special commemoration was held on the historic battlefield of Kosovo Polje. However, the annexation was not just a straightforward military affair; there were notable mass killings of civilians, with maybe 25,000 Albanians dead in total, as well as forcible conversions to Orthodoxy. Trotsky (a journalist in Vienna at the time) was convinced that, in order to improve the demographic mix, the Serbs "engaged quite simply in systematic extermination of the Muslim population". It was far from King Peter of Serbia's ringing declaration at the start of the war: "Christian and Moslem Albanians with whom our people have shared joy and sorrow for thirteen centuries now. To all of them we bring freedom, brotherhood and equality." It would be a long time before the League's ambitions came to fruition again.

On the other side of the river is the main city mosque, Sinan Pasha, its domes and elegant, narrow minaret rising above the tiled roofs around it against the dark mountain. Walking up the hill behind, it is clear that one is in a former Serb quarter. Shells of houses sit among others that have been newly restored. Much more of the damage in Prizren was caused after the war than during it; by the end of 1999, it was estimated that 97% of the local Serb population had left. High up, the 14th-century Orthodox Church of St Saviour is a roofless husk, although a small chapel inside had been cleaned up, and the remains of frescoes were still visible. Two figures in US uniforms walked in and I apologised, thinking I was trespassing, but they were exploring too, along with their Macedonian Albanian minder. The latter told me that he had done a lot of work for the *Daily Express* during the troubles but now worked with the US military. He excused his accent, saying that it had steadily migrated west alongside his employment.

I descended a desolate street with many abandoned houses. Planks were nailed roughly over doorways and ground-floor windows; on the first floor, window frames were blackened from fire. Back in the civilisation of the centre, I climbed in the car to visit the Monastery of the Holy Archangels, founded by Stefan Dušan, the last great Nemanjić tsar, who was buried here until his remains were moved to Belgrade in 1927. Under Dušan, the Serbian Empire was at its largest, stretching from the Danube to the Peloponnese, including Macedonia, Bulgaria and much of northern Greece. With his death in 1355, it fell rapidly apart.

The monastery lies down a narrow valley on an old trade route to Skopje and was razed to the ground under the Ottomans. It briefly became an active monastery again in 1998 but was burned and looted in both 1999 and 2004. Now, from the outside, it looked like an archaeological site, although the main entrance over a cobbled bridge consisted of a firmly locked black gate decorated with bronze crosses. Fearsome signs warned against attempted entry - "Danger, authorised use of firearms". Rolls of razor wire reinforced the point. A sign inside the gate was from another era, proscribing inappropriately revealing clothing. A Serbian flag hung limply from a scaffold on which a large bell was suspended. The whole scene was forlorn, but standing back amid clumps of deep purple thistles, one sensed the peace that must have once reigned on this plateau with the grey mountains all around.

I drove further away from Prizren along a river gorge so tight, one marvelled that a road could have been constructed there at all. A road sign indicated height and weight restrictions separately for trucks and tanks. The valley opened out and I came to the hamlet of Sredska, where I hoped to visit the early 16th-century frescoes in the Church of St George. All that was visible of the hamlet were three ruined houses and a police station by the road, from where I was pointed down a lane. I parked by a barrier, beside which an elderly man was occupied picking elderflowers in the hedgerow. Introducing himself as Dragan, he told me that he feared the church might be closed. He was visiting from Belgrade; his old house was still here at Sredska, as was his former school by the church and the hills that he had wandered as a boy. It had been a Serb village then, but everyone had gone now. His children all lived in Serbia, but he still liked to come back as he had been happy here. He trudged off into the woods plucking the occasional flower head, turning and waving back to me after every ten paces. The little stone church sat easily amidst fir trees in the green valley. Some of the slats were missing in the cupola; otherwise it looked in good repair, as did the churchyard. I noticed that many of the gravestones there were for couples. Some already had a pair of etched faces staring out from the black marble. Some were a work in progress, a picture on one side and a gap on the other, with the birth date already engraved in preparation for the partner's ultimate return.

Mitrovica

I drove back to Prishtina, fretting a little about my planned trip the next day to Mitrovica, which is now a divided town, having been mixed prior to 1999. A bridge over the Ibar River was guarded by UN troops; the south side is Albanian and the north Serb. My UN friend had told me that on her most recent visit to North Mitrovica, she had had to go in an armoured convoy. There were still meant to be seven wanted human rights violators there, four hiding up in the local hospital. My fears had been reinforced by looking at the British Foreign Office website, which recommended against visiting, warning of occasional violent clashes involving grenades and vehicle explosions and issuing particular admonitions about the dangers of rallies and other mass meetings. Nonetheless, another contact had said that it was pretty calm at present, and I was determined to visit Zvečan Castle, a Roman fort that had been refortified by Stefan Nemanja, the founder of the dynasty, and where he had celebrated victory over the Byzantines around 1170. North Mitrovica is now the only urban concentration of Serbs in Kosovo. Along with its satellite communities, it represents a little under half the total Serb population of 100,000 or so.

The next morning, I parked near the bridge in South Mitrovica. There seemed to be a building boom. Smart modern edifices, freshly painted or clad with glass and metal, lined broad streets. A glittering new mosque trumpeted its presence to the world with twin minarets and red and white detailing above the arches in a pale gold facade. Reconstruction was progressing apace. I walked through the corrugated iron barricades that shielded the view of the bridge to see half-a-dozen mixed police and NATO (KFOR) personnel in a relaxed group. I asked a Slovenian soldier if it was okay to cross the bridge. "Yeah, fine," he responded.

A hundred yards on, at the far end of the bridge, a mound of earth re-emphasised the defensive nature of the separation from the Serb point of view. Beyond it, I felt as if I had retreated forty years in ten paces. A snagged Serb banner was draped awkwardly on a wire high above. A long queue led into a bank. The cars on the road seemed to be mostly from Tito's era. Elderly, dark-clad figures sat on the kerb with bags of local produce and plastic bottles of opaque liquid for sale on the ground in front of them. Stallholders sat stoically on stools behind tables of basic clothing. The passers-by were disinterested. A sense of lassitude pervaded the town. I heard singing, shouting and a brass band. A flicker of fear went through me, but a group of young people danced past me harmlessly.

I found a taxi rank just up the hill and on it a driver who spoke a little English. Nenad was a stocky figure in a yellow polo shirt and jeans. He agreed to take me to Sokolica Monastery and Zvečan Castle but explained that I would have to give him money to put fuel in his vehicle before we could start. We set out in an antique Volkswagen, my view in front hampered by an extensive spider pattern in the damaged windscreen glass. Sokolica lay three miles up a track with striking views over the hills towards the Kopaonik mountain range and the Serbian border. We knocked on the door of the monastery and, after some time, a nun emerged and showed us the little church, within which is a much-revered 13th-century stone statue of the Virgin and Child. It has real primitive charm – both mother and son (more boy than infant) stare out wide-eyed and welcoming from their throne. Traces of paint suggested a much brighter past. The nun helped explain my plan to climb up to Zvečan Castle to Nenad, reassuring me that "he is a good man". As we said goodbye, she said that God knows better than us his plans and what is best, as if voicing the thoughts of the entire enclave.

Retracing our path, we soon came to the castle, whose ruins sit on the peak of a wooded cone that dominates the valley to the north. Nenad insisted on accompanying me but first removed his taxi sign and hid it in the boot, gesticulating that otherwise it was likely to be stolen. He said *"zmija"* and mimed that I should be careful of snakes on our climb. We wound our way up steep, indistinct paths to the summit, where a huge Serb flag flew proudly in the breeze. Some of Nemanja's castle walls are still standing but there is little left of the buildings, the site also of Stefan Dečanski's strangulation in 1331. It functioned as an Ottoman fort for several hundred years, but was abandoned in the 18th century and fell into disrepair. There are panoramic views at the top; Nenad pointed out to me the boundary between Serb and Albanian territory. Two small Albanian villages over the valley to the west looked especially isolated. They must at times have felt acutely vulnerable in recent decades.

As we descended, the red-banded grey chimney and extensive buildings of the Zvečan lead smelter were clearly visible. This was originally started with British backing in the 1930s to process ore from the local mines. The mines produced 40% of Germany's wartime lead demand, much of it mined by Serbs who had been sent to the concentration camp at Mitrovica. In the 1980s, it was the largest lead-smelting facility in Europe, and Trepča (the Yugoslav company operating the mines, smelter and associate facilities) was the dominant employer in the region. At one point, it accounted for 70% of Kosovo's gross domestic product, but with the division of Mitrovica in 1999, Trepča's operations became divided too. The Serbs continued to try and operate the facilities in their sector, even constructing a new power line into Serbia to enable this. In the summer of 2000, after arguments about ownership of the company's assets and with claims of high levels of pollution, UN troops stormed the premises and arrested the CEO, who was expelled into Serbia. The plant has been out of action since, a major factor in the downtrodden air of North Mitrovica.

As we drove back, we saw huge celebrations and bands in the village below. I tensed. Nenad grinned broadly, saying: "End of school." I thanked him warmly as he dropped me off, offering a choice of Serbian dinars or euros to pay my fare. He was very clear that he preferred the latter.

Back to the bridge, heavily graffitied on the north side with anti-EU slogans, and back past the various barricades to my car, I headed northwest to Stari Trg (literally, "old market"), the original mine from which operations had started again in the 1930s, although mines in the area had been operational in Roman times. West had been impressed by the benevolent operation there of a British company (Selection Trust, though unnamed in the book), with the provision of good-quality housing and education for employees and easy working relationships between Albanians and Serbs. She rhapsodised about "a garden city of white houses and pink roofs, set about with orchards". She had obviously been especially taken with the Scot in charge, "*Gospodin* [Mr] Mac".

Along a beautiful beech-lined valley, Cyrillic versions of place names on signs were painted out as usual. There was plenty of evidence of machinery and plant, some of it newish, but limited signs of activity. Above the road in the small town sat low stone buildings that could have been displaced from the Scottish Highlands. Sky-blue doors and cottage windows smiled under long, tiled roofs. Clay pots sat on windowsills. I felt very at home. I wandered around photographing what were evidently examples of West's model housing. Two youths asked what I was doing; after a conversation of sorts in cod German, they pointed me up the hill with the words "*Englisch Haus*". At the top, the land opened up and attractive modern villas surrounded by fruit trees stood with a view of fields and wooded ridges. Just below, in a sheltered and well-spaced position, stood the ruin of a substantial stone house with steps leading up to a terrace. The roof had gone and the ceilings were collapsing, but

I imagined that this was where West had sat discussing with Mrs Mac the trials and blessings of life in her long exile from Ayrshire. I fancied that I could still hear the click of her knitting needles on the terrace.

Kosovo Polje

Returning to Prishtina, the road was broadly the route that the Serbian army had taken as they fled south in 1916. At the start of the First World War, the Serbs repulsed the invading Austro-Hungarian forces better than anyone would have believed. The initial Austro-Hungarian invasion had been accompanied by massacres of civilians, mass rapes and torture in the fever for revenge stirred up by the killing of Franz Ferdinand. The aggressors eventually took Belgrade at the end of 1914 but were driven out again a month later. It was only in October 1915 that a new Austrian-German advance from the north combined with a Bulgarian attack from the south proved too unequal a challenge. Bulgaria had been induced to enter the fray with the promise of Macedonia, which they felt should have been theirs by right at the end of the First Balkan War. Even the British appeared to think that Bulgaria should have Macedonia. Duff Cooper's diary entry for 31st May opined: "The Bulgars are brutes, but ... they certainly got less than they deserved out of the Balkan War, though it was their own fault, and the population of eastern Macedonia is chiefly Bulgar."

In November, the decision was made to retreat strategically in an attempt to preserve as much as possible of the Serbian army. The main route fed through Kosovo and over the mountains to the west to the Adriatic coast. It was a brutal journey in midwinter. The American journalist Paul Fortier Jones travelled with them from Mitrovica to Prishtina. He described a valiant army becoming "a freezing, starving, hunted remnant". He recounted how "[s]cores of dead animals were strewn along the road, and ... many soldiers and prisoners, driven almost insane, tear the raw flesh from horses and oxen and eat it, if not with enjoyment, at least with satisfaction". He told of an elderly dying Serbian woman hurling curses at the soldier who tried to carry her instead of his gun;

his ability to fight was more important than her life. Much of the heavy equipment was ultimately dumped off the mountain road from Peja to Andrijevica. Unsurprisingly, the local population did not offer succour to the vanquished army. Edith Durham remarked: "That the Albanians spared the lives of the retreating Serbs who had previously shown them no mercy, is to their honour." In practice, however, there is evidence of revenge attacks by Albanians on the fleeing soldiers. By the summer of 1918, an exhausted Austro-Hungarian army was rolled back to the far side of the Danube with relative ease by Serbian, French and Italian forces. Kosovo was part of Greater Serbia again.

Five miles before Prishtina, a sturdy tower is visible to the east of the road. It stands on a low plateau amid fields of waving grass, within which a host of colours were apparent; not just the red of the poppies for which the plain is famous, but also varying shades of white and yellow and the blues and pinks of wild salvia. Against an overcast sky, it looked threatening, as well it might, for in many ways this site was the launchpad in 1989 for the decade of turmoil that was to follow.

The Gazimestan Monument was constructed in 1953 by the Yugoslav government on the site of the Battle of Kosovo. It is a plain construction of solid grey stone. The bare elevation at the front is broken by a line of three slit windows above a simple arch framed by two sturdy pillars. Inside the alcove, a shield with two crossed swords is mounted above an inscription in Cyrillic script. It is the curse ascribed to Lazar in the 19th-century folk song that reignited his legend.

> *Whoever is a Serb and of Serb birth,*
> *And of Serb blood and heritage,*
> *And comes not to fight at Kosovo,*
> *May he never have progeny born from love,*
> *Neither son nor daughter!*
> *May nothing grow that his hand sows,*
> *Neither young wine nor white wheat!*
> *And may his progeny be feeble until any left!*

From the top, one can easily envisage the disposition of the Serb and Ottoman forces back in 1389 on the "field of blackbirds" (Kosovo Polje). Some have claimed that the blackbirds were in fact vultures hovering above the dead left on the battlefield after fighting had ceased. Looking down, the scavengers seemed as likely to have been jackdaws, whose descendants still picked noisily over the ground. In the distance, I could see Prishtina and the power station that serves it. Much nearer was the dome of the mausoleum of Sultan Murad's standard-bearer as well as the peculiarly intrusive orange and glass bulk of a new office building.

In 1987, Slobodan Milošević, then head of the Serbian Communist Party, was sent to Kosovo to treat with local Serbs, who were protesting against perceived discrimination by the Albanian majority. The local police were struggling to contain the unruly mob outside the hall where he was speaking, and Milošević emerged to utter the fateful words: "No one should dare to beat you!" The reaction to that televised moment and the speech that followed seems to mark the point at which Milošević realised that he could use the Serb nationalist cause as his path to power in the uncertainties of the post-Tito era. By March 1989, despite considerable Albanian protests, he had engineered the passage through the Kosovo and Serbian assemblies of constitutional change that effectively removed Kosovo's autonomy. Three months later, on the 600th anniversary of the Battle of Kosovo, he held a huge rally here at the battle site, where he lionised the suffering and heroism of the Serb people through history since Lazar and the glories of the Nemanjić empire. More than half a million supporters roared their approval. Milošević's chilling words signalled the worst: "Six centuries later, again we are in battles and quarrels. They are not armed battles, though such things should not be excluded yet."

A little over a mile away, on the other side of the main road, is the mausoleum of Sultan Murad, on the spot where his tent was pitched and where he died on the day of the battle. Only his entrails are buried here under a stone covered with a black embroidered cloth. His other remains were removed to the imperial mausoleum at his birthplace of Bursa in Turkey. The custodian (or *turbedar*) of the mausoleum is a hereditary post, currently occupied by a Bosnian lady, who was inspecting her domain when I arrived. She appeared to be doing a much better job than the ancestor in charge when West had visited: "A fountain splashed from a wall, and there was nothing else pleasant there." The Muslim graves that still stand beside the mausoleum appear to have been cleaned and are still "of the handsome sort, having a slab as well as a column at the top and bottom". I endured a laborious tour given by a friendly Turk from Prishtina, who told me that there used to be big Turkish communities in Prizren and Gjakova, all now gone. The small museum on site boasted a costumed figure of Murad that would have looked more at home as a dummy in a local tailor's shop.

Prishtina II

Driving back into the city, I was greeted by a large poster, several storeys high, welcoming me to Bill Clinton Boulevard (formerly Lenin Street) with a grinning photograph of the ex-president. I assumed that he was not consciously endorsing the brand of coffee on the carefully colour-coordinated poster below.

I had one more pilgrimage to make before I left Kosovo. On a hill to the east of Prishtina lies the old Jewish cemetery, where the simple graves in a grassy field by a small wood are all that remain of the historical Jewish presence here. Many of them were Sephardic Jews who had fled the threat of forced conversion or death in Spain in the late 15th century. In May 1944, most of the 300 or so Jews still living in Prishtina were handed over to the Germans by Albanian collaborators. The majority died in Belsen. The very few remaining at the end of the war emigrated to Israel.

A short distance away is the Martyrs' Hill, where two rows of plain white marble sarcophagi hold the remains of members of the Kosovo Liberation Army (KLA) killed fighting the Serbs. Many were decorated with weather-beaten wreaths of plastic flowers. Many simply bore a name and dates and the words "DESHMOR I KOMBIT" (martyr of the nation). One of the dead had been barely sixteen. Other graves in the row were mounds of earth with head- and footstones in a traditional Muslim style. Only one was typically modern Balkan, where a moustachioed figure in uniform with a submachine gun stared out from a black marble tablet.

Slightly higher up the hill in a small formal park is the tomb of Ibrahim Rugova, a slab set atop a plinth, both of white marble. Rugova was the public face of Kosovan independence, but his strongly held views on non-violence set him at odds with the KLA, and there were fierce debates over whether his grave should be sited so close to the martyrs. Nonetheless, the outpouring of grief at his death from lung cancer in 2006 saw over half a million people line his funeral procession.

Rugova had been born at the tail end of the Second World War, and both his father and grandfather had been killed by Partisans shortly afterwards. He was an academic and had emerged as the leader of the Democratic League of Kosovo (LDK) in his role as head of the Writer's Union, quite possibly as the least threatening of the alternatives available. The organisation's name was a conscious echo of the League of Prizren. In the wake of Milošević's suppression of Kosovo's rights, the LDK became the central voice of Albanian discontent. After elections in 1992, illegal in Serb eyes, he became President of Kosovo and set about constructing a parallel Albanian state within a state while lobbying foreign powers to support Kosovan independence. Milošević tolerated the situation, not least as his war in Bosnia was occupying so much of his diplomatic and logistical resources. The Croats tried to encourage an Albanian attack on the Serbs, but Rugova was a strong advocate of peaceful resistance and horrified by the sectarian violence that had erupted in Bosnia. The armed resistance to Serbia in Kosovo began to coalesce around the KLA after its formation in 1993, though it remained a collection of groups throughout rather than a single, unified structure.

In the wake of the Dayton peace agreement in Bosnia in 1995, the arguments against armed resistance became weaker – fighting had made a difference. The subsequent collapse of Albania in 1997 led to a huge increase in the availability of cheap weapons. The number of violent incidents increased – bomb blasts and shootings of Serb policemen as well as the Serb rector of Prishtina University. In 1997, a spokesman for the KLA claimed responsibility, and later that year saw the first official KLA casualty, Adrian Krasniqi, after whom the street at Martyrs' Hill is named. The continued ratcheting-up of violence provoked inevitable and excessive Serb retaliation. Richard Holbrooke, who had delivered the Dayton agreement, led an international attempt to broker a peace deal in Kosovo, but it failed to hold. In the wake of the atrocities in Bosnia, there was considerable sympathy among Western leaders for the Albanian majority in Kosovo, although Madeleine Albright was probably not alone when she observed in her memoirs that the KLA "often ... seemed intent on provoking a massive Serb response so that international intervention would be unavoidable". They seemed to have learned the right buttons to push to maximise international support from their Bosniak co-religionists. Milošević continued to reject the idea of Kosovan autonomy, counting in part on Russian support.

In March 1999, NATO started bombing Serbia, Kosovo and parts of Montenegro. The action was not explicitly approved by the UN and was intended to be short-lived to force Serbia to agree to autonomy in Kosovo and forestall the sorts of atrocities that had been seen in Bosnia. Milošević apparently believed that a "polite" bombing campaign might boost his domestic support. In reaction, he embarked on a programme of full-scale ethnic cleansing with massacres of Albanians and mass deportation of over 800,000 (over four times the entire Serb population of Kosovo). The atrocities in the process were stomach-churning. The destruction of passports at the border sought to make the expulsions irreversible. In June, the Russians and the West presented Milošević with a non-negotiable deal. The bombing was over and KFOR would safeguard the key Serb colonies and cultural treasures. The United Nations would take over the administration of Kosovo. Some 10,000 people had died in the war, and the bloody reprisals as Albanians returned led many more Serbs to flee north. In the elections of 2000, the LDK won a significant majority, and Rugova became president again in 2002.

Violent riots in 2004 were sparked partly by ethnic tensions but also by dissatisfaction with the degree of autonomy that the Albanian population had in the new government structure. They were probably also fomented by organised crime gangs able to take advantage of the anarchic situation. In 2008, Kosovo declared independence from Serbia. To date, Serbia still refuses to recognise Kosovan sovereignty, though does recognise many of the Kosovan institutions of government. The negotiations to enshrine a settlement have been complicated by the indictment in 2020 of President Hashim Thaçi for war crimes by The Hague; he had been political director of the KLA during the war. He has also been accused of high-level involvement in organised crime. The path forward is still opaque.

I walked down the hill, past a market with stalls selling crates of fresh produce – strawberries, cherries, apricots, peppers, cucumbers, cabbages. The perfumed scent of the fruit and the dizzying array of colour was overwhelming. Back in the main square, across from Skanderbeg, stands a larger-than-life statue of Rugova, deep in thought with his eyes all but closed. His trademark silk scarf blows in the wind. When asked by Warren Zimmermann, the last US ambassador to Yugoslavia, why he wore it year-round, Rugova "looked embarrassed and said ... everybody needed a signature piece". Two very different fighters for Albanian independence stand in the heart of Prishtina, twin symbols of a finally independent Kosovo.

Serbia

*"... it is terrible, even in victory,
to be a small state among great empires."*

HUNGARY
CROATIA
NOVI SAD
ROMANIA
POŽAREVAC
BELGRADE
VALJEVO
RAVANICA
MONTENEGRO
NOVI PAZAR
NIŠ
BULGARIA
KOSOVO
NORTH MACEDONIA

Belgrade

I arrived in Belgrade on a late autumn day. Unable to stay where West had in the Serbian Crown Hotel, as it had been destroyed by the ferocious Nazi bombing of the city in 1941, I extravagantly opted for the Hotel Moskva, just up from Republic Square, the centre point of the old city. Above its Art Deco entrance rises a pristine flesh-coloured structure decorated with green-tiled panels and elaborate swagging. The steeply pitched roof is also green-tiled, flanked by two miniature celadon domes and topped off with twin copper spires. It is associated with the Secession movement founded in Vienna by Gustav Klimt and others a decade before the hotel's 1908 opening with the aim of breaking down artistic nationalism and aspiring to a "total art", unifying the various decorative and representational branches. A little more specialisation might have been helpful in this case, but it is an interesting historical curio. The building has hosted a range of the famous over the years, among them Einstein, Gorky, Indira Gandhi, Hitchcock, de Niro and Pavarotti, although the latter would have struggled to squeeze into the little garret room that I was allotted. A large beam angled down from the ceiling and pierced the floor a couple of feet in from the door, as if Wotan had lost his temper and hurled his spear through the roof. Outside the window, I looked down towards the railway station where West had first arrived, beyond it the grey flow of the River Sava.

Republic Square boasts the traditional equestrian statue, in this case of Prince Mihailo Obrenović, not a dominant figure in Serbian history, but one with symbolic value nonetheless. His reign proper lasted only eight years in the mid-19th century (after a three-year stint as a minor twenty years earlier), having spent much of the interim in exile in Vienna. On his return, he modernised the constitution and established the first Serbian army. With Austrian and Russian support, he achieved the withdrawal of Turkish forces from much of northern Serbia, including Belgrade. He also attempted to form an effective league with other Balkan nations to push out the Turks completely, but he was assassinated aged forty-five while out driving with his cousin and mistress, Katarina, before these plans could come to fruition. The motive was never entirely clear, but there was rising dissatisfaction with his increasingly absolutist policies. The prince faces south towards the lands that were still unliberated at his death, a symbol of Serb nationhood and independence.

Knez Mihailova, the main shopping street, was full of the fashion-conscious surveying its glossy boutiques. At the far end, it leads to Kalemegdan, the park containing the old fortress of Belgrade, which sits on a hill above the meeting point of the Sava and the Danube, the silver expanse of water reflecting the clouds above. With its commanding views to the west and north, it is easy to see why it was selected as a site well before the Romans arrived here. Their own fortress was sacked repeatedly by Huns and Goths in the first half of the 5th century, and some claim that Attila himself is buried beneath it. In the wake of the Battle of Kosovo in 1389, it became the base of Lazar's son, Stefan Lazarević, and thus the *de facto* capital of Serbia. Belgrade ("white fortress") takes its name from it. It was defended successfully against the Turks by the Hungarians in 1456 but came under Ottoman control with the fall of Serbia in 1521. It stayed that way until Prince Mihailo forced their withdrawal in 1867, other than for a brief interlude of Austrian occupation and rebuilding in the early 18th century.

In the park beside it, created by Mihailo to celebrate the departure of the Turks, stand two Meštrović statues, both commemorating the First World War. High on a pillar, a naked male figure, whose stylised face has the hard angles of an anvil, bears the grey falcon of Serb legend on his left hand and a lowered sword, tip on the ground, in his right. A symbol of freedom and peace, it was erected on the tenth anniversary of the start of the key advance from Macedonia in 1918 to liberate Serbia. Nearby, a female figure being cleansed in a torrent of water was erected in gratitude to the French soldiers who died in Yugoslavia during the same offensive. A reciprocal statue of Kings Peter and Alexander stands on Place de Colombie in Paris, joint testaments to the camaraderie felt by the two countries at the end of the First World War.

I went to dinner that night at a small traditional restaurant in the old town, just down the street from the only remaining mosque in

Belgrade. In the 17th century, it was described by many visitors as an oriental town, with a hundred mosques, as well as ten hammams, two bazaars and several caravanserais. The Occidentalisation of Belgrade had been started by the Austrians, after Prince Eugene's decisive victory over the Ottomans in 1717. The pace of modernisation slowed but accelerated again after the final departure of the Ottoman army, and the area in which I was dining had an ordered, tree-lined appearance that seemed to signal a distant Austro-Hungarian influence. As West put it, bemoaning its loss of Balkan authenticity, "Modern Belgrade has striped that promontory with streets that had already been built elsewhere much better". Her friend John Gunther, writing slightly earlier, had likened the city to "a pretty peasant girl with the carriage of a queen and the raiment of a dirty beggar".

The waiter who served me dinner poured me a glass, saying "Is red wine" in a tone more questioning than confirmatory. I read Misha Glenny's *The Balkans* while eating a perfect rare steak enlivened by a traditional cream cheese and paprika sauce. My visit to the men's room was also enlivening. There on the wall were century-old black and white photographs of men with fully visible and erect penises in a variety of poses with partially or un-dressed women. In one, a nurse was being ravished from behind while a woman in another appeared to be enjoying penetration from the front and rear. Some of the pictures looked as though a visitor had tried to remove them from the wall; whether from prudery or a desire to augment a personal collection was unclear. On emerging, I glanced into the Ladies to see a similar collection of women being fingered by participants of both sexes.

As I paid the bill, the waiter observed that I liked history. He told me that the house had belonged to Jevrem Obrenović (younger brother of Miloš, founder of the dynasty) and pointed out his picture on the wall. I remarked that he looked very like his nephew, Mihailo. My waiter then delivered an impromptu eulogy to the Obrenovićs, but said that things were very bad now. When I asked what he meant, he replied that Kosovo had gone and now Vojvodina wanted to go too (the northern "autonomous" province with a significant minority Hungarian population) and maybe even Raška (in the south-west, where Serbia's Muslims are concentrated). "They are determined we should be small and contained. That is why there are now two million people living in Belgrade.

In the village, peasants, if they can eat, are happy. In a city, people can be controlled." I questioned who "they" were; he retorted that I, as a reader of history, should know better than him. To my remark that I was still a century or so in the past, he replied, "Read on, it's all the same." He asked where I came from, saying that he liked the English – "at least the upright ones". I hoped that included me.

The continuum of history was a recurrent theme on my Balkan travels. The relevance of events 200 years earlier still has an immediacy to the man in the street today, in a way that the goings-on of the Hanoverian court do not at home. I suspect that this reflects the turmoil of the intervening period, where legends have been shaped to sell political agendas and are refreshed in the process. England is also probably a bad comparator as it is so long since it was last invaded. I often think that the key difference between England and its continental neighbours in its attitude towards Europe is the thousand years since it suffered any form of occupation by a hostile power. Nonetheless, my conversation with the waiter brought me in mind of Churchill's observations about the mindset of the Balkan states at the start of the First World War:

> Their governments were divided from one another by irreconcilable ambitions and jealousies. Every one of them at some ancient period in its history had been the head of a considerable Empire in these regions, and though Serbian and Bulgarian splendours had been of brief duration compared to the glories of Greece, each looked back to this period of greatness as marking the measure of its historic rights. All therefore simultaneously considered themselves entitled to the ownership of territories which they had in bygone centuries possessed only in succession.

Even now, in most museums of the region, you will find a prominent map highlighting the historical greatest extent of the relevant country's area of control.

Topola

The next day, I set off by bus to Topola, some 50 miles south of Belgrade. Many of my fellow passengers were mature ladies in their best coats on a communal outing, bringing with them a faint aroma of cleaning fluid. The villages en route were clean, with well-maintained houses and gardens. Many boasted surprisingly intensive displays of statuary, leaning heavily on the twin influences of classical tradition and Disney. The landscape opened up into rolling hills covered with woods. Topola means "poplar", and many of the nearby villages are named after trees. The impenetrability of the forests and the fierce independence of the inhabitants of these parts probably account for the belief until the mid-19th century that the mountains of the Peloponnese extended all the way up the Balkan peninsula.

It was a pig-dealer from Topola, Djordje Petrović (better known as Karadjordje or "Black George") who led the First Serbian Uprising in 1804. In the later stages of the Ottoman Empire, the weakened sultans had abdicated much of the control of their further-flung provinces to the janissaries. Originally the crack imperial troops, over time these had become a self-serving alliance of mercenaries, whose violence and greed led to a Serb revolt, initially with the sultan's blessing, triggered by the janissaries' pre-emptive execution of 150 Serb leaders. Karadjordje pulled together a disparate group of local Serb chiefs (or *knezes*) into an effective fighting force. He enforced loyalty and introduced the medieval Serbian cross into his coat of arms, along with the double-headed eagle to reinforce historical pride and legitimacy in the fight against the Ottomans. He could also be ruthless: he executed his brother for rape, leaving the hanging corpse in full view when the Serb leaders came to meet with him.

The success of the revolt against the janissaries was such that the Serbs broadened their ambitions to complete independence from the empire. The sultan sent an army to put down the uprising, but it was convincingly defeated by Karadjordje's army at the Battle of Ivankovac, 50 miles south-east of Topola. The ongoing revolt persisted, encouraged by the Russians, who were themselves at war with the Ottomans until 1812, when the tsar made peace so that his forces could concentrate on the threat from Napoleon. Despite Russia's former support for the rebels' cause, the peace treaty allowed for the return of Serbia to the Ottoman Empire. The renewed vigour of the Turkish attack in 1813 overwhelmed the Serbs, and Karadjordje fled to Austria. The retribution of the Ottomans was fearsome, with torched villages, rapes, impalings and mass sales of women and children into slavery. By 1815, the Serbs had risen again under the leadership of another illiterate swine farmer, Miloš Obrenović, a bitter rival of Karadjordje. Obrenović husbanded his forces cleverly and negotiated with the Sublime Porte (the Ottoman central government). In 1815, he achieved an agreement guaranteeing his effective rule in Serbia in return for his sworn loyalty to Istanbul. The more benign atmosphere in the country over the succeeding two years encouraged Karadjordje to make a surreptitious return. Obrenović learned of his arrival, had him killed and sent his stuffed head to the sultan as a demonstration of loyalty. This marked the start of a rivalry between the two clans that only ended with the bloody death of the last Obrenović king nearly ninety years later. Between them, the two families ruled Serbia (and subsequently Yugoslavia) for around 125 years.

Karadjordje's "palace" at Topola is an over-restored fortified farmhouse with a defensive tower attached. There is nothing pretentious about it, as one would expect from the down-to-earth nature of its original owner. Above it, a path leads up through the woods to the Karadjordjević family mausoleum, commissioned by Karadjordje's grandson, Peter l. The cornerstone of the Church of St George was laid here in 1907, but delays caused by the wars of 1913-8 and the complexity of the internal decoration meant that it was only finally dedicated in 1930 by Peter's son, Alexander. It is in a traditional style, of white marble topped with five copper domes that looked almost grey under a matching sky. The original copper had been stolen by the Austrians in 1915 during their occupation. Inside is a dazzling sight – mosaic copies were made of the finest frescoes of sixty old Serbian churches and now cover every inch of the interior. Natural light floods in from the arched windows around the cupolas. It is all very impressive, but there is a harshness in the texture that cannot compare to the originals. Gunther thought that it would "look well in a century or two, when time has dimmed the colour of its burning mosaics". West's husband's droll observation that it is "an encyclopaedia of medieval Serbian art over his family vault" is to the point. Mosaics of St Sava and the full line-up of Nemanjić rulers, as well as the Serbian rulers who came after (Lazar, his son and Djuradj Branković), each carry the model of the principal church that they founded. They proclaim the glorious legacy of the Serbian people and the Karadjordjević dynasty, while binding the Orthodox faith into the process. To the right of the main door, King Peter is led by St George to the Virgin bearing a model of the church in which I was standing. Time has come full circle. The innate tension between the Yugoslav ideal and the destiny of Greater Serbia is laid bare.

Peter Karadjordjević was nearly sixty when he came to the throne as a result of the assassination of Alexander, the last Obrenović king. There is no suggestion that he was complicit in the killing, which he described as ungentlemanly, although he had planned to take over the throne at an earlier stage in his life in conjunction with his father-in-law, Nikola of Montenegro, whose abandonment of the plan had caused a bitter rift between them. At one point, the reigning Obrenović, Milan, had him tried and sentenced to death *in absentia*. Peter had lived a full life. He had completed his education in Paris before attending the French military academy of Saint-Cyr, and later fought for the Foreign Legion in 1870 in the Franco-Prussian War, for which he was awarded the *Légion d'honneur*. He had also fought with the Bosnian Serbs against the Ottomans in 1875-6. He had been an exile in Geneva, living in straitened circumstances for almost ten years, when he was asked to assume the throne.

On becoming king, Peter instituted a new democratic constitution, rebuilt the army and began to seek out new regional allies in an attempt to jointly attach the neighbouring Slavic territories still occupied by the Turks. Both the Russians and Austrians sought to preserve the status quo, a source of considerable dismay to elements within Serbia, who viewed the Austrian occupation and subsequent annexation of Bosnia-Herzegovina after the Congress of Berlin as an affront. A trade war with Austria followed, particularly focused on pigs (Serbia's dominant export), but Serbia found new markets and a greater confidence in independent action as a result. After the Italians signalled the imminent dismembering of the Ottoman Empire with their invasion of Libya at the start of 1912, Serbia seized its chance. In the Balkan Wars of 1912-3 (the first with Bulgaria, Montenegro and Greece against the Ottomans, the second a swift destruction of Bulgarian forces by the Serbs and Greeks with opportunistic support from the Romanians and Turks), Serbia dramatically enlarged its territory to the south. The wars had demonstrated considerable military skill on the Serbs' part, but there was also a level of brutality and ethnic cleansing, involving forced conversion and mass migration impelled by atrocity, that helped set a precedent for the rest of the century. In 1914, Peter handed over responsibility to his second son, Alexander, his first son, George, having been disinherited for kicking his valet to death.

The Serb forces performed extraordinarily well in the early stages of the First World War. They were driven back by the Austrians for the first four months and forced to abandon Belgrade but, rallied by King Peter, who came out of retirement, they mounted a remarkable counter-offensive that retook Belgrade and drove the Austrians out of Serbia in the course of ten days in early December. Then came the desperate and costly retreat over the mountains in 1915. At the end of the war, Peter was proclaimed King of the Serbs, Croats and Slovenes (the forerunner of Yugoslavia) and returned to Belgrade, two years before his death in 1921. As a result of the military successes of his reign and the realisation of the dream of a united southern Slav kingdom, he is known as Peter the Liberator. He is perceived as the great latter-day Serbian monarch, but in the realisation of that greatness were sown the tragedies of the century's end – ethnic cleansing and the further estrangement of the Albanian and Bulgar populations in the south.

The remains of Peter and Karadjordje lie in two simple white marble sarcophagi on either side of the church. Between them hangs a colossal chandelier made of melted-down weapons from Peter's Balkan wars. Downstairs in the crypt, the mosaics are more muted in the dimmer setting, creating a reverent atmosphere. There are thirty-nine tombs prepared for members of the family, of which twenty-six are filled, including both Alexanders, father and son of Peter. For many years after the Second World War, no burials were allowed here, but in the last decade, Alexander's cousin, Paul, and the next generation of the monarchy have been permitted to be reinterred and lie with the rest of the Karadjordjević royals.

Alexander was educated in a Russian military academy, where he had been sent free of charge at the invitation of Tsar Nicholas II, who had known how impoverished the exiled Peter was. During his time in Russia, he appears to have fallen in love and suggested marriage with the tsar's daughter, Grand Duchess Tatiana. He was distraught at the news of the killing of the entire family by the Bolsheviks in 1918. He had fought with honour in the Balkan Wars and reviewed the Serbian troops at Kosovo Polje after they drove the Ottomans out in 1912; father and son were both strongly motivated by the legend of Lazar. Three years later, now regent, Alexander had retreated along with the Serb forces in the gruelling journey through the mountains in 1915. On his father's death in 1921, he became King of the Serbs, Croats and Slovenes. As West observed:

> He had come a very long way in his thirty-odd years. He had spent his childhood as the son of a pretender almost comic in his destitution, in a poky flat in Geneva, as a youth he had been lifted to a step of the Romanoff throne, and as a young man he had overthrown an imperial dominance that had pressed on his people for five hundred years, and before he was yet a ripe man had driven back another empire, the most formidable of Continental powers, and thereby reincarnated the glory of the Emperor Stephen Dushan.

The kingdom that he inherited was as disunited as its name suggested. Ivo Andrić referred to the "lusty chaos of a large new state, which so far had no clear frontiers, no internal order, not even a final name". In a short story, pity is expressed for the victors of the First World War, "for the conquered see what they're up against and what needs to be done, while the conquerors can hardly suspect what is in store for them". Croatia and Slovenia had both been part of the Hapsburg Empire for hundreds of years and had strong Roman Catholic traditions; they saw the new grouping as a defence against expansionist Italy, a factor that only grew in importance with Mussolini's rise to power. The Serbs viewed the Croats as tainted by Teutonisation, while the Croats called Serbs "Mexicans" and "bandits". In the south, the Kosovo Albanians resented the reassertion of Serb dominance after their brief moment of freedom and the Internal Macedonian Revolutionary Organisation (IMRO) sought to overthrow rule from Belgrade. Alexander liked to have a revolver close at hand whenever he ventured out.

The new king did attempt to develop a united entity and move beyond his Greater Serbian upbringing. He brought the radical Croat politician, Stjepan Radić, into government, but Croatian distrust of control from Belgrade was deeply ingrained, and Serb civil servants and army officers formed the backbone of the state. Tensions boiled over on 19th June 1928 when, amid a heated exchange of accusations in parliament relating to relations with Italy, a Montenegrin Serb member shot five Croat members – two dead and Radić himself, who was mortally wounded. In the ensuing chaos, and in response to the series of impossible demands from all sides over the next six months, Alexander dissolved parliament and established himself as a dictator, King of Yugoslavia. This added still more strain in the form of Serb resentment at loss of representation, and Yugoslavia continued to be rent by differences, exacerbated by the economic pressures of the global depression years. The nationalist Ustaše movement in Croatia sought to achieve independence through violent means. Its leader, Ante Pavelić, developed strong political links with the IMRO, was sentenced to death *in absentia* for promulgating violent revolt against the government and fled to Italy, where Mussolini provided support for his training camps. On a state visit to Marseille in 1934, Alexander was assassinated by the IMRO leader's Bulgarian chauffeur as he was driven from the port where he had just landed. The operation had been jointly planned with the Ustaše, but it is unclear if Mussolini was actively involved. The French foreign minister was also killed in the ensuing fracas. Around 500,000 people attended Alexander's funeral in Belgrade before he was buried here in the mausoleum whose completion he had overseen just four years earlier, a Yugoslav king in a temple to a Greater Serbia that he had sought to distance himself from. Among the attendees at the funeral was Hermann Goering, as Germany sought to foster links with Yugoslavia, believing that there was less risk of disruption to their plans elsewhere (notably in Czechoslovakia) if it remained stable and united. A militarising Germany became the dominant customer for Yugoslavia's mineral exports in the 1930s.

Alexander had tried to deliver a broader vision for the south Slavs, forging friendships with those who questioned his policy direction, including the Croatian sculptor Ivan Meštrović. He had also made tentative overtures to Serbia's longstanding adversary, Bulgaria, through King Boris, his cousin by marriage, in an attempt to find a mutually acceptable solution in Macedonia. In the end, his political skills were insufficiently developed to manage a way through the minefield of competing nationalist sentiments in his kingdom.

On his death, his cousin, Prince Paul, became regent on behalf of Alexander's son, Peter, who had just turned eleven. Paul was a cosmopolitan figure, educated at Oxford, a member of the renowned Bullingdon Club and friend of the British royal family; the future George VI, then Duke of York, had been best man at his wedding to Princess Olga of Greece and Denmark in Belgrade in 1923. She in turn was sister to Marina, who married George's younger brother, the Duke of Kent. Paul was also close friends with the bisexual socialite, Sir Henry "Chips" Channon, who described him as "the person I have loved most" and with whom he shared a flat in Westminster after they came down from university. In his diaries, Channon mused on the suitability of the Karadjordjevićs for power at this point: "They all talk English among themselves, read the Tatler, barely understand Slovenian and Serb, and dream of their next trip to London."

Paul was a great lover of art and clearly had a fine eye. He was friends with both Bernard Berenson and Kenneth Clark. His mother was a Demidoff, possibly the wealthiest family in pre-revolutionary Russia after the royal family, and Paul used his inheritance to build up a substantial collection of paintings, which now make up the core of the collection of the National Museum in Serbia. As he and his cousin had sought to find a role for him in Yugoslavia, he had established a museum of modern art and become head of the country's museums. Paul's upbringing coloured his approach in power, which was less dictatorial than his cousin. He had never wanted or expected to rule, viewing it as a seven-year sentence until he could pass on the mantle to his nephew. He also wanted to do anything possible to avoid involving Yugoslavia in another world war after the horrors of the last.

Paul's prime minister through most of his regency was Milan Stojadinović, according to Channon "a dark, huge man, not devoid of charm, but pro-Axis in his leanings and shaky financially". West reported him as "hated throughout the length and breadth of the country". He encouraged his key supporters to wear uniforms and lead repeated chants of *"vodja"* (leader) at meetings, a tactic that backfired as, on repetition, it sounded like *"djavole"* (devil). The corruption and repression may have been quite mild in the context of other fascist regimes and the longer sweep of Yugoslav history, but the transparency of his ambitions and an ill-advised and unauthorised flirtation with Mussolini led Prince Paul to remove him from office and send him into exile in Mauritius, a British colony, facilitated by his friend, King George VI. Post-war, Stojadinović escaped to Buenos Aires with the assistance of Juan Perón, where he lived by all accounts a very comfortable life, presumably funded by his time in office. Bizarrely, in 1954, he also met and may have planned to work with fellow Buenos Aires resident, Ante Pavelić, the Croat Ustaše leader responsible for the appalling atrocities against the Serbs in the Second World War. Some have suggested that this meeting was organised by Tito supporters to discredit the royalist cause.

Post-Stojadinović, Paul approved the creation of an autonomous Croatia within Yugoslavia, trying to solve his biggest internal problem but infuriating most other segments of the country in the process. He also failed to address the rights of minority groups, notably Croatian Serbs and Bosnian Muslims, whose fears would grow over the century, with cataclysmic results. In external matters, the Anglophile Paul tried to keep Yugoslavia neutral, balancing his personal sympathy with the reality of Yugoslavia's economic ties to Germany. He was put under acute pressure by Britain, who made repeated soft promises of trade and arms while delivering almost nothing. He was encouraged to form an alliance with the Greeks and Turks to form a joint front to fight the Germans at Salonika, although it should have been quite obvious that this would provoke a German invasion of Yugoslavia and involve surrendering its major cities at the outset.

Meanwhile, Hitler and Goering wooed Paul, who tried to play for time, recognising that neutrality was likely the best course to preserve his country. In 1939, he made the first royal state visit since Hitler had become Führer; when he and Olga lunched alone with him, a black-uniformed waiter was stationed behind each chair to circumvent issues of precedence with a simultaneous unveiling of the sturgeon main course. Olga had to sit next to Hitler at dinner for seven consecutive evenings. In March 1941, Paul was forced to return to Berchtesgaden as Hitler was gearing up to launch Operation Barbarossa on Russia at the same time as having to rescue the inept Italian invasion of Greece. The prince was told to sign a tripartite pact with Germany and Italy under threat of invasion. He managed to insist on terms that were surprisingly favourable to Yugoslavia: protecting its borders from Axis forces; no requirement for military contributions; no passage of troops across the country; and the expectation of Salonika (Thessaloniki) after the war. Ultimately, he and his crown council felt that they had no option other than to agree, not least as the Croats and Slovenes would be unlikely to back war against the Germans, and German troops were already in Bulgaria. Two days later, an anti-German military coup, backed by British intelligence, installed the 17-year-old Peter II as king in his own right.

Paul spent the next two years of the war under house arrest in Kenya, where he was billeted in Oserian, a gloomy Moorish house that had been freed up by the murder of its previous owner, the Earl of Erroll, only three months earlier. Post-war, he and Olga settled in Paris, a traitor in the eyes of the Tito government. His reputation was traduced in England too, where he was regularly described as the "quisling prince", an attack led as much as anyone by Churchill, who in his single-minded focus to defeat Hitler, refused to see that Paul had been trying to do right by his people. West too was grossly unfair to him. *Black Lamb and Grey Falcon* was published in 1941 in the depths of war; the resulting language is partisan and her account mendacious when she accuses Paul of being pro-Hitler and overriding his prime minister. This she justified in a letter to Harold Nicolson by her having witnessed his graceless behaviour before visiting Muslim worthies. Meštrović also found Paul snobbish, though this does not excuse West's tirade. With time, Paul was able to return to England to visit friends, including the royal family with whom he had been close almost all his life. His daughter, Elizabeth, once engaged to Richard Burton, finally persuaded the Serb authorities to allow her father to be buried at Topola in 2012. She was accompanied to the service by her daughter, Catherine Oxenberg, best known as one of the stars of the 1980s soap opera *Dynasty*. It feels like some compensation for an historic injustice to see Paul buried with honour at last in the country for which he tried so hard to do the right thing.

Hitler was enraged by the coup and the implied revoking of the pact. He immediately instigated the invasion of Yugoslavia or, as he termed it, destruction with "inexorable severity". The bombing of Belgrade began on 6th April; eleven days later, the surrender was signed. The young King Peter made his way to London. A shy boy who had received an indifferent education at home, he had begged to go into exile with his uncle. As the war progressed, the standing of his government-in-exile steadily slipped as Churchill resolved that Tito's Partisans were a more effective fighting force than the royalist Chetniks. Peter married Princess Alexandra of Greece and Denmark, a cousin of Paul's wife, an action that caused some disquiet as Serbian leaders were not expected to marry during a national emergency. Channon described her as "a merry, intelligent, slightly *méchante* minx". Peter's godfather, George VI, acted as best man again. Peter moved to America after the war when it became clear that he would not be allowed to return to Yugoslavia. His life as an exiled royal was troubled; he died in 1970 after a failed liver transplant, necessitated by his longstanding cirrhosis of the liver. He was reinterred at Topola in 2013. At the service there, Irinej, Patriarch of the Serbian Orthodox Church, advocated a return to a monarchical system, but this must be a pipedream. The mausoleum is a memorial to one incarnation of the lure of the Lazar myth, which foundered on the changes wrought by the intervening centuries. Unfortunately, worse was still to come.

I trudged back down to the unmarked bus stop where, after ten minutes or so, I fell into conversation with a fellow queuer. He had already been waiting an hour, a source of some irritation to him as he had only come to Topola to reregister his car, having failed to shift the registration to Belgrade. No one seemed to know when a bus might arrive, and it became clear that the local bus company was on strike. My new friend asked how I found Serbia and I replied that the people were charming. "They need to be, no? Everything else is very bad – health, transport…" I remarked how good I found Serbian food. "Ah yes, very full of fat, and our girls are pretty, but the economy is tragical."

I ended up sharing a taxi to get to a different bus route and thence to Mount Avala on the way back to Belgrade. It juts out sharply from the surrounding plain, which reminded West of lowland Scotland. At the peak is the Monument to the Unknown Hero by Meštrović, modelled on the tomb of Cyrus the Great and erected in 1938 on the site of a dynamited fortress. It had been commissioned by King Alexander, along with the Njegoš memorial in Montenegro and the French memorial at the Belgrade fort. When West visited, it was still under construction. She inspected a model of the planned building, admiring the calm peasant women on whose heads the roof was supported, and whom she imagined as the mothers of the Serb soldiers doing gargling drill against influenza in the sunshine not far away. She was outraged by the wreaths in a hut nearby from Nazi Germany and Italy, diplomatic niceties signalling nothing from the nations who would shortly wreak such havoc here. In the present, I ascended steps cut in the five-level black granite plinth, which symbolises the five centuries of Ottoman occupation. At the top, a simplified classical structure houses the sarcophagus. The entrances are flanked by two peasant women on each side representing the eight constituent parts of the former Yugoslavia. Their expressions suggest an indomitable resignation to the lot of women, who provide continuation while men destroy. Their gigantic toes cling onto the earth in sheer determination, while their mass and child-bearing hips indicate a life of hard work, giving and supporting life over the generations while their husbands and sons fight off invaders or pursue misbegotten century-old dreams. Now, they provide shelter to the representative male buried within. West was "filled with feminist rage":

> Since men are liberated from the toil of childbirth and child-rearing, they might reasonably be expected to provide an environment which would give children the possibility to survive ... The degree of failure to realize that expectation ... could not be matched by women unless ninety per cent of all births were miscarriages.

I had dinner that night in the improbably named "Pin Up Girls" Chinese restaurant.

Belgrade II

The next morning, I walked to the "New" Cemetery, the entrance flanked by rows of florists whose wreaths and bouquets added welcome colour on a grey day. Inside, well-maintained paths traversed the densely packed graveyard where memorials abound. A white temple houses the bones of Serbs who died fighting the Turks and Bulgarians in the 19th century, while massive structures commemorate each of the Serbian and Russian dead of the First World War. There are memorials to the liberators of Belgrade in 1944, to Holocaust victims and those of World War II bombings, as well as graveyards nearby for soldiers who fell in Serbia from each of France, Russia, Britain, Italy, Germany, Austria-Hungary and Bulgaria during the two wars. It is a sobering reminder of the scale of fighting here long before the more recent woes. Serbia lost up to 28% of its population in the First World War while Yugoslavia as a whole lost some 10% of its people in the Second.

Many of the graves were in the customary local style of a black granite headstone with photographs of the deceased looking out. Several showed young men in army uniform who had died in the 1990s, along with their parents who had outlived them. Elsewhere in the cemetery are the graves of many great figures, including Bosnian Nobel-winning novelist, Ivo Andrić (who provides the epigraph to this book), and Zoran Djindjić, whose short-lived prime-ministership of Serbia was ended by an assassin's bullet in 2003 at the behest of organised crime figures alarmed by his stated determination to clean up Serbia.

An old man came up to me and explained, in a mixture of German and Serbian, that he was visiting to clean the grave of his younger brother. He wandered beside me a while before clasping my hand to say goodbye in a haze of raki.

Walking down one of the central avenues, a particularly opulent memorial caught my eye. A gold-coloured bust in a polished black marble arch sat under a golden Orthodox cross. There was a far-off gaze in the man's eyes, and he wore a beautifully tailored uniform with greatcoat, braided kepi, high collar and medals around the neck and on his chest, like a military hero of old. His chiselled features suggested a career on screen and represented some departure from the original. This was the resting place of the infamous Arkan, leader of the Tigers, one of Serbia's most feared paramilitary forces in the Yugoslav Wars. After an extensive criminal career across Western Europe in his twenties, he returned to Belgrade, where he led a violence-filled life with a high degree of political protection. The Tigers were active in and around many of the racially mixed areas near the borders of Bosnia, Croatia and Serbia during the wars, and were renowned for their ferocity as they engaged in ethnic cleansing and forced expulsions, driven by the promise of loot. In one instance, Arkan was reported to have ordered all the men of one family to bite the testicles off each other. On his return to Belgrade after the wars, he cultivated a high profile, with folk hero status in some quarters. He married Ceca, the most famous popstar of turbo-folk (the Serbian nationalist music of the war years) and took over a lower-league Belgrade football club called Obilić, whom he manoeuvred to Yugoslav league champions through fair means and foul. It has subsequently plummeted to the lowest tier in the Serbian system.

Arkan was also extremely well connected; close to Milošević, whose dirty work he had been doing, and who described him as a "simple sweetshop owner" in one evasive answer. Even Djindjić described him as a friend, saying that Arkan had saved his life by helping him flee to Montenegro when Milošević wanted to kill him. After Arkan was shot in the lobby of the Intercontinental Hotel in Belgrade, the search of his wife's property revealed a considerable arsenal, as well as two Vukovar car licence plates, presumably kept as gruesome mementoes. Ceca retains a high profile and is a prominent supporter of the current Serbian president, Aleksandar Vučić, himself at the time of the Bosnian War a radical nationalist and open supporter of Ratko Mladić, the war criminal leader of the Serb forces in Bosnia. Vučić now professes a pro-European, progressive stance, but the maintenance of his historical links raises continued questions, as indeed does the lionising memorial to Serbia's most notorious war criminal in Belgrade's grandest cemetery, close by the Alley of the Greats, where many of the country's most eminent figures have been buried.

A few blocks away in Tašmajdan Park are two further memorials, both to victims of the 1999 bombing of Belgrade by NATO. Two simple conjoined grey stone eggs bear the legend "We were just children" in English and Serbian. It is dedicated to "the children killed in NATO aggression". On the north side of the park, the unrepaired side of the state television headquarters, bombed in April 1999, is another reminder of the trauma here twenty years ago. Sixteen workers were killed that day and eighteen injured, in part victims of regime indifference as NATO had prewarned the target. The simple stone tablet overlooking the hanging masonry asks "*Zašto?*" (Why?) with the names of the deceased. Next door, the cavernous interior of St Mark's Church houses the remains of Stefan Dušan, the most powerful of all Nemanjić kings, moved here from the ruins of the Monastery of the Holy Archangels in Prizren in 1927.

I took a cab to the Museum of Yugoslavia, whose main building, the House of Flowers, contains the grave of Tito. The cab driver was insistent that there was no Yugoslavia, only Serbia. "We say *do vidjenja* (goodbye) in Serbian," he told me as I paid the fare.

The site was deserted other than the gatekeeper, although I am told it is more popular at the weekend, with a particular cult following among Slovenian biker gangs. Tito is remembered more fondly by those parts of the former Yugoslavia outside Serbia and Kosovo, which may explain its mid-week inactivity. He is buried in a great white marble sarcophagus, very plain, and in some ways reminiscent of those of Karadjordje and King Peter in Topola. His name and dates in gold are the only relief. It stands under a pitched glass roof in a secular chapel of square white pillars and greenery. The terrace and garden are visible through the glass windows behind. It invites reverence, but this is somewhat undermined by its situation amidst displays about Tito's life. On the walls around one neighbouring room were tributes to his role in the Non-Aligned Movement, which he had founded with Nehru and Nasser in 1956 to provide an alternative grouping to countries that did not wish to identify with either of the two warring superpowers. Another area was dedicated to the batons that were run in relays to him across the country on his birthday each year, renamed National Youth Day after his first ten years in power. The scale of the celebrations as the baton was presented to him each year, with formation dancing, marching and flag-waving, gives the appearance of a personality cult, despite the museum's protestations to the contrary. The total collection numbers 22,000 batons, and competition was clearly intense, both to have a baton selected and to be worthy to present it to the great man at the end. Many are symbolic, one capped with rifle rounds, another shaped like a grenade, while others could almost be medieval sceptres. The whole emphasises Tito the statesman, man of peace and loved by the people. The truth is more complicated of course.

Tito was born Josip Broz in Croatia to the north of Zagreb near the Slovenian border in 1892. Both parents were of peasant stock, but his Slovenian mother's family were rather better off than his father's. He left home as a teenager to become a locksmith's apprentice and worked in a variety of engineering jobs around Austria-Hungary. In one of them, he mangled the tip of his left index finger in a machine, a fact that he would allude to from time to time when he wanted to emphasise his working-class roots. He had a reputation as a snappy dresser from early on and took dancing classes, while also becoming involved in union activities. Conscripted into the Austro-Hungarian army in 1913, his first posting was to the Serbian front, a fact that he sought to conceal later in life. He was the youngest sergeant major in his regiment, a fencing champion and a trained skier. Fighting the Russians on the Carpathian front, he was cited for his courage. He was taken prisoner, but escaped to Petrograd (de-Germanised from St Petersburg in 1914) with the advent of the revolution in Russia two years later. Here, he married a local girl, with whom he returned in 1920 to Yugoslavia, along with their infant son. Back in his homeland, he became involved with the illegal Communist Party, and was already a senior figure in the Zagreb branch by the end of the decade. He was arrested in 1928 after bombs were allegedly found in his apartment in the wake of his leading role in the protests following the killing of popular Croatian politician, Stjepan Radić. After five years in jail, he spent much of the remaining 1930s in Moscow, at the height of the Stalinist purges.

Returning once more to Yugoslavia, Tito assumed leadership of the Communist Party, and during the Second World War his Partisans gradually became the dominant resistance group against the Axis forces in Yugoslavia. He believed that "from the bloody imperialist slaughter a new world would be born". When the Nazis invaded Russia, he described them as "the German fascist capitalist band headed by the lunatic Hitler". It was during this period that he became known as Tito, for which differing explanations have been offered. Some say that it was his brusque manner of issuing orders: "*Ti to*" (You, do that). At an early stage, the British apparently thought that it was an acronym for the Secret International Terrorist Organisation (*Tajna Internacionalna Teroristicka Organizacija*). Tito himself said that it was simply a common name where he had grown up.

In addition to his Russian support, Tito managed to persuade the British that the Partisans, rather than the monarchist Chetniks, offered the best chance of victory. The Chetniks' policy of trying to avoid inciting German retribution against the local population had also laid them open to charges of collaboration. Churchill's private secretary, John Colville, reports "Tito telegraphing most politely" in early 1944 (in contrast to Stalin) with Fitzroy Maclean (Churchill's personal representative in Yugoslavia) describing the man as "congenial" with a sense of humour. The Partisans' policy of strategic withdrawal managed to avoid their being drawn into head-to-head battle with the Germans; Maclean said that, in Partisan eyes, any victory where their losses were more than a fifth of the enemy's was a failure. With time, the British kept up a steady flow of airdrops to augment their supplies. Churchill had told King Peter in London that he needed to reach agreement with Tito, advice that was rejected. Colville opined: "It would be hard to find two worse advertisements for hereditary monarchy than George of Greece and Peter of Yugoslavia." Tito referred disdainfully to the "Great Serb *émigré* government in London"; Britain was always going to be secondary in his eyes. Without warning, he "levanted" (as Churchill put it) from the Adriatic island of Vis, where the Partisans were holed up, waiting until they could return for the final push into Yugoslavia. It became clear that an unidentified Russian aircraft had ferried Tito to Russian-controlled Romania at the suggestion of Stalin, who had warned of the innate untrustworthiness of the British.

Maclean described the victory parade as Tito returned to a liberated Belgrade with a mixture of veterans and youth carrying an odd assortment of arms and equipment, and wearing torn and stained Italian and German uniforms, all taken from the enemy:

> They looked underfed and weary ... and held themselves proudly and smiled as they marched ... They had spent the whole of the last three years fighting ... Now, ... they were at last entering the capital as conquerors.

The new federal Yugoslavia balanced the interests of its constituent parts under the tight Stalinist rule of Tito and his Communist Party. The Yugoslav secret police, OZNA (Department for the Protection of the People), under the leadership of Aleksandar Ranković, executed over 50,000 people in the succeeding years and interned many times that number. Milovan Djilas, Tito's effective number two, quoted Stalin reprimanding a Polish delegation for their tepid measures toward their opponents, saying: "Tito is a tower of strength ... he wiped them all out!" However, Tito, a natural rebel against authority figures throughout his life, broke with Stalin within three years. His pursuit of regional Balkan policies and willingness to ignore Western sensitivities alarmed Stalin, who cut off all support, assuming that he "only had to lift his little finger" and Tito would cave in or be deposed. Tito told Djilas, "The Americans are not fools. They won't let the Russians reach the Adriatic", and started to plough his own furrow. As his biographer, Geoffrey Swain, said, "What made [Tito] different to other communist leaders was that his early experiences of Soviet Russia had given him sufficient knowledge of the Soviet experiment not to be bound by its spell."

The first twenty years of communist rule were extremely repressive. Discussion of war crimes was suppressed to help build the new federation, but this rankled with the Serbs in particular, given the horrors in Croatia during the war. Tito had Jasenovac concentration camp dismantled, where the Ustaše had murdered between 80,000 and 100,000 people, of whom half were Serbs. He also locked up as many as 50,000 Stalin sympathisers to shore up his own position. The Goli Otok prison and labour camp was notorious – Djilas described the fate of prisoners there as "evil beyond compare, unending shame ... [with] torture, the cruelty of which was matched by its perversity". Failed policies of agricultural collectivisation led to significant unrest and had to be wound back. John Gunther, in Belgrade in 1949, described "volunteer" workforces building New Belgrade with their bare hands. He also told how his wife had to stop wearing nail varnish on her toes because of the crowds that would gather to inspect her sandalled feet. Life was very hard, and there was mass migration to Germany in particular, on both a permanent basis and as *Gastarbeiter*. One rare highlight in the early years was the Yugoslav football team's triumph over the much-favoured Russian team in the first round of the 1952 Olympics, where they ended up as silver medallists.

Tito was skilled at balancing the competing nationalisms of the federation against each other. He was also ruthless at disposing of his inner circle when it suited him. In the mid-1950s, Djilas was arrested and subsequently jailed for promoting the decentralisation of decision-making. When Mao heard of Djilas' arrest, his face reportedly lit up at the demise of an anti-Stalinist. A decade later, Aleksandar Ranković, by then vice president, was ejected when Tito needed to be seen to be more open. It became clear subsequently that he had bugged the telephones of the entire communist leadership, including Tito's. Ranković's brutal treatment of the Albanians in Kosovo, using his largely Serb apparatus there, helped sow the seeds for the horrors at the end of the century. However, the less repressive regime that followed Ranković's fall allowed nationalisms and dissent to surface, and Tito felt the need to tighten again. He introduced a new, more complicated constitution with a revolving presidency, giving independent voices to Vojvodina and Kosovo (until then part of Serbia), in an attempt to demonstrate a more even balance of decision-making between the constituent parts of the federation. He also encouraged rivalry between the Serbs and both the Croats and the Albanians to help consolidate his own power. Towards the end of his life, he even jettisoned his third wife, Jovanka, when he felt that she had stepped out of role and tried to involve herself in politics.

Tito also became imperial. Even during the war, Djilas described "his predilection for palaces". On taking power, he took over most of the royal residences, although he left out Topola, presumably because it housed the Karadjordjević mausoleum. Next to the old royal hunting lodge at Belje, he erected a hunting chateau. His summer residence in the Brijuni Islands boasted a private zoo that bred animals for him to hunt, and housed two elephants given to him by Indira Gandhi. Celebrity guests there included Richard Burton, Elizabeth Taylor, Carlo Ponti, Sophia Loren and Gina Lollobrigida. Elizabeth Taylor particularly admired Tito as he had not signed a single death warrant, little realising that this was because he deputed the task to others. Even Khrushchev holidayed in the Brijuni in 1956 as relations with Russia thawed after Stalin's death. Tito also re-established the Karadjordjević royal practice of becoming godfather to the ninth child of any household, in honour of the nine Jugović brothers who fell at the Battle of Kosovo, though he had underestimated the number of potential godchildren and resultant favours asked, and so wound up the practice after twenty years. In many ways, he had reinvented the absolutist monarchy, using centralised power to silence any nationalist pressures that emerged. He appears to have believed that the various Slavs of Yugoslavia could evolve into a single people under the benign influence of communism in a way that could not have happened under a monarchy. As a non-Serb ruling from Belgrade, he held things in balance, but after his death aged eighty-seven in 1980, with no obvious heir, tensions re-emerged before long.

He left Yugoslavia with high unemployment, inefficient centralised industry and a convoluted political system that would need considerable mutual goodwill between the constituent entities in the absence of paternal coercion. As Djilas asserted prophetically at the time:

> Tito was a politician of staggering proportions ... but he created ... no lasting spiritual or institutional forms. Titoism will fade with time, if Titoism is understood to mean personal power.

The cult of Tito was dominant in Yugoslavia for over three decades, which is why it felt rather odd to see so little interest in the temple to his memory. His funeral had been attended by four kings, thirty-one presidents, six princes and twenty-two prime ministers, with representatives of over 120 countries in total. Almost half the population of Yugoslavia had visited his grave in the period after his death. For a generation, he had been the dominant figure in the lives of his subjects as they had learned about his battles in the war, celebrated his birthday each year and seen pictures of him wherever they went. There is an ambiguous attitude to him now – people are aware of how brutal his regime was, particularly in the first twenty years; but there is also nostalgia for a time when life was safe and ordered, if constrained, and Yugoslavia had real status in the world, courted by the West as the acceptable face of communism. The Belgrade writer Momo Kapor talks affectionately of his youth and the memories of "girlfriends' hair washed in rainwater and rinsed in diluted vinegar, so that lettuce for me still carries an association of early romance". In Bosnia in 1995, Anthony Loyd remarked on the much-graffitied slogan "TITO VOLIMO TE" (Tito, we love you), as the Muslims there harked back to a more peaceful and prosperous period. Meanwhile, in the condolence book near Tito's grave, messages pleaded for him to return and rescue the situation in these troubled times.

The mausoleum is on the edge of Dedinje, the most exclusive residential area of Belgrade, home to celebrities, politicians, the newly wealthy, both main football clubs and the American embassy. Tito is said to have given the American ambassador the second largest house on the hill as thanks for Truman aid post-war. Large detached houses stand in their well-guarded, thoroughly hedged domains. On the top of the hill is the Royal Compound, built between the world wars for

King Alexander Karadjordjević. Below it, on the edge of Topčider Park, is the original Belgrade home of Prince Miloš Obrenović, whose presence here at the start of the 19th century was the source of Dedinje's initial cachet. Topčider was only sparsely inhabited even a hundred years later, as it was in the forest that once stood here that Gavrilo Princip and his fellow plotters were taught how to use grenades and pistols ahead of their fateful return to Sarajevo. It seems poignant that this should have occurred so close to the house of the Serb who achieved *de facto* independence from the Ottoman Empire and the palace and mausoleum of the only two real rulers of the land of the south Slavs. The vision that had inspired Princip appeared to be sustainable in practice only by absolutist rule.

The Obrenović mansion sits at the bottom of a tree-topped slope. It has an unwelcoming aspect – under a tiled roof, a simple white exterior is set with undersized, black-framed windows. It shields its inhabitants from the world outside rather than welcoming it in. Inside, the feel is distinctively Turkish, richly decorated with dark wooden panelling and relatively little natural light. Low divans set around a bay window suggest an atmosphere of byzantine negotiation. It is quite unlike the plain rusticity of Karadjordje's home, but then they were very different, despite the ostensible similarities in their pig-farming backgrounds.

Following Karadjordje's flight from Serbia in 1813 and the savagery of the Turkish revenge, Miloš Obrenović emerged as the leader of the renewed uprising and adopted a very different approach. He did not seek big set-piece battles with the opposing forces and negotiated an agreement with the Ottoman Empire whereby he would manage Serbia in the interests of the Sublime Porte in return for their guarantee of his authority within Serbia (or more accurately, the Turkish province of Belgrade, which represented the central part of current Serbia). He used his position to amass a great fortune, balancing relations with the Turks and the Russians adroitly. He then used the fortune to buy from the sultan the inalienable hereditary rights for his family to rule Serbia. In the process, he made himself unpopular with his fellow Serbs and had to subdue a number of uprisings. Ultimately, he was forced to abdicate in favour of his sons; his young son, Mihailo, was deposed three years later in favour of Alexander Karadjordjević. After Alexander was forced out in turn, in large part for his wise reluctance to take on the great powers in support of neighbouring Slavic conflicts, Mihailo returned. When Mihailo was murdered, his teenage cousin Milan (grandson of Jevrem Obrenović) became king, but a series of military defeats and further peasant uprisings led to his abdication aged thirty-four in favour of his 13-year-old son, another Alexander.

With Alexander, described by West as "weak-kneed, stout [and] spectacled", came the end of the Obrenović dynasty. Edith Durham in 1902 reported that "through all the land I did not hear one good word spoken of him. That he was more fool than knave was the best said ... For him, there was nothing but contempt". He was perceived by his subjects as too close to Austria-Hungary, but the key factor in his downfall was his falling in love with and marriage to his mother's lady-in-waiting, Draga Mašin. She was ten years older than the king, an impoverished widow with a reputation for the variety of her liaisons. She was considered to be a disastrous choice as queen, not least by Alexander's father, who heard the news while trying to negotiate a match with a German princess. Soon after their marriage, it also became clear that she was unable to have children. Concern over her influence on the succession and a reorganisation of the army infuriated elements of the officer corps.

In the early hours of 11th June 1903, a large group of officers forced their way into the palace. Lieutenant Petar Živković opened the main door, earning himself the lifelong soubriquet "Peter the Door". The conspirators made their way to the royal bedroom, killing several loyal staff members en route, but when they arrived, the king and queen were nowhere to be seen. After an hour hunting around the palace without success, Alexander and Draga were discovered in a concealed wardrobe set in the bedroom wall. They were shot and horribly mutilated with swords before their corpses were thrown into the palace garden. Reports suggest that Aleksandar was not quite dead and clung onto the parapet until several of his fingers were severed. Edith Durham was told that one of the conspirators kept a piece of the queen's skin in his wallet for the rest of his life as a memento. With the end of the Obrenovićs came the return of the Karadjordjevićs in the shape of Peter, son of the earlier deposed Alexander and grandson of Karadjordje himself.

A number of the conspirators reappeared in Serbian history. Their leader, Dragutin Dimitrijević, was known as "Apis" (the Bull) because of his musclebound frame. He was badly wounded on the night of the assassination, carrying three bullets in his body for the rest of his life. He formed a secret society, the Black Hand, devoted to the cause of Greater Serbia, which provided the weapons that Princip and his fellow assassins used on Franz Ferdinand at Sarajevo. Dimitrijević himself was executed by firing squad in 1917 based on likely falsified allegations of an attempted assassination of Peter Karadjordjević's son, Alexander. Meanwhile, "Peter the Door" became disenchanted with the Black Hand and founded a rival society called the White Hand. He went on to become Prime Minister of Yugoslavia in the early 1930s and formed part of the Yugoslav government-in-exile during the Second World War.

The pictures of Alexander and Draga in the Obrenović house show an unimpressive figure with a vacant look behind his pince-nez. He moons over Draga in one picture as she looks up at him with a fixed gaze, leaving no doubt as to the balance of power in the relationship. Nearby, a cartoon on the wall shows extravagantly moustachioed uniformed officers hacking away at a figure that looks more like a tailor's dummy than a female corpse. A shocking end to the dynasty that had been instrumental in the creation of a Serbian nation, albeit one that had bought its way to power, with little to show for the country that had been delivered to them with relative ease by the steady crumbling of the Ottoman Empire.

On the other side of the Sava, in New Belgrade, the streets were wider, the architecture more utilitarian and the mood more depressed. Hunched figures in padded jackets, jeans and trainers stood or sat by a blue corrugated iron fence shielding a building site. In front of them, a selection of their possessions was laid out for sale – clothes, clocks, roller skates, pictures, old telephones and radios. It was a sobering reminder of the ongoing hardship of life for many. There were similar street markets in the steep, narrow lanes above the railway station. Little ever seemed to be transacted. West had described refugees in Hamburg after the war looking "as if they had not heard that there yet is peace, because there was so much bad news round them that they had no time to listen to good news". The aftermath of conflict lingers.

Zemun lies beyond New Belgrade on the banks of the Danube. Standing on the bank, I was surprised quite how far away the other side was, a wooded outline in the mist. The dark bulk of a barge thrummed slowly upstream. Small boats were moored near the embankment, and a fisherman cast a line with a wriggling silver fish at the end. His demeanour suggested that he was content to be there whether he caught anything or not. The town is charming, with cobbled streets and pastel-coloured buildings, many in a state of some disrepair, especially away from the river. Restaurants along the river must be full of life in the summer but were largely deserted on an autumn weekday.

Zemun had long been on the border between the Hapsburgs and the Ottomans, and was absorbed into the Austro-Hungarian Empire in 1717, only becoming part of the Kingdom of Serbs, Croats and Slovenes at the end of the First World War. Until late in the 19th century, travellers from the west would note that, after this point, the roads were "heaven-made", meaning "the hand of man had little to do with them". It was from Zemun that the first shell of the First World War was fired by the Austrians at an evacuated Belgrade in the early hours of 29th July, in response to Serbian troops blowing up the bridge over the Sava that linked the two. Its more recent past has been chequered. In the Second World War, half the Jewish population of Serbia were killed at the concentration camp on the fairground here. Thereafter, the same camp also housed over 30,000 other Serbs, many Partisans and Chetniks, of whom a third were killed or died from hunger or disease in atrocious conditions. In the 1990s, some 40,000 Serb refugees from the fighting elsewhere in Yugoslavia settled in the area. Many still live desperately hard lives.

The town also has a reputation as a centre for organised crime – the Zemun clan was one of the most notorious gangs in the Serbian underworld, with links to the Milošević regime and the Special Operations Unit (or Red Berets), the special forces police division that had evolved from the paramilitary units responsible for war crimes in the Croatian and Bosnian wars. Members were involved in the killing of both Ivan Stambolić (Milošević's erstwhile mentor and potential opponent in the 2000 election) and Prime Minister Zoran Djindjić (whose cooperation with the war crimes tribunal in The Hague threatened senior clan figures). The two heads of the clan were killed in a shoot-out with police following Djindjić's assassination. Many of the others have been killed or are in jail too, but rumours persist about high-level links between underworld gangs and the government.

On my return to Belgrade six months later on a bright May day, the city sparkled in the sunshine. I was staying in a quiet hotel slightly south of the main town, near to the massive bulk of the Church of St Sava, the much-revered patron saint of Serbia. Sava was the youngest son of Stefan Nemanja, first of the eponymous dynasty. He founded the Serbian Orthodox Church after spending many years on Mount Athos, where he restored the great monastery of Hilandar, to which his father retired as a monk in 1197. His remains were publicly burnt by the Turks in 1594, theoretically on the site of the church, in response to the Serbs fighting under the image of St Sava in a revolt the previous year. The ashes were scattered.

On the 300th anniversary of the burning, a movement crystallised to build a church to St Sava at this location. Since then, the progress has been tortuous; three competitions were held to find an appropriate design, with a total cessation of planning from 1912 to 1919 during the Balkan and First World Wars. Consensus finally formed around a church modelled on Hagia Sophia, the great cathedral built in Constantinople by Justinian in the 6th century, and the foundation stone was laid in 1935. Work came to a complete halt in the Second World War, by which time the walls were around 30 feet high, and the site was used as a parking lot by the Wehrmacht, then by the Russian and Yugoslav armies after the liberation of Belgrade. In the Tito era, all progress was blocked, despite repeated personal entreaties by the Church, which received no response. With Tito's passing, permission was at last granted in 1984, though the design had to be re-engineered to enable maximum use of pre-cast concrete rather than the mix of brick and reinforced concrete envisaged fifty years earlier. The main dome of copper-clad concrete was finally in place in 1989, but the exterior works were not fully completed until 2017, having been interrupted for two years by the NATO bombing of Belgrade and the reluctance of the Orthodox Church to be financing such an expensive project when their flock was suffering. The interiors are now nearing completion, with many of the mosaics being financed by and made in Russia. With the latest obstacle of COVID-19 delaying the planned formal opening in 2020, it is still not quite finished, a little over 125 years after the project first seriously launched.

The vast edifice looked impeccable from the outside, dominating the skyline from the river and New Belgrade on the other bank. The white marble facade underpins the massive grey dome above it with a scalloped base, the subsidiary domes around it emphasising the monumentality of the whole. Only Hagia Sophia has a larger dome in the Orthodox world, and St Sava's is similar in size to St Paul's Cathedral, though still well shy of St Peter's Basilica or the Duomo of Florence. The interior was a building site when I visited. Polythene-clad scaffolding stretched high above, almost vanishing into the gloom at the top of high arches. Bare concrete expanses awaited their canopies and mosaics. Two small candlelit areas were given over to the faithful, who shuffled along in line to offer a prayer and see the progress of the works. When it is finished, it will be able to seat 10,000, alongside a choir of 800. It would be nice to think that the final delivery of this project, stalled by all the troubles that have beset Serbia since 1895, might mark a new era of peace and engagement with the outside world.

I had been invited to lunch at the home of a local contact. Above a banded stone facade, an arched window was framed by mosaic panels of barely golden vases on a dark background. A similar border of panels ran around the building just below the roof. The upper storey was of muted russet-coloured plaster in which were set stone windows. Basking in the sun, it still had the welcoming panache envisaged when it had been built a century or so earlier. Around the corner, I rang the doorbell to the first-floor flat. At the top, I was greeted by a spare, distinguished figure in his sixties. "You have found me, Nick, bravo." Lazar briefly introduced me to his "Governess", who, it became clear, was preparing a remarkably good lunch for us. I was shown into a sitting room, where we sat on tapestry-covered chairs with large carved wooden arms under the watchful portraits of various distinguished forebears. In the corner was an exquisite black ceramic stove stretching to the ceiling. "Lord Snowdon also loved that; my family had one sent for each room from Vienna." We settled down to a long conversation over a glass of Serbian whisky.

We touched on mutual friends in England ("How is dear James? ... Bravo.") and Lazar's family history (a knighted great uncle and ambassadors all over the world). He talked of the Obrenovićs ("now extinct, bar a pretender") and the Karadjordjevićs ("They do wonderful things for the country, although some are suspicious [echoing Chips Channon's fears] because they speak poor Serbian"). He reminded me of the scale of British support for the Serbian cause in the First World War; Lady Paget, the wife of the British minister in Serbia, had helped set up a military hospital in Belgrade and in Skopje.

We went out to the terrace behind for lunch in the sun. An apartment block now stands on a large part of what was once the house's garden. The original must have been magnificent. It was at this house that the Serbs and Bulgarians signed the agreement to jointly liberate the remaining Slavic people from the Ottomans in 1912 at the outset of the Balkan Wars. A substantial plate of Parma ham and potato salad turned out to be only an appetiser to the chicken fillet in cheese sauce with fried potatoes and tomato salad that followed. Various themes recurred as we discussed the trauma of the previous century. There was a bitterness that Croatia and Slovenia, Germany's friends in the Second World War, appeared to have been rewarded with EU accession, while Serbia, Britain's loyal ally in two wars, continued to suffer. Lazar acknowledged that the Yugoslav government had been forced to accede to Hitler briefly (his grandfather had accompanied the regent Prince Paul to Germany at the start of the war), but the pressure had been impossible to resist. Yugoslavia should have stayed neutral, as choosing sides (ultimately for the Allies) had all but destroyed Serbia in the end.

In the Tito years, Lazar's family had lost everything except their name and their lives. He felt that, curiously, it had freed him and others like him to have more fun than friends who were children of Communist Party members and tended to be tightly controlled. Life had been glamorous in Yugoslavia in the 1960s. He had been a male model, being photographed on the Adriatic islands with beautiful Croatian and Slovenian girls. He opened a discotheque in the basement of this very house and attended masked balls. He remembered Margot Fonteyn and Michael Somes receiving thirty-three curtain calls on a visit to Belgrade, still bowing an hour after the curtain had gone down (apparently, Rudolf Nureyev declined to attend the afterparty in case the Russians tried to spirit him away). While the era held fond memories for him, it was Yugonostalgia with a twist. As a Serb, he did not have high regard for Tito himself – "That man whose name I cannot say, a federalist. His grave should be in Croatia or Slovenia; they love him there."

He talked of the dark days under Milošević, whom he believed had been under the spell of his wife ("a federalist, controlling communist with a strong agenda"). "When the bombing started, we all thought it would last for two weeks; instead, it lasted for 77 days." Lazar's mother had been ill, so he did not go down to the shelter. He remembered the sounds – a drone above, the whistle as the bomb fell near the house and then the boom of the explosion. His house is near to the Radio Television of Serbia building – "There was no reason for those people to be there, they were just pushing buttons." For him, the bosses were culpable. He also had particular animosity for Christiane Amanpour, the CNN anchor whose broadcasts from Bosnia were considered by many to have been more emotional than objective.

As I left, after several hours and a substantial dessert of chocolate cake, strawberries and baklava, he asked how many children I had. On hearing there were four, he clapped his hands with glee. "Bravo, Nick, bravo!" – the enthusiastic interjection that had interspersed much of our conversation. Lazar's thoughts seem to me to echo those of many of the Belgrade intelligentsia. Serbia has suffered horribly through the centuries and proved a key ally against Germany in two world wars. In the second of these, the anti-Serb atrocities in Croatia were horrifying. The behaviour of the Serbian government in the 1990s was indefensible, but it was driven by a narrow political and criminal fraternity unrepresentative of the country as a whole. Many Serbs felt part of a modern Europe, before bombs started to fall and life became impossible almost overnight. They feel hard done by in the broader sweep of history; the world must hope that they can focus on building a future rather than dwelling on the past.

As I walked back to my hotel, the air rang with the chants of Red Star Belgrade supporters. A packed yellow bus sped by. From its open window a hand-held flare emitted a pinkish flame and a smoke trail. I looked forward to my road trip the next day.

Novi Sad

The road north from Belgrade to Novi Sad, Serbia's second city, cuts straight across the fluvial plains of the Danube, where endless fields of corn grew in the dark soil. Crossing the river after 50 or so miles, I began to find myself in a different world. Stucco buildings on the approach to the city feel more central European than Slavic. Here, only an hour from the border, the capital of Vojvodina reflects its long history as part of Hungary, broken by two centuries under Ottoman rule. It has only been ruled from Belgrade since the end of the First World War, but even in Ottoman times it was probably the largest truly Serb city, known as the "Serbian Athens".

Vojvodina is majority-Serb, populated to a large extent over the centuries by refugees from Ottoman rule further south, but it also has a significant Hungarian minority. Each village has a different ethnic mix, with populations of Romanians, Slovaks, Croats, Ukrainians, Czechs and Roma as well. There was also once a sizeable German population, but that has gone, many fleeing with the German army at the end of the Second World War, and most others killed or rounded up into concentration camps by the communists thereafter. The *Schwaben*, those Germans who had settled along the Danube, had made up key regiments of the Hapsburg army in the Balkans as well, and there was considerable animosity after two world wars between them and the Serbs of the entire region. A friend told me how, in 1945, his blonde Slovak grandmother had nearly been taken in error, saved only by his grandfather punching the arresting policeman. A third of those Germans who went into the camps never came out, and very few stayed in Yugoslavia. An uncompromising paper in 1944 spelled it out, written by Vaso Čubrilović, whose past boasted the unusual blend of conspirator in the assassination of Franz Ferdinand, professor at Belgrade University and agriculture minister in Tito's first government: "In view of the atrocious crimes committed by the German Reich on Slavic lands with the help of local ethnic Germans, we have every reason to demand that [Vojvodina and Kosovo] be cleansed of this group."

Much of Novi Sad was destroyed by army bombardment during the Hungarian Revolution of 1848-9, explaining its well-planned, largely pedestrianised centre, which dates from the following decades. To me, the buildings feel over-presented, with a surfeit of statuary, pillars and decorative plasterwork clamouring for attention in typically Austrian style, but the main square is airy and welcoming, dominated by the tall spire of the Catholic cathedral. In the centre is a Meštrović statue of Svetozar Miletić, the leader of the Vojvodina Serbs through much of the late 19th century, an advocate of Serbian rights within the Austro-Hungarian constitution and a vocal opponent of Franz Joseph's policy of expansion into the Balkans, for which he was imprisoned. He stands mid-declamation, right fist raised from under his Ulster coat, the massive fingers of his left hand clenched with the passion of his delivery. He faces the cathedral with his back to the city hall (modelled on the one in Graz, Austria), as though reminded by both institutions of foreign domination. The statue was hidden during the Hungarian occupation in the Second World War but reinstated thereafter.

My hotel was on the main square, built in 1854 as part of the initial rebuild. From the outside, it looked palatial, a long, formal stretch of muted olive-green decorative plasterwork on a pale yellow base, severe rather than welcoming. Inside, the decor was a melee of styles. Prints of long-dead Hapsburgs hung at the bottom of a staircase with a protruding rail that appeared to have been installed for an undelivered chairlift. Halfway up, an abstract stained-glass window left no part of the colour spectrum untouched. The endless corridor to my clean, albeit basic room was a clinical strip-lit mint green. I had breakfast alone the next morning in a vast, bright, low-ceilinged dining room with red velour chairs and clean white linen, braving the three buffet guards who grudgingly acknowledged my presence.

I wandered around the town, passing the attractive Orthodox Bishop's Palace, with Moorish stone-coloured windows set in red brick, capped with a balustrade and miniature onion domes. All around, people smiled and chatted in the sunshine. Further out, the imposing synagogue of stone and white plaster was completed in 1909 in Secessionist style, traditionally influenced with Art Nouveau elements. The three naves are denoted by a central rose window at the heart of three stone arches. The cupola above is framed by its octagonal base, itself held in place by eight great stone buttresses high above the main building. These in turn frame triplets of leadlight windows below oversized white plaster pediments, each bearing a simple motif. It dominates the neighbourhood like a great cathedral. This was built by a community confident of its place in the world. Now, it is a concert venue, while the old Jewish school next door teaches ballet. Not far away, a golden dome glitters on an exquisite little white Orthodox church set in its own grassy grounds. Within it, Einstein's two sons were christened; his first wife, Mileva, hailed from Novi Sad.

On the banks of the Danube, a long, low memorial of bronze tablets records the names of the 1,200 Jewish and Serb victims of the Hungarian massacre in January 1942. It is interspersed with plaques of each of the Roman and Orthodox crosses and the Star of David. Here, the Royal Hungarian Army brought those that they had arrested, shot them in sub-freezing temperatures and pushed their bodies into the river, which had been shelled to break up the ice. It is thought that the severity of the action emanated from a desire to show Berlin that the scale of operations needed near home precluded the Hungarians from being posted to the Eastern front.

A sculpture of a family stands nearby. At its base is inscribed:

Memory is a monument harder than stone
If we are human, we must forgive, but not forget.

Out in the river, sturdy concrete pillars formed threatening dark masses against the light dazzling off the broad expanse of water. These were the piers of the Franz Joseph Bridge, destroyed by NATO bombing in 1999. White flags fluttered on a boat tethered to the bank beside it advertising a floating Citroën dealership, the cars and vans glinting in an orderly line on deck. Over the river atop a long, dark hill, Petrovaradin Fort lowered over the town, although its pale walls and regimented chimneys offered a veneer of benignity. Both Karadjordje and a young Tito had been imprisoned there. As I surveyed so many elements of the city's violent history, the message at my feet rang true. The past must be remembered, but life must move on. Looking at the carefree conversations at cafe tables on a sunny day as I walked back, it seemed possible that it could.

Fruška Gora

Eight miles south on the other bank of the Danube is the town of Sremski Karlovci, whose tree-lined centre could easily be mistaken for a sleepy Austrian town. It was here that the Ottomans and Austrians signed the Treaty of Karlowitz in 1699, ending Turkish control of much of central Europe and ushering in Hapsburg ascendancy in its place. It was also the base of the Serbian Orthodox Church in the Hapsburg Empire from the late 17th century, after Patriarch Arsenius was forced to flee Kosovo alongside the Austrian army ten years prior to the treaty. By the latter stages of the Austro-Hungarian Empire, the patriarchate here was perceived to be under Franz Joseph's control, and in the wake of the First World War the Serbian Orthodox Church recentred on Belgrade, although the palace here continues to act as the summer residence.

West visited the palace, which she described as "built in the Byzantine style with Austrian solidity, rich in arch and balcony"; I imagine that it looks little different now, despite its eye-bruising colour, more yellow than cream. She described wandering around the garden unable to gain access, but being shown the printing press, where "young girls bound ... pamphlets, not very skilfully but most devoutly". The finished product was "lying about not in disarray but in only amateurish array". The palace seemed deserted, so after noting the remarkable effusion of the iconostasis in the cathedral next door, where surprisingly Westernised images rose high to the ceiling in elaborate gold frames, I followed her footsteps south to Fruška Gora ("Frankish Hills").

Climbing from the plain, one turns back in time again from the regimented structure of Austro-Hungarian towns to the wilderness of the hills and the Byzantine monasteries among them, even if some have been rebuilt many times, having clearly borrowed from the style of their Hapsburg overlords. The monasteries here were founded by refugees from Ottoman occupation further south, who established an independent Orthodox Church around these communities in the hills.

The Monastery of Krušedol is set in parkland through an impressive deep red domed gateway. The main entrance to the low compound was a portico detailed in muted yellow ochre and topped with a simple black cross. I knocked on the door to be admitted by a disgruntled monk in a purple-black velvet hat over greasy hair. The little white church in the centre of the enclosure contains the tomb of King Milan Obrenović, as well as the remains of St Angelina, the devout and much-venerated sister-in-law of Skanderbeg and widow of Stefan the Blind, a descendant of Lazar who ruled Serbia very briefly in the mid-15th century. My escort shrugged his shoulders at any mention of either, but a tablet on the wall by the front door had been clearly erected by Franz Joseph to "Kral (King) Milan". Inside the church, a look of horror crossed the monk's face when I motioned to lift the cover on a relic case, which I presume contained "the Duchess Angelina's narrow and elegant hand, black and mummified, loaded with the inalienable rings of her rank". West also reported that when she had visited the monastic treasury, it had contained the contents of King Milan's last home, which he had left to Franz Joseph in "an act of testamentary whimsy". There was no sign of this legacy, but in the years after West's visit, the monastery was looted and turned post-war into a children's home, before returning to its original function in the 1970s. I imagine Milan's table service and furniture are spread far and wide.

Nearby, in the small church of the Novo Hopovo Monastery, a faded fresco by the local baroque master, Teodor Kračun, evokes the horror of the Massacre of the Innocents with perverse beauty; red-robed soldiers pull babies from their resisting mothers, who twist and turn in desperation while Herod looks on impassive. Down the road at Irig, in the heart of the local wine country, great pillars of deep pink petunias down the high street stood guard over freshly painted rows of old houses; the tiled roofs of each at different heights and angles and of different shades of grey and orange, as if they had grown together over the centuries. Around the corner, a handsome 19th-century merchant's house was deserted. It had been painted deep yellow and boasted still intact stone mouldings of stylised flowers and plants, but now the glass was broken, the plaster was falling off and the two houses beside had been demolished. It felt as if the last residents had left in a hurry.

At the Monastery of Sremska Ravanica-Vrdnik, both church and quadrangle gleamed white; the orderly tower and neo-classical finish to the exterior betokened an Austro-Hungarian influence again, as did much of the artwork inside. The design allowed light to fill the interior, in contrast to the older monasteries in the south, rejecting, as West put it, "the Byzantine prescription that magic must be made in darkness". When she came, King Lazar lay here, his remains having been brought for safety in 1690 from Ravanica, the monastery that he had founded in central Serbia near his base of Kruševac. They lay here until the Second World War, when they were removed to Belgrade with German help, after Croatian Ustaše members had stolen his gold rings. Now, only a surprisingly fibrous piece of his shoulder was displayed in a gold and blue casket before the iconostasis. Its natural colouring, presumably evidence to the faithful of his incorruptibility, made me feel slightly queasy in comparison with the more evidently aged relics encountered elsewhere. The rest of Lazar's remains have now returned to Ravanica, having been sent on a nationwide tour by President Milošević in 1989 in the early stages of his nationalist drive for greatness. In the northern choir apse, a mural showed an unsuspecting and morose Lazar praying to heaven as a cheery Turk in an orange robe and red fez bounded up behind him with sword held high, moments before delivering the *coup de grâce*.

Jazak, described by West as an "exquisite mongrel church", has layers of influence. The bronze of the onion shaped cupola and belfry cap are supported by Hapsburg-influenced towers that rise in turn out of a more traditional Serb Orthodox structure of stone and decorative brick. Here are the remains of St Uroš, otherwise known as Stefan "the Weak", son of Dušan, under whom the Nemanjić empire disintegrated. West had questioned why he was venerated, to be told: "He was of our ancient dynasty, he was a Nemanya, and the Nemanyas were sacred. Not only were they the instruments of our national power, they have a religious significance to us." The painting of him in the church above his ornate blue and gold sarcophagus showed a haloed figure in a green and gold robe, with an ermine-lined cape, crown and sceptre. He looks questioning but eager to please, saintly rather than martial.

As I set out to drive south, I was struck again by the multiplicity of odd overlaps between power and religion in the Serbian Church. I would like to hope that, in this day and age, the household fittings of a venal 19th-century king would no longer belong in a monastic treasury. Yet the veneration of all members of the Nemanjić dynasty, seemingly regardless of their achievements or innate spirituality, helped to explain how, even now, medieval legend might be a dangerous force should another cynical power-seeker look to exploit it.

I passed by Šabac, site of particular horrors in the Second World War, where over 1,000 mainly Viennese Jews seeking to escape to Israel (the Kladovo Transport) were caught by the Nazis in 1941 after their boat had got frozen in on the Danube. Almost none survived. Later, in 1941, a joint Chetnik and Partisan force launched a failed attack on the German garrison at Šabac. In retribution, the Germans ordered the arrest of the entire male population of the town between the ages of fourteen and seventy. 21,500 were incarcerated and a further 1,130 executed alongside mass burning of towns and villages.

A little way on, one climbs into the foothills of the main Balkan mountain range that stretches west through Bosnia and Herzegovina to the Dalmatian coast and south through Montenegro, western Kosovo and Albania to Greece. This was where the resistance to the Nazis was kept alive during the war.

Valjevo

Valjevo, an hour to the south, also suffered savage reprisals in the Second World War after its brief liberation from Nazi control in 1941. In a sense, history was repeating itself, as it was here that the murder and decapitation of two local chieftains (*knezes*) sparked the First Serbian Uprising in 1804. The heart of the town is attractive, with pavioured pedestrian areas on either side of the small river that runs through it. I checked in at the Hotel Grand, a name accurate only in the context of the town, forced as I was to walk up to my room due to the lift that was broken, as were many of the light switches that could have helped me manoeuvre down the long corridor. The room was comfortable and looked as though a Tito-era designer had channelled Empire-style luxury with deep yellow velour curtains, bedspread and chair covers. A list of admonitions included: "It is not allowed for quests to make unpleasant noise and disturb piece and order." A prominently placed ashtray had a sign attached prohibiting smoking. Over the river in a street of low houses and shops that showed its Ottoman past, I found a friendly local restaurant, where a party in the adjoining room was singing enthusiastically to accordion and guitar. My mixed grill consisted of local sausage, two chicken breasts, five kebabs (four of minced meat and one regular) and a pork fillet, all served with a fresh loaf of bread and a vast plate of tomato and cucumber. It was utterly delicious, albeit unfinished, and I waddled back to the hotel to the sound of accordions duelling with the sound system of a local club.

The next morning, I was served an excellent omelette by a cadaverous waiter before wandering out to inspect the town. The main civic buildings had a solidity and even grandeur that evidenced a pride in the community dating back to the 19th century, but outside the centre it felt run down, with several unloved ruins that I was told were owned by "others". It is surrounded by low hills, atop which white-painted villas sat serenely in the morning haze. Behind the hotel is the oldest preserved building in Valjevo, the 18th-century Muselim's House, now a museum to the slaughter of the *knezes*. It is a low white rectangular building whose tiled roof extends over wooden posts to create a simple awning in front. Its small windows are barred and shuttered. This was the headquarters of the region's Turkish administrator, and in its cellar two local *knezes*, Aleksa Nenadović and Ilija Birčanin, were imprisoned by the *dahi* (janissary leader), Mehmed-aga Fočić, who knew that Valjevo was the centre of plans to rebel against the janissaries, and had been smuggling arms in from Austria-Hungary in preparation. After their execution, the heads of the two Serbs were displayed on the roof of the building. By the end of the month, Fočić and the three other *dahis* had killed a hundred or so *knezes* and several hundred peasants across Serbia, but they had failed to catch Karadjordje.

In the cellar, two figures sat chained to the wall, both dressed in the Ottoman style with loose collarless shirts and sashes around their waists, one wearing a waistcoat, the other a fez. On the wall beside is an extract from the famous poem *The Beginning of the Revolt against the Dahis*, written down by Vuk Karadžić in 1815 not long after the events that it describes. It sits with *The Mountain Wreath* as among the most important of early Serb nationalist songs. They were banned by Miloš Obrenović in case they encouraged people to rise against the Turks, with whom he had negotiated a convenient accommodation. In the poem, the *dahis* rage:

> *We will slaughter all the Serbian* knezes,
> *All the* knezes, *all the Serbian leaders,*
> *All the* kmets [headmen] *who are a danger to us,*
> *All the village priests, those Serbian teachers;*
>
> *Only will we spare the helpless children,*
> *Children weak of seven years and under;*
> *Then the Serbs in truth will be a* rayah [Christian peasantry],
> *Truly will they serve their Turkish masters.*

The poem goes on to describe the executions of various *knezes*, including the two presented here. Birčanin is beheaded after Fočić asks if he would like to ransom his own life, only to be told: "Who would let a mountain-wolf escape him?" Nenadović is killed in turn while crying out to his brother:

> May God kill every Christian
> Who depends upon a Turkish promise!

A subsequent verse depicts the escape of Karadjordje, who had drunk a pre-dawn glass of brandy before setting off to fulfil his destiny. At the end of the poem, his final words are:

> Drina water, O thou noble barrier,
> Thou that partest Bosnia from Serbia!
> Soon the day will dawn, O Drina water,
> Soon will dawn the day when I shall cross thee,
> Pass through all the noble land of Bosnia.

This is clearly intended as an ambition to liberate the Slavs from Ottoman control, but the lines have ominous overtones in hindsight.

As I left the building, the aging attendant was sitting in the sun engaged in desultory conversation with a friend. He pressed a flask on me and insisted that I drink from it. I did so, part in tribute, part to clear my head. I was reminded of Patrick Leigh Fermor's memorable description of a shot dropping "to its destination with the smoothness of a tracer-bullet and the somnolent organism is roused with the same shock as that of an oyster under the lemon, summoning startled gasps from the novice and making his eyes leap from their sockets".

Over dinner the previous night, I had realised that the following day was 13th May and, just as importantly, a Saturday. It was on this day in 1941 that Dragoljub "Draža" Mihailović had gathered his royalist forces together on Ravna Gora ("Flat Hill"), 25 miles south-east of Valjevo, and instigated the Chetnik resistance to German occupation. On the Saturday of (or following) that date each year, a substantial collection of sympathisers gather there to commemorate their hero. It felt like serendipity. I left town, passing the old Nenadović Tower, where the Turks had shown off their collection of impaled heads a couple of centuries ago. As I drove into the wooded hills, fields of purplish grass rippled in the breeze and the far hills were an astonishing blue, adding additional depths to the brilliance of the sky above. By the road, the pale green of new leaves in false acacia trees were almost hidden by their clouds of hanging white blossom.

Mihailović had had a distinguished military record in both Balkan Wars, participated in the retreat to Albania in 1915 and been decorated for his bravery on the Salonika front towards the end of the First World War. After the Yugoslav surrender to the Germans in 1941, he had led a small group of officers into these hills, from where he gradually recruited a disparate collection of men to fight under his umbrella. The royal government-in-exile blessed his role as commander of the "Yugoslav Army in the Fatherland". Despite the title, Mihailović was primarily driven by the survival of the Serb people. Given the historic links between Croatia, Slovenia and the German-speaking world, and the atrocities being unleashed by the Ustaše, it is not hard to see why he might have felt that the Serbs were under threat. A 1941 Chetnik manifesto talked of the need for transfers and exchanges of population between mixed Serb and Croat areas, saying that "Croats and Moslems have undertaken in a calculated way the extermination of the Serbs".

The Serb nationalist streak in the Chetniks was in large part at the root of their eclipse by the Partisans, with whom they operated some joint missions. The two groups had even discussed merging forces at an early stage, but this was rejected by Mihailović, for whom Tito's Stalinist agenda was diametrically opposed to his own monarchist views. With time, he came to view the Partisans as an additional and even principal enemy. Hitler had been so alarmed by the scale of resistance in Yugoslavia that he announced a reprisal system, whereby 100 locals would be executed for each German life lost and fifty for each wounded. The Chetniks were reluctant to bring reprisals on the local population; as a result, some became disinclined to fight and grew overly close to the occupying forces in their desire to save lives and encourage the Germans to focus their attentions on the Partisans. Tito took the view that German reprisals helped recruit more men to his cause and continued to focus on guerrilla attacks. His Partisans were also more representative of broader Yugoslavia, although underrepresented by Albanians and Serbs.

The British supported the Chetniks initially, not least because they were the official resistance; but by the beginning of 1944, Churchill's "ambassador-leader" to the Yugoslav guerrillas, Fitzroy Maclean, had reached his conclusion:

> The Partisans, whatever their politics, were fighting [the Germans], and fighting them most effectively, while the Četniks, however admirable their motives, were largely not fighting at all or fighting with the Germans against their own countrymen. Moreover, regarded as a military force, the Partisans were more numerous, better organized, better disciplined and better led than the Četniks.

British support swung exclusively behind Tito, who of course already had Russian backing; from that point on, the Partisans became the dominant resistance force. At the end of the war, Mihailović was hunted down and finally caught by the Partisans in March 1946. He was put on trial for war crimes. It is clear that there were Chetnik atrocities, particularly against Bosnian Muslims, justified as reprisals for Ustaše atrocities against Serbs. Mihailović in one instance said he knew that the local Serb commander had wanted to "settle accounts", but "never thought he would clear it up in this way". He was found guilty of high treason and war crimes, executed and buried in a secret grave. His last words at his trial were: "I have been blown away by the gale of the world." The man remains an ambiguous figure; it is not clear how much he knew or could control of what happened in remote Chetnik units, and his trial was politically motivated with only one possible outcome. West, a committed monarchist, had been a vocal supporter of Mihailović and kept a photograph of his dead body with her papers. His star rose again in the 1990s, with attempts by Serb nationalist politicians like Vuk Drašković to use the Chetniks and Mihailović as part of the heroic story of the quest for Greater Serbia. In 2015, the High Court in Belgrade rehabilitated him on the grounds of an unfair trial. Police guarded the courtroom, outside which a crowd of Chetnik supporters and anti-nationalist protestors had gathered. Prince Aleksandar Karadjordjević, son of Peter II, said that it reversed "an injustice towards one patriotic man" and should help national reconciliation.

I wound down narrow lanes, noticing the increasing police presence at junctions. They waved me through a makeshift roadblock, but I soon found myself in a queue of traffic at yet another. A burly figure knocked on the window asking me for 200 Serbian dinars (£2.00), and I was channelled on down a muddy road, with cars and buses already parked along one side as far as I could see. The traffic dispersed into fields. Tents were being erected and barbecues built. One might have mistaken it for a heavy metal rock festival were it not for the absence of guitar solos. The attendees were predominantly male and almost entirely dressed in some form of paramilitary gear. Many looked as though they had retrieved now retired military uniforms from their bedroom cupboards; others wore a beret or a combat jacket over jeans or tracksuit bottoms. Individuality seemed to be expressed primarily through headwear, which ranged widely from furry domes to kepis to mob caps. Other than me, one of the few bare-headed figures was the imposing bronze statue of Mihailović, erected here in the 1990s. He looked contemplative and regal, standing in uniform with a greatcoat over his shoulders and a pipe in his left hand. I was surprised to see that he was not wearing the iconic glasses without which he could see little, and his well-coiffed beard and moustache resembled those of an early 20th-century monarch more than the shapeless growth evident in photographs of the man himself. Great beribboned wreaths lay in front of the crested plinth on which he stands. Groups of uniformed men queued to be photographed in front of it and then moved on to light candles in the small chapel nearby. The legend lives on.

Nearby, an early starter was already flat on his back, unconscious on a pile of logs in the midday sun. By the gate to the monument, a legless figure held out a cup, asking for change. I walked down the track past trestle tables loaded with military paraphernalia for sale, endless piles of black and camouflage, belts, flags, headwear, uniforms, but other memorabilia too. Many stalls sold T-shirts, embroidered jackets, more flags and plaques emblazoned with a photograph of Mihailović or the royal double-headed eagle. One vendor looked a little out of place selling salamis and cheeses off a red-checked tablecloth, beside which two whole pigs rotated on enormous spits over a bed of ashes, propelled by a sputtering engine via belts and bicycle chains. Already at noon, the beer tents were full, and sides of pig were being hacked up to the sound of patriotic singing in the distinctive rhythm of alcohol-fuelled atavistic emotion. Serbian flags flew everywhere, from posts, tents and trees, and brandished out of the car windows of the steady stream of new arrivals. Out in the fields, some groups picnicked quietly, while others swayed with arms around each other. All seemed to hark back to the legend of a past that has not existed for many years and has borne black shadows in all its recent manifestations – the Greater Serbia of the Nemanjas, Lazar, King Peter, Mihailović and Milošević. There was a strong sense of camaraderie among the attendees, and I suspected that many were ex-Serb military reliving the past in a way that must be hard to do openly day to day. I wondered how many of them must have seen terrible things, what they thought about them now and whether they spoke of them, but the mood felt more celebratory than confessional. I felt quite conspicuous, clean-shaven in an open-necked shirt, but everyone was friendly. I feared that, with time and drink, things might become less comfortable, and so headed off south, passing the once Partisan stronghold of Užice 50 miles away through the steep wooded hills.

Mileševa

The scenery was stunning as I drove on through occasional peaceful villages and endless valleys, some so steep that the continued presence of tree cover seemed impossible. Snow-capped mountains started to appear in the distance. The road passed under rocky overhangs along astonishing gorges with splashes of vegetation on the grey cliffs and the bright blue water of the River Lim below. A railway track followed the same route; the train would disappear into tunnels and reappear like a video game at a surprise angle or distance that seemed to bear no relation to its previous position.

A few miles beyond the scenic town of Prijepolje stands the Mileševa Monastery on the southern slope of Mount Zlatar. Large Serbian flags flew high on poles, a conscious statement of ancient rights in this largely Muslim area. A police block on the way out of town had concerned me, but they seemed only concerned about the state of the road ahead – "no *dobro*". They indicated that I could go to the monastery but it was unfit for cars beyond. My planned journey on to Novi Pazar would now involve a big loop to the north, retracing a significant part of my drive so far. However, my mood was lifted again by the sight of the newly painted white monastery compound shining happily in the sun, its red-tiled roofs and the outline of the cross on the belltower appearing to emanate heat against the blue sky and toothlike peak of the mountain behind. Flowers spilled over the long first-floor balconies and the white-pillared arcade below was studded with brilliant deep pink begonias. The simple church rose out of a lush green lawn.

Mileševa was founded around 1235 by King Vladislav, grandson of Stefan Nemanja and nephew of St Sava. He was the middle of three brothers who ruled Serbia, each being toppled by revolts in turn. Vladislav shared his mausoleum with his uncle Sava, whose remains were returned to Serbia after he died in Bulgaria on his way back from a pilgrimage to Jerusalem. When St Sava's remains were burned by the Turks in Belgrade, it is thought that his left hand was saved, and it lies here too. Both sarcophagi are made of red marble and adorned with fresh flowers. St Sava's is almost pre-Raphaelite in appearance with borders of twining vines. Flames glistened from the red glass holders of the silver candelabra on its lid, but they were utterly eclipsed by the strength of the light shining in from the window opposite, creating a natural halo around the resting place of the final remains of Serbia's patron saint. The feeling of reverence is enhanced by the frescoes around, which also date from the 13th century and are believed to be accurate portraits of their Nemanjić subjects. A tonsured St Sava with an aquiline nose and pink cheeks looks otherworldly as he raises his right hand in blessing, as though his mind is dwelling on spiritual matters. To his left, only half the image of Stefan Nemanja remains. He looks haunted in a monk's habit with a long white beard and a deeply set eye beneath a bushy grey eyebrow, as if he has had too much time in his monastic retreat to dwell on the past. Meanwhile, a wide-eyed Vladislav is led by the Virgin to Jesus bearing a model of Mileševa; he looks understandably overawed, like a bashful teenager being introduced to a girl he has admired from afar. In the narthex, an angel shoves false prophets and apostles towards hell, their number including priests who cover their eyes with horror at the realisation.

Above Vladislav, women bear myrrh to Christ's grave, which is guarded by a white-robed angel sitting on a block of polished red stone, possibly the same raw material from which the two sarcophagi were carved. A thick gold band on the upper arm seems to denote rank, while the gold wings are white-tipped and partially spread. Long curly hair frames an androgynous face, whose cool stare and tight lips have a mesmeric quality, both solemn and sympathetic. It seems to stare straight into your soul. Beautiful though it is, I had to move on from its scrutiny after a while. It is known as the White Angel, and its image was part of the first satellite broadcast across the Atlantic in 1963. It has also been beamed into outer space in an as yet unsuccessful attempt to communicate with other civilisations.

The road on as I headed east was beautiful too, with more gently rolling contours covered with a mixture of pasture and woodland. Scattered farms were guarded by massive hayricks propped up with greying boughs and daintily topped with brightly coloured polythene headscarves to stop rain penetrating their cores. I gave an elderly man a lift for a while, who was concerned that I should use the Serbian name "Raška" to refer to the area, rather than the Turkish alternative, "Sandžak". This was still part of the Ottoman Empire until the First Balkan War of 1912, when Montenegrin and Serbian troops overran it with relative ease and considerable brutality. The century since has seen significant migrations to Turkey and Bosnia, although the Muslim population is of Slav not Albanian origin. When I dropped my passenger off, he told me that he still had another four kilometres to walk, but that there, "...I am president."

Novi Pazar

Ten miles before Novi Pazar ("New Bazaar") is the Sopoćani Monastery, founded by Stefan Uroš the Great, younger brother of Vladislav (of Mileševa fame), whom he had overthrown in 1243. Uroš reigned for thirty-three years, a period of Serbian prosperity and relative peace. He did not have grand tastes; a Byzantine visitor recounted how the king lived "a simple life, in a way that would be a disgrace for a middling official in Constantinople"; his daughter-in-law (Princess Catherine of Hungary) worked "at her spinning wheel in a cheap dress"; and the royal household ate "like a pack of hunters or sheep-stealers". He was ultimately deposed by his son Dragutin, who, impatient for power, enlisted the military support of his Hungarian in-laws in rebellion. The monastery was badly damaged and deserted in 1689, when its monks joined the exodus north that populated the Orthodox communities of Fruška Gora. It was roofless for two centuries, until Alexander Karadjordjević sponsored restoration works from 1926. The name comes from the Old Slavic word *sopot* ("spring"), referring to the source of the Raška River nearby. Uroš is buried here together with his mother, Anna Dandolo, a granddaughter of the Doge of Venice and third wife of King Stefan the First-Crowned. The Nemanjas understood the worldly advantages of a well-planned marriage.

The pale stone building looks pristine against the wooded slope that rises to moorland behind. Inside, some of the frescoes are in poor repair, but many are better than one could have imagined given their exposure to the elements for so long. The 13th-century artists who painted here are unknown, but their combination of colour, detail and character seems to hark back to the masters of the Eastern Church from centuries earlier, while also in some ways appearing to foreshadow the Renaissance. The centrepiece is the Dormition of the Virgin on the back wall of the nave, where a host of mourning figures in garments of faded apricot, lilac and sea green surround an impassive Mary. Their anguish is evident in expression and posture as they tighten their robes around themselves or bury their faces in the folds. The figures of St Peter and St Paul on the pilasters flanking the altar are painted in subtle hues. Both look resolute – Peter with a sense of immediate purpose in muttonchop whiskers, while a contemplative Paul shows the strain of a life on the road, with lines etched so deeply into his face that they might be tattoos. Elsewhere, a shepherd clad in sheepskin and a straw hat looks up into the face of the angel telling him patiently where to find the infant Christ. The angel has his hand on the shepherd's shoulder to reassure him, while the latter appears willing but barely comprehending as he holds a finger up, as if to ask another question. There is wonderful humanity in the detail. Inevitably, there is also a strong Nemanjić presence. Nearby is Ras, the ruined ancient 9th-century capital of the Nemanjas, but for an untrained archaeological eye like mine, there is little to see, so I pushed on to Novi Pazar.

My first instinct was that I had crossed a border. Elegant minarets punctuated the landscape while the main street had the busy, low-rise hubbub of a Turkish town. Lines of coffeehouses and restaurants seemed populated primarily by groups of heavily smoking men, and many of the women wore hijabs as they went about their business. I visited the old mosque, Altun Alem. It is square and solid, of grey stone, with high, white-painted arches opening on to a spacious porch. A boy appeared and unlocked it for me, telling me the story of its origins, when the three beautiful unmarried daughters of a wealthy man decided that one would build the mosque, one a fountain for washing and drinking, and one a gathering place for the faithful. I was waiting for the punchline when he proceeded to tell me that he was in charge as the imam had gone to Mecca, and he needed to hurry as he had to take the microphone for the fourth call to prayers.

At the Turkish restaurant that I had been recommended for dinner that night, the waiter spoke no English, but a neighbouring group of diners suggested a rich beef stew with paprika, vegetables and potatoes, and the cinnamon-dusted rice pudding. They were excellent choices and we fell into conversation. The most talkative had been a professional footballer in Germany but was home visiting his parents in the city. He appeared to be at a crossroads in his career and was debating whether to return to Germany to get his coaching licence, as it offered better prospects than locally. At a similar juncture in my own life, I sympathised with his dilemma, wondering if I had the energy to devote a decade to building a new business; I was coming to the conclusion that I did not. As I travelled, I felt increasingly that it would be good to try new challenges of a more fulfilling nature. My life on the road was instilling a new curiosity, a desire to be less hidebound by schedule, and a sense that, if I might be three quarters of the way through my active life, I should ensure that I made the most of the quarter that remained. I wanted to devote more time to different interests and to spend more of it with my family and friends. My new acquaintance was twenty years younger.

Walking back to my hotel past dimly lit buildings, the pavements overhung by protruding upper storeys and roofs with deep timber eaves, it was hard to remember that this was a corner of Serbia. History had taken this pocket of land and radically changed the culture of the local Slav population, although I suppose Belgrade was not dissimilar on a larger scale in the early 19th century. The intervening years and another century of Ottoman occupation had rooted Islam more strongly here, while the changes further north seemed to have passed it by. It was a smallish knot in the greater tangle of Balkan religious and racial separations. Its exoticism was beguiling, but the region has tended to suffer from under-investment because of its different nature, which in turn risks fostering further separation. Local Muslims have looked to Sarajevo as much as Belgrade, and the area suffered collateral damage from the Bosnian War, which lingers in local memories. Montenegro's independence had divided the historical Sandžak in two, while the imposition of a relatively hard border with Kosovo just ten miles down the road had removed the major historical market for their clothing factories. There are periodic movements for autonomy, although it is unclear how such autonomy could have any economic viability if it involved true independence. The only real solution would seem to involve a measure of decentralisation, fair treatment economically and significant goodwill on all sides.

The next morning, I turned north to start the long loop back to Belgrade. A couple of miles from the town centre, just past the sizeable red-roofed houses of a comfortable suburb, stands the small Church of the Holy Apostles Peter and Paul, with pastures and hills stretching out behind it. It is the oldest church in the country, built in the 9th century, with foundations some 300 years older, clearly pre-Nemanjić. For 900 years, it was the base of the bishops of Raška, and St Sava is supposed to have been christened here. It is also possible that Stefan Nemanja was rebaptised here as an adult; although raised Roman Catholic, he converted to the Byzantine tradition after a period in Constantinople as a prisoner of the Emperor Manuel.

On arrival, I was greeted by a beaming uniformed figure with his head in the bonnet of a car. In very broken English, he conveyed to me that the man with the key to the church had disappeared but would return in five minutes, the time signalled with an emphatic spread of his fingers. He gestured at me to wait, so I wandered around the graveyard. Centuries-old stones were crammed together drunkenly. Most were carved in the shape of crosses, some simple, others almost floral as their outlines reflected the relative complexity of the carvings on the face of the stone. Some had sunk into the ground to their

1. Rebecca West, 1934

MONTENEGRO

2. Bay of Kotor

3. King Nikola of Montenegro and his family, c. 1910

4. British Embassy in Cetinje

5. Statue of Njegoš on Mount Lovćen

6. Gravestone with hanged patriot at Andrijevica

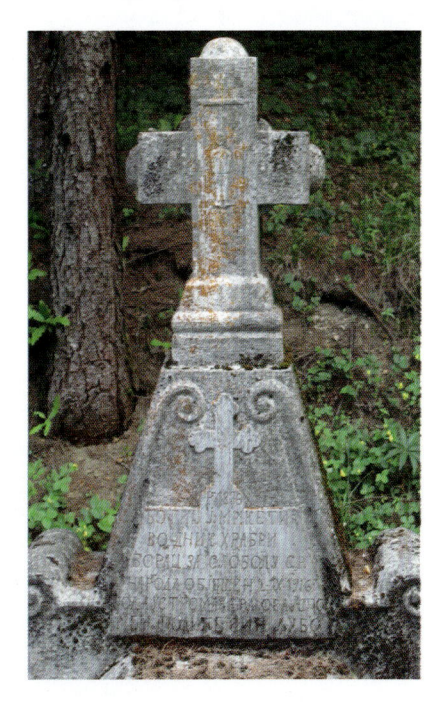

7. Lake Skadar

KOSOVO

8. Adem Jashari (*l*) of the Kosovo Liberation Army and comrades

9. National Library of Kosovo, Prishtina

10. Gračanica

11. Remains of Lazar's mine at Novo Brdo

12. Monks awaiting the bishop at Visoki Dečani

13. Tombs of chief dervishes, Bektashi Tekke, Gjakova

14. Gazimestan monument inscription: *"Whoever is a Serb..."*

Ph. Marianovitch
LA RETRAITE SERBE. — DÉTACHEMENT SERBE PASSANT LE PONT DU VIZIR SUR LE DRIM NOIR, EN ALBANIE

15. The Serb army retreat over the Drina, World War I, 1915

16. Ibrahim Rugova, 2001

SERBIA

17. Yugoslav women bear the lintel of Meštrović's *Monument to the Unknown Hero*, Mount Avala

18. Prince Paul of Yugoslavia with Hitler, 1939

19. Grave of Arkan, Belgrade

20. Assassination of Draga Mašin, 1903

21. St Sava Temple, Belgrade

22. Tito meets Winston Churchill at Caserta, near Naples, 1944

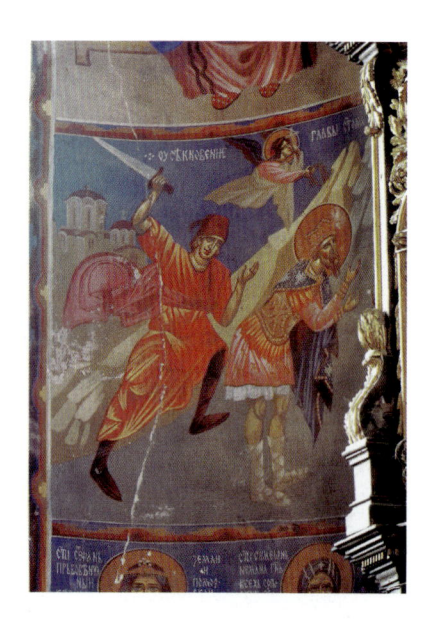

23. Death of Lazar, Monastery of Sremska Ravanica-Vrdnik

24. Draža Mihailović statue at Ravna Gora

25. Tito statue in Užice

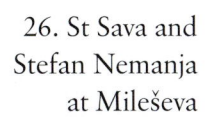

26. St Sava and Stefan Nemanja at Mileševa

27. Grave of Nikolai Rayevski at Gornji Adrovac

28. Concrete fists of Niš

29. Slobodan Milošević, 1997

30. Entrance to Bambiland, Požarevac

31. President Aleksandar Vučić of Serbia, 2017

crossbars, others leaned at unlikely angles. I was struck by how much more attractive they were than their black marble counterparts, the recurring feature of modern Serbia.

My new friend with the car was clearly concerned by the length of time that I was having to wait and started pressing chocolate biscuits on me, determined that I should eat more than the one I had already accepted out of politeness. I think I discerned his name as Ivan, while he determined that mine was Niki (pronounced as a diminutive of Nikita). To pass the time, he started to tell me the age of the church and its various artefacts with an increasingly characteristic use of his fingers to clarify numbers. He then moved on to relaying the distance to other monasteries, which required considerable concentration on my part, his outstretched hands contracting and extending with ever greater frequency as the journey times increased. Raška (and Kosovo) are the heart of the old Nemanja kingdom, and so the density of ancient foundations is particularly great here – I planned to visit three further famous examples that day. The presence of so many of the greatest Serbian Orthodox treasures in the part of the country that spent the longest period under Ottoman control must increase their totemic value, in much the same way as Jerusalem for the sponsors of the Crusades. In fairness to the Ottomans, they had allowed considerable freedom of worship within their empire, while preserving economic advantages for conversion to Islam.

After half an hour, the priest finally arrived and handed Ivan the keys to show me around. I felt rather guilty, suspecting that he was already late for work, although he gave no sign of it. Inside the patchwork metal door of the church, he showed me more 18th- and 19th-century gravestones with facial representations carved into the stone. All were stylised portraits with wide eyes, but their sophistication varied considerably. One resembled a Cycladic head with the addition of eyes alone. Several could have been three-dimensional versions of turn-of-the-century caricatures with elongated noses, stylised moustaches and spectacles, although always with a wide-eyed expression of surprise. Further into the gloom, St Sava's font was an unspectacular blue glass bowl. On the wall beside, he looked out as if assessing the onlooker. As we emerged into the daylight, Ivan disappeared at high speed with a friendly wave, presumably needing to report for duty at last.

Studenica

An hour on, I came to Studenica, the first of the great monasteries. It was founded by Nemanja himself, patriarch of the dynasty. His remains rest here along with those of his wife, Anastasia, and his son, Stefan the First-Crowned, the first Nemanjić king. St Sava was the archimandrite for seven years in the early 13th century and established it as the centre of learning in medieval Serbia. It sits on the lower slopes of the hills that rise up to the west of the Ibar valley, several miles up a long road that zigzags through the woods above one of its tributaries. As I walked into the monastery compound, sheep were grazing on the lawn by the church. An old stone watchtower rose above the residential and administrative buildings, reminding one that for centuries there had been an omnipresent threat here, although Studenica was never completely abandoned like its southern counterparts.

Its main church, the Church of the Mother of God, looked much grander than those of the other great monasteries that followed it, of pale grey marble rather than the usual combination of stone and brick. It gleamed in the sunshine, its burnt-ochre cupola adding a surprising harmonious contrast. It was built at the end of the 12th century, although it suffered a poorly conceived stone extension by Nemanja's grandson, Radoslav, thirty-odd years later. The exterior of the original building has remarkable carvings. Over the main entrance, the Virgin sits on a much-decorated throne, staring out with endless compassion; the lower half of the Christ child is still evident on her knee, but the statue has suffered damage over the years. The Archangels Michael and Gabriel flank her in ardent attendance. Around archways, fantastical figures and forms entwine. A centaur in a Scythian-style cap shoots an arrow at a bemused lion, while his companion fends off its more purposeful partner with a round shield; a large dog carries a sheep in its mouth; a dragon gnaws on a human torso; a sprightly-looking cock treads on the woebegone head of a lion, symbolising the victory of good over evil.

Inside, the frescoes have a more static but also more exotic quality than those at later churches. High up, Jesus calls a tightly bound Lazarus from the tomb while one of his sisters prostrates herself, kissing the Lord's feet, and a servant boy covers his nose, presumably in anticipation rather than the actuality of the likely stench. Beside it, Christ enters Bethlehem on Palm Sunday riding a clearly weary horse that could have come from an Islamic painting. The palms appear to have rooted in the ground like grass, and the faithful have spread robes on the ground to welcome him. On the western wall, Jesus hangs on the cross against a background of a deep blue starlit sky. The gold of the eight-pointed stars is mirrored in the gold and blue halo that frames the stoically suffering Christ, his eyes barely open. The colours have the depth of reality. On two pilasters are depictions of St Joseph and St Barlaam, the former an Indian prince convinced to renounce his wealth and embrace religion by the hermit Barlaam in a likely Christianisation of the Buddha story. The legend was a particular inspiration to St Sava, and later, when popularised in writing in the Middle Ages, convinced wealthy youths around Europe to follow a religious path.

After his abdication, Nemanja retired to Hilandar Monastery on Mount Athos and became a monk, taking the name Simeon. He was an educated man; Robert Kaplan observed that he could sign his name while Barbarossa could only manage a thumbprint. Nemanja's body was brought here to be buried and his tomb was reputed to exude a miracle-inducing oil, although it ceased to flow some 300 years back. There are still receptacles below the plain stone sarcophagus to catch the precious essence should it reappear. He is known as St Simeon the Myrrh-Flowing. His image on the wall has much in common with that at Mileševa, slightly fuller-faced, but with the same long, narrow nose, pronounced nostrils, long, flowing white hair and beard, and a guarded watchfulness. His wife and son lie in more modern, ornate caskets.

I left the monastery almost breathless at its beauty but struck anew by the anchoring of church and state together, whereby saints were rulers and vice-versa. Sava identified his father with Abraham and the Serbs as "an elected People". When added to the neo-crucifixion legend of Lazar, the Bible story was Serbianised, laying the foundations for a holy land and an endless quest in pursuit thereof.

Kraljevo

Some 20 miles down the Ibar valley, the river curves around a hill on the far bank. Silhouetted against the sky is the imposing early Nemanjić fortress of Maglič, built to protect the valley and its treasures. Beyond it, the last great treasure of the day awaited me at Kraljevo, the Monastery of Žiča, the least protected of those that I had visited. Here, Sava founded the patriarchate on his return from Mount Athos, and here was the coronation site for the Nemanjić kings. The code of canon and civil law that Sava drew up here, the Nomocanon, formed the basis for the subsequent intertwining of church and state. Žiča was built in the early years of the 13th-century but was burnt down by the Tatars little more than twenty years later, whereupon the patriarchate moved to Peć. It was rebuilt and plundered several more times in its life, then abandoned for 300 years under Ottoman rule; when Edith Durham visited in 1904, she described it as "a melancholy monument of former greatness", where the church still stood but the monastery was "but a few rocky masses of wall". She described the blocked-up openings in the side wall where a new door was created for the entry of each new king upon his coronation, only to be filled in again straight after. After a 500-year interlude, Alexander Obrenović was formally launched on his brief, unhappy reign here in an attempt to don the Nemanjić mantle; King Peter I (Karadjordjević) chose not to tempt providence by following him.

The monastery is attractive from a distance, standing in its own space outside and above the main town. It has been thoroughly restored and its deep brick-red tower and cupola stand out in the trees around its pristine compound of tile-capped stone, brick and white plaster. The surprisingly large carpark is some way off, and one accesses the monastery through a pedestrian underpass and unexceptional urban landscaping. Inside, there appears to be a thriving community, but the gleaming newness diminishes the sense of a centuries-old spiritual connection. It felt like a monument *to* the past rather than *of* the past, albeit no longer melancholy. The few remaining 13th-century frescoes, much trumpeted in the guidebook and the monastery's own literature, were roped off in a choir chapel to the right of the altar. My request to approach closer was rejected and I struggled to discern any detail in the blinding light that reflected off the wall. I didn't stay long. Later, I chanced upon Prince Paul's suggestions to Bernard Berenson about a proposed tour of the great ecclesiastical foundations of southern Yugoslavia: "[I] feel it my duty to discourage you from going to Žiča ... the discomforts of the journey will not be repaid by all the 'restorations', and bad ones too, of the church."

Kruševac

The drive over to Kruševac is only 40 miles or so, but slow and of relatively little interest as one passes through the string of small towns that seem to merge into one along the West Morava valley. On arrival, I discovered that the large state hotel in the centre of town where I had planned to stay was in the process of demolition, but I found a simple alternative in a side street with ease. The streets outside felt animated. Kruševac is a university town, and the small lanes of cafes and bars were filled with groups of young people drinking, debating and laughing.

In a park at the centre of the town are the few remains of Lazar's fortress. It was here in the legend that two ravens flew to the white tower where his wife, Milica, received the news of the fateful Battle of Kosovo Polje. "We have seen the meeting of the mighty armies, and the leader of either is slain." Now, as Durham told us, "there stands one shattered lonely fragment of the white castle up against the sky" and it stands there still – Lazar's church. From the outside, it looks timeless, with bands of brick and stone, a high cupola and much-carved surrounds to the windows and doors. It was used as a powder magazine by the Turks and the interior was entirely destroyed. It was restored in the mid-19th century, but inside it looks more modern and is unlovely.

The museum at the edge of the park was more interesting. It purports to hold an original robe of Lazar, which has an oriental appearance, pale jade in colour, bordered with gold brocade, embroidered with golden gryphons and buttoned down the front to the ankles. It suggests an owner of education and taste, but one who clearly wished to impress.

The exhibit that I was keenest to see there was the original model of the planned Meštrović monument to the Battle of Kosovo that he had unveiled at the Roman International Exhibition in 1911. This was to combine the glorious legend of Lazar with the dream of a southern Slav state. It was a controversial project, created while he was still a subject of the Austro-Hungarian Empire to build a memorial mausoleum (the Vidovdan Temple) in what was still part of the Ottoman Empire, promoting a concept that would be anathema to both. Meštrović had refused to show it in the Austrian or Hungarian pavilions, ultimately settling on the Serbian section in an act of Slavic solidarity. He won first prize for sculpture in Rome, alongside Klimt, who won the prize for painting. The key statuary was also shown at the Great War Exhibition at the Victoria and Albert Museum in 1915 to enthuse the British public in their support for an important ally. There were sculptures of the key figures in the battle, but also fallen soldiers, grieving widows and the poets who commemorated the glory and the struggles through the subsequent centuries of repression. The wooden model shows a domed structure not unlike an Orthodox church, with long arcades and ranks of caryatids lining the long approach to the central buildings and supporting each of the five tiers of the square tower that would rise high above the main dome.

With this vision of Yugoslavia given a physical reality, it is little wonder that Meštrović developed a close relationship with King Alexander Karadjordjević after the war, but the reality of the internal tensions in the new state led the sculptor further away from his earlier southern Slav idealism with time. The monument was never built due to lack of funds and would clearly have been out of the question after the arrival of the communists in 1945. I had assumed that the model would be easy to find as it is five metres long and two high (planning for an actuality some fifty times that size), but it was nowhere to be seen, and the museum curator told me that it was off being repaired. He remarked that it was a relief that it had never been built given all that had happened since, an unarguable sentiment, although I also felt that it was true on aesthetic grounds. Much as I admire a lot of Meštrović's work, pictures of the model building's Art Deco lines feel uncomfortably close to fascist architecture of the subsequent decades, while the ranks of caryatids rising into the sky remind me of Busby Berkeley's showgirls. Far better to be a curiosity than a source of still more tragedy.

In the main square of the town stands a 1904 monument to the heroes of Kosovo. A winged angel guards a uniformed soldier of the 19th century. A moustachioed bard sits at the base, playing a *gusle* and looking hopefully into the future beneath the inscribed date of 1389, that of the legendary battle. On the other side, a bare-breasted figure of victory stretches out an arm in triumph, her sword resting at her side. Above her is the date 1882, the year when Serbia became an independent kingdom once more.

Upstream on the South Morava River, I found a sign to the Russian Church. High on a ridge looking over the broad valley was a slightly garish construction of red and yellow bricks with stone edging and features and a small, pillared portico in each corner. It sat down a straight, tree-lined path in a large grass meadow and seemed little used. Walking in, with the hum of insects the only thing to disturb the peace, I felt the unusual blend of reverence and solemnity that attends a graveyard. To the right of the path, in front of the church, stands a simple stone headstone underneath a large cross, not quite supported by the pillars that frame an inscription:

> THE RUSSIAN COLONEL NIKOLAI RAYEVSKI
> DIED AT THIS PLACE ON 20 AUGUST 1876
> IN THE FIGHT AGAINST THE TURKS.

This was the grave of the original inspiration for Tolstoy's Count Alexei Vronsky, who had died here fighting alongside the Serbs in their disastrous attempt to liberate those Slavs still under Ottoman rule in 1876. The poorly organised Serb peasant army, under the command of pan-Slavist Russian General Chernyaev, stood no chance as it marched on the strongly fortified Ottoman base of Niš, 25 miles south of here. The attack was unsupported by the major powers, but Chernyaev had brought with him 700 Russian officer volunteers, including Rayevski/Vronsky, happy to die for the great cause of the freedom of "the little Slav brothers" after the heartbreak of his lover's suicide.

As a man, ... I'm good in the sense that life is worth nothing to me. As to my having sufficient physical energy left in me to hack my way into an enemy formation and kill or fall – I know I have that. I am glad there is something I can lay down my life for; it's not so much that I don't want it, but that I am tired of it. Someone will find a use for it ... As a tool I may be of some use. But as a man, I am a ruin.

I had been reading *Anna Karenina* as I travelled, being moved by it far more now than as a youth forty years earlier. I marvelled at Tolstoy's ability to let us understand and sympathise with characters and situations from different viewpoints. I had fallen in love with Anna myself, struck by a *coup de foudre* along with Vronsky, and felt wrenched by her increasing unlovability as her unhappiness manifested in neediness and recrimination. Most of all, I had grown to like and admire Vronsky, who had evolved from a thoughtless seducer at the outset to a figure who behaved with dignity and loyalty in adversity in a way that I hoped I would have done. To me, there were universal truths about relationships within its pages, although West would have disagreed. She disliked Tolstoy's works intensely, believing that *Anna Karenina* had been written "simply to convince [himself] that there was nothing in this expensive and troublesome business of adultery".

Now I stood at Vronsky's grave, where he had been buried after being hit by shrapnel from a Turkish cannonball. A few yards away was the trench where he had gazed out at the Turkish and Serbian lines down in the valley below. Far away, I could just discern the hazy blue hills that stretch to Bulgaria. Rayevski's sister built the church here in 1903, and his picture is on the wall inside (slightly confusingly labelled 21st August 1876). He has dark hair receding under his shako, a full moustache and side whiskers, and wears a blue uniform with plenty of gold rope and braid, but he looks younger and less sure of himself than I had visualised. He is described as "a dark, stockily built man of medium height, with a good-natured and handsome, very composed and determined face". The portrait shows fine features but also a haunted quality. Maybe this is in part "the lost, docile expression ... of an intelligent dog when it feels guilty" that was observed after his illicit love for Anna first became apparent, but it seemed to me to be the gaze of a man for whom life had lost all meaning. I shivered at the inevitable end to his futile romantic trip to the Balkans, the coda to the life that I had been sharing.

In one corner of the church, above a bench and table with empty beer and wine bottles, three marble tablets recorded the dead of the First World War. In another corner, a framed picture displayed black and white photographs in the shape of a cross of those who had died in Kosovo. In front of the church is a dedication to Rayevski. The rear two porches contained blank tablets, as if in recognition of Serbia's endless need for new memorials.

I returned down the path deep in thought. As I emerged through the gate, a figure appeared from the house on the other side. He was a curious sight, short, sixty-ish, with a moustache, hawkish features and greying hair cascading over his shoulders. In his purple V-neck jersey, red socks and galoshes, he greeted me warmly. He insisted on taking me back to the church and showing it all to me once again, indicating with a sweep of an imaginary broom that he was the caretaker. After a warm and all but unintelligible conversation, in which the only two familiar words were *dobro* and raki, he led me to his house, where he showed me his living room and, extracting from it his best chair, shepherded me into the garden. He left me sitting in comfort by an old wooden table and stool in the long grass amid some spindly trees to reappear shortly with a plastic bottle and a couple of grimy glasses. He poured a full glass for himself and half for me (after I had mimed my driving wheel), with much talk of *stari* (old), holding ten fingers up to convey its age. He showed me the pea-sized growths on the plum tree beside us, which would provide this year's vintage of raki, a successor to the surprisingly delicate spirit that I was admiring. We pursued a lively conversation whose general thread was clear – *Ruski* and *dobro* being the most oft-repeated words. After a while and many iterations of *hvala* (thank you), I managed to extract myself without accepting the second glass that he was determined to force on me, and with firm handshakes and much waving I set off back down the hill. Descending through sunny farmland, trails of dust signalled the cutting and turning of hay in fields. Distant figures picked over crops in others. Great blue splashes of Balkan clary illuminated the verges. Tractors passed me, red-cheeked wives sharing the single seat with their smiling husbands in evident conjugal harmony. It felt like a scene from the other side of Tolstoy. I thought that Levin, whose love was so nearly disrupted by Vronsky's emotional carelessness early in *Anna Karenina*, would have been quite at home here. I hoped that Rayevski had found a measure of peace in the end.

Niš

The city of Niš is attractive and friendly. It was long a key junction on the routes across the Balkans, the road south leading on to Thessaloniki and Athens, the eastern turn to Sofia and Istanbul. The River Nišava flows through it shortly before it joins the Morava, separating the old Ottoman fortress from the city centre. After it was eventually absorbed back into Serbia in 1878, Niš was rapidly remodelled, with the old wooden houses and mosques demolished and replaced with squares, wide streets and stone buildings. By the time Edith Durham arrived in 1904, "two slim minarets show[ed] that it was once Mohammedan, and a fat new church, bloated with cupolas, proclaims its orthodoxy". She remarked that some of its features still "give it picturesqueness and a dash of the Orient; but you must not tell it so, unless you wish to hurt its feelings". I thought that I could detect a hint of its exotic past in the crowded, narrow, cafe-lined streets around (yet another) Republic Square, but much of the centre is light and airy. Only one working mosque remains of the nineteen that existed here in Ottoman times.

Crossing the river, one is confronted by the old main gate of the fort, handsome but strictly practical, with battlements high above guarding the deep gateway whose minimal decoration offers no aid to any attacker. The fortress was rebuilt by the Ottomans in the years following the end of the Austro-Turkish War in 1718, recognising the strategic position of Niš. Through the gate is a grassy, tree-filled park, where people strolled happily in the sun or sat in cafes under the old fortress walls. An open-air theatre occupied the angle of the wall to the right of the gate. The structure (though not the minaret) of an old mosque sat alone in the broad green expanse, now an art gallery. Its pale stone walls, pierced windows and red-tiled dome were a gentle reminder of the centuries of occupation. Not far away, a stone monument in the shape of an oversize rifle bullet commemorated King Milan Obrenović, whose army had finally liberated Niš. Its blunt pink granite tip had an unmartial appearance, more lipstick than ammunition, perhaps an apt metaphor for modern Niš, where the enjoyment of peace now occupies the military structure of the past (as in Belgrade).

Back on the south bank in a small green park, a bespectacled bronze figure in a suit and open-necked shirt sings into a microphone. It is a statue of Šaban Bajramović, the gold-toothed, scar-faced, hard-living, Niš-born "king of Romani music". He developed his musical skills in the prison orchestra on Tito's notorious island jail of Goli Otok, where he had been sent for desertion aged nineteen after running off to find his girlfriend. His most famous song, *Djelem, Djelem* ("I travelled, I travelled"), is the *de facto* national anthem of the Roma people. Listening to him sing it in his smoky tenor voice, I hear ancient echoes of India, as well as early soul music and the accordion of European nights. He sings of the destruction of the Roma people by the Nazis and calls them back to walk alongside him with the rawness of personal loss. His hometown was always important to him. There is a story of his driving into the Gypsy ghetto in Niš in a new Mercedes to emerge the next morning with only the shirt on his back, having lost his suit, jewellery and car in an all-night poker game. During the troubled Milošević era, he returned here again, making music and breeding pigeons, but he fell on hard times and died in poverty in 2008.

Beside it is a monument to Niš's other famous son, the Emperor Constantine, erected to mark the 1,700th anniversary of the Edict of Milan in 313, which granted full tolerance to all religions and legalised Christianity in the Roman Empire. The aesthetically challenging monument is hard to decode – a cross tops a totem pole of three busts, the middle of which is superimposed on a cloud-textured form of indistinct shape. To me it looked as though a poodle had been impaled on it.

Constantine's birthplace was just outside Niš at Mediana. In Roman times, this was Naissus, where he built himself a large villa, to which he returned several times in his reign. Edith Durham claimed that Constantine's mother, St Helena, the discoverer of the True Cross, was the daughter of an innkeeper from Naissus, but this does not seem to be generally accepted. What is accepted is that she gave birth to Constantine in Mediana, where her husband, Constantius, was stationed in the province of Dardania. Constantius would later become emperor; he died in York on his return from an expedition to subdue the Picts. He was accompanied on the British mission by Constantine, whom he anointed as his successor. Six years later, Constantine entered Rome as emperor after his victory over Maxentius at the Battle of the Milvian Bridge, his army's shields emblazoned with the first two initials of Christ following a vision the previous evening.

On the road back into Niš is a darker relic of its Ottoman past, the *Ćele kula* ("Tower of Skulls"). During the course of Karadjordje's uprising, the two sides fought each other near Niš. As the battle progressed, the Serbian commander, Stevan Sindjelić, realised that he was facing defeat. To avoid he and his men being impaled alive, and to inflict maximum damage on the Turks, he fired his pistol into the powder magazine as they poured into his trench, blowing up large numbers of his own soldiers and considerably more of the enemy. Hurshid Pasha, commander of the Ottoman fortress at Niš, livid at the cost of his victory, determined to set a warning to others who might try to rebel. He collected the heads of the dead Serbs and made a four-sided tower of 952 skulls. When the French poet Alphonse de Lamartine passed through Niš twenty-five years later, he described:

> ... a large tower rising in the midst of the plain, as white as Parian marble ... composed of regular rows of human skulls; these skulls bleached by the rain and sun, and cemented by a little sand and lime, formed entirely the triumphal arch which now sheltered me from the sun. In some places portions of hair were still hanging and waved, like lichen or moss, with every breath of wind. The mountain breeze, which was then blowing fresh, penetrated the innumerable cavities of the skulls, and sounded like mournful and plaintive sighs.

The monument was rebuilt in 1892 on Milan Obrenović's instructions and enclosed in a simple cream-coloured chapel, as a tribute to Serbian bravery and to keep the anti-Ottoman flame burning. Its deterrent purpose had failed to such an extent that the last Ottoman governor of Niš had had it dismantled some thirty years earlier. Only fifty-eight skulls remain now, smiling eerily out of a tower of otherwise empty stone sockets, having the last laugh at the expense of the tower's constructor. Many of the missing heads were retrieved over time by families wanting to bury the dead properly; they may not have been overconcerned that they got the right one. Presumably, others were taken by trophy hunters. Sindjelić's skull, which had sat at the apex of the tower, is now displayed separately. A plaque outside quotes Lamartine: "This monument must remain. It will teach their children the value of independence to a people, showing what price their fathers paid for it." I left the ghoulish scene drained but confident that the original owners of the remaining skulls would be proud of the continued evidence of their courage.

There was still one more aspect of Niš's troubled history that I felt I had to understand better. Logor Crveni Krst ("Red Cross Camp") was the site of the concentration camp at Niš during the Second World War, named as a possibly deliberate ironical reference to the Red Cross facility nearby. I approached it down a long path of pink concrete tiles through a patchy expanse of grass, just down the road from the smart facade of the headquarters of the Philip Morris tobacco firm. The long grey outer concrete wall looks forbidding but also lower than one would expect, until calibrated against its darker grey steel gate, with the inset open door offering entry to the compound beyond. Inside, the low, red-tiled buildings that enclose a grass square on three sides look almost homely as they face the severe bulk of the main building. Guard towers sit at the corners of the external walls, still eliciting uneasy upward glances. A double wire fence separated the camp from the barracks of German and Bulgarian soldiers.

During the war, 30,000 people passed through here: Jews, Roma, the citizenry of Niš and members of the resistance, both communist and Chetnik. Of that number, a third were executed on Bubanj Hill in the south-western outskirts of the city; women and children were typically sent on to Belgrade to be killed, while others were dispatched to other parts of the German camp network, notably Mauthausen in Austria. I read scratched on one wall: *"tomorrow I go to Germany (4.J.42)"*.

Inside, the building was divided into bare concrete boxes with straw spread around the edge for sleeping. The inmates would be classified and placed accordingly in separate rooms: captured Partisans, local activists, Jews, Romani, those sentenced to death, hostages, women,

Chetniks, etc. Room 7 was known as the "sabotage room" as it housed railway workers and officials who had tried to disrupt German traffic movement. Political and military prisoners suffered daily torture, primarily beating with poles, boots, fists and pistol grips. There were also solitary confinement cells.

An incident on 12th February 1942 saw a mass escape from the camp. General Paul Bader, the German commander in Serbia, had ordered the execution of 3,484 people in reprisal for Nazis killed during the resistance uprising of 1941, although the number does not quite tally with the precise multiples of 50 or 100 that Hitler had specified in his guidelines. Of these, 700 were to be dispatched in Niš. Word got out and the inmates planned a breakout. Their plans were betrayed, but the prisoners overpowered a guard, shot him with his own gun, and large numbers jumped in desperation onto the wire fence, which gave way at one point, allowing a stream of naked and barefoot prisoners to run out into the fields beyond. Forty-two inmates perished but 105 escaped. Most went on to join the Partisans, although six were subsequently recaptured and killed. Over the following week, 800 prisoners were executed in reprisal, 100 for the death of the guard added to the original quota. The wire fences and wooden towers were replaced with the concrete walls and stone towers now in evidence.

I shivered as I walked through the grim structure. It felt cold in here on a sunny spring day and must have been bitter in midwinter. The memory of evil and misery seemed to linger in the utilitarian rooms of grey concrete, whitewashed above chest level, presumably to facilitate counting of the inmates. The photographs of those who had passed though on their way to death seemed to be a broad cross-section of society: the firm gaze of a reservist lieutenant colonel, a smiling youth, a self-composed matron, dashing officers, a knitwear-encased toddler. The heritage that I shared with so many of the victims gave an immediacy to the horror of their grisly fate, ordained from far away purely by circumstances of birth, although the fate of many of the other victims was hardly less arbitrary. The weak features of the camp commandant made me wonder if for once the excuse of following orders might be valid, although still unjustifiable. My fortune of British birth, a country untouched by foreign occupation for almost a millennium, had never seemed happier.

As I left Niš, I stopped at Bubanj Hill. A long track winds up through thick woods, wide enough for two vehicles but now used only by pedestrians. The occasional bench was empty, unsurprisingly as it was dark and claustrophobic below the trees. I imagined all too easily the fear that must have engulfed the lorryloads of prisoners crawling along this road to the old army shooting range. Most must already have known their fate, and the gloom and secrecy of the journey can only have exacerbated their sense of doom.

At the top, a long, low white wall and three giant concrete fists sat in a sunlit clearing. This was the Nazi place of execution, where 10,000 people were killed between 1942 and 1945. The monument had a visceral effect on me. I walked the length of the white marble frieze, which showed in turn groups of helmeted figures crouched with guns, hanging figures, corpses and fists. Raised letters spell out the words of a local poet:

> *From the blood of communists and patriots the fists were born:*
> *fists of rebellion and warning, fists of revolution, fists of freedom.*
> *We were shot but never killed, never subdued.*
> *We crushed the darkness and paved the way for the Sun.*

Beside it, three colossal concrete structures loom over the grassy space – fists, but with an uncanny resemblance to security cameras. They are differently sized to represent men, women and children, and were inspired by an unknown prisoner who raised his clenched fist to the sky to embrace his imminent freedom just before the fusillade that ended his life. The impact is undeniable, although reading the inscription of the 1963 monument, the political message feels over-strong; many Partisans were undoubtedly killed here, but so were many others too.

Joggers passed by and lovers lay on the grass staring into each other's eyes while music enveloped them, seemingly oblivious of the history of their surroundings. I hoped it signalled that this generation could abandon the guns.

Ravanica

An hour north of Niš, ten minutes off the main road to Belgrade, is the Monastery of Ravanica, the once and present resting place of Lazar, sitting snugly below the wooded foothills of Mount Beljanica. The church is contained within the ruined walls of the old fortifications and is rather dwarfed by the large new apricot-hued monastic block beside it. The red, blue and white stripes of an enormous Serbian flag gleamed in the sun above the remains of the front gate. The monastery was badly damaged at the end of the 17th century, along with so many others, although it was only abandoned for thirty years before the first monk returned to start repairs. It is stylistically influenced by Gračanica, which was sited near the mines of Novo Brdo in Kosovo, the principal source of Lazar's wealth. The similarity of the template is clear, but the striated colours and elongated cupolas of Ravanica feel less fine to me than their equivalents at the earlier monastery.

The frescoes are not in great condition, but the long windows of the cupolas created a dazzling aura of light far above the nave, lending a mystical quality to the dark blue colour of the church around it. Lazar's coffin sat under an illuminated portrait, in which he bears a model of Ravanica. Oil lamps hung on either side. The sarcophagus was made of dark wood, banded with silver and inlaid with pictures that seem to emphasise the regal and martial quite as much as the spiritual. His remains travelled north with the monks fleeing the Turks in 1690. West had seen him in Fruška Gora on her travels:

> He lies in a robe of faded red and gold brocade. A dark cloth hides his head ... His mummified brown hands, nearly black, are crossed above his loins ... He is shrunken beyond belief; his hipbones and his shoulders raise the brocade in sharp points. He is piteous as a knot of men standing at a street-corner in Jarrow or a Welsh mining town. Like them he means failure, the disappointment of hopes, the waste of powers. He means death also, but

that is not so important ... When this man met defeat it was not only he whose will was frustrated, it was a whole people, a whole faith, a wide movement of the human spirit.

I stood and pondered my encounter with the remains of the legend of Kosovo. I could not shake the thought from my head that there was an innate selfishness about Lazar choosing heaven for himself while condemning his people to defeat by the Turks and centuries of hardship thereafter in a quest to fulfil his original failed mission.

Ahead of the 600th anniversary of the Battle of Kosovo, Milošević sent the sarcophagus on a nationwide procession from Belgrade Cathedral, where it had lain for safety since the Second World War, carefully ignored by the communist regime. It travelled through Serbia, Bosnia and as far as Krka Monastery in Croatia, accompanied by considerable Orthodox ritual, ending back here 300 years after it had left. It highlights the destructive nature of Milošević's ambitions that the most potent symbol of Greater Serbia should be sent so broadly around Yugoslavia just as it was entering its death throes. This was a call to all the Serb peoples of the federation.

I try to carry a torch when I visit old monasteries so that I can see the detail of frescoes in their underlit interiors. As I clicked it on, a lady with a tight-wrapped lilac headscarf rushed up, thinking that I was wielding a camera. Embarrassed by her error, she turned all the lights on and grabbed my arm to show me the faint outlines of Lazar, his wife and two children on the back wall. In a haze of garlic, she indicated a brightly coloured picture in a book that purported to be the same image. I selected a few postcards from the range of Lazar-related memorabilia on offer and escaped into the fresh air. Another lady approached me and chatted in English, puzzled by my presence. She was a retired economist from a nearby town and had visited England in the past. She offered me a handful of walnuts, which she said came from the tree behind the church and were especially good as the air was so clean. On a bright sunny day, this typical display of Serbian generosity and warmth sent me on my way smiling.

Kragujevac

An hour to the west, I came to Kragujevac, the major city of the wooded central area of Serbia known as Šumadija, heart of the original Karadjordje uprising and the original Obrenović capital of Serbia. The town itself is cheerful, although much of the old centre was destroyed by war, and then further to allow for industrial development. When West came here, it was home to a great munitions works, which evolved with time into the Red Flag military factory and then into the Zastava ("Flag") car plant, now part of Fiat. The old factory still stands there, imperial in style with neo-classical figures leaning on a clock high on the facade and a flagpole rising above the square dome behind it. In front of the building, the statue of a Yugoslav car worker stands proudly in apron, moustache and cap, burly forearms emerging from rolled-up sleeves. It is communist realism at its finest, the subject matter of posters across Eastern Europe and much of Asia for decades. Aging Yugos and Zastavas from the plant are still a common sight on the streets and roads of Serbia.

To the north of the city is a much more sobering sight. In a large park, an assortment of red-brick towers of different heights could be mistaken for a modernist reinterpretation of the Giant's Causeway. It is in fact a memorial to the victims of the worst German crime in Serbia in the Second World War. On 21st October 1941, the German army massacred almost 2,800 Serbian men and boys around here, many on this grassy rise. Inside the building, the story is told; copies of German orders set out the sequence.

As far back as April that year, a month after the invasion of Yugoslavia, Second German Army Command had issued an order saying that "the increasing number of treacherous attacks on German soldiers calls for the harshest countermeasures". By September, the language had become more violent; General Böhme, the commander in Serbia, sent out an order to his key subordinates saying: "Your task is to travel throughout the country, in which German blood flowed in streams in 1914 due to the treachery of the Serbs, male and female. You are the avengers of those dead. A horrifying example must be made for all over Serbia, which must be the hardest blow for the entire population." It is captioned: "When reported, destroy."

In October, Böhme detailed the appalling prescribed ratios of revenge. He also specified that hostages should be taken by all garrisons and numbers were to be reported to headquarters three times a month. He said that anyone shot should be buried "purposely in isolated places" and that "communists imprisoned by troops in a struggle should generally be hanged on the spot or shot".

On 21st October, the chief of local command in Kragujevac detailed the shooting of 2,300 people in retaliation for the loss of ten German soldiers and injuries to twenty-six sustained fighting the Yugoslav resistance some way to the west of Kragujevac. Captain von Bischofhausen, the district commander in Kragujevac, did express concern, saying that "the shooting of completely innocent people from this town may have dreadful consequences", believing that reprisals would only be effective in the vicinity of the initial precipitating action. However, on 27th October, Major König, battalion commander of the 724th Infantry Regiment, reported the detail of the 2,780 men who had been shot over the week, reassuring his superior: "With that, the action is finished."

Particular details illuminate the horror: a formal, urgent request from the superintendent of police for lists of specific pupil categories at the male grammar school; an order from Major König: "On Oct. 21st at 7 a.m. selection and shooting of the prisoners will begin"; photographs of the arrested walking out to the execution place; and the messages in handwritten notes: "Remember me, my dears, because I don't exist anymore", "Don't send me any bread tomorrow", "Goodbye Mica, I died today", "My dear daddy and mammy, regards the last time".

The massacre at Kragujevac was in response to a joint Chetnik-Partisan attack on the Germans. Both resistance movements were well explained in the memorial exhibition, when the Chetniks are often airbrushed out. A Chetnik recruiting poster was displayed, evoking the memory of the Nemanjić family, heroes of the Battle of Kosovo and the Karadjordje uprising, as one would expect from a royalist organisation. The atrocity here marked a turning point. The scale of the reprisals was a key factor in Mihailović's withdrawal from guerrilla action that might bring significant harm to the general population. Meanwhile, the more politically motivated Tito would have agreed with von Bischofhausen's sentiments that the resulting bitterness would lead to acts of revenge, recognising that it would ultimately help to build his forces further. From then on, their paths diverged. Post-war, a jailed General Böhme threw himself from a fourth storey to avoid extradition to Yugoslavia.

The extreme scale of this particular atrocity and the random selection of its victims appal, but as I travelled around Serbia, I realised the extent to which the horrors of life under German occupation were systematic and countrywide – Belgrade, Novi Sad, Valjevo, Kraljevo, Kruševac, Niš and now Kragujevac. I thought again of my friend Lazar's assertion in Belgrade that Serbia should have remained neutral in the war, given that it was nearly destroyed by it. I thought again of the Anglophile Prince Paul, who had sought to balance his deep dislike of the Nazi regime with the desire to protect his country, and I returned to the conclusion that Serbia would in all likelihood have been better off accepting the surprisingly accommodating pact that the regent had negotiated. Of course, no pact with Hitler offered any real security, but as long as the output from the mines flowed, the Germans would probably have used their military resources elsewhere. Churchill described Paul as being a man in a cage with a tiger, "hoping not to provoke [Hitler] while steadily dinner time approaches". With hindsight, Paul's actions are not hard to justify, and the coup that Britain helped sponsor to overthrow him could be seen as yet another of the quasi-imperial interventions that served the relevant great power much better than those who had to live with the day-to-day consequences.

Požarevac

I drove north through endless cornfields, surprised again at the sheer volume of memorial tablets to the victims of road accidents along the side of the motorway. One was on the central reservation, which must have impeded laying flowers. As I pulled off for the last stop of my Serbian travels, another black slab was sandwiched in the triangle of grass between the slip road and the motorway proper.

Požarevac, an hour east of Belgrade, was my final destination. It was the scene of the treaty signed between Austria, Venice and the Ottoman Empire in 1718 that established Austrian rule in Serbia, although only for about twenty years as it transpired. Venice surrendered much of its Greek empire to the Turks in the same agreement. Later, the city was the second capital of Miloš Obrenović; a statue of him stands in the green gardens at the centre of town, pointing the way with a commanding finger. The pale pink town hall beside it has a regimented Viennese solidity, while many of the town's older buildings have a late 19th-century Austrian sensibility.

A short walk away is the prosperous residential street, Nemanjina. It felt secure but not grand. Small shops and a car mechanic's premises were interspersed with detached houses that sat in well-kept gardens behind black wrought iron fences and white walls with louvred panels. At the end of a side street, a modest tile-capped gatehouse with green metal gates formed the entrance to the home of Slobodan Milošević. He and his wife, Mirjana ("Mira") Marković, are buried in the backyard of the family house in the town in which both were born during the Nazi occupation of Serbia, and where they met in high school.

Milošević was Montenegrin by birth, but his father was posted to Serbia by the education ministry, for which he worked. He abandoned the family soon afterwards, leaving Milošević and his brother to be brought up by their mother in considerable poverty. Mira's parents were both Partisans. Her mother had been caught by the Germans during the war and killed. It is unclear whether she was executed by the Nazis or by Partisans who suspected her of having betrayed them under torture. Post-war, her father was a government minister and disinterested in his daughter, so she was brought up by an aunt who was close to, and possibly a mistress of, Tito. With their difficult home backgrounds, Slobodan and Mira were inseparable from early on in their relationship. Milošević was a diligent student and went on to Belgrade University to study law. While there, he became an active organisational member of the Communist Party. He also became close friends with Ivan Stambolić, the nephew of a prime minister of both Serbia and Yugoslavia. Stambolić was both his best man and mentor, and went on to become President of Serbia, before Milošević turned on him.

Post-university, Milošević completed his year of military service, at which he did not excel. As Dušan Mitević, head of the Serbian public broadcaster during the early stages of the break-up of Yugoslavia, remarked: "The student who got the worst marks for pre-military training ended up as the commander-in-chief." After stints at Belgrade city hall and the national industrial gas company, Milošević got a senior role at the Belgrade-based consortium bank, UBB, which involved frequent business trips to the US. He appears to have been a constructive force at the bank, helping to introduce a more rigorous business approach. In 1984, Stambolić became president of the Serbian Communist Party and installed Milošević as the head of the party in Belgrade, launching his career as a full-time politician. His reputation was political but pragmatic, and he was perceived as relatively succinct in an organisation that tended in the opposite direction. With the benefit of hindsight, it is clear that he always kept his eye on power as he steered a course between the aging Titoists and the reformers, no doubt encouraged by Mira, who had been brought up in the workings of the party. Milošević also courted the military.

In 1987, on a trip to Kosovo, he appears to have realised that his opportunity for power lay in the divide between the Yugoslav and Serbian views on the ancestral lands there. His return four days later marked the real turning point, but it seems that the speech he made to the protestors outside the hall was not pre-meditated:

> This is your land ... your memories are here ... You should ... stay here because of your ancestors and because of your descendants ... I do not propose, comrades, that in staying you should suffer and tolerate a situation in which you are not satisfied. On the contrary: you should change it.

With those words, he shone the spotlight on the innate conflict between the Yugoslav ideal and the sense of destiny felt by swathes of the broad Serb community. Milošević may well have thought that he could use nationalist sentiment and mob power to eventually rule Yugoslavia; instead, he destroyed it.

Over the next two years, he consolidated his power base after ousting Stambolić. In the delicately balanced constitution of Yugoslavia, Serbia essentially had four votes out of eight, representing the two "autonomous regions" of Kosovo and Vojvodina in addition to its own vote and that of its inseparable ally, Montenegro. It could usually count on the support of one of the other four republics if it played politics correctly. By 1989, after a series of meetings characterised by simultaneous violent "rallies for truth", Milošević had a tight control over all four votes. He also exerted an ever-tighter control over the media. When he returned for the 600th anniversary of the Battle of Kosovo, greeted by crowds waving posters of Prince Lazar in one hand and his picture in the other, it was a coronation, symbolised by the presence of the Serbian Orthodox patriarch. Although Milošević had orchestrated it, he would have protested against any such characterisation, striving as he did to maintain his image as man of the people.

The disintegration now began. Slovenia, the wealthiest and most ethnically self-contained of the Yugoslav republics, started to move towards independence, fearful of Serbian domination and unhappy about its continued subsidisation of its poorer southern siblings. Milošević posed as a defender of Yugoslavia, with the support of the federal army, but when the moment came in 1991, it suited him to let Slovenia leave and enshrine Serbian dominance in the remainder. The fight to keep Yugoslavia intact lasted only ten days. However, in the course of the negotiations, Milošević had changed the political boundaries, referring to "the interest of the Serbian people" and not just to Serbia. This was irrelevant in the context of Slovenia, but it set the scene for the quest for Greater Serbia and the horrors to come.

With Croatia, the position was much more complex. It had strong ties with the German-speaking world, but also a significant Serb minority, who would only feel safe in Yugoslavia. The identification of Croatia with the Croats, which was apparent in the independent constitution proposed by its president, Franjo Tudjman, would be anathema to its Serb inhabitants, many of whom had an innate suspicion of Croat nationalism dating back in particular to the atrocities of the Nazi-sponsored Ustaše in the Second World War. This fear was further fuelled by Tudjman's adoption of the red-checked medieval banner of Croatia as the new national flag, which the wartime regime had also adopted, and by his abolition of the official use of the Cyrillic script. The Croatian declaration of independence led to Serb uprisings in those parts of the country that they dominated, with the support of the Yugoslav army under the guise of preserving Yugoslavia. Particular war arenas caught the attention of the world, notably the shelling and slaughter in Vukovar and the bombing of Dubrovnik, and by January 1992 the UN-sponsored Vance Plan had achieved a largely successful ceasefire with a *de facto* separation of the respective Serb- and Croat-controlled areas of Croatia.

Serbian atrocities had received particularly broad exposure in the world media, but there is no doubt that it was two-sided. The local media in both Croatia and Serbia stoked up nationalist sentiment relentlessly; Misha Glenny refers to the main television stations on each side as "the two greatest war criminals of them all". Mass demonstrations on the streets of Belgrade in March 1991 against the propagandist nature of the media were given additional fuel by the perception of Milošević as an old-style communist, but he had won a convincing mandate in the 1990 general election and, with the help of the army, he faced the protestors down.

The relationship between Tudjman and Milošević is hard to fathom. They appeared to have had a civil personal relationship. Tudjman did not support Slovenia, when he had apparently committed to do so, and he failed to reinforce Vukovar in controversial circumstances when it was under Serb attack. It has been suggested that the two leaders were content to play out their visions of a Greater Croatia and a Greater Serbia, which could coexist reasonably happily in their minds. That, though, would involve the dismembering of Bosnia and Herzegovina.

Bosnia is an all but landlocked triangle, surrounded by Croatia on two sides and sharing a border with Serbia and Montenegro on the other. Its population split at the time was 44% (primarily urban) Muslim, 31% Serb and 17% Croat. The latter two communities were mostly rural, the Croats largely concentrated in the south-west and north of the republic. As the country inched towards an uneasy independence in early 1992 that was feared by the Bosnian Serbs, the latter planned a pre-emptive strike. They declared an independent state and by autumn were in control of 70% of the country. Much of their force was the re-badged Yugoslav army under the control of and paid for by Belgrade. Croatia seized its opportunity and supported and fought with the Bosnian Croats to carve out a Croat homeland. The Muslims (Bosniaks) were forced to defend themselves. All sides committed atrocities, but the Serb paramilitary forces were essentially criminal enterprises run closely by Milošević. The scale of rape, murder and the use of concentration camps by the Serb side was of a different order to that elsewhere. Repeated foreign attempts to stop the fighting failed, and there was particular international outrage at the near four-year Serb siege of Sarajevo.

In 1994, American pressure forced Tudjman to wind back any plans to absorb parts of Bosnia into Croatia and to form a new federation with the Bosniaks in non-Serb-controlled areas. The *quid pro quo* was seen the following year when Croatian troops took back key areas of Croatia that had been occupied by the Serbs several years earlier. Milošević did not attempt to defend them; the economic damage caused by sanctions and mass printing of money at home was no longer tolerable. That summer, the end of the war became inevitable when the Serb massacre at Srebrenica and renewed shelling of Sarajevo brought NATO air attacks on the Bosnian Serbs. Srebrenica at least cannot easily be charged to Milošević; it appears that his men on the ground were out of control by then, notably Ratko Mladić, the Bosnian Serb commander. The final settlement involved the surrender of the rest of Serb-occupied Croatia, but it denominated 49% of Bosnia as Republika Srpska, nominally part of the country, but self-governing and looking in reality to Belgrade as the parent. Richard Holbrooke, chief architect of the Dayton peace agreement, described Milošević as making "a stunning first impression on those who do not have the information to refute his often erroneous assertions".

In the years that followed, disenchantment inside Serbia grew; unhappiness with the wars and the economic turmoil of the Milošević years was compounded by increasing authoritarianism, corruption and links with organised crime. The latter was evidenced by a series of high-level street assassinations. Meanwhile, the situation in Kosovo was ratcheting up, and in the summer of 1998, Milošević sent in his armed police and special units to target areas with KLA sympathies. The Americans wanted to restore peace before they had another Bosnia on their hands. Given his identification with the Kosovan Serbs from the start of his rise to power, Milošević was in a bind. When he refused to sign the UN-sponsored peace plan in March 1999, it is clear he knew that NATO would start bombing Serbia itself. It seems he believed that his longstanding knowledge of America and his relationship with the Clinton administration since the Bosnian negotiations would be enough to keep the bombing "polite". In one sense, they were. There appears to have been a prewarning system of some sort that minimised civilian deaths, though not in Kosovo, where Serb forces, now including the army, embarked on a programme of mass ethnic cleansing. Hundreds of thousands of Kosovars were driven out of the country, but ultimately Milošević had taken on an adversary of a different quantum. He was also staying at a different location each night to avoid being targeted. At the beginning of June, he finally agreed to the proposed NATO deal, which would give Kosovo significant autonomy under UN protection, while remaining technically part of Serbia, the mirror image of the Republika Srpska solution. Meanwhile, he had been indicted on 24th May for war crimes by the chief prosecutor in The Hague.

The remainder of his presidency was marked by further repression at home. He finally lost power in the election in October the following year after the opposition united around Vojislav Koštunica, a moderate anti-communist nationalist. Koštunica had replaced Milošević's old mentor, Ivan Stambolić, as the candidate following the latter's disappearance; it later turned out that Stambolić had been kidnapped and murdered by the Red Berets on Milošević's orders. The election result needed to be enforced by mass protests and strikes as Milošević manoeuvred. On 5th October, 10% of the population of Serbia demonstrated in Belgrade; a group of them stormed the federal parliament, setting it on fire. Milošević's reign was finally over. Six months after leaving office, he was arrested on domestic financial and economic grounds and taken into custody, after a shoot-out, with the assurance that he would not be handed over to any authority outside Serbia. Soon after this, the discovery of mass graves of Kosovo Albanians in Serbia provided clear evidence of Milošević's knowledge of atrocities and his authorisation of attempts to cover them up. On 28th June 2001, he was flown to the Netherlands, twelve years to the day after his pageant at Gazimestan, apparently in the same helicopter that had taken him there. His trial started in 2002 on charges of war crimes in Kosovo and Croatia and genocide in Bosnia. As he sat in the dock, pale-faced, wearing a blazer with a tie the colours of the Serbian flag, he presented himself and Serbia as victims and the current proceedings as a show trial. He claimed that he had brought peace to Bosnia rather than war, focusing on Dayton rather than the years of bloodshed that preceded it. Did he really believe it? Had endless hours of self-justification warped his truth so far? Or was this a calculating opportunist playing his best cards for survival? He was found dead of a heart attack in his cell in March 2006 before the trial had concluded; he had been suffering from high blood pressure and heart problems. He was buried in a family funeral here at Požarevac, although tens of thousands had attended a farewell ceremony in Belgrade just beforehand.

By then, Mira had fled to Moscow to join their son. She died there in 2019 and her remains were cremated and buried alongside her husband in Požarevac. Long considered the power behind the throne, she was commonly referred to as the "Red Witch of Belgrade" or "Lady Macbeth of the Balkans". She had been a professor of sociology at Belgrade University and written a diary column for many years in the Serbian magazine *Duga*, continuing to write for *Pravda* and online in exile. Her views were hard-line communist, reflecting her upbringing, with much handwringing about the death of the Yugoslav ideal of harmony between races. Despite this, she justified her husband's policies, drawing a narrow distinction between nationalism and patriotism. The two of them appear to have had an entirely self-contained social life. Both Milošević's parents committed suicide when he was a young man; as a result, other than his brother Boris and their children, neither of them had any real direct family. Outside a taste for acquiring properties, Milošević's main pleasure seems to have been a quiet family dinner at home with a cigarillo and a glass of raki. If meetings overran, he would swiftly ring Mira to explain, an act quite atypical for a Balkan male.

Undoubtedly, Milošević could be charming when he wanted, as recounted by many international politicians and by those involved in the various peace talks. He also knew how to use his business experience of America to his advantage. Ultimately, however, he only appears to have been close to his immediate family. When one seeks to analyse why he presided over such a calamitous and inhumane decade, a simple answer does not come easily. Warren Zimmermann found him:

> ... a man of extraordinary coldness ... For the most part ..., people were groups ("Serbs," "Muslims") or simply abstractions to him. I [n]ever heard him say a charitable or generous word about an individual human being, not even a Serb ... For Milošević, the truth has a relative and instrumental rather than an absolute value. If it serves his objectives, it is put to use; if not, it can be discarded.

Milošević was able to distance himself from the human consequences of his actions; maybe, for Serb nationalism, as with communism, the principle could be used to justify all, even if it was ultimately a fig leaf for power. Maybe once he had taken the initial step to use uncontrollable forces for his own ends, everything else unfolded by following the ghastly logic to its natural conclusion, compounded by a fear of the consequences of losing power. Organised crime clearly benefited from the chaos, and it is likely that Milošević's criminal connections would have played a key part in some of his more unpalatable decisions. Towards the end of his time in power, he seems to have been drinking heavily, but that feels like a reaction to the situation in which he found himself rather than a cause of it. By then, it must have been clear that all likely scenarios were bleak.

A few minutes from Nemanjina is an area of town devoted to sporting activities. Players were practising behind the red and white walls of the local football club, the stand's seats faded to pale pink over the years by the sun. Nearby was a riding school and a recreation centre. Opposite the latter, two narrow crenelated wooden towers formed an open gateway about 12 feet tall. Suspended between them was a cartoon fawn, wide-eyed and poised to leap, against the background of a yellow and orange globe. The name of the park was obscured by a red and black banner captioned "EXTREMƎ". Through the gate was a concrete path leading to abandoned areas behind wire fencing. Paint peeled off a children's roundabout. Chains hung loose on another ride, the awning gradually disintegrating on its frame. Scrubby bushes were pushing up through what might once have been well-tended lawns. Two small bridges spanned the greenish water of a children's swimming pool.

This was Bambipark, a six-acre themed recreation space for the young, one of the more bizarre business diversifications of Marko Milošević, the notorious and much-indulged only son of Slobodan and Mira. Its name was changed from the originally proposed "Bambiland" to avoid a Western name after the NATO bombing started, despite the dubious etymological logic involved.

It opened in 1999 soon after the end of the war in Kosovo, joining a number of Marko's other business ventures, such as Madona, also in Požarevac, the biggest nightclub in Serbia, and the monopoly on Serbia's duty-free shopping business. He had a reputation for trading on his family's position to advance his interests, for mixing with organised crime, for his extensive gun collection and for crashing expensive cars. He had dropped out of secondary school early, complaining of the innate conflict between schoolwork and pleasure. He was deeply unpopular in Požarevac, which he ran as a personal fiefdom, exerting control by threats and violence. The launch of Bambipark may have been in part an attempt at repairing his image, which had been damaged still further by accusations that, despite posing in military uniform as the country embarked on the war in Kosovo, Marko had spent much of the conflict at his family's villa in Greece, where he had also been seen out shopping for powerboats. He fled to Russia soon after his father was arrested. Požarevac demonstrators trashed Bambipark and many of his other local interests in the succeeding months. Now, it sat quietly decaying, a forlorn reminder of Serbia's recent decade of horror.

On my way out of town, I gave a lift to a hitchhiker called Jasmina. She worked selling cosmetics in Požarevac, hitching to and from her home an hour away each day. She talked of her daughter working as an estate agent in Dubai, but it was clear that her life was very difficult. She asked my age and was surprised to hear that I was already in my mid-fifties. I delicately asked hers in turn, pegging her at a decade or so older. She was only forty-nine. As I drove on to Belgrade having dropped her off, I mulled over the cost of the Milošević years, not just in the loss of so many lives and the streams of refugees in the series of failed wars, but also in the fate of the mass of Serbs at home whose economy had been pillaged and run into the ground at the same time, casting a blight on an entire population.

I had dinner with a journalist contact in Belgrade. We sat on the wooden terrace of a small restaurant not far from St Sava drinking beer on a warm evening. He talked of the tentative signs of early-stage reconciliation, of dialogue in Mostar and rescue operations in recent flooding that had spanned communities. He talked about avoiding conscription in the Milošević years; he had lived in an apartment block above Belgrade from where it was easy to see the military police coming, so he and his friends would run into the forest to hide until they had gone. He talked of Bekim Fehmiu, the great Kosovan Albanian actor who had gone to Hollywood but quit the stage permanently mid-performance at a Belgrade theatre in 1987, traumatised by Milošević's anti-Albanian rhetoric. He talked about the scale of corruption in the war years – Bosniak forces had been able to rent armed and manned Serbian tanks. He felt that there were some signs of progress against corruption in the arrests of a number of local politicians. He hoped that a reshaping of anti-Western attitudes would allow for some sort of deal in Kosovo.

The situation remains difficult. The EU's inability to agree to admit Serbia in 2019 has strengthened Russia's influence and diminished moderate voices. Many Serbs have gone abroad in search of work, although there are signs of life in the IT sector in particular. President Aleksandar Vučić is seen as improving the lot of many Serbs, and has had some success in attracting international money into the country, most obviously in the huge Belgrade Waterfront project behind the old railway station being financed by Abu Dhabi. But he is still viewed by some as the latest in a long line of autocratic leaders, with tight control over the media. Levels of corruption and political violence are still perceived to be high. Like Serbian leaders over the years, Vučić seeks to balance the interests of his country between Europe, the major trading partner, and Russia, the centuries-old sponsor of their Orthodox Slav little brothers. China is now added to the mix. A long-term formal solution to Kosovo is still out of reach, which hampers Serbia's European ambitions. Talk of a land swap between the two and formal recognition of Kosovo's independence comes up against the twin challenges of leaving an orphan Serb community in southern Kosovo and the likely knock-on effect of disrupting the uneasy status quo of Republika Srpska's position in Bosnia. More time is likely needed. A more recent focus on a sub-regional grouping with Albania and North Macedonia may be a clever way to defuse tensions between the Slav and Albanian communities and create some economic critical mass, but it is unlikely to be a straightforward process.

A generation down, familiar themes play out. Anastasija Ražnatović, daughter of Arkan and Ceca, is a YouTube star, posting bikini shots in Dubai and promoting products to her million followers on Instagram. Murals of Ratko Mladić, the war criminal Bosnian Serb military leader, have appeared on the streets of Belgrade and elsewhere. The highest profile Serbian of all, of course, is Novak Djoković, who enjoys almost godlike status at home. When he was detained in Melbourne ahead of the 2022 Australian Open for failing to comply with COVID rules, supporters lit candles at St Sava seeking divine intervention on his behalf. Meanwhile, President Vučić claimed that the tennis star was a political victim, the implication being that his country continued to be cast in a similar vein. Beyond his borders, the invasion of Ukraine has made it hard to balance the historic friendship with Russia with the desire to be part of Europe. Those of us who love so much about Serbia must hope that it can cast off the yoke of perceived victimhood and accelerate its evolution as a constructive westward-facing regional power.

North Macedonia

"... *cupped in her destitution as in the hollow of a boulder there are the last drops of the Byzantine tradition.*"

SERBIA
KOSOVO
BULGARIA
TETOVO
SKOPJE
ALBANIA
PRILEP
BITOLA
OHRID
GREECE

Skopje

As the cab left Skopje Airport and joined the motorway, I was struck by the signpost to Athens, a reminder of the proximity to the southern border of the former Yugoslavia. Somewhat different complexities had played out here over the years, with Greek and Bulgarian influences as well as Albanian and Serb. Macedonians have often referred to their four main neighbours as the four wolves, and at different times in history each in their own way has sought to control at least part of what is now officially called North Macedonia, in addition to Turkey, which ruled here for well over five centuries.

We turned off the Autostrada Nënë Terezë ("Mother Teresa") towards the city centre. The music in the cab had a much stronger sense of the Mediterranean; lilting, offbeat plucked strings underpinned a flute playing an exotic melody. I had been asked to shut the windows of the cab at the outset, but twenty minutes later the air conditioning was making no discernible impact, so I rebelled and breathed in the warmth of a late summer afternoon. We turned left at the Hostel Bimbo and arrived at the more decorously named Hotel Rose.

On the walk into town, the first roundabout showcased a vast statue of a freedom fighter in the Remington idiom, firing a pistol from a galloping horse. On investigation, it was a statue of Vasil Chekalarov, one of the early leaders of the Internal Macedonian Revolutionary Organisation (IMRO), described by British journalist H. N. Brailsford as the "cruel but competent general" of the Bulgarian Macedonian independence forces at the beginning of the 20th century, fighting in turn against the Ottomans and the Greeks in the Balkan Wars.

The relatively small centre of Skopje boasted statues in all directions – freedom fighters, saints, ancient kings, statesmen, writers and more. A vast figure of an early warrior-king on horseback, high on a pedestal with bands of marble reliefs, was clearly the great Alexander on Bucephalus, although tactfully not named as such. Four lions admired the ever-changing display from the jets of water that surrounded him.

Nearby, two gold-hued girls exchanged frozen words as they encountered each other out shopping. A fountain celebrated motherhood, water splashing out of an elevated basin over bronze women suckling, hugging and playing with their infant children. Philip of Macedon towered above on another pedestal, left hand on his sword and right fist above his head as he emphasised an ancient declaration. By the river, a group of figures commemorate an anti-Ottoman bombing campaign of 1903, although the introspective assembly on the plinth ignore each other so completely that you would doubt their ability to collaborate at all.

A thirteen-arched 15th-century bridge crosses the River Vardar. It was lined with railings to display the impaled heads of offenders in Ottoman times, most notably that of Karpoš, King of Kumanovo, who was executed here after leading a failed rebellion in 1689 in alliance with the Austrians. His equestrian statue stands nearby too. Looking over the bridge parapet, a red-bikinied bather was poised before a dive into the river to join her companion, whose feet were still visible above the water's surface. The variety of the statuary and the unfinished nature of much of the new construction on the periphery of open spaces suggested a theme park that had opened on time despite manifest delays to the scheduled works.

North Macedonia's relationship with Alexander the Great had been a major bone of contention with its southern neighbour Greece for some time. The previous regime sought to burnish its reputation by co-opting the most famous Macedonian in history. This was a dubious enterprise on several levels. The Slav and Bulgar ancestors of the majority of the current population had only arrived in the 6th and 7th centuries, displacing the Albanians into the mountains and the Greek-speaking peoples further south. The current Macedonian language has much in common with Bulgarian, and this land was ruled by Bulgaria from the mid-9th until the early 11th century, when the Byzantine Emperor Basil "the Bulgar-Slayer" re-established rule from Constantinople.

Further back in time, the ancient Macedonians would have classified themselves as separate from the rest of Greece in status, but they clearly acknowledged their Greek ancestry. Their ancient capitals of Aigai (present-day Vergina) and Pella were 150 miles to the south of Skopje in northern Greece, only 20 miles from the coast. Ancient Macedonia would have claimed control over the southernmost part of current North Macedonia after their defeats of the Illyrian kings, Bardylis and Cleitus, and might have had some tribal brigades from this area in its army, but neither Alexander nor his father are believed to have travelled further north than Lake Ohrid. The Battle of Pellion, at which Alexander defeated Cleitus' Illyrians, is believed to be slightly to the west of the lake in modern-day Albania. Macedonia was seen in ancient Greece as a buffer against the uncivilised tribes beyond them, and the Macedonians in turn would have viewed their unreliable tribal allies in the highlands as an important bulwark against barbarian threats from still further north. The relationship between ancient Macedonia and its Greek allies was complicated, with many Greeks having fought on the Persian side against Alexander's crusade. The major motivation was likely to have been financial, but southern Greeks tended to dislike the Macedonians, whom they saw as outsiders.

The modern-day Greek government understandably resented Macedonian appropriation of one of their greatest heroes, which included naming Skopje International Airport after him. The Greeks also disliked the implied legitimacy of Slav arrivistes using the simple name of "Macedonia" to describe an area that only included a modest part of the ancient kingdom and only represented a portion of the area that became known as Macedonia during the 19th century. Prior to that, it had been part of the larger Ottoman region of Rumelia, which encompassed the entire Balkan peninsula. In 1992, a million Greeks marched through Thessaloniki in protest at the perceived misappropriation. For many years, Greece blocked the prospect of Macedonian accession to the EU until the name issue was resolved. In 2018, the two countries reached an agreement that the Former Yugoslav Republic of Macedonia (FYROM) would change its name to North Macedonia, having cleansed the name of the airport in February that year. Two years later, the EU finally agreed to begin accession talks, some sixteen years after the original membership application was submitted.

The old Turkish area of Čaršija extends up the hill to the north of the river. The narrow streets are full of cafes, old inns and a wide variety of shops. Some of the older curiosities still seem to represent the phenomenon that West observed of "a shopkeeper [spending] incredible ingenuity in displaying articles of only one or two kinds, and ... [putting] the most appetizing of them along side others that have been unsaleable not for mere months but actual decades". Delicious smells lure one in different directions and the pace is unhurried. I sat over Turkish coffee and baklava in the market observing the scenes around me. The elegance of many of the young Muslim women in elegant headscarves and sharply cut coats with military buttons contrasted with the black coverings and dull-coloured raincoats of the older generation.

Tucked up to one side is Sveti Spas ("Holy Saviour"), a 17th-century church built on older foundations and set deep in the ground, as churches at that time were not permitted to presume to the same status as mosques. The iconostasis within is remarkable. West described it as "Byzantine in its recognition of the moral obligation to decorate, as extensively and intensively as possible, yet in its spirit it is purely peasant". It is crudely rustic in some ways and extraordinarily complex. Vines ascend twisted trunks in its depths, while a profusion of animal and plant life host a series of homespun scenes. In one corner, the three brothers who created the whole are busy with hammers and chisels, two hard at work while the third seems to have paused in alarm at something that one of the others has done. As West observed, Abraham looks irritated at being disturbed in the middle of sacrificing his son by an angel whose wings appear to have been modelled on those of a chicken. In a scene from the life of St Nicholas, another would-be killer looks upset to be stopped from finishing off three martyrs, and the stone-faced guard who brings the head of John the Baptist to a governessy Salome seems utterly unmoved.

In the courtyard outside near a pomegranate tree laden with fruit is the cross-hatched marble sarcophagus of Goce Delčev, leader of the IMRO until he was shot by the Turks in 1903, shortly before the Ilinden uprising that he had helped plan. He was Bulgarian yet espoused an inclusive multi-ethnic regionalism and self-determination for the broad area of Macedonia that included the current North Macedonia but stretched into Greece as far as Salonika, as well as into south-west Bulgaria. The debates about Macedonian and Bulgarian identity date back many years.

Further up the hill is Mustafa Pasha Mosque. In the garden "of this not extraordinary mosque", visitors washed themselves at the marble fountain. "Prosperous middle-aged men were sitting on the domed and pillared white porch, and talking not more dramatically than two Londoners at a club window." The scene seemed to have changed little from West's visit, but the much-restored and elaborately decorated interior had a somewhat clinical feel. The view from the terrace over which West rhapsodised is still fine. The city stretches grey, white and ochre far to the "bare blue mountains beyond, shadowed violet by the passing clouds", but the right angles and glazed glare of modern buildings detract from the harmony of old.

I was buttonholed by an earnest young man who, after offering a brief history of the mosque, felt that I would benefit from an exposition of the Koran and its scientific accuracy. A mosque elder moved us outside as the disquisition was disturbing the faithful. After straining to follow the evidence that the Koran foretold Einstein's theory of relativity, I made my excuses and moved on, with the expressed (and sincere) intention of reading the holy book myself.

At the peak is Kale Fortress, which has been occupied since the Bronze Age and thought to have been built originally by Justinian in the 6th century CE. Stefan Dušan, the last great Nemanjić monarch, crowned himself emperor here in 1346, establishing a new capital roughly at the centre of his Serbian Empire, which stretched from Belgrade to Lamia in Greece. The empire effectively died with him twenty-five years later. Recently, the fort has been the site of tension between elements of the Albanian and Macedonian communities, both of whom claim centuries- and even millennia-old historical rights over the site in a manner somewhat reminiscent of the more violent disagreement at Ayodhya in India.

I followed the sound of folk music and found the source in a carpark on the ridge by the entrance. A group of thirty or so Albanian women of all ages were dancing in a circle to an insistent rhythm from a car stereo system. The older women wore black dresses to their ankles and headscarves of different colours. Younger women in denim favoured a red tint in their long dark hair. They held hands together in the air and laughed as they turned. Small children joined in or ran around waving vivid red Albanian flags, which also festooned the cars parked nearby. It seemed to be part of a wedding celebration and emanated pure joy. I took a few photographs from a distance but was politely asked if I would delete them by a powerful-looking attendee.

I made a brief tour of the castle battlements, which sit impressively above the city, but there is little to see other than the walls and the view. The punctuation of the city landscape with minarets had its customary appeal. By the time I emerged, the wedding procession was descending the hill, a cavalcade of cars with horns blaring, flags waving, bodies swinging out of windows and collective screaming. The reception proper promised to be quite a party.

Back near the river, I found the Museum of the Macedonian Struggle. The next compulsorily guided tour was still half an hour off, so I walked over the square to St Dimitri, clearly the church where West had scrambled to a midnight Easter service after her late arrival at Skopje railway station. She had described it somewhat unfairly as looking like "an opulent two-storied farm building". It is late 19th-century, bland in appearance and pale salmon pink in colour. I was surprised to notice the entrance to a lawyer's office at the edge of the grassy graveyard. The church's only real external character is derived from its adjacent Italian-style basilica uneasily topped by an awning in the form of a Byzantine dome. Inside, away from the hubbub of the main square, the mood changes. The filigreed metal stairs spiral up a pillar to an improbably high pulpit, which must give most priests vertigo and have been influenced by the height of its Muslim equivalents. The iconostasis is a gallery of pictures ascending into the gloom above, where one can faintly discern the outline of an Orthodox cross. Candlelight reflected off pillars and glass. The sense of spirituality within belied the unpromising exterior.

Not so at the museum, where we were given a brisk, partisan canter through a hundred-odd years of Macedonian oppression and resistance thereto. The building was only a few years old, of a grand post-imperial style and smelt strongly of cat's urine. The history was told through a combination of waxworks and oil paintings, with photographs and exhibits to illustrate key incidents. Our attention was drawn strongly to any that refuted Greek or Bulgarian claims to Macedonia, including a 1903 Macedonian language book and the formation of the Macedonian Committee that met around then in Salonika, while conveniently skirting over its Greek membership and initial incarnation as the Hellenic Macedonian Committee. It is hard not to sympathise with the Macedonians, victimised in turn by the Ottomans, Bulgarians, Serbs and Greeks, but a more balanced approach would have been more persuasive. I was reminded that the IMRO slogan "Macedonia for the Macedonians" had been the original creation of Gladstone in 1897, although he was criticised at the time for the difficulty of anyone to understand whom he meant by "the Macedonians". The photographs of the naked victims of the reprisals by Turkish bashi-bouzouks after the 1903 Ilinden uprising and of the inmates of Tito's Goli Otok prison camp were particularly upsetting.

The treatment of the 1934 assassination of King Alexander Karadjordjević appeared to be difficult to position correctly. There was a waxwork of the Bulgarian assassin in pride of place, the gun in a bunch of flowers, and a display of photographs. There were also waxworks of Alexander and fellow victim, French Foreign Minister Barthou, but blame seemed to be firmly attributed to Croatia, Mussolini and Hitler. As we emerged from the darkness and bloodshed into a circular hall, waxworks of relevant great figures stood around a balcony. Mussolini appeared to be high-fiving Hitler in celebration of the success of their plot, observed by Churchill calmly smoking the inevitable cigar. There was a curious moral relativism at work, which allowed for the celebration of a violent uprising against the Turks over a century ago but some embarrassment at the targeted killing of a Serb ruler thirty-odd years later. Maybe this reflected the changing character of the IMRO. Its members had started as freedom fighters, but by the 1930s the Macedonians living in Sofia's slums were providing hitmen for hire in service of radical causes throughout Europe. As *New York Times* journalist C. L. Sulzberger had remarked: "For some strange reason, the Bulgars are Europe's finest murderers."

Outside, I could see the location by the old bridge where, after the First World War, the Serbs

> ... in their joy at turning out the Turks and becoming the masters of Macedonia, pulled down the beautiful mosque that had stood for three centuries in this commanding position, and replaced it by an Officers' Club which is one of the most hideous buildings in the whole of Europe. It is built of turnip-coloured cement and looks like a cross between a fish-kettle and a mausoleum, say the tomb of a very large cod.

It was flattened by the 1963 earthquake, and the site has been the subject of periodic debate as to whether either of the previous two incumbents should be reconstructed here.

Tetovo

The car hire attendant reassured me that Macedonians were good drivers compared to the crazy Albanians. The road west passed through a landscape of gentle hills and endless corn fields. Approaching Tetovo, sitting below the Šar Mountains, the scenery became an evident extension of that which I had admired around Prizren in Kosovo, only 20 miles away as the crow flies, but 70 miles or more by road. The peak behind the town is known as Tito's Summit and is the highest peak fully in the former Yugoslavia. The mountain's name has changed with the times. It was originally called Big Turk but renamed Mount Alexander in the wake of the king's assassination in 1934. The Bulgarian occupation saw a reversion to the original name in the Second World War, before it was honoured by the communist authorities in its latest incarnation. As the lady in the Skopje museum had told me, everyone had to be a communist Partisan after the war.

The west side of North Macedonia, beneath the mountains that divide it from Kosovo and Albania, is where much of the Albanian minority live. Tetovo has been a centre for the expression of protest against Albanian repression since it came under Serb control in 1913, after which it saw mass migration, particularly to the US and Canada. Since the Second World War, there have been periodic flare-ups, against communist repression and again in solidarity with the Kosovar Albanians in the 1990s. It was an important point of supply for the KLA and later housed many refugees.

Close by a small river, I found a mosque with "a strange and dissolute air, for it was covered with paintings ... Not an inch but had its diamond centred with a lozenge or a star, all in the most coquettish, interior decorator's polychrome". The exterior walls were covered with painted square panels resembling an expensive set of playing cards in pastel shades. The paint and glaze required to create the effect apparently required over 30,000 eggs when it was built in the 15th century. Old men sat on benches by the water enjoying sporadic conversations, in no hurry to unfurl their rods to see if anything could be caught in the sparkling flow. The mosque was guarded by a low wall of robust wooden grilles set in sturdy pillars below a tiled ridge; it was defensive but also enticing, affording further glimpses of the jewel inside. A slim stone minaret pierced the sky above the hilltop behind.

Inside the compound, low barstools stood by two ancient marble basins. Clean white towels hung above the taps that fed them from the old stone fountain. Petunias and roses gleamed in the sun. A figure appeared and waited while I rinsed my hands before showing me into the main building. My jaw dropped; it was as if one had stepped into a *Vogue* fashion shoot. West had described it as "being inside a building made of a lot of enormous tea-trays put together, the very most whimsical tea-trays that the gift department of Messrs. Fortnum & Mason would wish to provide". In more contemporary terms, it is how I imagine Gianni Versace would have designed a ballroom in his Florida mansion. Every inch of the walls and ceiling is covered with ornate stonework and vegetation on backgrounds of yellow and burnt ochre framing medallions of showy vases and graceful townscapes. A frieze runs high around the room with a landscape of elegant palaces and ships sailing with flags fluttering. The women's balconies resemble Montgolfier balloons. It is an extraordinary confection. As West said: "In this erection a fierce people had met to worship their militant prophet. I understand nothing, nothing at all."

On the edge of town, the Bektashi Tekke, a Sufi monastery, was founded by a brother-in-law of Suleiman the Magnificent in the early 16th century, although the majority of its buildings date from 250 years later. The Bektashi were hugely influential in Ottoman times and still had dozens of foundations at the beginning of the 20th century, many takeovers of earlier Christian establishments, some of whose practices had been incorporated into their own. I entered a large garden compound, where stone paths led me past an antique fountain and old guesthouses with carpeted wooden platforms for meditation. In the communist era, it had been taken over by the state as a hotel and museum. The Bektashi have regained control, although they are in dispute with the state, as well as with a group of Sunni Muslims who have established a mosque on the site. Loudspeakers on a high chimney marked out the makeshift minaret of the encroachment.

A figure waved from a window and descended to welcome me, introducing himself as an Albanian from Long Island who was staying to help the sect in their legal travails. He gestured me through a small gate flanked by the barred grave of an earlier leader. I walked down a passage to be greeted by a smiling, full-bearded figure with a large golden amulet nestling in his sober waistcoat; it was clear that he was the resident dervish. Together we established our best language for communication as French from an extensive list of options that excluded English. He explained to me the key concepts of the sect. All are equal under one law, both men and women. They perceive themselves to moderate between the two poles of extreme Islam and extreme Christianity. He talked of the need for spirituality and of existence and non-existence, which I understood to mean that only in finding God do we find true fulfilment (or existence). His calmness and evident spirituality seemed to me much more likely to provide a path to greater understanding than the exhortations of strident extremists of either religious camp. He showed me photographs of visitors to the *tekke*, among whom I recognised the unlikely pair of James Belushi and President Erdoğan of Turkey. As our discussion wound to an end, a Turkish tour group appeared. I had a cup of coffee with the young American, who told me that the sect has 1,000 adherents in Tetovo and 50,000 in Albania, where the head baba (or spiritual guide) is based. They have opened a monastery in Michigan. They are not allowed to run their own schools in Macedonia but may practise their rituals, which somewhat surprisingly include the use of bread and wine. I left with some reluctance, feeling that I had glimpsed a spiritual channel of substance and would have liked to learn more of this relatively unknown corner of Islam.

Continuing south, villages climbed the wooded slopes above the road. Many of the houses resembled *kullas*, the traditional Albanian tower houses, but with a more homely aspect. Most had a white-plastered top floor above two or three plain and barely windowed lower storeys, as if a farmhouse had been built on a fortress. The style fitted the landscape in practical terms too; given the steepness of the valley, the houses were sunk into it on the lower levels, which were used for animals or storage. The topmost alone was for the family.

Near Debar, the valley widened out and two slow streams wound through mud formations. Doubtless they form a torrent in early spring. Near here, close to the border with Albania, Skanderbeg had won two of his great victories over the Ottomans, commemorated by a statue in the town centre. It had also long been a centre for Greater Albanian nationalism. Senior figures from the town had helped to found the League of Prizren, and Debar was briefly Albanian during the Balkan Wars before being included in the Kingdom of Serbs, Croats and Slovenes after 1918. The situation in this region was especially complex in the Second World War; the Italian and German occupiers included western Macedonia in Albania, which appealed to some local chieftains. The Albanian resistance groupings broadly divided into three: communist, republican and royalist, of which the former did not subscribe to the concept of Greater Albania. To this mix was added Tito's Macedonian Partisans, distrusted by many for perceived Serb or Slav communist associations. The local British liaison officers working in the area took longer to command airborne support than Fitzroy Maclean further north, but ultimately were able to support a joint operation by Albanian and Macedonian Partisans to displace the Germans from Debar with supply drops and a rocket attack on their barracks. It is clear that local Albanian nationalist interests (both anti-German around Debar and German-supported around Gostivar) were important factors throughout and remain so to this day.

I had been looking forward to my visit. Debar had been described by West as "a double town, its white houses collected in an upper pool and a lower one, its minarets and its poplars placed so that the heart contracted, and it became an anguish to think that one would not be able to recollect perfectly its perfection". It retains a rundown charm, with tree-lined streets leading off a decaying central plaza. A group of bored-looking policemen yawned over lunch at the table beside me. On a street corner, barrows of watermelons and boxes of tomatoes seemed too numerous for the customers available. I bought a bag of dark plums almost exploding with the juice inside. Narrow streets of white houses were somewhat scuffed, with plaster patches and a density of wires fanning out over alleyways, detracting from the original character. The occasional feature was a reminder of the town's importance in the past. A series of twin stone-arched windows looked down from the first floor at a builders merchants' pavement display of corrugated iron and pipes. The octagonal bronze cap and louvred shutters atop the belltower of the Orthodox church had seen better days, but they had obviously existed.

Each town in turn down the west side of Macedonia felt neglected, with barely designed structures of concrete, glass and metal gradually inching out the evident charm that had preceded it. This was still more apparent at my next port of call, Struga, which sits at the north-western corner of Lake Ohrid, once "white and clean like a peeled almond". As I drove into town, a large photograph of a beaming princess in tiara and pearl-strewn high collar tried to signal me to the Club Caffe Lady Di.

The greyness of the day did not favour the pebble beach occupied by ranks of unused white plastic deckchairs and flanked by a low, dark disco bar from which a thudding beat vainly attempted to incite an early-afternoon party. The setting was undeniably pretty though, and the water of the little river that flowed into the lake looked beautifully clean, so I took heart and wandered up its banks and around the town. West had described the houses as "white and periwinkle blue, ... a country town ... pretty enough to eat". Sadly no more; an old bathhouse looked sturdy enough, but many of its windows were smashed and the old mosque was closed for repairs behind a corrugated iron fence. Meanwhile, the new constructions that enveloped the town made one question whether the mayor was a glazier. Buildings staggered under the weight of the mirrored bay windows that they had been asked to support. The local shopping centre appeared to be made of large pink boxes glued onto a squat smoked-glass cylinder. No periwinkle shade was visible, only the garish blue tiles of the roof of an over-reflective hotel. I drove out through a collection of dismal mustard-coloured blocks as rain pattered on my windscreen. I have since been told that a number of the villages in the area have become centres for drugs and prostitution, and that the influx of black money has destroyed what was still beautiful twenty years ago. I wound my way around the lake to Ohrid, full of foreboding that it too had been irretrievably spoiled by the 80-year gap between West's visit and mine. As I drove down to the harbour, however, my heart lifted.

Ohrid

The sky cleared and the sun irradiated the mirrored surface of the lake out to the misty outline of the far shore. Small groups wandered down to the lake's edge to take advantage of the sudden improvement. Behind me, a cobbled street led away from the waterfront, the upper storeys leaning out over the street, the whole a harmonious blend of stone, timber and whitewash. Waiters emerged into the refreshed air to wipe down tables and set them for the evening. I was in a Mediterranean idiom, but with an added sense of calm that may have stemmed from the density of churches here, whose faded brick cupolas stood out above the skyline in each direction. West described the old town as "stuck as thickly with churches as a pomander with cloves".

In her letters, she also describes how she was jumped in Ohrid by Stanislav Vinaver who, as head of the Yugoslav press bureau, had been her guide for her travels in *Black Lamb and Grey Falcon*. He is a major character in the book under the pseudonym "Constantine". "He was a man of forty-five, short, fat, like a Jewish Mr Pickwick, with a head like a cone with the apex cut off thatched with coarse black curls." He was clearly a great talker: "In the morning he comes out of his bedroom in the middle of a sentence; and at night he backs into it, so that he can just finish one more". For two consecutive nights, she had to drive him out of her bedroom with her fists and tried to work out how she could escape from him with only limited cash at her disposal. Happily, he "quieted down" by the time that they returned to Skopje, and she found some excuse for him: "apparently all French women journalists sleep with the officials of the Pressburo, and at first he was genuinely amazed to find I didn't intend to be agreeable." The situation got worse again in Belgrade, where West contracted erysipelas and Vinaver appeared daily at the hospital protesting his love through her fever, claiming that she treated his feelings "as England treated Lord Byron". She was finally rescued in her convalescence by John Balfour, the British *chargé d'affaires* in Belgrade.

West had spent romantic evenings in Belgrade, but with a former lover, Prince Antoine Bibesco, Romanian diplomat, friend of Proust and married to Asquith's daughter, once described by West as "a boudoir athlete". She was no stranger to men's intentions, having conducted a ten-year affair with H. G. Wells, with whom she had a child. She had also had relationships with each of Charlie Chaplin, Lord Beaverbrook and the journalist John Gunther. Her romantic attachments were rarely straightforward, probably coloured by her ambivalent feelings towards her father, who had abandoned his family when she was eight. In her view, "the mind of man is on the whole less tortuous when he is love-making than at any other time". She was capable of saying no, as evidenced by her rejection of Ford Madox Ford, complaining that being embraced by him was like being the toast under a poached egg. Despite the contretemps with Vinaver, West and her husband offered him asylum in England during the Second World War, as they did to a number of other Yugoslavs, but he chose to remain, enlisted in the army and was a prisoner of war in Germany from 1941. West sent him food parcels but they never met again, and the last decade of his life was difficult under the new communist regime. He is buried at the New Cemetery in Belgrade.

Lake Ohrid has been inhabited since prehistoric times, and the town was conquered by Philip II's forces and later by the Romans. It gained in importance with the building of churches here from the 5th century, whose work became more missionary after the Slavs settled the region a century or so later. Ohrid developed into a significant centre of learning for the Church once St Kliment (Clement) and St Naum arrived at the end of the 9th century. They were disciples of St Kiril and St Metodi (Cyril and Methodius), two brothers from Salonika who had enabled the Slav peoples to engage with Christianity by translating the scriptures and the liturgy into a Slavonic language. In the process, they devised a Glagolitic alphabet to enable an accurate rendition. This alphabet later evolved into the Cyrillic script. The multiplicity of languages allowed by the Orthodox Church, in marked contrast to Rome's insistence on Latin, explains much of its success in broadening its appeal. The Archbishopric of Ohrid remained important over the centuries, with its authority stretching as far as Venice, Malta and Sicily, but it was abolished in 1767. Soon after, the Ottomans placed both Ohrid and Peć under the control of the Greek Church because they were too independent of Istanbul, the stated reason being the improbable fear that both were seeking to switch allegiance to Rome.

In the heart of the old town not far from the waterfront, I found the 11th-century St Sophia, the cathedral church for four centuries before it was taken over as a mosque. It was used as a warehouse in the Second Balkan War and retains a slightly secular appearance from the outside. It is surprisingly reticent, sitting in a small green garden, its entrance below ground level, and its brick cupola barely sticking its head above the main body of the church beside it. Inside, the Ottoman whitewash was removed fifty years ago to reveal the thousand-year-old frescoes below. They are beautiful, somehow simpler and less psychologically freighted than those of the later Nemanjić foundations. Above the sanctuary, a vast, solemn Mary holds a knowing infant. Below this, Christ offers communion to the apostles, but it is a posed affair. At a lower level still, well-spaced church worthies keep watchful eyes on the congregation. Elsewhere, Abraham looks guiltily over his shoulder as he grips Isaac with his right hand and wields his sword in the other. Presumably, he has heard the approach of the angel closing in from above with right hand outstretched. The story of Abraham, with its message of late rescue from sacrifice, appears to have had particular resonance around Macedonia.

As I pondered the severity of the faces of the angels in their various interactions with biblical characters or supervising the process of justice, a beautiful sound started to fill the cathedral. Unseen by me, four men had started to sing in harmony; the music drew on strands of sacred choral music through the ages, but its Slavic tonality added a plangent freshness. I sat alone in the church and time ceased to have any meaning. Somewhere in the shifting blend of notes was an eternal truth and a sight of the hereafter. After a while both instantaneous and infinite, the music came to an end. I was reminded of Beethoven's view that "music is the one incorporeal entrance into a higher world of knowledge which comprehends mankind, but which mankind cannot comprehend".

I thanked the singers, who it turned out were rehearsing for a concert of Rimsky-Korsakov choruses that evening, and I returned later to hear their advertised performance. It was uplifting again, but the magic of the moment was much reduced from earlier in a full church, with the promoter pacing up and down the aisle in a lilac shirt, instructing a photographer on the detail that he sought in mid-performance shots. Afterwards, I sat outside on a terrace in the warmth of the evening and ate a fresh pink grilled trout from the lake, which had more flavour than I had thought possible in a fish that has a habit of disappointing.

The following morning, I walked out to the south-western point of the town, where the exquisite little Church of St John sits on its own above the brightness of the lake, loosely framed by cypress trees. Its bricks and tiles reflect a spectrum of shades from pink to deep brown through orange that would challenge the subtlest of painters. Regarding her time in Ohrid, West's letters refer to a curious lunch in the porch of a church by the sea that the then bishop was especially fond of because he had succeeded in ridding it of a poltergeist who used to snatch the marriage-crowns from the heads of people being wed there, but I cannot be sure that this was the right setting. I sat for a while, trying to imprint its perfect image on my memory, before ascending to the remains of the Fortress of Tsar Samoil, the Bulgarian emperor who had based himself at Ohrid and at Prespa a little to the east. He reigned for seventeen years from 997 to 1014, and even before that as co-ruler had inflicted a number of defeats on Byzantine armies as he sought to defend Bulgarian independence. In the end, the superior strength of the enemy told, and Samoil's troops were defeated in the Battle of Kleidion. The Byzantine Emperor Basil, apparently infuriated by the death of his favourite general in the battle, blinded the Bulgarian captives, leaving one in every hundred with a single eye to lead the others home. Samoil died of a heart attack thought to have been brought on by witnessing their return.

Looking out from his fort, Ohrid's tiled roofs shade the broad valley extensively as it feeds down to the curve of the bay, but it still sits naturally in the contours as it has done through the ages. The old Roman amphitheatre below the fort offers spectacular views out across the lake if ever the action on stage palls. A little further on is the Church of St Bogoroditsa Perybleptos, which became both the cathedral church and the repository for the remains of St Clement after the Ottoman arrival. West thought that the domes "are bubbles [but] the porch is of extravagant clumsiness, approached by squat steps and pressed by a wide flat roof, which is utterly unecclesiastical and might be proper in a cow-byre". It is hard to disagree. Passing through a gate in the old town wall, within minutes I was back in the unhurried streets of the resort, where one could pass leisurely days and evenings drifting from cafe to lake, with only the statues of the great saints in the waterside gardens to highlight the town's importance over the centuries. It was an unusual juxtaposition, intense spiritual history side by side with the restaurants, water and sunshine of a holiday destination. Much as I enjoyed Ohrid, its worldlier side and the inevitable, if slight, commercialisation of its ecclesiastical history had somewhat diminished my sense of connection to the principles of its deep past.

St Naum

At the southern end of the lake is the Monastery of St Naum, tight up against the Albanian border. The drive there led past lakeside hotels and little villages that embraced pristine beaches. Men were cutting wood in the sunshine ahead of the onset of winter. Strings of red peppers hung over balconies as they dried. At the monastery, once the site of the church founded by Naum, the companion and possibly brother of St Clement, I was greeted by a long, paved avenue between twin lines of juvenile cypress trees, with the lake on my right. On the other side, a long row of boxy stalls with orange shutters and roofs testified to its popularity as a tourist destination, as did the unusual practice of charging for entry. Beyond the commercial area, the mist rose off the dark waters where the springs rise that feed the lake. They are surrounded by woods, extending up the Galičica Mountains behind, through whose rocks the water from Lake Prespa on the far side is filtered until it emerges here bright and clean. For one fanciful moment, I thought an arm might appear from the lake elevating a sword, but instead the peace was broken by the arrival of two small pleasure boats. I crossed the small, fast river that flowed into the lake proper, heeding the sign that warned of the danger of peacocks to myself and children, and came to the monastery. It is substantial, much of it new, of white plaster and stone. West had complained about its deformation "by a concrete tower livid in colour and vile in design" erected by a bishop to celebrate its thousandth year. It was an unappealing and dominant feature of photographs of the monastery at that time, but it has since been demolished, and the compound is more harmonious as a result.

The small Church of the Holy Archangels is enclosed in a courtyard. It is built of stone and brick and its two cupolas give it a shape "like a locomotive". It has been thoroughly restored and is dwarfed by the buildings of the main monastery around it. The remains of the original 10th-century church lie beneath the current structure, which evolved over the centuries, the tomb chapel of St Naum and its frescoes being completed in around 1800. He himself lay under a gold-embroidered red velvet cloth. On the wall behind is a fresco of him on his deathbed surrounded by great Slavic teachers. St Cyril reads the requiem, St Methodius is richly robed, St Clement blesses his closest companion, and their fellow Antiquarius wipes a tear from his eye. They seem to be joined by St Sava – surprisingly, as the event occurred some 300 years before he lived. Sadly, West was mistaken when she referred to the thousand-year image of St Naum, but the chapel has a strong aura of sanctity and healing accumulated over the ages; the saint's tomb has a particular reputation for cases of madness.

The iconostasis in the dark depths of the church is extraordinary. At the base, the many winged heads of the cherubim and seraphim decorate bare boards. Above them, an elaborate gold-painted carving of vegetation, birds, shells and even hands frame the great gallery of rich portraits. Over the main doors, two red-tongued dragons balance a scroll showing the year of its creation, 1711. High above, two larger and fiercer specimens appear to support the great cross on the force of their fierce breath. A fresco caught my attention. Jesus is riding into Jerusalem on Palm Sunday, welcomed by a young figure with a look of wonder on his face, who spreads his red robe under the ass's hoofs in an act of devotion. The dignitaries behind him look put out by such spontaneity, while Jesus looks back at the apostles, who follow him as if to remark on the impromptu act. In the foreground, two small boys wrestle, oblivious of the significance of the event beside them. The palms strewn on the ground look like bulrushes, the obvious local template for an artist.

Outside the church, I stared across the lake, the low white clouds giving it a brilliant sheen as it stretched far into the distance to the marginally deeper hues of the shoreline. West had written of standing by the water and finding a slab of a ram and ewe copulating, which she believed to be the relic of an ancient fertility cult. There is an old relief that would be easy to interpret that way, but it seems to be a depiction of a miracle of St Naum, who harnessed a fierce bear that was terrorising a farmer and his ox, and induced it to pull the plough in tandem with the scared animal.

As West had looked out, she had had a revelatory moment inspired by the scenery and the old church, essentially "a belief that life, painful as it is, is not too painful for the endurance of the mind, and is indeed essentially delightful". As I emerged from the dark womb of the church - where one could address one's deepest fears and in so doing leave much of their burden behind - to enter into the startling brightness and unity of the water and sky before me, I too felt a renewed energy and sense of oneness with the world.

Bitola

I wound my way back around the lake for a few miles before heading east over the mountains, skirting the wilder shore of Lake Prespa and coming down through the wooded hills beyond to Bitola, the second city of North Macedonia. It was an important centre in Ottoman times when it was known as Manastir, still its Albanian name. I searched out the city museum, a fresh primrose yellow and white neo-classical building that belied its previous role as a military academy.

Mustafa Kemal Atatürk trained here for three years early in his career, arriving from his hometown of Salonika aged sixteen. During his time in Manastir, he was introduced to the works of Voltaire and Rousseau by a Dominican monk with whom he had become friends. They were dangerous reading for a young army student, whose career could have been finished if found in his possession, and they seem to have sparked a strong reaction in him against the autocratic rule of Sultan Abdul Hamid II in Istanbul. The museum displays a love letter from his local girlfriend, whose father "snapped me from you, locked me up and didn't let me out for a month". She tells him that her father has died, and she will always wait for him. It is not at all clear whether he received the letter, nor even whether he reciprocated the feelings; this was a man who never shared himself with another easily. Having done brilliantly in his final examinations, he had been selected for staff college in Constantinople. Atatürk did return to Salonika in 1907, shortly before the outbreak of the Young Turk revolution, and it was there that he first came into conflict with his long-term rival, Enver Bey, who played a leading part in it. Atatürk was sympathetic to their ambitions but did not take an especially public role.

The Young Turk movement was particularly strong in Salonika and Manastir, the key garrisons for the Ottoman Third Army, which were at the forefront of the revolt against the sultan's despotism. A local army officer, Niyazi Bey, had led a group of soldiers into the mountains to form a guerrilla band at the start of July 1908 after his participation in the anti-imperial conspiracy had been discovered. Four days later, the assassination of the sultan's key local general outside the Manastir telegraph office proved to be the final trigger in turning sentiment to the Young Turks. Seventeen days on, the sultan bowed to the mass popular uprising, which had spread to Istanbul, and restored the reformist constitution that he had abolished thirty years earlier, bringing an end to absolute rule. A year later, he was forced to abdicate in favour of his brother and was exiled to Salonika. Pictures show the streets of Manastir thronged with people celebrating their liberation on 22nd July 1908 as Niyazi Bey's units took control of the town under the slogan "Freedom, Brotherhood, Unity". Unfortunately, the end of autocracy was not accompanied by a unified vison, and the death throes of the Ottoman Empire continued until 1922. A photograph at the museum shows Atatürk on the battlefield in 1922, just ahead of his victory over the Greeks that led to the foundation of the Turkish Republic. A later photograph shows him alert but tight-lipped in the back of an open-topped car with Edward VIII of England; the latter, in a bold chalk-stripe suit, looks down and away as if struggling to maintain any sort of conversation.

Macedonia had become an epicentre of regional unrest at the start of the 20th century, where the nationalist ambitions of Greece, Serbia and Bulgaria eyed the opportunities thrown up by the Ottoman decline. National experts produced widely varying racial breakdowns of the Macedonian population, demonstrating in each case a majority of their own ethnic brethren. The great powers promoted their own interests. The Germans and Austrians attempted to exploit their friendship with Istanbul to achieve a land route to the Middle East. The sea-going powers of Britain and Russia sought to frustrate them by keeping the Sublime Porte in its weakened condition, the one seeking to contain the other by protecting free passage through the Dardanelles and latterly access to Middle Eastern oil. Their ally, France, was the largest foreign investor in the Ottoman sphere, but the growth of German influence in Turkey steadily shifted the balance.

Meanwhile, the local desire for autonomy took many forms. For Slavs, that would tend to mean true independence for all inhabitants of Macedonia or a separate identity for Macedonia within Bulgaria; for Albanians, however, that might involve some form of Greater Albania in the west. Others wanted an evolution of the status quo. This led to the possibility of conflicts between almost any combination of Macedonians, Albanians, Bulgarians, Serbs, Greeks and Turks. Most occurred at some point.

Five years before the Young Turk revolution, there had been a series of uprisings in Macedonia against the Ottomans under the auspices of the IMRO. 1902 and early 1903 saw several uncoordinated incidents: a local uprising near the (now Greek) town of Kastoria, another close to the Bulgarian border, and a series of terrorist attacks in Salonika, where a French steamer was holed by a bomb and the main gas pipeline ruptured, followed by explosions at the central station, a cafe, the bar of a popular hotel and the complete destruction of the French-controlled Banque Ottomane. In each case, the Turks were able to restore order with relative ease, generally accompanied by on-the-spot executions and mass arrests, but they looked less and less in control of the territory.

On 2nd August 1903, St Elijah's Day (Ilinden), burning haystacks near Manastir signalled the start of a broader uprising. Fires were lit all over western Macedonia, bridges blown up, telegraph lines cut, and roads blocked. A 300-strong guerrilla band took control of Kruševo, a town 30 miles north of Bitola, and declared a republic. Within two weeks, the Ottomans had suppressed the rebellion with considerable brutality, and the Greeks likewise, but the Ilinden uprising remains a rallying point for Macedonian nationalism to this day. There is a well-attended re-enactment at Kruševo each year. The call to arms is displayed on the museum wall:

> *Blood of our innocent fallen brothers from the Turkish tyranny is waiting for the revenge. The trampled honour of our mothers and sisters is calling out ... A thousand times better death than shameful slave life.*

In many ways, it is fitting that the end of Ottoman rule in Macedonia came here at Bitola in the First Balkan War. In November 1912, the Serb army of 110,000 confronted the final stand of the smaller Turk forces. Three days later, the Ottomans surrendered, having lost 17,000 men with a further 45,000 taken prisoner. Serb losses totalled 12,000. However, the Serbs were fighting here because the Greeks had made less progress than expected, and its Bulgarian allies viewed Bitola, along with much of Macedonia, as rightfully theirs. The ending of the Ottoman presence merely sowed the seeds for the next century of conflict.

West refers to her visit to Bitola, "a lovely but villainous town", so designated because the waiter had palmed the money with which they were settling their bill. She described buying clothes at a fair from a man who said, "When you come back here, you'll be able to find me quite easily, I've a very uncommon name – Abraham Cohen." Like Salonika, Bitola had a significant Jewish community since the migration of the Sephardic Jews from Spain in the 15th century. A poignant display in the museum draws attention to their fate here. Seven years after West's visit, in March 1943, the entire Jewish population, over 3,000 in number, was rounded up and sent to Treblinka, Mr Cohen presumably among them.

Out in the sunshine, Bitola's importance through the years was evident. Its main shopping street of Širok Sokak ("Wide Street") was handsome, the long progression of 19th-century three-storey buildings admiring the restrained decoration of their opposite numbers. Two century-old solemn bearded figures looked down from the tops of the pillars that flank the door of the local dentist, mouths firmly closed as if in warning to those who enter. The street has undergone many name changes, having honoured since the start of the 20th century each of Abdul Hamid, King Peter of Serbia, Tsar Boris of Bulgaria and Tito, in a potted history of the country's domination from outside. At the top, in the main square, Philip II of Macedonia sat astride a rearing horse; across the square was the Yeni ("New") Mosque, now an art gallery. When I visited, its smashed darkened windows still attested to the anti-Albanian riots here in 2001, accompanied by ethnic cleansing by Slav paramilitaries, in response to the death of nine local soldiers in an ambush.

In the wake of the Kosovo War, troubles erupted in North Macedonia, where tensions between the Albanian and Slav populations were exacerbated by the role of elements of the Albanian population in smuggling weapons to the KLA in Kosovo, and also reportedly to Muslim insurgents in southern Serbia. The situation was complicated by rivalry between different Albanian political groupings, and made uglier by the interior minister, Ljube Boškoski, sending in his paramilitary thugs, the Lions. Like the Red Berets in Serbia who had trained them, this group occupied a dark area where politics and organised crime meet. Fearful of another Kosovo, the international community mobilised rapidly; six months after the violence had started, the key parties signed the Ohrid Agreement, launching an uneasy cooperation. The Lions were disbanded in 2003. The total number killed in the troubles was around 140, split roughly evenly between the Albanian and Macedonian communities. Boškoski was acquitted of charges of responsibility for war crimes at The Hague, although his fellow defendant was found guilty; he was subsequently jailed for seven years for illegal party funding. The combined population of Albanians and Turks in Bitola is now only around 6%, down from almost 16% fifty years earlier.

Behind the main square, large porticoed mansions mark the old diplomatic area; prior to the First World War, there were a dozen consulates here. Bitola and Prilep are the strongholds of Macedonian nationalism, and one of the more handsome buildings carries the red and gold banner of the VMRO Party, successor to the IMRO, which has evolved from its original 19th-century ideal of representing all those who lived in Macedonia to a narrow focus on the interests of the Macedonian majority. It held power in North Macedonia for much of the 21st century and was the progenitor of the "antiquisation" policy that claimed the ancient Macedonian dynasty as their own. VMRO's loss in the 2016 assembly elections paved the way for the agreement with Greece. Sadly, it continues to protest that it will unwind the agreement if it returns to power. However, the party will be without its erstwhile leader and former prime minister, Nikola Gruevski, who was sentenced to jail for corruption in 2018 and fled to Hungary.

Over the river lies the old bazaar area. The long, winding, narrow streets retain an Ottoman feel. Groups of middle-aged men sat on benches around the water fountain, apparently content to chat all day, despite the activity around them. The vegetable market was filled with colour in the pepper season; the density of hanging chili peppers formed awnings beneath which stallholders sold their plumper brethren in great mounds of green, yellow and red. It was here that West was rescued by a large group of people from the attention of an elderly Muslim woman who had been following her around town after the generosity of an initial handout. When the beggar caught a cab across the bridge to approach an unaware West for the fourth time, the local population felt that she had crossed the bounds of acceptability.

West had also visited the old German cemetery twenty minutes out of town; having no confidence in my own ability to find it, I hired a cab to lead me there. It sits just beside the main road from Ohrid to Prilep, and I scrambled up through long, desiccated grass to a pine grove, through which I could see a fortress-like wall at the top of a small hill. A solid stone tower guards the entrance, broken only by a narrow archway just big enough for one person to pass through. Inside, a sarcophagus-sized concrete block is set in a floor of red clay paviours. It is inscribed with "1914 1918" and, in each of German and Macedonian, "Here rest 3,406 German soldiers". The ceiling has an abstract geometric design in grey and white marble. Three long, narrow arches lead out into an unloved scrubland enclosed in a circular wall. The whole feels defensive.

West loathed it, describing it as "one of the most monstrous indecencies that has ever been perpetuated", feeling that it commemorated an ugly German invasion of Serbia and Macedonia:

> It has seemed good for them to bury their dead on the top of a hill where their guns were mounted for the martyrdom of the city, and to build a wall round it which gives it the appearance of a fortress. Nothing could say more plainly that they have no regret for what they did there, and intend to come back and do it all over again as soon as they are given the chance.

She felt that it insulted both Macedonia and the soldiers buried within, who had lost all individuality without the honour of a list of names and regiments, but then many may have been unidentifiable. It is an odd monument to find here, martial in its statement of German strength and military tradition, a natural extension of Bismarckian values. The architect, Robert Tischler, built a number of these hilltop castles of the dead (*Totenburgen*) to commemorate the fallen of the First World War. This one was inaugurated in 1936, conveniently compatible with the Nazi aesthetic. West was looking at it from a contemporary British perspective, and though her warning about the Germans' return would be borne out by events, she was undeniably seeing things through the eyes of an ardent Serb sympathiser.

At the outbreak of the First World War, one of the difficulties faced by the Serbs as they reacted to the Austro-Hungarian attack was that so many of their troops were deployed in the "newly liberated territory" of Macedonia, where their presence was unwelcome locally. They were displaced by the Bulgarians in 1915, who were eager to avenge their defeat in the Second Balkan War; Macedonia was a significant part of the price of the Bulgarian alliance with the Central Powers. The Bulgarian forces took back what they viewed as rightfully theirs as the Germans and Austro-Hungarians attacked Serbia from the north. Most Macedonians are likely to have wanted some sort of autonomy from either of their covetous neighbours, although if forced to choose would have been inclined to opt for Bulgaria. Having achieved their aims, the Bulgarian resolve weakened considerably, as did the local population's support for their heavy-handed occupiers. Significant German reinforcement was needed. Meanwhile, the Allies gradually built up their forces in Salonika.

In November 1916, Serbian forces, with French and Russian support, had managed to force their enemy to evacuate Bitola. This had political but no real strategic value, and the town was bombarded for the next two years by German and Bulgarian guns. Attempts by British troops to make progress further to the east in the spring of 1917 over extremely difficult territory on the western side of Lake Doiran were repulsed. British casualties of over 5,000 were nearly four times those of the Bulgarian defenders.

The winters could be bitterly cold. An officer reported: "Our overcoats are frozen hard, and when some of the men tried to beat theirs to make them pliable to lie down in they split like matchwood." In the summer, malaria impacted tens of thousands of men.

On the morning of 14th September 1918, the Allied forces commenced bombardment of the German and Bulgarian forces from the mountain ridges that divide Bitola from the Vardar valley, 60 miles or so to the east. The artillery had been emplaced at night in secret over the previous two months in support of planned attacks by southern Slav and French forces in the west and British and Greek in the east three days later. The western assault achieved the key breakthrough, rushing the armed Bulgarian positions up a steep 200-metre slope at the Battle of Dobro Polje ("Good Field"), 20 miles east of Bitola. The Serbs were commanded by General Mišić, who had inflicted the humiliating defeat on Austria at the Battle of Kolubara in 1914 and had then led the Serbian army in retreat over the mountains under protest in 1915. The Greeks and British were held at the Second Battle of Doiran with even heavier losses than the previous year, but as the Serbian and French troops pressed on, the fragile Bulgarian morale collapsed, not least because of acute hunger. The eastern forces found themselves pursuing the fleeing Bulgarians only two days after they had been forced to retreat. By the end of the month, Bulgaria sought an armistice, and within a week the Germans, also under severe pressure on the Western front, started to treat for peace. The Kaiser sent a telegram to Tsar Ferdinand of Bulgaria: "Disgraceful, 62,000 Serbs decided the war." Serbia was well rewarded for the Allied victory, regaining a difficult possession of North Macedonia until the return of the Germans in 1941.

The interwar years saw an unpopular and ultimately unsuccessful attempt to Serbianise North Macedonia. Many Macedonians had to change their names to end in "-itch" not "-off", and there was significant Muslim migration to Turkey from Macedonia, as well as from Serbia's other newly acquired southern territories. This was amplified in Greek Macedonia, where the population swaps in the aftermath of Greece's disastrous attempt to annex Anatolia shifted the demographic majority decisively and permanently from Slav to Greek. Despite that, the supporters of the Athenian football teams still chant "Turks" or "Bulgars" at games with Thessaloniki.

Prilep

After Bitola, the country opened up and fields were filled with corn, the hanging black heads of sunflowers and the crisp colours of ornamental cabbages. As I got closer to Prilep, its dominant industry became apparent. The pink-white flowers and fresh green heads of tobacco plants stretched into the distance, their stalks stripped of the leaves that hung on frames under polythene by the side of the road. Prilep was still "an agreeable country town", its Turkish heritage clear in the centre's old streets, overlooked by a sturdy and clearly much-loved clocktower capped with a golden cross, in sharp contrast to the unrestored grace of the minaret that rose from the ruins of an old mosque nearby.

I was searching for the Monastery of St Michael the Archangel, which West had visited to be excited by "a carving representing a round and jolly rogue, stark naked, riding a very large horse", a relic from an earlier monastery on the same site that she took to be a representation of the Thracian Rider, an ancient deity. I asked for directions, but it was clearly not straightforward. A father summoned his son with whom he was working hard on a building project and who spoke somewhat better English. After a minute's incomprehension, the son jumped into a car, saying that he would lead the way, apparently delighted to escape his labours a while. We ascended to the monastery past further drying racks, which seemed to cover every pavement, front garden and field as we neared the factory that consumed their loads. Shortly before we reached the site, my guide stopped, indicating the way, and entered a nearby house, largely confirming my earlier suspicion of an ulterior motive.

The monastery sits below the ruins of King Marko's fortress, built on a rocky outcrop that dominates the town. Marko was the son of a Herzegovinian lord who had managed to elevate himself to co-ruler with Stefan Uroš in the growing chaos after the death of Stefan Dušan. His father died in 1371 when the Ottomans inflicted a severe defeat on the Serbian army, and Marko ended up the strictly nominal King of Serbia from his base in Prilep, though controlling a chunk of west Macedonia as an Ottoman vassal. As such, he is likely to have supplied troops to Sultan Murad for the Battle of Kosovo and may even have fought on the Ottoman side. He died fighting for the Ottomans against Wallachia in 1395. He and his talking piebald horse, Šarac, became much-loved figures in the folklore of Serbia, despite the dubious Kosovo connection, as well as in Bulgaria, often seeming to draw on older tales. He has been adopted by the North Macedonians as an important marker on their long path to independence. He was also the centrepiece of Meštrović's uncompleted Temple of Kosovo – rather bizarrely, given his back story.

The monastery was highly restored. A nun showed me an ancient Cyrillic inscription on a pillar, the tombstone of a 10th-century bishop. I asked her if there was a carving of a man on horseback, omitting the detail of his nudity, but she looked at me blankly, despite, or perhaps because of, my pantomime gestures. Descending the hill, I noticed a great white marble block set back from the road at the bottom of a rocky slope. A large man, naked other than his moustache, sat astride a horse that is powering its way up a mountainside. The rider clasped what I took to be a boulder, which Marko made a sport of throwing in legend. It might have been a hundred years old, but it did not seem possible that it could be from the 12th century. I hoped that it was a copy of the original with which West had been so taken.

In the hills above is the abandoned Monastery of Treskavec, five miles along a narrow highland track. As I approached, only its orange roof marked it out from the grey landscape, where it sat low on a boulder-strewn ridge. The jutting mass of the rocks behind resembled petrified giants. The sky was overcast, reminding me still further of Scotland, and from the monastic vantage point I could see the shading of the light beneath the clouds over the valley that signalled the arrival of rain. In the distance, the misty brightness of the far hills suggested the showers had already passed them. Despite its remoteness, there has been a place of Christian worship here since the 6th century, and it was part of an even older town. It was admired by Stefan Dušan, protected by the Turks and still welcomes an annual pilgrimage.

In a rock sheltered by an overhang was a haloed figure painted red and white, her arms held aloft as she sang to the Lord. The monastery was quite empty. Mary and an angel guarded the garlanded but locked main door; above them, a dull red cross relieved a sky-blue pediment.

Candle stubs stood in shelters, attesting to the church's occasional use, and the squat brick cupolas were intact. Neatly stacked piles of stone indicated an intention of future restoration, but the size and precariousness of the remaining shell of the monastic quarters, destroyed by fire in 2010, suggested that it was unlikely to ever return to its full former glory. Dahlias, roses and magnolias occupied one corner, too content not to have been nurtured. A niche in the wall contained an all but monochrome sketch of the two elderly men who founded the 14th-century church, whose model they hold between them. Sadly, I was unable to enter their gift to see the frescoes within, which are meant to be deteriorating badly. As I sat in the cobbled compound, there was sanctity in the air, despite the desolation. I could see the attractions of a contemplative life up here in the wild; close to nature, close to the sky and close to God. As I progressed on my journey, I had come to realise the value of time to think, to pray and just to be, in contrast to the overscheduled existence that had been mine for so long. I left through the open doorway beneath the roofless belltower with the benediction of the painted figure in its archway.

The wilderness of the scenery up here reminded me of one of the odder episodes in the IMRO's early amateurish efforts to fund their fight for independence, which had occurred in the mountains to the east. Among ideas that the group had considered and discarded were the kidnap and ransoming of King Alexander I of Serbia; "kidnapping" one of their own members who held a Russian passport in the hope that a ransom could be extracted from Moscow; and sending Macedonian volunteers to America to fight in the Spanish-American War as mercenaries. An early attempt at kidnapping for ransom had failed when the captor fell asleep, allowing the victim, the son of a wealthy Turk, to steal his gun and escape. Another unsuccessful attempt to capture a bey for ransom was abandoned after a month. The compromise victim, a Greek moneylender, yielded only $700 (rather than the hoped-for $8,000), saying dismissively that he did not have it and could not get any more.

The next target was Ellen Stone, an overweight 55-year-old spinster from Roxbury, Massachusetts. She had been in Bulgaria since 1878 doing evangelical work with women in the Salonika area. She and her small party were ambushed on the road from Bansko to Gorna Dzhumaya on 3rd September 1901 by twenty-two men led by Yane Sandanski and Hristo Chernopeev, five of them dressed in Turkish uniforms in an attempt to divert suspicion elsewhere. (Bansko is now a popular ski resort and home of the "hedonistic" Horizon electronic dance music festival in the snow. Gorna Dzhumaya was renamed Blagoevgrad in 1950 after the founder of the Bulgarian Communist Party.)

Stone and one of her travelling companions, Katerina Tsilka, were separated from the rest of the party and led off on horseback. Tsilka was five months pregnant, and both women were in light summer attire. Prior to that, the gang had searched the party, leaving valuables untouched, but taking the food and eating some, including pork, thereby undermining much of the pretence at being Turkish. Stone and Tsilka were left with a Bible and an umbrella. The rest of the party were released and instructed to say that they had been seized by Turkish-speaking bandits.

The gang clearly tried to look after the two women, picking them bunches of flowers and pressing food upon them. They asked what they would like for dinner each night as they zigzagged through the mountains between Ottoman and Bulgarian territory for the subsequent six months. They even made their beds for them and apparently tucked them in at night on occasion. Meanwhile, after a few days, they asked Stone to write a letter in support of their demand for a ransom of $100,000. The first letter sent to Bansko appears to have been ignored due to the recipient's fear of getting into trouble with the Turkish authorities. A subsequent letter to a Protestant minister in Samokov was relayed immediately to Constantinople, setting in train a protracted saga, as various interested parties tried to get involved in finding the kidnappers and raising and delivering the ransom.

$66,000 was collected from the faithful in America, but Charles Dickinson, the US consul general in Constantinople, determined to lead the bargaining with the kidnappers. His insistence on being in sole charge led to significant delays in the ransoming process, alienating in turn the Bulgarian government, the Russian ambassador in Sofia, most local missionaries, the US legation in Constantinople and the Department of State (whose minister in St Petersburg was the extravagantly named Charlemagne Tower!).

Meanwhile, the weather worsened in the mountains. The gang provided coarse woollen material and cheesecloth (the latter traditionally used to clean guns) so that the women could make themselves winter clothing. A book swap was less successful. Asenov (one of the gang members) felt that the Bible demonstrated God to be an old man in need of man's help to achieve his ends, while Stone found the writings of Marxist theoretician Karl Kautsky nonsensical. At one point, the gang had to fight off a local bandit and his men who thought that they would snatch the women and redeem the ransom themselves. Somewhere around the New Year, Tsilka's baby, Elena (or *Kesmetchka*, "the lucky one"), was born, named after her companion. Sandanski rocked the baby by the fire and the whole gang blessed her and passed her around the party along with a wine gourd. A local midwife hung a piece of string threaded with a silver coin and garlic to ward off evil spirits.

The ransom was finally handed over on 2nd February at the Protestant Centre in Bansko, with lead replacing the gold in the delivery cases, which were then sent back to Constantinople as if the exchange had failed (to minimise the risk of disruption). It was another three weeks before the women were freed near Strumica in North Macedonia, delayed in part by intensive Turkish troop movements in the area. They made a strange sight riding into town in goat-hair cloaks with white kerchiefs around their heads. Neither of them gave much in the way of detailed information about their captors, and the kidnappers were never arrested. Both women lectured subsequently in America, Stone now a keen advocate for Macedonian independence. Baby Elena, who was wildly acclaimed by audiences when presented on stage during her mother's talks, died in Tirana at the age of twenty-four from tuberculosis.

The money raised was assigned to buy money for the Ilinden uprising the next year. Bitola appeared to do best, getting nearly half of the total, which may well account for its relative success in the insurgency. Meanwhile, the US Congress finally passed a bill in 1912, at the fourth time of trying, to authorise repayment of contributions to the American donors who had provided the ransom. Sandanski became the leader of the IMRO's left wing and was killed in 1915, probably in revenge for his assassinations of members of the centralist IMARO faction. Chernopeev became a representative of the Bulgarian National Assembly and also died in 1915, fighting on the front in the First World War.

Skopje II

I re-entered Skopje on Alexander of Macedonia Motorway, now diplomatically renamed the Friendship Motorway, the main road from Belgrade to Athens, and was happy to settle back in at the homely Hotel Rose. The next morning, a table was laid for one downstairs. I picked a Macedonian breakfast from the selection on offer; after ten minutes, no inch of the table was left uncovered. I gazed at the spread: watermelon, fruit bowl, eggs, ham, cheese, olives, nuts, tomatoes, celery, cucumber, slices of red pepper, spicy tomato paste, bread, pastries, sesame- and poppy-seeded twists, buns filled with cream cheese, butter, jam, orange juice and coffee. "So much?" I asked. "This is what Macedonians have for breakfast," came the reply. The profusion reminded me that Macedonia had given its name to a salad of mixed vegetables and fruit, although it is unclear if that refers to the varied ethnic composition of Alexander's empire or the 19th-century Ottoman region.

Properly fortified, I set off to Lake Matka, ten miles or so to the south-west. It is formed by a dam on the River Treska, which was under construction when West visited, a symbol of Yugoslav achievement, although West was aware that the Albanians doing much of the work did not relish their newly imposed nationality. This seems to have been reflected again by the turnout for the 1991 independence referendum, in which a very strong majority voted in favour, disquieted by the effective control of Serbia and Montenegro in Yugoslavia after the departure of Slovenia and Croatia. However, nearly a quarter of the population had not voted, believed to be the Albanian community, who felt that the options of being a minority in Yugoslavia or in the new state were equally unpalatable. Despite this internal apathy, Macedonia's departure from the federation proved remarkably bloodless, a mere sideshow given the turmoil further north. A similar factor was at work with the 2018 referendum on the name of North Macedonia, where the 91% vote in favour of the change was less authoritative than it might have seemed, being achieved on only a 37% turnout.

I crossed over the dam and climbed for forty-five minutes along a path through scrubby woodland. The bright pink markings of ivy-leafed cyclamen glinted amidst the green in sunny clearings. The steep valley offered ever more enticing views of the mountains beyond, almost turquoise in the distance beneath the bluer sky. High in front, a small church came into sight on a pass, its cupola oddly dainty, dwarfed by the rocky masses that rose above it on each side. Animals frolicked around a plaited stone window high on one wall, while a patchy ochre-painted plaster arch framed the grille that protected its deserted interior. The wooden side of an outbuilding was painted in the yellow and red sun design of the North Macedonian flag. From the green meadow in front, I could see the small Church of St Andrew, my next destination, far below on the other side of the lake, but I would have to retrace my path to get there. I sat on a bench relishing the sun and the solitude for a while, before turning back downhill.

Back over the river, I threaded along a narrow gorge beneath overhanging rocks, emerging to see the same translucent mountains framed much more tightly by the dark bulk on each side. The church sat in the sun where the lake widened. It was clearly a popular destination; boats were for hire at the water's edge on one side and a restaurant terrace stretched over the lake on the other. Inside, the fresco of Mary lifting Christ down from the Cross is intensely moving:

> ... death is shown working on the body that is bound to the spirit of Christ, wringing the breath out of the lungs as a laundress wrings water out of a shirt ... There is demonstrated that separateness of flesh which Proust once noted, in a passage which describes how we think in our youth that our bodies are identical with ourselves, ... but discover later in life that they are heartless companions who have been accidentally yoked with us ...

That separation is made starker by its setting between the health of Jesus's ascent to Golgotha and the pitiful sight of Mary laying his bandaged corpse in the tomb.

Just south of Skopje is the 12th-century Monastery of St Panteleimon, the patron saint of physicians. I found my way there with some difficulty, turning left after a long blue factory to climb halfway up a mountain, following a country lane with countless unsigned junctions to flip a coin at. After several enquiries, the church finally appeared, pink and fresh in a large stone paved courtyard, with "domes that are plainly bubbles blown by the breath of God". A substantial monastic complex sat above it and an elegant terraced restaurant below. I found the door locked, but a passer-by told me to ring Žarko on the number pinned to the door. I sat reading in the shade until a figure in black shirt and shades drove up and let me in.

When West visited, the 12th-century frescoes were being "uncovered very slowly, to wean the peasants from the late eighteenth-century ... frescoes which had been painted over them". The church itself is much ruder than West about the now removed images, describing them as "the work of a very unskilled painter and they have extremely degraded the church interior". But they are gone, and the restored originals are glorious. St John and the Virgin Mary each take a hand of the dead Christ, whom Joseph of Arimathea is lowering from a ladder propped up against the Cross. Another apostle is engaged with a pair of pliers in removing the nail from his left foot that still secures him. The foot of Christ is positioned in parallel with that of Joseph, so alike but one clearly alive and one dead, indicated by the slightest difference in shade and tone. In the Lamentation, the peaceful body is laid out, while Mary clasps it, pressing her face to her dead son's, contorted with grief. Back in the Garden of Gethsemane, Jesus looks almost irritated at the sight of the apostles dozing and chatting in a group as if taking time out at a rock festival.

West's favourite image of a child being washed by "a woman who is a fury" is remarkable; the powerful arms and distant gaze of the woman bathing the impassive child could be by William Blake, but it is the birth of the Virgin, not her son as West had believed. The raising of Lazarus shows "an elderly woman lifting a beautiful astonished face at the spectacle", though she might be as astonished by the highly designed shroud and tomb (which would not look out of place in a King's Road shop) as she is by the surprise reappearance. Meanwhile, the learned St Panteleimon looks out intently, the auburn waves of his hair forming an inner lining to his halo; he could be a prize pupil in a Victorian children's book. The painting is wonderfully naturalistic; these are real people, and one cares about the stories that are unfolding on the wall, though they date back over 850 years. The unknown chief artist was sent from Constantinople by Alexios, son of the Byzantine princess, Theodora Komnene, and his skill ensures the memory of a patron that might otherwise have faded long ago.

Circling back to central Skopje, I found Šuto Orizari (or Šutka), the area where the homes of the city's Roma population are concentrated. I had been led to believe that the narrow streets behind the market contained picturesque houses evoking carefree and artistic lives. One or two were in evidence, little white cottages sitting in sunlit grassy squares, probably built on years of labour working away from home in the German-speaking world, but the times have moved on rapidly. The still simple streets were now lined with modern mansions behind secure walls and fences in what were rendered undersized plots. The predilection for reflective glass has spread here too, giving many of the new homes a commercial air, often with a nautical twist from the variety of metal-framed balconies that they incorporate. Colour schemes are bold. Some were unfinished but with no sign of building in progress, as if waiting for another year's instalment before recommencing work. From the streets and the bazaar, it is evident that Šutka is a poor community overall, but some of the community were making money surprisingly fast.

Before leaving, I sought out the birthplace of Mother Teresa, arguably history's most famous North Macedonian, who was born here in Skopje on 26th August 1910. The site of her original home is now marked by a plaque on the wall of a boutique in the smart central shopping area. Not far away, a memorial house has been built to honour her memory on the site of the Catholic church that she attended as a girl. It is modern and tastefully executed with a small chapel on the top floor above the exhibits on her life. It was at the old church here that the young Gonxha Bojaxhiu, an Albanian Catholic, was inspired by the letters that were read out from Yugoslav missionaries working in India, and set her out on her life's path.

At the age of eighteen, she resolved to leave home and work as a teacher in India. She was accompanied to Zagreb on the train by her mother and sister; she would see neither of them again, as they subsequently moved to Tirana to live with Teresa's brother, and the Hoxha government refused to guarantee that she would be allowed to leave if she visited them. She travelled on to the Sisters of Loreto convent at Rathfarnham to the south of Dublin, where she learned some English over a seven-week stay, before embarking for India. Three years later, she adopted her monastic name. She was evidently a good teacher, becoming principal of one of the order's schools, but she was shocked by the conditions in which the poor lived in Calcutta, and increasingly felt it was her mission to help them. "There is so much beauty and joy in the mud." She was particularly upset by the bloodshed and starvation resulting from the sectarian riots in the city at the time of Partition in 1947, saying that she had seen 200 children die of hunger before her eyes.

In 1948, she left the Loreto Convent and adopted the simple, blue-bordered white sari that allowed her to work more easily with those who had nothing. After several months in Patna getting basic medical training, she returned to Calcutta and founded the Missionaries of Charity. The provision of food and education to the poor was the starting point, but it also evolved into the provision of homes for the dying after Mother Teresa realised the sheer number of people abandoned to die in the streets of Calcutta. She also sought to work with leprosy patients (and latterly with AIDS sufferers), who were ostracised by society, feeling that "the worst illness of all is not leprosy, but loneliness – when somebody is forgotten by everybody" (a message reinforced all too clearly in our recent pandemic-dominated times). By 1990, there were 456 centres worldwide, which fed 500,000 families, educated 200,000 children and treated 90,000 leprosy patients. Her missionaries had also rescued over 23,000 people from the streets of Calcutta, of whom around half died. She won the Nobel Prize for Peace in 1979, investing the prize money in more homes, and was canonised by the Catholic Church in 1999, two years after her death in Calcutta, the city of which she had become the symbol.

There were controversies – she accepted donations from some questionable sources and had hard-line Catholic views on birth control and divorce. But she indisputably eased the conditions of many, while raising awareness of the appalling conditions endured by the poor in India and elsewhere. At home, she is rather harder to place – a Catholic Albanian, whose father may have been Albanian or Vlach (yet another Balkan ethnic group) and whose mother came from Kosovo, but she is still a cherished local daughter.

I walked on down Makedonija, once Marshal Tito Street, the traditional route of the evening corso, but that has now migrated into the area's cafes. At the far end is the station where West arrived on Easter Saturday all those years ago, although the rather homely white building that she must have passed through was replaced a few years later by a modern Byzantine construction. That in turn was badly damaged in the 1963 earthquake that killed over 1,000 people and left three quarters of Skopje's residences unusable, many of them destroyed, resulting in up to 200,000 homeless. The clock hands on the external wall are still frozen at 5:17, the time that it hit.

I had arranged to have a drink with a local journalist contact. We sat in a modern glass-fronted cafe looking out at the statues of ancient Macedonian kings. He talked of the concept of Macedonia: Greater Macedonia was not a realistic prospect any longer, and Macedonians feel very distinct from Bulgaria, despite the linguistic overlap. It was an unknown quantity for fifty years, as was Albania. Meanwhile, there was an inevitable discomfort with Serbian politics, and any accord with Greece was likely to be fragile for some time.

There are still internal tensions between the Macedonian Slavs and the minority groups. There has been a longstanding disagreement between the Macedonian and local Bulgarian communities over whether to erect a statue to Mara Buneva, a prominent member of the IMRO, who shot the Serbian chief of police in the back in 1928. She is a heroine in Bulgaria but a controversial figure in North Macedonia for her strong pro-Bulgarian sympathies. Controversy is also stirred up by the figure of Ivan Mihailov, ex-leader of the IMRO, active collaborator with Mussolini and Hitler, employer of Vlada Georgiev, who assassinated Alexander of Serbia, and "a butcher", now elevated to patriot by nationalist politicians, who might describe him as John Gunther did: "a sort of Robin Hood murderer, never attacking the virtuous, but only the Serbs."

There are all sorts of historic tensions in the relations with Greece too. Memories are still surprisingly fresh about the ethnic cleansing of Macedonian communists in the Greek Civil War. Inside Greece, there was an identification of Slavs with communism after the Second World War, sensitive to their borders with communist Yugoslavia and Bulgaria, as well as Albania. Stalin had made it clear that he would not support the communist rebels in Greece as he had given his word to Churchill not to interfere there, but Tito had no such constraints, a key factor in the subsequent Yugoslav split from the Russians. The Americans stepped in to support the Greek army, arguably launching the Cold War in so doing, and the brutality of the conflict leaves a legacy of bitterness to this day, both in Greece and here across the border. This must have only added to Greek sensitivity over the name issue, not just cultural but also related to a bloody, relatively recent history; though, of course, the latter is also true for the (now) North Macedonians.

Internally, politicians are inclined to use the Albanian-Macedonian split to seek advantage, although the demographic divide in the country is not wholly clear. There has not been a census since 2002, and considerable economic migration overseas has taken place. The Ohrid Agreement put integration first and promised more jobs in the public sector to Albanians, which in turn has fuelled jealousy in the Macedonian majority. There have been large protests almost every year in Skopje: by Albanians who mistrust the court system (as do many Macedonians); by Macedonians who fear creeping Albanian influence (for example, the introduction of Albanian as a nationwide second language); and over the name change to North Macedonia. Different variations on the theme play out each year, but at their root they all reflect the politicisation of race, the curse of the Balkans. Politicians fabricate what they perceive as controllable tension, but it is at the expense of the harmony of the whole. It is complicated by politics to the north. If the long-term solution for Kosovo is to be more closely aligned to the West, the prospect of a Greater Albania increases. Meanwhile, the number of mosques, Albanian flags and giant Orthodox crosses seems to keep growing. Even the statues have been used as counters in the game. Skanderbeg in Prishtina faces south, leading some of the more recent Skopje statuary to be positioned in retaliation.

The relationship with Serbia is undefined. At a personal level, relationships tend to be good. At various moments of crisis, such as the 2014 floods, North Macedonia has been quick to offer support, but the history of Serb control is still an unwelcome memory that can rise again, most obviously in the longstanding fight for the Macedonian Orthodox Church to be recognised as autonomous from its Serbian counterpart.

There is still considerable nostalgia for Yugoslavia. After the shift from repression in the mid-1960s, memories of life are of prosperity and openness, with pride in the military and the Non-Aligned Movement, no evident Albanian issue and a confidence in being Macedonian as part of an entity within the broader Federal Republic rather than an ethnic grouping. People wore jeans and drank Coke, and there is still a desire now to be aligned to the prosperous West. We must hope that the opportunity offered by the recent Greek accord can ultimately lead to EU accession, and along with it a restraint on the darker forces below the surface. Perhaps the two main communities can heed the dying wishes of Alexander the Great, who sought to bring together two continents (or their legacies) "to common concord and family friendship by mixed marriages and the ties of kith and kin".

Bosnia and Herzegovina

*"The people ... adhered with intensity to certain faiths ...
But in all other ways they were highly individualistic."*

CROATIA
SERBIA
JAJCE
TRAVNIK
SARAJEVO
VIŠEGRAD
JABLANICA
MOSTAR
ADRIATIC SEA
MONTENEGRO

Trebinje

I landed in Dubrovnik on a late April afternoon, turning away from the coast shortly before I reached the city to wind my way up to the heights that mark the border of Croatia with Herzegovina. As I climbed, the vulnerability of the city to aggression from above was all too apparent. Trebinje, the southernmost town of Bosnia and Herzegovina is only 15 miles from Dubrovnik, but it is a different world. The name Herzegovina comes from the German *Herzog* ("duke") and was a title taken by a local ruler of Serbian extraction in the mid-15th century. Like the Montenegrins with whom they share much history, the people up here had a long record of independence and unrest against the Ottomans. They have tended to ally with the Serbs inland rather than the inhabitants of the coast below them. It was from the heights here that the Mayor of Trebinje, known as "lorry-driver" for his former occupation, led hundreds of men to join the Yugoslav army in bombarding Dubrovnik in late 1991 as the relationship between Croatia and the disintegrating Yugoslavia broke down. Trebinje in turn suffered from a prolonged siege by Croatian forces during the Bosnian War as they sought to safeguard a reclaimed Dubrovnik.

At the border post, a bedraggled guard took my papers and disappeared into his hut. By the time he emerged a couple of minutes later, he was smiling and singing a folk song in unison with his colleague, presumably *šljiva*-fuelled. He raised the barrier and I drove on into Herzegovina, although the sign welcomed me to Republika Srpska, as Bosnia and Herzegovina have been two in another sense since the Dayton peace agreement, with a new political separation more critical than the historical boundary of the original merged states. The Serb-dominated parts of the country (49%) are essentially self-governing, although technically they remain part of the greater whole, while the Federation of Bosnia and Herzegovina governs the Muslim- and Croat-majority areas.

The rocky landscape was already turning green, the new leaves on small trees almost transparent in the sunshine. I drove past a small group of men strimming around a black marble tombstone that bore the image of a young man on a motorcycle, the likely mode of transport when he met his end. Entering Trebinje, I noticed a policeman with a speed camera and a broad grin on his face, unusually more interested in waving to his friends than securing a conviction. At the hotel, I struggled with the door, but an elegant figure appeared and opened it without difficulty, saying, "I appear to be stronger than you, no?" Presumably, this was Maja, whose email confirming my reservation had addressed me as "Recpected Nicholas" with a hint of Cyrillic charm. I was honoured to be shown to the Monica Bellucci room where the glamorous actress had stayed while shooting *On the Milky Road*, a film about war, love and living as a hermit by the famous Serbian director, Emir Kusturica.

The town was appealing, with leafy squares and an old, fortified centre set above the clear running Trebišnjica River. The hill behind it was a dazzling gold in the evening sun, creating a vivid block of colour as it reflected off the water. The streets were full of young enjoying the spring warmth. Over dinner, I fell into conversation with a visitor from County Mayo, who was repeating a pilgrimage to the famous site of Medjugorje, some 70 miles to the north-east. He told me that the previous year he had hired a taxi to take him back from there to Dubrovnik at the end of his stay, and they had flown along at an alarming speed until past Trebinje; at which point, the driver had stopped and unscrewed his taxi plates. Once over the border, the final leg of the drive was taken at a sedate 30 mph. Clearly, cross-border relations remained strained.

I set off around town the next morning in a light drizzle, which soon intensified to a point that I needed better protection. Trebinje's many sportswear shops were little help, as were the two ladies' boutiques that I tried, but I was eventually signalled to a general-purpose store, where I was greeted with the words "Umbrella, you need". Emerging better equipped, I walked along the river to the Arslanagić Bridge, another Ottoman legacy to the Balkans. It was built by Sokollu Mehmed Pasha (or Mehmed- paša Sokolović to the Serbs), the Orthodox boy from Herzegovina who had risen to become imperial grand vizier to three successive sultans in the 16th century, married a granddaughter of Suleiman the Magnificent, and enabled the re-establishment of the independent Serbian Church from Peć. He was also responsible for the building of the legendary bridge over the Drina at Višegrad a few years after this one. The bridge at Trebinje spans the river with two large arches flanked by two smaller ones, and further semi-circular apertures echoing these to create the customary Ottoman lightness of touch. From a distance, it was at one with the vanishing misty ridges of the mountains behind, impossibly insubstantial for something so practical. I was struck that the two most beautiful things that I had seen in the town, the bridge and the town fountain, were both Turkish.

Fig trees hedged in the path as I strolled back. Swallows dipped to the water surface and frogs carolled from the far bank. Walking up to the old town, I noticed several streets where stone walls marked the shells of former homes, what West had described in post-war Berlin as "mere diagrams of habitation". Daylight was bright through the spaces where windows and roofs once provided protection, and vegetation was steadily encroaching. The small, restored pink mosque looked clean and well maintained but was carefully secured following its destruction in 1993. Here was a reminder of the fate of the local Muslim community when the recent war started. Those unwilling to be conscripted into the Yugoslav army were liable to be executed. Those who had not fled were expelled by Serb militiamen in 1993. Many of their homes were reportedly taken over by Serb families from Croat-dominated areas. The Muslim population of Trebinje was 18% of the whole in 1991; twenty years later, it was only 3%.

I may have imagined it, but I sensed a generational divide in the attitude to visitors. As I walked through the old streets, the middle-aged and elderly looked ahead rigidly, unwilling to exchange a gesture or a greeting, while the younger generation seemed as carefree as anywhere in Europe. I visited the local museum, housed in what was once the Austrian military headquarters. Rather too much of it is made up of locally bequeathed art collections, but the display of Greek bronze helmets was a reminder of how long ago civilisation had reached the town. The photographs of 19th-century life made me wish that I had been here with West eighty years ago, when much must still have looked similar, with the varied communities, both rural and urban, each wearing their traditional garb. That being said, had we travelled together in the flesh, West's great love for the detail of local costume, fabric and needlework may have prompted me to divert into various bars to kill time on occasion.

The narrative panels on the history of Herzegovina were distinctly – if understandably – Serbo-centric, raging against the Austro-Hungarian retaliation for Franz Ferdinand's assassination, against Croatian and Muslim atrocities against Serbs in the Second World War, and displaying bitterness at the division of eastern Herzegovina in the Dayton accord. I hoped that the younger generation would be able to understand the horrors of their recent history with rather more balance.

Walking back to the hotel, I passed two memorials. The monument to the fallen of the Second World War showed assorted fighters, full of glory, hope and exhaustion, among them a resolute girl in traditional costume and a bowed elderly figure who looked to have walked in from an earlier conflict. Not far away, an angled pink stone wedge stretched up from a curved stone base. It represents a sword blade held in a pair of fists and honours the Serb dead who fought in the Bosnian Wars.

Back in the main square, the town market was in operation, vendors sheltering under large umbrellas along with their wares. West had visited it and admired the soberly handsome women selling their produce, but both of us saw a version diluted by the weather. Historically, this would have been a twice-weekly destination for the inhabitants of Dubrovnik, a trade that is understandably diminished. I bought a jar of figs closely packed in deep brown honey and moved on.

I wanted to visit the Duži Monastery before starting my journey north. It appeared to be deserted when I arrived. The simple church had a bell-shaped arcade at one end of its roof housing three bells in arches, the complementary outlines clear against the sky. I knocked on the main door and a flustered nun appeared, chewing vigorously while apologising at the same time for her hunger. It turned out that she was one of only three remaining nuns in the community and that nothing had really changed for a hundred years, since they were self-sufficient.

The church dates back to the late 17th century but was ransacked by the Ottomans several times in the 1800s in response to monastic support for various Herzegovinian uprisings. One of the leaders of the 1875-8 uprising, Mićo Ljubibratić, had made his headquarters here. He was a strong advocate of joint Serb-Bosniak collaboration in the fight for independence and was the first person in the Balkans to translate the Koran into Serbian. The interior was covered with frescoes that had recently been restored. The originals had been painted a century earlier by Russian monks who had sought refuge here following the October Revolution, arriving at Duži with nothing but the clothes on their backs. A large painting of the Crucifixion had also been painted by one of their number in a style faintly reminiscent of Picasso's blue period.

I lit a candle and was saying a few prayers when an elderly blind man with a full white beard and a faded brown jacket was led in. He stood at the icon stand in front of the sanctuary, where he crossed himself, touched the floor and sang for ten minutes in an exquisite light baritone voice. The church filled with his verses. I stood quietly by a pillar, transported by the spirituality of the moment, admiring not just the beauty of his voice but also the nature of his relationship with God that enabled a direct address of such evident emotion. I thought of my own religious practice – respectful, straightforward, occasionally sceptical – and wondered at the openness on display and the easy transition to ecstasy. As I drove on, I wondered if this too was tied up with the conditioning and tight self-management of decades of formal education and business life. The glimpses of spirituality that I was encountering on my travels seemed to show me a need to be freer, not just in planning my life, but also with my attitudes to the unknown.

Before I left, the nun showed me her terraced vegetable garden, still somewhat bare this early in the season. Her left hand was badly swollen from a bee sting the previous day. In a meadow below were two long lines of hives, occasional boxes of yellow and blue standing out against the green freshness of the woods behind them. Beyond the trees, the grey mass of the mountains looked simultaneously protective and forbidding. Here were both the sources of the nuns' food and the wherewithal to trade for other necessities. When the time came to leave, I made a small donation, prompting my friend to rush back into her quarters and re-emerge with two eggs, hand-painted in red leaf patterns in memory of *"Sancti"*, which, so soon after Easter, I took to mean the risen Christ.

I passed again through the bleak landscape – striated hills whose grey stripes angled down to form cones that could have come from a Japanese woodblock print. Finally, the valley opened up into flatter terrain, initially grazed by cattle and then quite intensively cultivated. Historically, one of Herzegovina's best-known agricultural exports has been tobacco, and this was prime growing country. Vienna court cigarettes were made from Herzegovinian product when Austria ruled here, and Stalin smoked Herzegovina Flor cigarettes, crumbling the tobacco from two at a time into his Dunhill pipe bowl. At that time, much of the local industry was destined for the senior Soviet cadres. Times have changed, and the growth in popularity of light-tasting tobacco over the strong, Turkish-style leaf produced here has led to the near demise of the local industry, although I see that empty black and green vintage packets of Stalin's favourite brand can still command £25 on eBay.

Mostar

I stopped at the small town of Stolac for lunch. Sitting in the square, I could have been in Turkey. The tight spiral of my cheese burek seemed incompatible with the lightness of the cream cheese and the flakiness of the pastry that encased it. I followed it with Turkish coffee and an astonishingly rich chocolate and cherry cake. On the hill above were the ruins of the 14th-century fortress of Vidoški typical of many others that fell into disrepair under the Ottomans as the Bosnian aristocracy's need for large defensive hilltop bases disappeared. The finger of the local minaret was broken by a green flag with a crescent moon secured to its muezzin terrace. I was surprised to see a symbol that appeared so alien in Europe, but the independence revolts of the 19th century against the Ottomans had been fought under flags of this style, indicating the relative harmony between Orthodox and Islam for many centuries. Sadly, the destruction of that harmony was all too apparent as I tried to walk my cake off along the riverbank and witnessed the plaster walls of low-level apartment blocks peppered with bullet scars.

On arrival in Mostar, a similar phenomenon struck me. Strolling down the incline to the instantly recognisable bridge and wandering through the streets of the old town above it, one would have no sense of the violence that took place here so recently. As I wandered more widely through the city, however, a very different picture emerged. All that remained of Tito's villa on the main square was a stubby L-shape of walls with purple flowers growing out of the upper storeys. The remains of the orange and yellow striped facade of the once grand Hotel Neretva next door posted signs saying "Dangerous building and structure" and "Do not enter or park here", although restoration work has apparently since started. I crossed the river and turned along Šantića Street (the frontline between the Muslim and Croat sides in the war). Houses on both sides were so pockmarked with bullet wounds as to be more scar than original. The black maw of an empty second-storey window was surrounded by areas of bare brickwork where the plaster had been shot away, the sheer volume of such holes evidencing exchanges of fire that must have lasted weeks, if not months. Balconies appeared to have been crowbarred in and the interiors to have regressed to an entirely raw state. However, amidst all this dereliction, the occasional floor high up showed signs of occupation, with new white-framed windows and pot plants, incongruous in the pocked concrete around it and likely hazardous to access through the destruction below. As I turned towards the old bridge, a large cross was visible on the hill above, as if to taunt the Muslim inhabitants of the city from the place where the Croat artillery had shelled it. Closer to the bridge, a rusty assemblage of bullet casings and shell parts sat on a stone emblazoned "DON'T FORGET '93".

The old bridge (*Stari most*) has been wonderfully restored; in an instant, one understands why it was iconic even before the added impetus of its recent past. As West observed:

> It is one of the most beautiful bridges in the world. A slender arch lies between two round towers, its parapet bent in a shallow angle in the centre. To look at it is good; to stand on it is as good. Over the grey-green river swoop hundreds of swallows, and on the banks mosques and white houses stand among glades of trees and bushes.

It was built between 1557 and 1567 on the orders of Suleiman the Magnificent, and the unprecedented scale of the arch that he instructed led the builder to fear for his life lest his careful calculations result in failure on its opening day. The towers on either side were used as a powder store and a dungeon. The town is probably not named after the bridge itself but after the bridge keepers (*mostari*) of an earlier incarnation. Now, any visitor is likely to be badgered by local boys for money to watch them dive off into the river below, a courtship so protracted that they appear to lose most of their potential sponsors before sealing a deal.

In the early stages of the Bosnian War, Mostar came under attack from Serb and Montenegrin units from the Yugoslav army in the initial surge to grab as much of Bosnia as possible to make a Serb state. They were driven back in June 1992 by a joint Croat-Muslim defence reinforced by UN pressure to withdraw. Many of the Serb residents of the city were forced to leave at the time. However, the Herzegovinian Croats, with support from Croatian President Tudjman, increasingly looked to form their own state that could link with Croatia to the west in much the same way as the Serbs intended to do with Serbia to the east. The Muslim community were forced to look to their own interests, and the two sides turned on each other as they tried to establish their own geographies. In Mostar, the Muslim-controlled east bank of the river faced off against the Croat west bank, with mass expulsions and killings by the Croats and a distinctly lopsided war given the greatly superior Croat artillery. East Mostar was largely ruined, culminating in the Croat destruction in November 1993 of the old bridge, national symbol of the country and a famous image worldwide. The deliberate vandalism of the shelling combined with the filming of the act by its gloating perpetrators tarnished the Croat image badly, which until now had stood up well given the easy comparison with the Serbs. Over the next few months, American and German pressure on Tudjman and the Muslim Bosnian president, Alija Izetbegović, managed to achieve a federation of the Croats and Bosniaks, even if it would be better characterised as a ceasefire. That in turn started to lay the foundations for the Dayton agreement, which was ultimately concluded almost two years after the bridge had fallen.

At the museum nearby, it was shocking to see the footage of the bridge before, during and after its shelling. Tempting as it is to see the destruction as symbolic of Croat repudiation of the town's Ottoman heritage and of their desire to sever communication with their long-time Muslim neighbours, this may be too contrived. Every bit as shocking was the footage of guerrillas running down the alleys and streets of Mostar amidst the crackle of rifle-fire only twenty-five years before. The film of the bridge's reopening in 2004 is joyous, though

I was grateful to see an edited version of what appeared to be an overlong ceremony, graced by Prince Charles and John Cleese among others, with dancers, divers with flares and endless fireworks to the soundtrack of Beethoven's *Ode to Joy*.

The largely restored town centre feels authentic. Merchants sell the usual assortment of paintings, carvings, carpets and produce. At the 17th-century Koski Mehmed Pasha Mosque, the gravestones are now all upright again, the resting places of men distinguished from those of women by the turbans atop their stone stumps. I climbed the minaret to look over the city; from up here, it was good to see so many red-tiled roofs and intact minarets, yet there were still large, derelict buildings in each direction. At my hotel, I had been told that the private buildings were largely restored now, although one or two graffitied and abandoned old houses had trees growing out through the windows, likely once the home of Serb families. Most of the neglected sites belong to the government, whose budget is too pressured to allow for significant restoration.

Before leaving, I sat by the bank downstream from the bridge to enjoy a cup of coffee and drink in the famous view once more. It was hard to believe that mortal men could have created a span of such delicacy between the high sides of the original canyon. Its height emphasised the startling aquamarine of the River Neretva in the morning light as it swirled towards me. I pondered the inevitable continued divisions within the city, which is run by dual administrations despite their ostensibly peaceful coexistence. Looking back, the tensions had been fuelled by the arrival of the Austro-Hungarians over a century earlier, opposed by both Muslims and Serbs. At the time, they were natural allies in a desire for different forms of independence in this part of the country, although the former tended to be resented by the latter as the landlord class. In the Second World War, the local Muslim clergy here had issued a resolution about the ill treatment of the Serbs by the Croat Ustaše. When Yugoslavia started to break up, the longstanding antagonism between Croatia and Serbia became the focal point of most of the early fighting, and the Bosniaks, from the same Slav bloodstock but whose forebears would have converted in Ottoman times, were caught in the middle.

Jablanica

I ignored the call of the road to savour the scene for longer, but ultimately tore myself away to head upstream to Jablanica, the scene of a rather different sort of river crossing. I drove north past stalls selling multi-coloured produce: bright bags of oranges, trays of green apples, the differing reds of berries and tomatoes alongside an assortment of home-produced jars and bottles of honey, jams and liquids of varying lethality.

The mountains were striking; one could sense the force that must have thrust them out of the earth at an angle. Their alternating bands of grey and green were so defined as to appear a deliberate design decision from above. Occasionally, a vertical cluster of elongated molten-rock domes interrupted the broader scenery, growing out of thickets like a landscape from an ancient Chinese scroll. Each village that I passed through seemed to boast its own mosque, and I had a meat burek at Jablanica to the strains of the muezzin before visiting the local museum.

This was the site of the Partisans' great retreat to safety over the River Neretva in March 1943, taking with them their wounded and sick (many with typhus). They had blown up the railway bridge here themselves to fool the pursuing German forces as to where they intended to cross the river. They then built a temporary wooden bridge over to the far bank, where the remaining steel structure hangs near vertically downwards into the fast-flowing water. Looking at the skeleton, like a section of an outsize Meccano construction with another barely recognisable frame twisted away at its base downstream, it must have been a truly arduous experience, even without the large numbers that they carried with them on stretchers. After climbing the steep bank, they faced the high dark mountains, even more testing in still wintry conditions.

All was not quite as it seemed, however. The bridge had been constructed and demolished twice in the shooting of the 1969 film of the battle, which starred Yul Brynner as the senior engineer in the pioneer company destroying German tanks with his mines on the retreat from Bihać before blowing up the bridge. Orson Welles, as the leader of the

Chetniks, roused his men to fight with the exhortation that, alongside the Germans and Italians, they could not fail to destroy the Partisans. The politics had to fit, as Tito himself had authorised the production of the most expensive movie ever made in Yugoslavia. I noticed that a Partisan cannon was emblazoned "Karadjordje"; whether this had been captured from the Chetniks or indicated that, in Partisan eyes, the great man had been more freedom fighter than royalist was unclear. One of the film's posters had been designed by Picasso, apparently in return for a case of finest Yugoslav wine. The first attempt to shoot the bridge scenes had to be redone because the volume of smoke had made the footage unusable; when the same problem occurred again on the rebuilt and redestroyed bridge, key segments had to be shot in a studio instead.

Inside the museum, much is made of the fact that the combined forces faced by the Partisans were not just Italian and German but also Chetnik and Ustaše. There is no shortage of photographs of Chetniks fraternising with Italians; undoubtedly, the Chetniks did work closely with the Axis forces at times, especially with the Italians in Montenegro, although it is not clear that Mihailović approved of this. However, in early 1943, the Germans were trying to clear local resistance away from the Dalmatian coast, fearing an Allied landing there and needing cleaner control. Meanwhile, Tito himself was fearful of Allied forces should they link up with the Chetniks, as a joint victory by the two at that stage would scupper his goal of a communist Yugoslavia. He had sent representatives to tell the Germans that, if the Allies did land, he would "cooperate" with the Germans against them. His retreat to the southeast was targeting the Chetnik forces, although his customary strategy of avoiding head-on confrontation with massed occupying forces would also have guided him inland.

Nonetheless, the Partisans did inflict significant damage on the Chetniks during the Battle of the Neretva, and Tito reached out again to the Germans in the aftermath to suggest that they leave him "a free hand" against Mihailović. But Hitler distrusted all Yugoslav resistance groups. After the Partisans broke out through the ring of much larger forces attempting to destroy them at Mount Durmitor in the summer, it became clear that they were the more effective local fighting unit, and they began to attract Allied support. The domestic agenda was always paramount though; even in 1944, a senior German official noted that

Tito was as concerned about an Allied landing as he was about the Germans. This is not to say that the Partisans had any affection for the Germans. Fitzroy Maclean tells of a conversation with a Partisan lieutenant in 1944, who, given the atrocities that he had seen, hated Germans "more than anything else on earth". When asked what he did with his prisoners, he said: "'If they surrender in large groups, ... we send them back to base; but if ... there are only a few of them, we don't bother,' and he winked." In the most famous quote of the film, German General Lohring (Curt Jürgens) is quoted as saying that they must win by "the back stairs", war against children and civilians. "Each Partisan's life you spare may avenge you next time with a hand grenade or a few shots from a machine gun."

In the room next door, a smaller exhibition about the Bosnian War consisted largely of photographs of young Bosniaks who had died fighting. There was no real attempt to militarise the images; most of the boys looked as if they had come out of a high school yearbook. Some had long hair, most looked innocent and hopeful. The faces said as much about war as all the words on the explanatory boards could.

Sarajevo

Shortly before Sarajevo proper, I made a small detour to Ilidža, the site of an old Austro-Hungarian pleasure garden by the source of the River Bosna that West had visited, and where Franz Ferdinand and his wife, Sophie Chotek (latterly Duchess of Hohenberg), had stayed for the three nights before their ill-fated visit to the Bosnian capital. As I turned off the main road, a billboard displayed an obscenely magnified image of a skinned, skewered and barbecued chicken advertising a local restaurant. I thought that it would lead the most hardened carnivore to question their diet.

The remains of the old spa are still visible. Over-tall, re-roofed buildings near the parking lot were painted in different hues of yellow with white facings, and an almost doll-like restaurant area nearby featured an eye-watering combination of salmon pink and ochre. Constantine had described Ilidža to West as a "Potemkin village ... built to show the foreign visitors how well [the Austrians] had imposed civilization on our barbarism". He was right – like so much Austrian architecture in the Balkans, it feels both stolid and showy, designed to create an impression of history and taste while failing to achieve either. As West said: "The builders of these horrible hotels ... had come to Sarajevo, the town of a hundred mosques, to teach and not to learn."

There are further villas of this type as one walks to the springs, well over a mile down a long avenue lined with plane and horse chestnut trees. Empire-style horse-drawn buggies drove lovers and families backwards and forwards, while couples on benches screen-tested poses for selfies. Elderly gentlemen were taking laboured constitutionals, some on bicycles pedalling perilously slowly, the zigzagging front wheel only inches away from disaster. At the far end, the springs have been over-developed, with banking, bridges and a restaurant detracting from the evident beauty of nature's original. Here too, families and couples wandered about happily. I assumed that the majority were Muslim, but the practice of religion is so moderate in Bosnia that relatively few women cover their heads. In most towns, the easiest way to gauge the population mix is to count the relative numbers of minarets, onion domes and crosses on the skyline.

In Sarajevo, I was staying at the functional Bosnia Hotel (formerly the Beograd). Awaking in the morning, I thought it time to get my progressively more disordered stomach sorted out. When I asked in the lobby if it was possible to get a doctor's appointment, the receptionist tried a couple of numbers, though without success. I made it clear that it was not urgent, but she was now determined to deliver and, after a few consultative calls, seemed to make contact with a medical expert. She asked my age, at a volume that would have turned heads in the street outside, before informing me that a doctor would appear shortly, so I was not to go far. Ten minutes and a dry bread roll later, I reappeared in the reception to find three medics in red uniforms determined to take me to hospital. As a compromise, the lead doctor eventually suggested that she might examine me in my room, so we traipsed upstairs, where after a certain amount of prodding and questioning she wrote out a prescription and made to exit. I apologised again, hoping that I had not distracted her from more important duties, but I was cut short by a homily on the duty of Sarajevo to its visitors – "We work, even if no one else does." My surprised enquiry as to whether it was a holiday elicited disbelief that I had not heard of 1st May. I muttered feebly that English bank holidays tended to be on Mondays, thanked her again and headed out into the drizzle to find the *apoteka*.

Sarajevo flanks the Miljacka River, a tributary of the Bosna. Along its north bank, many of the buildings that face out over the main promenade date from the Austrian period here, but they are varied and light and have a pleasing well-to-do aspect. Behind them is the heart, the wide streets of the Austrian city to the east and the more tortuous layout of the old Ottoman town to the west. Prior to the Austrians' arrival, it had been known as "Damascus of the North", with large houses and gardens running down to the unconstrained river, which now runs in an orderly fashion through its embankments. Halfway through the 19th century, there were still only two carriages in the town, one belonging to each of the vizier of Bosnia and the Austrian consul. These were purely for show, as progress through the labyrinthine old town could only be undertaken on foot, and there was only a single usable road out of town, which became impassable after an hour. The Austrians Westernised much of Sarajevo rapidly. Ivo Andrić described the mood here at the start of the 20th century:

> The people of Sarajevo, already burdened with the Turkish legacy of habitual indolence and with the Slavic hankering for excesses, had lately adopted the formal Austrian notions of society and social obligations, according to which one's personal prestige and the dignity of one's class were measured by a rising scale of senseless and nonproductive spending, often by an empty and ludicrous extravagance that was devoid of all sense and good taste.

The south bank rises relatively swiftly towards the high ground behind, but in almost every direction there are hilltops and mountains visible, one of the reasons that made it such a successful host for the 1984 Winter Olympics, but also so vulnerable to siege in the following decade. As I passed the many handsome Ottoman bridges spanning the river, I thought about the awful dilemmas that people had had to deal with as snipers waited to pick random pedestrians off through a telescopic sight;

the choice of route, the choice of bridge, the choice of moment as to when to make the dash across an exposed area. Seeing the narrowness and number of the bridges brought home the daily quandaries that people must have faced as they weighed up whether each dangerous outing could be justified.

One of those bridges was the Latin Bridge, whose four arches rise out of diamond shaped piers, the centre pair pierced with portholes to relieve its stone mass. It was here that Gavrilo Princip fired the shots in 1914 that set the world on a path to war. Not far beyond is the old city hall from where the archduke and his pregnant wife had set out shortly before. It has been fully restored and remains every bit as hideous as West's description:

> ... designed by an Austrian architect, ... it is stuffed with beer and sausages down to its toes. It is harshly particoloured and has a lumpish two-storied loggia with crudely fretted arches, ... and its highly ornamented cornices are Oriental in a pejorative sense. The minaret of the mosque beside it has the air of a cat that watches a dog make a fool of itself.

The garishness of its ochre and terracotta stripes induced me to look at old photographs to see if the restoration could be held responsible for so aesthetically displeasing a building, but photographs of the original confirmed that its architect was to blame.

Austria-Hungary had taken control of Bosnia almost by default at the Congress of Berlin in 1878, more as an attempt to balance the ambitions of Russia and her client Bulgaria than through any strong desire to possess it. The occupation was deeply unpopular with both the local Muslim community, who typically wanted some sort of self-government within the Ottoman Empire, and with the Orthodox community, who wanted no imperial control of any sort, and many of whom were sympathetic to the developing notion of a broader Slav entity. There was significant emigration from both communities, some Muslims fearful of life in a Christian state, many Orthodox adherents fleeing poverty in search of a better life. The Austrians reinforced the status quo in rural areas and, in the process, the relative prosperity of Muslim landlords over Serbian peasantry. When Austria annexed Bosnia fully in 1908 in the wake of the Young Turk revolution, it was especially badly received in Serbia, whose relationship with the Hapsburg Empire had already deteriorated. Serbia and Montenegro's success in the two Balkan Wars further inflamed Slavic nationalism and Muslim fears. In response, the Austro-Hungarian government imposed a state of emergency in Bosnia with a strong anti-Serb tilt.

In 1907, aged thirteen, Gavrilo Princip had been sent to high school in Sarajevo from the family village of Obljaj, 150 miles or so to the west near the Croatian border. While here, the bright student had become radicalised and joined *Mlada Bosna* ("Young Bosnia"), an anti-imperialist movement that had links with, among others, Leon Trotsky, then based in Vienna. He was outraged by the fate of Bogdan Žerajić, a would-be assassin of the Austro-Hungarian governor in 1910, who, having failed to hit his target with his first five shots, used the sixth on himself. As a threat to other young Serbs, his decapitated skull was subsequently used as an inkpot by the Sarajevo chief of detectives.

By 1912, Princip's anti-Austrian views had crystallised into south Slav nationalism, and he made his way to Belgrade, the centre of the movement's ambition. There, he made contact with Milan Ciganović, a Serb veteran and member of the Black Hand movement, which had been responsible for the assassination of King Alexander Obrenović and Queen Draga ten years earlier. Ciganović provided training, weapons, cyanide tablets and the means for Princip and his two co-conspirators to cross the border back to Bosnia. It is highly unlikely that an assassination attempt was blessed by the Serbian government, despite the ambiguous position of the Black Hand in Serb circles. Nor is it clear if the attempt was actually planned by the Black Hand, despite claims to that effect by its leader, Apis; but it would doubtless have met with their approval, even if Princip's broader ideal was not the pure Serb nationalism that they promulgated.

By the time Princip and his friends set out, the plan for Archduke Franz Ferdinand to inspect the summer manoeuvres of the Austro-Hungarian army in Bosnia had been published. He had become heir to the Austrian throne after the suicide of his cousin, Rudolf, and the later death from typhoid of his own father, brother to Emperor Franz Joseph. His abiding interest was hunting; he was a greedy shot, and his game records detailed the almost 275,000 creatures that had fallen to his gun. He had fallen in love with the lady-in-waiting of one of his cousins and married her, despite the emperor's disapproval, on the clear dictum that their children could not inherit the throne. Politically, the archduke wanted to centralise more power in Vienna, primarily because he felt that the dual nature of the monarchy hampered its effectiveness. His instincts towards Serbia seem to have been relatively emollient, not wishing to provoke greater conflict with its Russian ally. Nonetheless, he was the ultimate symbol of the oppressing empire, as well as the biggest Hapsburg obstruction to war for those who favoured it in Belgrade or Vienna. His visit to Sarajevo was symbolically ill-timed for 28th June, St Vitus' Day, the anniversary of the Battle of Kosovo, and also by chance his wedding anniversary.

In retrospect, it seems extraordinary that such a clear opportunity was presented to Princip. One of his fellow conspirators had thrown a bomb at the open-topped royal limousine in the motorcade that morning; it had bounced off and exploded under the car behind, injuring several of its occupants. The party proceeded to the city hall, where the welcoming mayor delivered his prepared – and now inadequate – speech, only to be interrupted by Franz Ferdinand: "I come here as your guest and you welcome me with bombs." Nonetheless, all parties regained their composure, and the afternoon's programme was adjusted to replace a tour of the old city with a visit to the morning's injured victims in hospital. Unaccountably, no one informed the drivers.

When they emerged half an hour later and proceeded down the Appel Quay, there was added security in the form of a bodyguard positioned on the running board of the archduke's car. The driver turned to go down Franz Joseph Street in line with the initial schedule, prompting the Governor of Bosnia in the front seat to order him to reverse and continue down the embankment. The car came to a halt right beside Princip; its royal occupant must have proved a clear target in his green plumed helmet. The assassin fired two fatal shots, hitting Franz Ferdinand in the jugular and Sophie in her stomach artery. A crowd overwhelmed him before he could get a third shot off. He was beaten up so badly by both the mob and the police that by the evening, only his mouth and lips could be discerned on his heavily bandaged head. At his trial, he admitted the plot but regretted that the bullet intended for the governor had hit Sophie. Three of his fellow defendants were hanged, but Princip was too young for the death penalty and was sentenced to twenty years in jail. He died of tuberculosis six months before the end of the war that his act had triggered.

Meanwhile, the bodies of the dead couple were returned to Vienna, where Prince Alfred of Montenuovo, first *Obersthofmeister* of the court and Napoleon's step-grandson, was responsible for the arrangements. Montenuovo had had an acrimonious relationship with Franz Ferdinand. Having deeply disapproved of his marriage, he had made a point of humiliating Sophie in life, although she was of aristocratic stock, prohibiting her from sitting near her husband on numerous public occasions. He continued to use court etiquette to make his point beyond the grave, forbidding the officer corps to salute the funeral train. At the funeral mass, Sophie's coffin was deliberately positioned below her husband's, and the chapel was closed after the service to preclude any public viewing. In agreeing to a morganatic marriage, Franz Ferdinand had known that he and Sophie could not be buried together in the imperial crypt. As such, his will specified his desire to be laid to rest at their summer residence of Artstetten Castle. The coffins were conveyed there in the middle of a stormy night. In an echo of the events at Sarajevo, however, no one knew the way from the station in the dark, and they finally arrived well behind schedule at the new family crypt, constructed six years earlier after the stillbirth of their fourth child.

In Vienna, attitudes against Serbia hardened quickly. The Serbian government made some show of mourning and held a memorial service at the Catholic church in Belgrade, but the mood in the streets was jubilant. When the news had reached the Kosovo fields, where the symbolic battle was being celebrated with especial vigour following the triumph of the Second Balkan War, it had sparked an outpouring of joy. Serbia's protests that it had no official involvement in a crime committed in the Austro-Hungarian Empire were undermined by the relatively half-hearted nature of its investigations into any links. Vienna had been seeking to rein in expansionist Serbia for some time; the combination of the assassination itself and the absence of Franz Ferdinand's relatively conciliatory voice served to crystalise the resolve that the moment to take action was now.

An ultimatum to Serbia was crafted to preserve the diplomatic niceties, although there is little doubt that, in Austrian eyes, only complete capitulation would have prevented action. The author, Baron Alexander von Musulin, was a Croat and strongly opposed to Serbian expansionism. Meanwhile, Vienna corresponded with the other great powers, especially Germany, whose backing would be needed in any fallout. It is likely that Austria believed, at least in the early stages, that it could be contained to a bilateral affair, although subsequent events showed that this might well have embarrassed Austria badly. Many of the demands of the ultimatum were uncontentious, but two in particular involved some surrender of sovereignty, one compelling Austro-Hungarian collaboration in suppressing anti-Austrian movements in Serbia, the other insisting that Vienna would delegate participants in the local investigation into the crime. Serbia's response was conciliatory on all fronts save the latter, while seeking clarification on a number of details. The long-serving and notably cautious prime minister, Nikola Pašić, delivered the note that he himself had largely crafted to the Austrian General Giesl with the words: "Part of your demands we have accepted ... For the rest we place our hopes on your loyalty and chivalry as an Austrian general."

Russia by now had indicated its support to Serbia and that it was preparing to mobilise. A telegram in formal French arrived from Austria saying that the Serbian response was not satisfactory; it now sits in the National Museum in Belgrade. A month to the day after Princip pulled the trigger, Emperor Franz Joseph signed the declaration of war on Serbia. Within fifteen days, each of Germany, Russia, Britain and France had followed suit. As Misha Glenny puts it: "The Balkans were not the powder keg ... They were merely the powder trail that the great powers themselves had laid. The powder keg was Europe."

In a small museum near the fateful bridge is an exhibition on the subject of the assassination. Among the exhibits are Princip's clothes, the gun and the attractive striped woven bag in which he presumably carried it. West had written of visiting Princip's grave, the slightly raised central slab of a group of three under which the conspirators were buried by the palings of the old Serbian graveyard. St Mark's Cemetery is accessed through a large market beneath a flyover to the north of the city centre. The sturdy stones of its well-spaced graves stretched way into the distance under the gaze of the suburban tower blocks on the low hill behind it. Two ladies were having an animated discussion in the central pathway. I enquired "Princip?" and was indicated to the far right. I looked for a series of three stones, reluctant to appear too prurient as an elderly lady was hugging a gravestone in quiet desperation 50 yards away. I walked around a small stone chapel in a loosely Orthodox style to find a rust-brown cross painted on its end some 15 feet high. Beneath it was a wreath and a black marble slab engraved with the heading "Heroes of St Vitus' Day" and the names of Gavrilo Princip and ten companions, his co-conspirators, now joined by Bogdan Žerajić, whose skull had been so ill-used. Along the top runs a quote from Njegoš: "Blessed is he who lives forever. He had something to be born for." Meanwhile, in Belgrade, a statue of Princip was erected in 2015. An imperial terrorist is also a nationalist hero, albeit not a nationalism that Princip himself would likely have embraced.

I went to explore more of Sarajevo. It had only really developed rapidly after the arrival of the Turks and was a largely Muslim town until the end of the 16th century, bolstered further in the following century by Islamic refugees from territories lost by the Ottomans to the Austrians and Venetians. Prince Eugene had burnt it to the ground in 1697 to be accompanied by many of the Catholic residents as he retreated. After the destruction, the Bosnian viziers had shifted their capital to Travnik and, despite Sarajevo's greater wealth and importance, the city resisted their return and was significantly self-governing. Thereafter, it was a city in which different cultures – Muslim, Catholic, Orthodox and Jewish – cohabited reasonably happily, although the differences between the communities became more evident as it moved into the 20th century. This was partly because the Christian population tended to adopt Western clothing more rapidly than the Muslims and Jews, creating some sense of otherness, but also due to the increased political divide between Croatia and Serbia.

The emergence of an independent Serbia and the nationalist sentiment that accompanied it, coupled with the arrival of Austro-Hungarian rule in Bosnia in 1878, led to an increasing identification of the Catholic and Orthodox communities as Croat and Serb respectively. This was reinforced in the royalist interwar years, when Croatian hostility to Serbian dominance was the most critical political issue in what became Yugoslavia. Inevitably, the Muslims had to politicise and tended to incline to the Croatian side in disputes. They also feared excessive control from Belgrade, having suffered localised anti-Muslim attacks in the aftermath of 1918.

In the Second World War, Bosnia was divided into Italian and German military zones, but Hitler's man, the Croatian, Ante Pavelić, was Führer of all from Zagreb. His primary concern was dealing with Serbs and Jews. Initially, most Bosnian Croats were content to be absorbed into Croatia, but the lawless and vicious nature of the regime led many to join the Partisans as time went on. Bosnian Serbs joined both of the two main internal resistance groupings, but for the Muslims the Chetniks appeared too Serbian (despite periodic attempts to reassure them), and local militias in Herzegovina had been responsible for a recurrence of anti-Muslim attacks. Some Muslims joined the Partisans, some formed independent defence units, and some looked to Germany as the only possible guarantor of Bosnian independence, though these latter Muslim recruits were misled and sent off to train in France and Germany rather than being allowed to defend their villages. Once it became clear that the Partisans were the most effective resistance force, taking possession of weaponry from the surrendering Italians in September 1943 and enjoying Allied backing, the numbers of Muslims joining them increased significantly.

Post-war, there was considerable repression of religious practice, but the status of the Muslim community improved after Tito championed the Non-Aligned Movement. They were even recognised as a nation of their own in 1971 under his increasingly complex federal balancing act. With his demise, the old cracks resurfaced.

As one walks around the city, its multi-cultural nature is evident. On the old Sarajevo Bank building by the river, sculpted heads above each doorway represent the three main communities. A few blocks north, the Eternal Flame burns in an alcove at a conspicuous point on Marshal Tito Avenue, celebrating the liberation of Sarajevo in 1945 by the Yugoslav army "with the joint efforts and sacrifices of Sarajevan patriots, Serbs, Muslims and Croats". There are substantial churches of both main Christian denominations, as well as a number of fine mosques and a synagogue. The old Serbian Orthodox church stands just by the heart of the old market. It is a darkly intimate two-level construction dating back to the 18th century, replacing earlier versions that had burnt down, and houses two fragments of the True Cross. Nearby, the handsome

Begova Mosque originally dates from 1530, although it too has been rebuilt many times. It imparts a feeling of calm and contemplation, with figures prostrate in prayer on the carpets on its stately stone terrace on a sunny May afternoon. The larger Orthodox church a few blocks to the west was a subject of some argument when it was built at the tail end of Ottoman control. The mosque's hard-line imam objected to the novel prospect of Christian bells being rung in an Ottoman city. He also complained that the Christian belfry would be taller than his minaret but was sent packing by the then governor with the words "Silence, you donkey", remarking that he would clearly be happy to ring the bells himself for a pittance. The iconostasis of the 19th-century church sports a familiar medley of oil paintings of the spiritual and the royal.

Given its recent history, it is remarkable how Sarajevo has regained its poise and feels so welcoming. Young people thronged the streets, chatting and buying snacks from street vendors, which they consumed in laughing groups. The restaurants in the old town were opening up for the evening and happy voices emerged from their interiors along with tantalising smells. The many minarets were almost ethereal in the fading light as they pointed to heaven. As the call to prayer came from different quarters of the city, they combined in a transfixing if unintended harmony.

However, it is not long before one turns a corner to find a concrete wall riddled with bullet holes or the grey patches where repairs have been made to a painted surface. The city pavements are brightened by Sarajevo Roses, where scars left by shell explosions have been filled with blood-red resin, leaving jagged petals beneath one's feet. Down the main shopping street, marble tablets on a column between two shops list the names of the twenty-six Sarajevan citizens killed by "Serb criminals" on 27th May 1993. Somehow, the city has regained its composure without forgetting the horrors that it endured so recently. The blitz spirit seems to have preserved a sense of community, despite the appalling circumstances. It is the one city that I have visited in the former Yugoslavia that feels harmoniously multi-ethnic. Incidentally, it is also the only capital of the now seven constituent parts without an equestrian statue as a centrepiece.

The Bosnian election in 1990 had returned an assembly that was not unlike the split of the electorate; the Muslims won 99 seats, Serbs 85,

Croats 49 and "Yugoslavs" 7. Alija Izetbegović became president of an all-party coalition in the very testing circumstances of Yugoslavia's break-up. He was from an impoverished aristocratic family and had written a treatise in 1970 that tried to reconcile Islamic tradition with Western advances; some of its language was uncomfortably theocratic, although Izetbegović insisted that it was theoretical and not a template for Bosnia. He had been convicted in 1983 for hostile Bosnian nationalism in a much-criticised court case and spent the following five years in prison. As president, his natural instinct to side with Croatia and Slovenia in the Yugoslav federation was at one with his fear of remaining in a Serb-dominated structure if they left. He made clear his support for Bosnian sovereignty if that were to be the case. Zimmermann described him as "[m]ild-mannered to a fault, deferential and perpetually anxious ... [He] wore the mantle of Bosnian president with extreme discomfort". British General Sir Michael Rose was less charitable, believing "that his talk of creating a multi-religious, multi-cultural State in Bosnia was a disguise for the extension of his own political power and the furtherance of Islam". The later presence of the Iranian intelligence service and military trainers in support of the Bosniak forces lend credence to his belief.

The Bosnian Serbs, steered by Radovan Karadžić, the leader of the largest political party in the Bosnian assembly, followed the lead of Serb enclaves in Croatia towards the end of 1991 and declared four "Serb Autonomous Regions" in Bosnia. When Izetbegović objected, the Serbs boycotted parliament and set up their own. Karadžić's final speech threatened: "The Muslims cannot defend themselves if there is war." He portrayed the Bosniaks as seeking to impose a fundamentalist Islamic regime. The Serb "parliament" voted to remain in Yugoslavia, but the referendum in early 1992 on Bosnian independence, boycotted by many Serbs but with a high 64% turnout nationwide, resulted in an almost unanimous vote to leave the federation, as Croatia and Slovenia had done. The Serbs were deeply fearful of being in a minority; within weeks, their assembly had declared a new entity – Republika Srpska.

By this stage, the Yugoslav army had militarised Serb areas and installed heavy artillery in key positions, including the high ground around Sarajevo. The commanding general, Ratko Mladić, described by Rose as being "in the classic Soviet mould of generals: fat, swaggering and coarse", flew to Belgrade on Tuesdays to receive orders.

Karadžić left Sarajevo for his new capital of Pale, a ski resort in the hills about ten miles to the east, where he set up his presidential office in the former Hotel Panorama.

Karadžić was actually Montenegrin, born shortly after the end of the Second World War into a harsh environment, made worse by his Chetnik father spending the immediate post-war years in jail. Aged fifteen, he moved to Sarajevo, where he attended medical school and also joined the Communist Party, but was expelled after participation in Sarajevo's version of the 1968 student demonstrations sweeping the world. He secured his medical degree and also started writing, spending ten months in the US on a literary scholarship to Columbia University. He spent over a year in jail for fraud in the mid-1980s and was also employed as a psychologist for Red Star Belgrade during a brief stint in Serbia. Back in Sarajevo, he returned to work in the psychiatric clinic of a leading local hospital. He became progressively more involved in politics, with the specific aim of enabling Bosnian and Croatian Serbs to remain part of Yugoslavia (or Greater Serbia) in the event that their home republics achieved independence. In Pale, Karadžić appeared to rely closely on his wife, Ljiljana, one of a number of parallels to Milošević. She accompanied him to many meetings, and access to him was arranged through his daughter and chief press secretary, Sonja. He dressed smartly, was proud of his full locks of hair, enjoyed cognac and Cuban cigars, and had a reputation for taking a cut on deals that needed his approval, although his "raw and bleeding" fingernails suggested to Rose that he suffered from "extreme anxiety beneath his calm exterior". He was interviewed by David Frost in Pale in 1995, clearly hooked on protocol and the entitlements of office, and became angry when Frost questioned him too hard on ethnic strife. His bodyguard cocked their rifles and told Frost's team to "knock it off". To Frost's credit, he did not.

In Paweł Pawlikowski's documentary about Karadžić, *Serbian Epics*, another manifestation of the Lazar myth is displayed. Karadžić boasts of his (marginal) kinship with Vuk Karadžić, the 19th-century collector of Serbian poems and folktales, comparing their cleft chins as proof. He makes frequent references to the darkness of his own youthful poetry. He looks down from the heights on the smoke rising from the shelling of Sarajevo and pronounces in English:

That was Serbian country when Turks came ... We own this country ... Turks have been here, occupiers, and Muslims are successors of those occupiers ... After Turks came, after Kosovo Battle, those Serbs who didn't accept Islam have been pushed to the mountains.

A contrived version of events of the 14th century being used to justify a late 20th-century atrocity. The troops with him sing:

Oh, beautiful Turkish daughter,
Our monks will soon baptise you.
Sarajevo, in the valley,
The Serbs have encircled you.

Meanwhile, ahead of negotiations in Geneva, he stakes a claim to "some 12 kilometres of coastline south of Dubrovnik. It's not right that Croatia should have all the coast and we have none". This is again nonsensical without reference to the deep past, either in the form of Dušan or the mid-14th-century King Tvrtko of Bosnia, who had controlled (and devastated) varying sections of the Adriatic coast during his 30-year reign. As Karadžić flies off to Geneva, his tame *gusle* player wishes him well, singing: "Hey Radovan, you man of steel, the greatest leader since Karadjordje." One is led to conclude that this amoral and opportunistic individual had been seduced by a combination of historical legend, love of the spotlight and the material gain that it afforded, while somehow managing to entirely blot from his mind the consequences of his actions.

The siege of Sarajevo went on for three and a half years, the longest in modern times. The European Community recognised Bosnia and Herzegovina as an independent state on 6th April 1992; on the same day, the shelling of Sarajevo started. There had already been instances of violence in the city as Serb police and paramilitaries had faced off against protestors, but within days war had engulfed the country, as the Bosnian Serbs, supported by the Yugoslav army and with the active participation of paramilitaries, sought to gain control of swathes of territory and terrify non-Serbs (predominantly Muslim in the key areas) into fleeing. The arms embargo that the UN had imposed on Yugoslavia in 1991 was also applied to Bosnia, a decision that locked in the

Serbs' logistical advantage, since the army had stockpiled ordnance in advance. The international community persisted in characterising the conflict as a "civil war", when in fact it was more a disguised land grab by an aggressive neighbour. The success of the original Serb offensive was such that the Bosniak leadership would find it all but impossible to accept a solution based on the status quo. Over 100 ceasefires were negotiated, none of which proved lasting. For Sarajevo, this led to occasional lulls in the shelling, but the threat from sniper fire in the streets was ever present, even in these interludes.

In total, around 10,000 people were killed in Sarajevo over the course of the siege, mostly civilians. Many more were injured. Nearly 90% of the buildings in the city suffered damage. The population of close to 400,000 were without electricity and running water for much of that time. One of the key reasons to go out and risk sniper fire was to fill up water containers; the old brewery high on the south side of the river sat on top of a large spring, providing a source of water to thousands. This was founded in 1864 before the Austrians arrived here, becoming the largest brewery in their empire by the start of the 20th century. Today, it exudes civic pride in local commerce, its clean brick-red and white-painted exterior enhanced by a clocktower with a rakish oriental cap.

Most of the trees in the city were cut down for firewood, with even their roots torn out. The winter atmosphere was spiked with the scent of random articles being burnt on fires or in stoves. Anthony Loyd described the typical meal at the time as "beans, bread, UHT milk and meat-fat". A journalist friend described corpses lying for days in the corner of hotel lobbies or out in the streets until finally it felt safe to deal with them properly. Fog and rain became the Sarajevans' ally. Stray dogs roamed the streets; many had been pedigreed pets whose owners could no longer afford to feed them. The only link to the outside world was a small tunnel built under the airport in 1993, some 340 metres long, approached by covered trenches at each end. Through it, key supplies could come in and people could get out (on payment of a substantial fee), but it was subject to flooding and the air quality was so poor that all users had to wear masks.

Western efforts initially focused on the plan developed by the UN and EC negotiators, former US Secretary of State Cyrus Vance and former British Foreign Secretary David Owen. This envisaged dividing the country into ethnic areas, which reinforced an incentive to grab land, leading to conflict between the Croats and Muslims, who until now had presented a reasonably united front to the Serbs. The plan was opposed by the Serbs, who wanted full independence from the rest of Bosnia, and by the Muslims, who had been penned back into a rump of their former country, pockets of which were surrounded by Serb territory and now effectively giant refugee camps. A visit by international journalists to visit Serb camps in the north of Bosnia had produced evidence of the horrors that were occurring there, with Muslims held in utterly degrading conditions, semi-starved and subject to beatings, torture and summary executions. On a visit to London, Karadžić had invited the media to visit and so lay to rest stories of concentration camps; it is hard to believe that having done so, he stage-managed the event so ineptly. By the end of 1992, the Serbs, who at the start of the war had represented 31% of the population, controlled 70% of Bosnia's landmass, despite many of their number having fled the conflict. They pressed for a division of Sarajevo.

As the war moved towards the end of its second year, a mortar strike on a market in Sarajevo killed sixty-eight people. In response, NATO ordered an exclusion zone for heavy artillery around Sarajevo with the threat of airstrikes. Soon after, international pressure forced an accommodation between the Croats and Muslims. Meanwhile, the UN peacekeeping force (UNPROFOR), though clearly improving the situation dramatically for refugees, was unable to be fully effective without sufficient strength or a clear mandate to take decisive action, which would have been for NATO anyway. It was further hampered by the Bosniak strategy of provoking conflict in order to stimulate greater international intervention. UN participants also provided a periodic source of hostages for the Serbs.

By 1995, things began to shift. The Clinton administration, which had used the Bosnian situation in the presidential campaign against George H. W. Bush, could see that the cycle of failed ceasefires was not working. Bush's secretary of state, James Baker, had refused to intervene with the memorable words: "We don't have a dog in that fight." Madeleine Albright, the US ambassador to the UN, had been to Sarajevo in March 1994 to dedicate the future site of the US embassy there. She had been shocked by what she saw: "destroyed buildings and shattered glass everywhere ... Apartment buildings were gutted, with massive holes where windows should have been." In the autumn of that year, the experienced US diplomat Richard Holbrooke was appointed as chief negotiator. The latest ceasefire held reasonably well over the early winter months of 1995, but as the weather improved, the Serbs started shelling again. After repeated violations, the UN allowed NATO to bomb Serb ammunition dumps near Pale. The Serbs retaliated by upping artillery attacks on a number of targets through Bosnia and chaining UN peacekeepers to the sites that they wished to protect, threatening their lives unless bombing raids ceased.

The US increased pressure on both sides to come to a negotiated deal. The Serb General Mladić, emboldened by his hostage strategy, was determined to secure strategic geographies before a deal was inked. On 9th July, he attacked Srebrenica, a former silver-mining town that had been the most important centre in the western Balkans in the 15th century, now a Muslim enclave at the base of a finger of eastern Bosnia that projected into Serbia. The Serbs took thirty-two Dutch UN peacekeepers hostage in an effort to force the UN to call off airstrikes. Mladić's forces killed around 8,000 Muslim men and boys, burying them in mass graves, and expelled another 5,000 Muslim women and children along with the elderly and infirm. Satellite photographs confirmed the account of the very few escapees from the slaughter. A television camera captured Mladić saying: "I give this town to the Serbian people as a gift for St Vitus' Day. We finally took revenge on the Turks."

On the other side of the country, the Bosnian government forces were supported by the Croatian army to protect the Muslim enclave of Bihać, and the Croatians swept on to retake that part of their country that local Serbs had grabbed in 1991. On 28th August, five Serb mortar shells hit Markale Market in Sarajevo, killing thirty-seven people and wounding twice that, in a repetition of the even more lethal attack in the same spot in February 1994. Mladić's refusal to remove his artillery from the exclusion zone finally led to much more intensive bombing of Serb positions. The United Nations had proved a significant drag on any action; their peacekeeping mission demanded an even-handed approach. Holbrooke reported that the statement of UN Secretary-General Boutros Boutros-Ghali in the wake of the Serb mortar attack,

... typically, meant almost exactly the opposite of what it seemed to say; he 'unreservedly condemned the shelling' and ordered his military commanders to 'investigate this attack immediately and take appropriate action without delay.' In fact, this was a device to avoid taking action.

It reflects the considerable difference between the peacekeeping mission of the UN and the military aims of NATO, a distinction that could get lost all too easily in heated discussions, and one that the US did not always wish to acknowledge.

The Croatian-Bosnian forces continued to make considerable progress in the west of the country, with active but managed encouragement from the US. Holbrooke had urged Tudjman to stop before Banja Luka, fearing an even worse human rights catastrophe. Serb morale was low and Belgrade had no appetite to persist with a war that was so unpopular both at home and abroad when sanctions were biting. Milošević was reported as responding to a remark about his Bosnian Serb friends with the words: "They are not my friends. They are not my colleagues. It is awful just to be in the same room with them for so long. They are shit." Since the 1994 shelling of Sarajevo, he had become progressively more disenchanted with his tools; they had become less biddable and were now a liability. In July, he imposed an economic embargo on them.

On 21st November, Holbrooke was able to announce that a division of the country and a peace agreement had been reached by all parties at Dayton, Ohio. The Bosnian Serbs were represented by Milošević, as Karadžić had by then been indicted by The Hague as a war criminal. The two entities would have joint monetary, trade and foreign policies, but were otherwise autonomous. One is left to speculate what might have happened with a push on to an increasingly possible victory over the Serb forces. Instead, the status quo all but delivered the aggressors what they sought and left a state with near insoluble divisions. Paddy Ashdown, the international community's High Representative in Bosnia, subsequently described the agreement as "not so much a help as an impediment", but it did bring an end to the fighting. In all, 100,000 people had died in the conflict, of whom over 60% were Muslim. Over a million had had to leave their homes.

The Americans had refused to let anyone leave Dayton until they had reached agreement. The meetings were clearly well lubricated, with Milošević appearing to enjoy late-night negotiations. He had a legally adept mind and a strong head. Izetbegović would not touch his food in his presence; it is unclear if this was understandable distaste at the company or a fear of dirty tricks. Milošević enjoyed singing the Nat King Cole song *Tenderly* with the pianist at the officers' club there, but he had always enjoyed showing off his comfort with American culture. Holbrooke was puzzled at Milošević ceding Sarajevo to the Muslims, speculating "that he was fed up with the Bosnian Serbs and decided to weaken their Pale base ... [and] Karadžić and strengthen the Serbs in other parts of Bosnia, especially Banja Luka". Milošević was adamant that he would not give up Karadžić and Mladić to an international tribunal and was very resistant to looking at evidence linking Arkan to the Yugoslav army or war crimes. He was clearly concerned to hide any trail that led back to him. After his death, the International Criminal Tribunal would conclude that he could not be linked directly to genocide in Bosnia, but was guilty of failing to cooperate in bringing perpetrators to justice, notably Mladić.

In March 1996, the Bosnian Serbs lowered their flag in Grbavica, the principal Serb suburb of Sarajevo, to a rendition of the old royalist Yugoslav anthem. They left for Pale, destroying Serb property before leaving. Karadžić commented: "We saved this area militarily, but we lost it at Dayton."

The net took its time to tighten around the worst perpetrators of war crimes. Dario Kordić, the military commander of the Bosnian Croats, surrendered in October 1997. His public remarks at Split Airport en route to The Hague were translated by Croatian President Tudjman's personal interpreter, appearing to signal a potential complicity between them. He was subsequently found guilty of war crimes and sentenced to twenty-five years' imprisonment. He was granted early release in 2014. Tudjman had died in 1999; it is unclear whether there would have been an attempt to indict him had he lived longer.

Karadžić remained in power in Pale until the summer of 1996, when the US pressured Milošević to make him step down from his roles. For a while, he was spotted around Pale, but he disappeared from view in 1997. He appears to have moved to Belgrade in secret, initially under Milošević's protection, but as things became more difficult, he adopted a new persona, Dragan Dabić, a bushy-bearded, pony-tailed practitioner of alternative medicine. He was finally arrested in 2008, found guilty of genocide and war crimes in 2016 at The Hague, and is now serving a life sentence.

Despite Karadžić's attempts to dislodge him when the war started going badly for the Serbs in 1995, Mladić remained as head of the Bosnian Serb army until the end of 1996, when he was retired on a pension that he continued to receive until 2005. He went into hiding in Serbia and Republika Srpska, helped by supporters in the Serbian army, but as the political climate changed in Belgrade, he lived a more peripatetic existence, relying on his extended family to provide shelter. He was finally arrested in May 2011, over fifteen years after the end of the war. He was also found guilty of genocide and war crimes at The Hague and sentenced to life imprisonment.

While the fugitives were sought, another hunt was going on. In 1996, the International Commission on Missing Persons (ICMP) was formed, at the instigation of President Clinton, to find and identify the victims of the war at Srebrenica and elsewhere, many of whom had been buried in mass graves. In the case of Srebrenica, those graves had been dug up again and the remains moved to a large number of secondary sites in an attempt to hide the original crime. Often in the earth-moving process, individual bodies had been divided and reburied in more than one location. Given the scale of the task, the ICMP had to build an enormous DNA database, both of living relatives of the missing and of the human remains that they recovered, and try to match them up. By September 2019, some 6,643 victims had received a proper burial at the memorial cemetery at Srebrenica, allowing some closure to their families.

Before leaving Sarajevo, I went to stand on Vrbanja Bridge, a nondescript road over the river where six protestors were shot by Serb snipers on 5th April 1992, the day before Bosnia was recognised as an independent state by the EC; two of them died, the first victims of the siege. Three years later, Bosnian Serb troops dressed as French UN peacekeepers captured French guards stationed on the bridge and used them as hostages. The ensuing battle between the two sides saw three French and four Serb deaths before the French regained control. France suffered the heaviest casualties of the UN participants in Bosnia.

Over the river a few blocks away is the beautifully proportioned 16th-century Ali Pasha Mosque. It was badly damaged in the siege, sitting as it did at one of the most vulnerable spots in the city. Hastily implemented barricades of buses and corrugated iron beside it had provided shelter from snipers for pedestrians. A little beyond it in a park is a memorial to the children who died in the siege. Water bubbles in a pool, out of which an elongated green glass iceberg juts, fractured along its length as if to show the rending of child from mother. The names of the dead are inscribed on six rotating silver cylinders beside it, prayer wheels for the prematurely departed. As one walks around Sarajevo, one is repeatedly reminded of the past, when the constant possibility of imminent death existed in such a familiar urban milieu. The scars still run deep, for those both in the capital and where entire communities were murdered, but here I seemed to glimpse a brighter future, an echo of what a better present might have been, an embrace of the multi-cultural.

Local politics offer limited glimmers of hope; the head of the regional government in Sarajevo represents a deliberately non-ethnic party called *Naša stranka* ("Our Party") in a five-party coalition, but it is small nationally. Meanwhile, nationalist issues place constant strain on the fragile status quo of the country as a whole. The veteran leader of the Bosnian Serbs, Milorad Dodik, once considered moderate, has become more strident in his talk of secession and bans teaching about the siege of Sarajevo or the horror of Srebrenica. He is actively supported by Russia. Bakir Izetbegović, having inherited his father's mantle as leader of the Muslim community, has developed close ties with President Erdoğan of Turkey, who even held an election rally in Sarajevo in 2018. The old imperial divides seem to have adapted to the complexities of the new century.

Višegrad

Before tracking north, I wanted to make another literary pilgrimage, to Višegrad, 70 miles to the east. To my right as I set out was Mount Trebević, which West had visited, and had been the location of the Olympic bobsleigh events in 1984. During the siege, snipers with telescopic sights had tried to pick off pedestrians from its heights, and it was so thoroughly mined that much of it became a no-go area for decades afterwards. The boundary between the two Bosnian entities bisects it, which complicated the reopening of the gondola from the city to its slopes, but in 2018 the mountain became accessible again as one of the primary country parks for Sarajevans.

The drive east was spectacular, yellow-speckled mountain meadows dotted with wide, red-roofed houses giving way to the striking valley of the River Drina. This is wild country; at night, you can hear the howls of wolves in the hills. I drove ten miles past Višegrad to the 14th-century Dobrun Monastery, close to the Serbian border. The main gate was open but there was no sign of life. After some time, a nun appeared, dark-clad other than her denim skirt. Making no visible acknowledgement of my presence, she walked slowly to the newly painted white church and unlocked it for me. The building was simple and of indeterminate age; it has been much restored over the years. At the near end were beautiful if damaged frescoes of the last great Nemanjić tsar with his wife and son. Dušan and his queen, the Bulgarian princess, Helena, look steely-eyed and formidable, while the boy Uroš sandwiched between them is doughy-featured, clutching his belt as if unsure where to put his hands. He appears utterly cowed by the strength of his parents. Looking at the painting, no one would be surprised that, sixteen years after he inherited his father's empire, it had all but vanished. Still wordlessly, I left.

I gave two large youths a lift back to Višegrad. They spoke no English, so after a brief awkward silence, they engaged in an animated discussion with each other while I ferried them, trying to discern the occasional familiar word. On arrival, they thanked me effusively. I turned to gaze finally on the "Bridge over the Drina" itself, as much a masterpiece as the eponymous novel that it inspired. The structure itself consists of eleven all but hemispherical arches that span the fast-flowing pale green Drina from the steep mountain behind the road on one side to the town spread over a rare flat expanse on the other. The faint arc of the bridge's width belies its sturdiness.

Ivo Andrić's great chronicle refracts three and a half centuries of history through the bridge and the town that it serves. He describes the decoration on the piers, "finely carved blind windows, narrow as loopholes, in which the wild doves now nest", as well as the tall stone in the middle where the bridge widens out into a gathering place, or *kapia*. A plaque high up pays tribute to its 16th-century builder, Sokollu Mehmed Pasha, who had been taken to Istanbul as a boy from a local village. Below it is a fountain with a snake-shaped waterspout, used by a coffeemaker in the novel to serve those passing the hours on the stone sofa below the parapet. In the central pier, twin infants were reputed to have been walled up to placate the angry river spirits.

The saga begins in the Ottoman years, during which the various communities of Višegrad (Christian, Muslim and Jewish) accommodate each other reasonably well, although during construction a saboteur is caught and impaled on the bridge. Things become more complex after Karadjordje's uprising in Serbia, when the Ottomans display the heads of likely rebels on stakes, but it is the arrival of the Austro-Hungarians in 1878 that proves most disruptive, with modernisation threatening centuries-old habits. As the Hapsburg forces retreat from the Serbians at the start of the First World War, they blow up the central portion of the bridge behind them, removing the one constant: "they had ... blown it all into the skies as if it had been some stone in a mountain quarry and not a thing of beauty and value, a bequest ... to take things away even from God." A brief summary cannot do justice to the humanity of the whole and the subtlety with which the relationships of a diverse community unfold as events far away ripple out to their remote corner.

Andrić, a Bosnian Croat, spent most of his childhood here in Višegrad, but was educated in Sarajevo, Zagreb and Vienna. He was a member of the Young Bosnia movement and knew Princip, although he was a few years older than him. At the outbreak of the Second World War, he had been Yugoslavia's ambassador in Berlin. He declined the offer of safe harbour to neutral Switzerland and spent the remainder of the war closeted in his Belgrade flat working on his two great works, both of which were published in 1945. He received the Nobel Prize in Literature in 1961. His heritage has been claimed by Serbia, as he spent the majority of his working life in Belgrade, which may have served to damage his image among some Muslims, who have claimed that there is a strong negative bias to his depiction of their fellow believers. That is not readily apparent from my reading of his major works. There are probably accurate depictions of the cruelty of Turkish executions and of occupying forces in general, but the local Slav Muslims are sympathetic figures and cut from a similar cloth to their Christian neighbours. Most of the Roman Catholic villages in the Drina valley had only become Muslim in the 19th century anyway, due to ill treatment. His attitude seems best summed up for me by this quote from his book as the consequences of Franz Ferdinand's assassination become clearer:

> It is true that there had always been concealed enmities and jealousies and religious intolerance, coarseness and cruelty, but there had also been courage and fellowship and a feeling for measure and order, which restrained all these instincts within the limits of the supportable and, in the end, calmed them down and submitted them to the general interest of life in common.

The bridge took on its grimmest role in the Bosnian War. As a mixed town near the Serbian border, although two-thirds Muslim, Višegrad was an early target for Serb ethnic cleansing, and Muslims would be brought to the bridge to be tortured and killed. The volume of bodies tipped over the edge clogged the culverts of the hydroelectric plant downstream, said to have turned the river red. The town also housed a notorious rape camp and saw local Muslims crowded into houses and burned alive. The local paramilitary leader, Milan Lukić, was a disciple of Karadžić and Mladić, apparently linked to a drug-running operation that was part of the hidden side of Karadžić's network. His cousin, Sreten Lukić, was a senior minister in Belgrade and helped protect him from arrest after he was indicted by The Hague in 1998, but that protection vanished after the cousin was indicted in turn for war crimes. Lukić was finally tracked down in Buenos Aires in 2005, where he was living under a false name. He was sentenced to life imprisonment along with yet another cousin, who received thirty years. Meanwhile, the ex-minister is serving twenty years for his role in the campaign of terror and violence in Kosovo.

I strolled out to the centre of the bridge. I had read Andrić's book recently and was surprised at how small the seating area was and how wide the parapet along which a one-eyed drunkard had danced one night in a memorable scene. The shrunken size of the setting imparted a new intimacy to my visualisation. I fell into conversation with a vendor, a homely figure who offered to translate the tablets on the central stone.

I demurred, knowing the meaning already. She indicated where the twins were meant to be interred. I asked if there were many Muslims left in the town and she said almost none. In the past, they had lived on the north bank and the Serbs on the south, but almost all were gone now. She herself had come to Višegrad to get married but she had been born in western Bosnia. The troubles had started when she was five; at the age of seven, she had seen "things no child should ever see". Her mother had been shot, losing the twins that she was carrying, and the family had been forced to flee. "Everybody has stories they don't want to tell." I bought a small bottle from her limited selection, decorated with a wrapping of alternately coloured strings like an exhibit in a school craft show. I walked back towards the town wondering quite how the relative harmony of so many centuries could have been undone with such violence.

I went into the town looking for Andrić's classroom, but it was closed for a holiday. A sturdy square building of faded orange with formal ochre accoutrements signalled the historic Austrian occupation. I noticed that there were two small mosques, secured but in apparently good order. The atmosphere seemed sullen, as I have sensed in other ethnically cleansed towns. I suspect that this is due in part to the smattering of empty buildings in poor repair and the shrunken population, but it feels as though the dark memories of the past endure in their fabric.

I walked on to Andrićgrad, a new development pointed out to me by my friend on the bridge with the half-hearted recommendation: "It is much nicer inside than it looks." It was a large compound of plain stone buildings on a peninsula a few hundred yards downstream from the bridge. The upper-storey windows were mere slits, while the entrance was through an arch in the otherwise solid facade, giving it a defensive appearance. Inside, I was surprised to find boutiques, cafes, restaurants, a cinema and large numbers of people enjoying the sunshine. At the far end stood a new Orthodox church, in front of which was a statue of Njegoš, the 19th-century Montenegrin prince-bishop and author of *The Mountain Wreath*. He was sitting reading a book, traditionally dressed, his literary rather than martial side on display, although that may be a narrow distinction given the tenor of his most famous work. The view of the bridge from here is breath-taking, its low line absorbing some of the jade green of the river as it creates a border with the richer green of the wooded escarpment rising steeply behind.

Andrićgrad is a project of Emir Kusturica, the Serbian film director whose most famous film, *Underground*, tells the story of Yugoslavia from the onset of the Second World War to the break-up of Yugoslavia through the lives of two friends, one of whom spends decades underground in a cellar complex in the belief that the Nazis are still in power. It is funny, tragic, overflowing with energy, and lunatic. It won Kusturica one of his two Palme d'Or at Cannes. He and his film have been accused of downplaying Serbian atrocities, but it certainly does not ignore or glorify them. In its very different style, it is almost a coda to Andrić's work, its madness reflecting the history that it was depicting.

The development is Kusturica's homage to Andrić, with Islamic, Byzantine and Austro-Hungarian architectural nods to the history of Višegrad. A curious mural boasts Kusturica participating in a tug of war in an idealised rural setting alongside tennis player Novak Djoković, Gerard Depardieu and the hard-line Bosnian Serb leader, Milorad Dodik. Kusturica claims that it is a pacifist project, and he has strong educational ambitions for it, although it seems to ignore the violence of the post-Tito years rather than addressing it. He is hard to pigeonhole; born into a Sarajevan Muslim family, he converted to Orthodoxy aged fifty.

In a short story published soon after the war, Andrić wrote a fictional letter from a young Jewish doctor explaining that he left Bosnia because of the deep, innate hatreds that were part of its fabric. He talks of their differences defined by religion:

> Your holy of holies is, as a rule, three hundred rivers and mountains away, but the objects of your repulsion and hatred are right beside you, in the same town, often on the other side of your courtyard wall. So your love remains inert, but your hatred is easily spurred into action ... This poor backward country, in which four different faiths live cheek by jowl, needs four times as much love, mutual understanding and tolerance as other countries.

Kusturica claims that *Underground* shows the triggers of wildness. In their respective times, I suspect that both he and Andrić would claim to be Yugoslavs rather than one of the constituent south Slav tribes, and both would advocate education and understanding as the best way to heal and avoid repetition of the cycle of violence. Time will tell

NORTH MACEDONIA

32. Statue of Alexander the Great in Skopje

33. Market Street in Skopje, early 20th century

34. Painted mosque, Tetovo

35. St Jovan Kaneo, Ohrid

36. King Edward VII and Kemal Atatürk, Istanbul, 1936

37. Serb soldiers embark in Corfu for Salonika, 1916

38. Pepper stall in Bitola

39. Treskavec Monastery

40. Katerina and Elena Tsilka with Ellen Stone shortly after their release

41. Saint Panteleimon in his monastery near Skopje

BOSNIA AND HERZEGOVINA

42. The bridge at Mostar

43. Santica Street, Mostar

44. The bridge over the Neretva

45. Sarajevo Town Hall

46. The Latin Bridge at Sarajevo

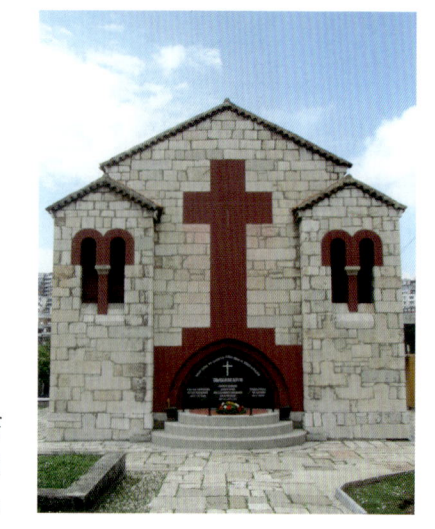

47. Resting place of Gavrilo Princip and fellows, Sarajevo

48. Alija Izetbegović, 1997

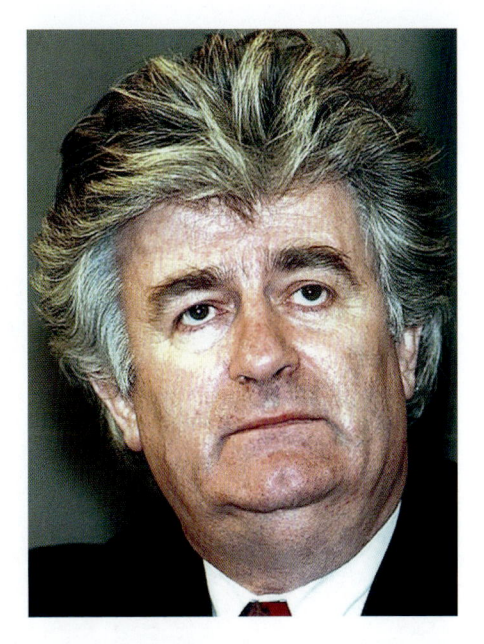

49. Radovan Karadžić, 1994

50. The Bridge over the Drina at Višegrad

51. The author at Bobovac

52. Coloured Mosque at Travnik

53. Museum of the 2nd AVNOJ session, Jajce

54. Milorad Dodik, Chairman of the Presidency of Bosnia and Herzegovina, 2016

CROATIA

56. Vukovar war cemetery

55. Vukovar water tower

57. Bishop Josip Juraj Strossmayer by Meštrović, Zagreb

58. Blessed Alojzije Stepinac, c.1937

54. Hitler and Ante Pavelić listen to Goering, June 1941

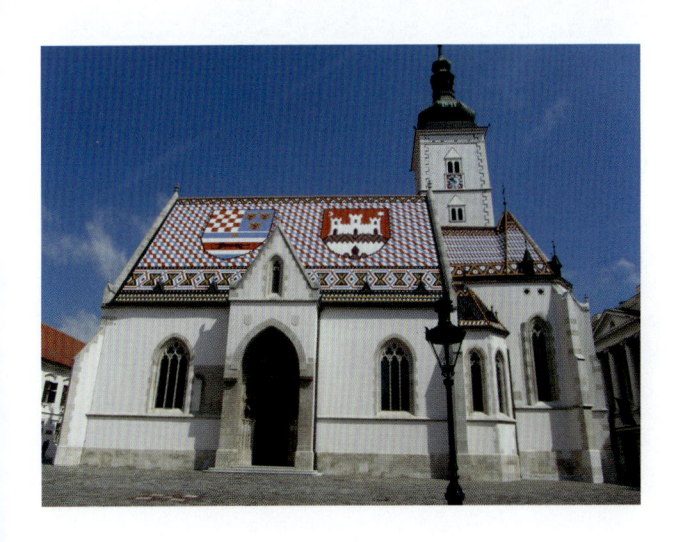

60. St Mark's Church, Zagreb

61. Grave of Franjo Tudjman, Zagreb

62. D'Annunzio's palace, Rijeka

63. Deposition of Christ at Rab

64. Bellflowers at Rab

65. Knin Fortress

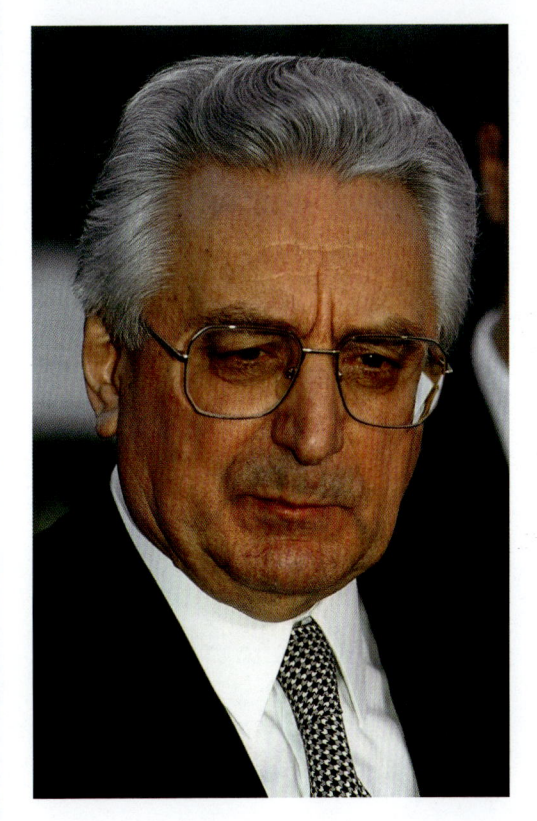

66. Franjo Tudjman

67. Split

68. *Job* by Meštrović

69. Marmont's gloriette at Trogir

70. Fitzroy Maclean and partisan

571. Siege of Dubrovnik, November 1991

72. Hilandar Monastery on Mount Athos, Greece

whether this surreal themed development, a great tourist hope for the much-vilified Republika Srpska, reinforces ancient prejudices or helps to heal them. If it is to succeed, one feels that at the very least it needs to acknowledge them properly, a sentiment presumably shared by the UN High Representative in Bosnia, who criminalised genocide denial in July 2021, stirring up Serb resentment in the process. Andrić's doctor referred to "deeply rooted injustices and abuses which only torrents of hatred can uproot and wash away. And when these torrents dwindle and dry up, room for freedom remains, for the creation of a better life". We have seen the torrents; we must hope that they have run dry.

I returned to the bridge and sat on a terrace, admiring it through a veil of willow trees while working my way through a pizza adorned with a gelatinous egg, a gluey spiral of tomato ketchup winding its way slowly to the edge of the disc. I remembered another passage from the eponymous book:

> Its shining line in the composition of the town did not change, any more than the outlines of the mountains against the sky. In the changes and the quick burgeoning of human generations, it remained as unchanged as the waters that flowed beneath it. It too grew old, naturally, but on a scale of time that was much greater not only than the span of human existence but also than the passing of a whole series of generations, so that its ageing could not be seen by human eye. Its life, though mortal in itself, resembled eternity for its end could not be perceived.

Before leaving Višegrad, I drove up to the small Serbian military cemetery above the town, where orderly rows of black slabs, each bearing a white cross on the left shoulder, bore witness to the fallen of the remaining community in the years of horror. Their engraved images seemed to fall into two categories: warriors, presenting a gun or leaning on a tank, and civilians, fresh-faced in sports gear. Presumably, some of these reflected the nature of the grave's occupant, and rather more the memories that their families wished to preserve. Twenty years on, every grave was still decorated with flowers. Even the aggressors had to grieve, and many may not have been natural aggressors. The past still resurfaces though. At the Muslim graveyard to the north of Višegrad, the local mayor had the word "genocide" removed from the white stone memorial to the victims here in 2014. Periodically, an anonymous black ink marker reinstates it in defiance.

Back in Sarajevo, I had dinner of polenta with smoked beef, an egg and sour cream in a tiny restaurant down a small passage in the old town. It was almost overwhelmingly rich but rendered bearable by the crispness of the cabbage salad that accompanied it and some heroically bodied red wine. It seemed to echo the city whose rich blend of cultures could be brought into harmony by common sense, humanity and just enough forgetting.

Kraljeva Sutjeska

Forty miles north of Sarajevo is the village of Kraljeva Sutjeska, the ancient capital of Bosnia and the base of the Franciscans here for almost 700 years. The River Bosna snakes up the valley so vigorously that the motorway tracking it must have been a bridgebuilder's dream. I stopped at the gloomy town of Kakanj to ensure that I was travelling on the right road and a blond Muslim boy insisted on climbing into my car for a mile or so. He pointed confidently in the direction that I was facing, and I emerged from the town proper to find myself in a landscape from an earlier industrial age: a crumbling brick building was surrounded by piles of coal while conveyor belts cased in corrugated iron angled across the road from one stained disused concrete installation to another. I drove under these decaying fingers, but around the corner was a newer version of the same. Presumably, it was a replacement for its dying neighbour, whose advancing decrepitude looked likely to impede access to its offspring at some point without more active intervention.

A few miles on, I could have been in a different century and country. A lane ran beside a rushing stream with white-painted houses and black timber farm buildings well spaced along each bank and scattered up the tree-lined meadows above them. It was a rural paradise. At the top of the little valley, the twin black pyramids on the white turrets of the Franciscan monastery seemed to signal a fustier era. The guidebook had indicated that it was open for six hours on Fridays, but all the doors were locked. I walked down the drive and greeted a man cutting the grass at the bottom. We established quickly that we had no natural linguistic meeting point, but he was a friendly figure, somewhat younger than me, with smiling eyes and pink cheeks (no doubt in part through his exertions with the mower), dressed in jeans and a striped rugby shirt. He stuck out his hand and said, "Josip", to which I responded, "Nick, English". I added "Bobovac?" hopefully, referring to the ruins of an old fort nearby, at which point Josip looked quite animated and indicated that I should get my car. We set off, pausing only to put away the mower and collect a large key from his home.

We turned onto a rough track, having by now established between us a polyglot language blending Serbo-Croat, English, Italian, German and mime. He complained about the lack of government support for tourism. I learned that his village was mostly Catholic now - "We had big trouble, boom boom" - but many of the surrounding villages were Muslim. Over the day, we saw a number of impossibly picturesque rural mosques whose wooden minarets resembled outsized chimneys on what might otherwise be comfortable farmhouses. He told me that he had a wife and four children and a taste for *šljivovica* ("Bosnian whisky"), despite the apparent attempts of his wife to control it ("medicine").

We walked through the woods and emerged above the remains of the old walled city. This was the 14th-century stronghold of Ban Stjepan Kotromanić, the ruler and unifier of Bosnia and Herzegovina, and his nephew and successor, Tvrtko, King of Bosnia and Serbia (the latter in name only), a kinsman of the Nemanjas and ally of Lazar. This marked the high point of Bosnian independence, controlling the Dalmatian coast - bar Ragusa (Dubrovnik) - and parts of northern Croatia. After his death in 1391, Tvrtko's successors attempted to contain or manipulate the competing ambitions of Hungary and the Ottomans for their territory. Finally, on 20th May 1463, Bobovac fell to a large Turkish army under Mehmed II, angry that the last Bosnian king, Stjepan Tomašević, had refused to pay the customary tribute. The king fled north but, realising that his cause was hopeless, eventually surrendered on the promise of safety. Nonetheless, he was beheaded, reputedly by the mullah who had issued a fatwah justifying the revocation of the earlier assurance. Bosnia remained Ottoman for the next four centuries.

The view was breath-taking. The ruins are strung along the spine of a ridge, itself set in a deep valley. Brooks far below on either side fed into a steep, tree-covered gully dominated by the furthest point of the old settlement. To one side were wooded hills, in which two hamlets nestled far in the distance, the only sign of human habitation. On the other, forbidding mountains stretched to the horizon. A small, heavily restored stone mausoleum was opened with Josip's key. It was once the resting place for the remains of the Bosnian kings, but now there was little to see beyond an information board, piles of debris and building materials, among which I could discern pieces of carved masonry and burial stones. All were covered with a thick layer of dust and protected by sheets of equally dusty glass, rendering any real inspection impractical. Outside, there was little sign of the four palaces that had made up the royal capital, but the next mound accommodated the ruins of the citadel, and some way below a round pool of water marked the original well structure. Josip and I sat companionably in the sunshine admiring the surrounding scenery.

On arriving back at the village, Josip made a call, said "super good" and sat me in the surprisingly large tourist centre-cum-village hall, indicating that I should wait five minutes. Apparently, we had been lined up to see the monastery with the "*custos*, good super" and an Austrian tour group at 4 o'clock. He reappeared five minutes later with a plate of sliced smoked bacon and cheese smothered with sour cream, accompanied by a delicious brioche-like bread, a glass of *citron pressé* and a small bottle of *šljivovica*. We toasted life and ate; he told me that he was a director of a local tourist agency and that I should help him build a business here in Kraljeva Sutjeska. Well-fortified, we walked up to the monastery, where a monk told us that the Austrian group were running late and asked us to wait a while.

The Franciscans had originally been allowed to come to Bosnia in 1340 by Stjepan Kotromanić to placate the pope, who was concerned about the schismatic nature of the Bosnian Church, understandably isolated from both east and west up here in the mountains, though probably not Bogomil (Manichaean), despite West's belief to the contrary. The Franciscans expanded rapidly in Bosnia, supported in particular by the penultimate king, who allowed forcible conversion on pain of expulsion. It has been suggested that the relative fragility of belief that this engendered accounted for the much higher proportion of Muslim converts here than elsewhere in the Balkans (bar Albania). There may be some truth to this, although the Islamisation of Bosnia took 150 years. Noel Malcolm suggests convincingly that the relatively weak support of both the Western and Eastern Churches for their local organisations coupled with the economic advantages of conversion are probably the root causes. The numbers of Bosnian Muslims were later bolstered by the migration of converted Slavs from the north and west as the Ottoman Empire started to contract at the end of the 17th century.

We wandered up above the monastery to see the terraces of the less defensible old Bosnian royal palace, now just levelled ground. By our descent, the group had still failed to appear, so the monk talked of the history of the Franciscans here while we waited. Historically, they had been the main link for this part of the world with Western Europe, as most recruits had been sent from Bosnia for further education in Italy, Vienna or Hungary. In Ottoman times, the Franciscans were accepted, but Catholics were clearly second-class citizens, their religion perceived by Istanbul as a much greater political threat than the Orthodox Church. The order had consciously resisted Austro-Hungarian attempts to politicise religion for all the reasons that have become so evident since the end of the 19th century, when religious groupings developed into national identities.

After the Hapsburgs acquired Bosnia, the Catholic landscape became more competitive and Vienna-centred, and the tension with the Serbs more evident, especially after the arrival of the Jesuits. This period also saw the last of the church's many rebuildings here. It is a typical basilica for its age and provenance, and the romantic interior fittings are distinctly faded and too sweet for most modern eyes. The arrival of the much-delayed coach party finally allowed us to be whisked round the library and treasury, which were well worth waiting for. The former contains over thirty books that predate the 14th century. In the latter, a small, rough-hewn 9th-century cross from Syria looks slightly out of place in the opulent company around it, as a devout friar might amidst a crowd of robed ecclesiastical grandees.

Before leaving, Josip showed me the oldest house in central Bosnia, built 300 years ago, largely of wood. One terrace ran the breadth of the building on the first floor while another occupied a conically capped dormer projecting from its wood-shingled roof. It was a dovecote for humans. I inspected the tourist accommodation Josip had organised in the village with such enthusiasm that I was offered a directorship in his company. I promised to consider it and to return one day with my family. He had been a very engaging companion for the day.

Travnik

I drove on to Travnik down another beautiful valley, interrupted for a couple of miles by the sprawl of light industry along the road at Vitaz, a site of vicious Croat-Muslim fighting in the war. Travnik was the old Ottoman capital and relatively undamaged during the conflict. West's characterisation still held true: "it has a definite urban distinction, yet it is countrified as junket." My hotel was uncomfortably near the main road, but convenient for walking around the town. I went in search of dinner at Plava Voda ("Blue Water"), where a mountain spring feeds a stream lined with small restaurants on the edge of the town. I sat eating two small trout, freshly caught and fried, to the sound of the water racing down from above. Walking back afterwards, I crossed yet another stream after a hundred yards, when it struck me that running water had provided the soundtrack to my journey through Bosnia - inevitably, I suppose, in a country that is home to such a variety of spectacular valleys and the mountains that created them.

Breakfast the next morning was less appetising; the orange "juice" tasted as if it had been created in a factory, while the tub of chicken paste that I made the mistake of sampling appeared to be made from parts of the bird that would otherwise be unsellable.

The fortress sits above Travnik, its weathered grey walls blending with the outcrops of rock on the mountain behind. The fort is accessed by a stone viaduct whose high arch spans yet another swift stream. Opposite the entrance was the spray-painted legend "Never forget Srebrenica". Despite that, the descriptions of the fort and town in the armoury emphasised the lack of damage to monuments and buildings in the most recent conflict, and by implication the relative harmony of the communities here. The outline of the fort is clear but, other than the walls, only the armoury and the minaret of the original mosque remain standing. "[T]he hard vertical whiteness" of many more minarets contrast with the languid expanse of the town that seems to have settled in the valley below as if it were a living thing. One of them, the 16th-century Jeni Mosque, provided some variation in the line of handsome merchants' houses on the steep street that led me down to the town centre via an underpass. Travnik's historic prosperity was driven in part by its position on the north-south road, but the latest incarnation bisects the town rather too decisively.

Its heart is delightful. A coloured mosque is adorned with painted vines, a profusion of brightly coloured bunches of grapes decorating the upper levels; the building is suspended on sturdy stone pillars, under which runs a bazaar. Supposedly, it guards some hairs from the beard of the Prophet. In the ochre and blue alcove of its attendant fountain, taps emerge from stone scallops for the faithful to wash themselves. An elderly woman in a black scarf sat on a solid black bag catching her breath, holding a walking stick in her trembling hand. By the time I moved on an hour later, she had only moved 50 yards along the street, pausing after every 20 paces to recover again. Groups of men nodded their heads over cups of coffee as they must have done for centuries. The coffeehouses of Travnik were famous in Ottoman times as fora for political debate and as a major source of influence on local policy. The heady mix of coffee and tobacco filled the air, the scent of gossip and conspiracy. Open-arched pavilions set in the pavement on either side of the street marked the burial places of long-gone viziers. As I strolled past a small park, I noticed that the face of a large sandstone bust on a plinth had been hacked off. It was a monument to a Serb Partisan leader who had died in the liberation of Travnik in 1944.

The museum gave disappointingly little insight into the town's history, being essentially devoted to stuffed animals of the world and contemporary local art, but the curator explained to a local taxi driver how to find the Jewish cemetery, which I was struggling to achieve solo. It sits above the town on the opposite side to the fortress. West had been to lunch with a highly cultured Sephardic couple in Travnik, the parents of a woman whom she had met in Sarajevo. He, "a handsome man in his late fifties, whose likeness I had seen often enough in the Persian miniatures, gazelle-eyed and full-bodied"; she, "the more beautiful mother of the most beautiful daughter". At that time, the Jewish community had numbered almost 400; within a few years, all that remained were the low stone mounds of their forebears' graves.

A monument to the victims of the Holocaust was erected here in 1979. I hoped that West's hosts had escaped somehow, but I feared that it was most unlikely. No one really had. In *Travnik Chronicle* (Andrić's other great work, also known as *Bosnian Chronicle*), an elderly Jew says:

> ... big lords are like a big wind; they blow, they break things, they blow themselves out. And we lie low and keep on working and put something away for a rainy day. That's why we last longer and always have something.

Only suddenly, after centuries here, it did not work.

My family had all moved to England more than a century earlier, but it could have been very different. I could understand the reluctance of my father to acknowledge his background, in what must have been a defensive reaction. I think that he wanted to be an indistinguishable part of the British community that he had been brought up in, not least as he had been bullied for his background at school. I could also understand the fierce antagonism felt by those who had lost large numbers of family members in the Holocaust. At times, I had seen that metamorphose into anti-Catholicism, because of the brutality and scale of the camps in Poland in particular, but also because of the perceived equivocal positioning of the Vatican at the time. There must have been many moments when a Jewish Catholic would have questioned his or her faith, but I suppose all religious institutions are by definition human and therefore flawed. We - and they - need to refocus regularly on the underlying principles on which they were founded.

Before leaving, I wanted to visit the Ivo Andrić Museum, in what purports to be his reconstructed birth home, a black and white house with a small courtyard. He moved to Višegrad aged two, but located his second masterpiece here. It is set in Napoleonic times and tells of the machinations between the Ottoman vizier and the Austrian and French diplomats stationed here, while the local community observe and endure. In it he observes:

If anyone wanted to find out about Travnik from two travelers, one of whom had spent the winter there and the other the summer, he would get two completely opposite views of the town. The first would say that he had lived in hell, and the other that he had been close to paradise.

It is clearly viciously cold here in winter, but happily, in early May, I had glimpsed its heavenly countenance.

Before I moved on, I sat in the sun down in the market eating *ćevapi*, small spicy sausages in a split wheel of pleasingly oily bread. The road west there sported the commonplace evidence of recent history in the form of signs whose Cyrillic script had been graffitied over, leaving only the Roman alphabet to provide guidance. It seemed to be the wedding season - I passed two processions of cars with hazard lights flashing, noisy escorts to the mobile confections of lace and flowers bearing the day's precious cargo.

Turning north along the Vrbas valley that ultimately flows into the Sava at the Croatian border, hedges formed an irregular patchwork of high meadows. The ground was so steep in places that it seemed astonishing that the trees clung on instead of joining me in the road. The pale green leaves of spring on those nearer me looked edible. Wisps of low cloud hung in the dips of the hills ahead, radiant in the all but visible sun.

Jajce

Fitzroy Maclean had come to Jajce the day after his parachute drop into Yugoslavia. He had arrived at night and looked "up at the dark shape of a ruined castle rising high above the road. Round it clustered some houses, while the lights of others showed from the other side of a mountain stream. From somewhere nearby came the roar of a waterfall". He had climbed up through the trees and been guided through the crumbling walls, after producing the required password to a sentry who emerged from the shadows. He found Tito "sitting under a tree studying a map by the light of a flickering lamp ... After a couple of rounds of plum brandy we were deep in conversation".

As they talked late into the evening, Maclean had been struck by his "readiness to discuss any question on its merits and, if necessary, to take a decision there and then". He was surprised to find "such independence, in a Communist". At the end of their conversation, Maclean asked whether the new Yugoslavia would be an independent state or part of the Soviet Union. Tito paused before saying:

> You must remember ... the sacrifices which we are making in this struggle for our independence. Hundreds of thousands of Jugoslavs have suffered torture and death, men, women and children. Vast areas of our countryside have been laid waste. You need not suppose that we shall lightly cast aside a prize which has been won at such cost.

I had come by daylight, ascending the paved streets that led to the castle on foot. There was not a car in sight. The fort commands views on all sides from its broad battlements. A group passed me saying "Game of Thrones" with enthusiasm, and it is certainly a telegenic setting, looking out over the steep black pyramids of the roofs, the wooden minaret of an old mosque and the mist-decked hills in the distance. Each house seemed to boast a well-tended vegetable garden with ordered rows of onions and rings of twigs guarding young plants from predation. A few were in obviously poor condition, rusty corrugated iron sheets just about clinging on above an abandoned structure. Others were still marked with bullet wounds.

Jajce had a hard time of it in the Bosnian War. It was besieged by Serb forces virtually from the outset, resulting in the departure of its minority Serb population either voluntarily or by force. It finally fell at the end of October 1992 amidst heavy bombardment, resulting in a column of 30,000 refugees fleeing to Travnik. It was recaptured by the Croat-Bosniak forces late in 1995, although in 1997 returning Muslims were initially barred from entry in violent scenes orchestrated by the Croat war criminal, Dario Kordić. The population is now roughly split between Muslims and Croats, but around a third smaller in total than it was before the war.

The upper town cannot look very different to the scene that welcomed West or Maclean. The medieval belltower of St Luke below the fort marks the site of old St Mary's Church, where Stjepan Tomašević, last King of Bosnia, was crowned in 1461. Two years earlier, he had married the 12-year-old daughter of a late Serbian despot, who brought with her a relic of St Luke and the right to use again the inaccurate title of King of Serbia, albeit only briefly as it transpired. By the age of sixteen, she was a widow and living in a Venetian monastery, while her hosts negotiated the purchase of the family heirloom. Jajce clung on as a semi-independent Hungarian protectorate for another sixty years, surviving on food convoys from the north, before finally falling to the Ottomans in 1527. The church became a mosque but, since a fire in 1832, only the stone shell remains.

Close-by are the catacombs. Access required the reluctant assistance of a lady from the town museum, who unlocked the gate in the little stone temple that guards its entry. Down in the dark, the ante room has indistinct carvings of the coat of arms of a 15th-century duke (a replica of those over the gate in the fort above) and a female figure with a lily in her hand. Below them, vaults are carved out of the rock. Still deeper lies the dark crypt, where a massive rock shelf forms an altar of one piece with the slab that juts up behind. In it is carved a rudimentary cross flanked by a sun and crescent moon, made more mysterious by their negative space. To West, it had evoked "a temple excavated from the ebony night, where priests swathed and silent, though putatively *basso profundo*, inducted the neophyte by torchlight ... to the inmost and blackest sanctuary, where, by bodiless whisper or by magic rite brightly enacted against the darkness, The Secret was revealed". She went on to ask herself "why, if this Master of Mysteries was so powerful, he had to do his work downstairs?" She was right; the darkness evoked mystery and superstition. Enlightenment belongs where its name suggests. This was a place of burial rather than worship.

Down the hill is a temple of Mithras, from the 3rd or 4th century, newly uncovered in West's day during the course of a building project; she was shown it in a shed in an orchard. Now it is in a side street sitting above the Hotel Turist in its own glass enclosure. The figure of Mithras appears to have arrived at speed, his cloak high above him as he bestrides a bull, grasping its jaw with his left hand to present its neck, while his right hand is poised in the seconds before sacrifice. A snake underfoot lends a sinister air, while a torchbearer stands formally on each side with a stance that suggests they might disclaim responsibility. Mithras is both creator and destroyer, but the key image of bull-slaughter is thought to hark back to a Zoroastrian legend. Mithraism had all but died out by the 5th century as Christianity became dominant and no longer tolerated alternate beliefs. It was a religion that favoured worship and rituals in the dark and it echoed the mood of the catacombs. I was happy to return to the light.

The lower town had its charms too: an imposing stone tower guarded the entrance arch and an Ottoman water fountain still provided mountain water for thirsty passers-by. The Franciscan monastery, built along classic late-19th-century Austrian lines, was clearly an all but total rebuild of raw grey concrete and vivid orange bricks awaiting its decorative finish. It houses the bones of Stjepan Tomašević. The principal mosque required total rebuilding after the war as well. By the fast-flowing river, cafes operated from caves in the cliff face; customers were served on terraces that look out on the mini waterfalls that presage the imminent thundering of the River Pliva into the Vrbas 60 feet below, in the same explosion of foam and spray that Maclean had once heard. It is said that during an Ottoman siege, the young women of the town went to dance in the meadows here to mislead the attacking forces. Each was armed with a concealed knife to protect their honour in the event that the plan failed. When the Turks ran down to seize the women, their menfolk emerged from hiding and slaughtered the would-be rapists.

On the far side of the River Pliva sat a stone building, whose unassuming facade embodied civic duty. Early in its life, it was the local headquarters of the Falcon Society, which promoted physical exercise and national awareness among Slavic peoples. It was founded in 1862 in response to the perceived Germanisation of the Slavic nations under the Austro-Hungarian Empire, its symbol all too evidently harking back to a glorious past. In some ways, this made the building a fitting location for Tito to gather together delegates from around Yugoslavia at the end of November 1943 after his successful retreat into Bosnia following the Battle of Sutjeska. It is now the pithily named "Museum of the Second AVNOJ Session" (AVNOJ being an acronym for the "Anti-Fascist Council for the National Liberation of Yugoslavia").

The interior could be a town hall from anywhere in Europe, albeit dressed for the past. Rows of hard chairs faced a narrow stage, on which stood a long, red-swathed table with a backdrop of two Yugoslav flags, bright red and blue draped against a plain white wall. A bust of Tito stared out, dressed in a suit and tie with high cheekbones and a razor-sharp parting, as good-looking as any film star, confident of both his appeal and his audience. Some of the attendees must have had very difficult journeys to get here, coming from different corners of their war-torn country. Here, they elected Tito marshal of the newly agreed Federation of Yugoslavia; here, Bosnia and Herzegovina achieved full recognition as a state within the federation; and here, the delegates decided to do away with the monarchy, subject to a post-war referendum. At the ceremonial lunch following the session, Tito sent his visitors off saying: "See you, comrades, in Belgrade at the third session." Two years later to the day, the first constituent assembly of the new Republic of Yugoslavia duly convened there.

There are many photographs on show of William Deakin, Churchill's representative in Jajce, and a number of references to Maclean. A letter from Churchill to Tito is displayed. Dated 8th January 1944, it thanks Tito for "your kind message about my health from yourself and the heroic Patriot and Partisan army of Yugoslavia". He promises all aid, by sea, by air and by commandos, with Maclean to be joined by his son, Randolph, at Tito's headquarters. He talks of the "[o]ne supreme object ... before us, namely, to cleanse the soil of Europe from the filthy Nazi-Fascist taint" and emphasises that he has "no desire to dictate the future government of Yugoslavia". He also talks of his resolve to give "no further military support to Mihailović", while making it clear that he will retain official relations with the young King Peter in London. Maclean described "the broad smile of unaffected delight [that] spread slowly over [Tito's] face, which became broader still when he found a large signed photograph of Mr. Churchill in a separate envelope".

I left Jajce pondering how a small town could have been pivotal at so many moments in history, in many ways encapsulating all the major currents that had shaped this part of the world over two millennia. From the Romans to independence, from Ottomans to Hapsburgs, from Tito's launching pad to unimaginable dislocation at the end of the

20th century, Jajce had seen it all. It somehow remained, nonetheless, as pretty a town as I had seen on my travels, surrounded by remarkable countryside. With peace, prosperity should surely follow.

Banja Luka

The valley north became still steeper as I descended between sheer cliffs fringed with trees. At one point, it opened up where a ruined tower high above guarded an old river crossing. As I got closer to Banja Luka, the capital of the Bosnian Serb administration, spotlights strung along the river indicated a particularly well-known stretch for white-water rafting. I was welcomed back into Republika Srpska and noted how the federation never seems to greet one in reverse. Presumably, there are hidden messages here, one of independence and the other of underlying indivisibility. As so often, the police were out speed-trapping in force, thought by locals to represent a revenue-raising exercise rather than any underlying campaign for greater safety.

I entered Banja Luka and was immediately struck by the remarkable number of towns and cities with which it is twinned; a dozen or more, ranging from Moscow to towns in Germany, Greece, Israel, Italy, Slovenia, Ukraine, three in Italy and no fewer than four in Serbia. It felt like a teenage girl trying to prove her popularity by mustering the maximum number of best friends. After several attempts in the pouring rain, I finally managed to locate the Museum of Republika Srpska. One leg of the journey involved walking in the front of the museum of theatre puppetry and being escorted out the back past an obstructive security guard by a pitying passer-by. When I finally arrived at my destination, it was locked. The caretaker, proud possessor of a single tooth (in his upper gum), informed me that it was closed on safety grounds; rain was leaking into the building and it was dangerous. I asked if I could wander around if I did not touch anything, but he said, "No, big danger, walls electric", while patting the walls as if to prove that they were not. I wandered off disappointed, somewhat surprised by the poster-calendar of Slobodan Milošević hanging in the lobby. I sheltered from the rain over a delicious pizza enhanced by a central cone of *kajmak* and a black olive. The background music sounded like the Beatles, but I could have sworn that they were singing "All you need is Slav"!

During the war, Richard Holbrooke had seen Banja Luka as the centre of moderate anti-Pale sentiment within the Serb community, but even here he reported of a visit in 1992 where he had encountered "the occasional house left completely undamaged in a row of ruined ones – its occupant a Serb not a Muslim. Such destruction is clearly not the result of fighting, but of a systematic and methodical pogrom in which Serbs fingered their Muslim neighbours". The 16th-century Ferhat Pasha Mosque, thought by many to be the finest in Bosnia, had been demolished in 1993 by the authorities, although it has subsequently been rebuilt. I found the mood of the town morose, as I had others of its persuasion, but that may just have been the weather.

I wandered around the remains of the old castle briefly but was deterred by the rain and retreated to my car to head north to the border. The almost empty highway stopped in the middle of nowhere, not far from the town of Gradiška, so I tracked to the west following the course of the River Sava and then its tributary, the River Una. Both mark the border between Bosnia and Croatia, and this was the frontier land (Krajina) between the Austrian and Ottoman Empires, where both powers encouraged settlement during the 15th and 16th centuries. In the case of the Ottomans, this was to repopulate land that had suffered emigration into the Christian lands further north; for the Austrians, it was to bolster defensibility. Most of the incomers were Serb-speaking adherents of the Orthodox faith, many of them not Serb but Vlach (traditionally semi-nomadic herdsmen). On the Croatian side, the region had a long history of limited self-governance. It was part of the short-lived Republic of Serbian Krajina, which had declared independence from Croatia at the start of the wars in 1991, supported by Belgrade-directed Yugoslav forces. Croatia had retaken it at the end of the Bosnian War in 1995.

The constitution that was put in place then by the Dayton agreement feels like a staging post, albeit one that has delivered an extended period without armed conflict. The three-man presidency consists of representatives of the main ethnic groups, with checks and balances to try and safeguard the interests of each. It has particular responsibility for foreign policy and the armed forces, leaving the two constituent states to focus on day-to-day domestic affairs. The structure is economically inefficient for a country of fewer than four million people and requires continued supervision by the United Nations, but the US and the international community have invested a considerable amount in this peace and will not want to see renewed conflict. In 2021, Milorad Dodik, the presidency's Serb representative, threatened to pull Republika Srpska out of the joint army, which would feel like the first step to outright secession. Ultimately, the three communities must have an open discussion to find a way forward that they can all live with. To some extent, this is an age-old difference of views between a relatively educated urban (Muslim) community and two communities with small-scale agriculture at their heart. It is made still more complicated by the fact that the latter have neighbouring "parent" countries, while the Bosniaks have only Bosnia.

I drove past the sodden fields that flanked the river on the Bosnian side. The weather was vile. A cluster of hunched egrets had puffed themselves up into near spheres in an attempt to keep out the driving rain. At times, the river vanishes from view, and you feel that you could walk across a couple of fields and start to climb the wooded hills of Croatia on the far bank, but only twenty years earlier, this had been a real front line. I reached the crossing point at Kostajnica, where I joined a long line of cars waiting – mostly – patiently to cross the border. The high street looked quite unremarkable, apart from the local appetite for pale purple paintwork. Eventually, I turned the corner into the town square, a collection of largely empty cafes and bars centred around a grim grey block capped with a red star – the town war memorial for the dead of the Second World War. Exiting the square on the far side, the checkpoint was sandwiched between the Caffe Bar Gelija and a boutique. The Bosnian and Croatian guard stations stood ten metres apart under a single structure. Neither guard showed any interest in my passport as I inched past, nor in those of the various couples who walked through in each direction. A far cry from the regular exchange of shots and shouts and the destruction of the bridge over the river here in 1995.

I drove slowly to the far bank from the 14th-century fort on one side, built by the Frankopans to keep out the Turks, to the large, evidently restored Catholic church flanked by derelict houses on the other. Between 1991 and 1995, much of the old town on the Croatian side had been wantonly destroyed by the Serbs, then a majority of the population, now representing only a quarter. I ascended the hill, noting how there was something about the orderliness of the streets and buildings that instantly signalled one had crossed the historical line between the Ottoman and Austrian domains. An hour and a half later, I was in Zagreb.

Croatia

"... formality ... comes of being watched all the time by people who thought they were better than you ..."

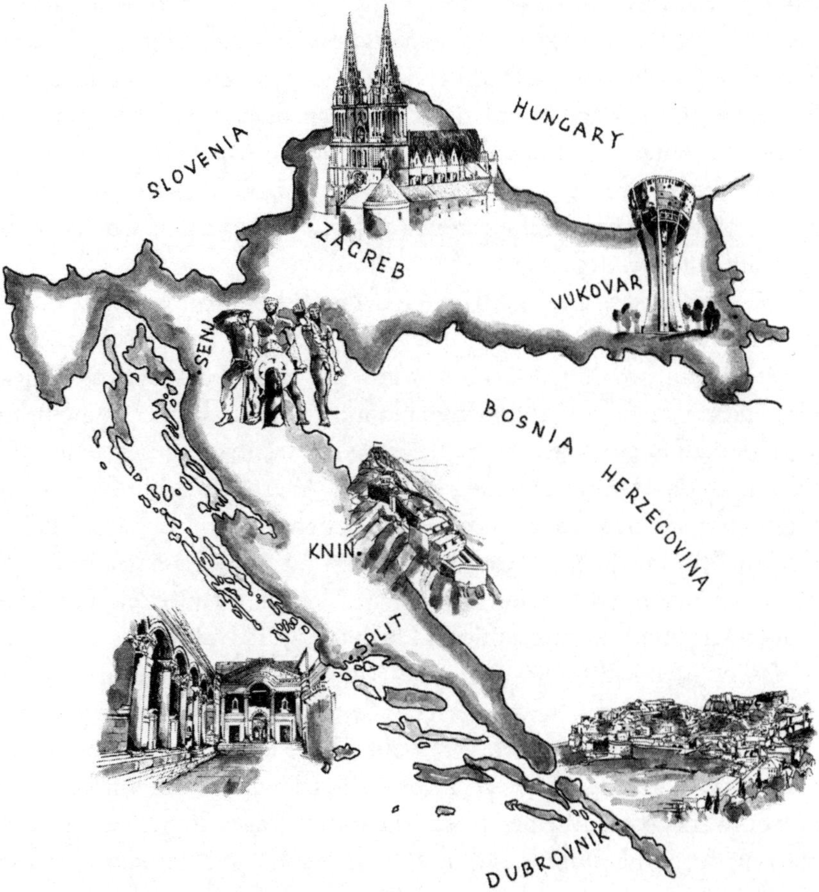

SLOVENIA
HUNGARY
ZAGREB
VUKOVAR
SENJ
BOSNIA
HERZEGOVINA
KNIN
SPLIT
DUBROVNIK

Osijek

After many weeks of solitary travel, my wife, Sarah, agreed to accompany me on the last leg of my exploration. It seemed fitting, as West had travelled with her husband on one of her three trips to Yugoslavia. Moreover, both Zagreb and the Dalmatian coast were well tuned to foreign travellers, so I should for most of the trip be able to deliver a consistent degree of comfort that had not been available until now. However, there were still elements of history ahead that would be no less difficult to experience.

We drove east from Zagreb on the Belgrade-bound motorway through the broad agricultural plains of eastern Slavonia. Endless fields were broken by an occasional stand of trees. We turned off towards Osijek, the region's main city, following an almost deserted road. Sometimes, a car parked at the edge of a field seemed to testify to the presence of a fisherman or a farmer checking his crops. After passing through undistinguished suburbs, we rounded a slight bend to find ourselves in the city's handsome, late-19th-century centre. A turn down a narrow alley by the watermelon-red Pansion Strossmayer led us off to explore, with a strict instruction from reception to be back by 11 o'clock.

Osijek is only 20 miles from the Hungarian border and its heart is Austrian, built in two main phases. The first involved the construction of the sprawling fortress of Tvrda after the Hapsburgs had cemented their control of Croatia at the Treaty of Karlowitz in 1699. It was built as a bulwark against the perceived threat to the agricultural heartland of Slavonia from the Ottomans only 100 miles away in Belgrade. The commercial centre developed almost 200 years later, spurred by Osijek's importance as a centre for timber and wood-working industries. The not drastically over-ornamented civic buildings show the prosperity of the city as it entered the 20th century, although the restored yellow ochre of the town theatre was slightly compromised by the McDonald's that had taken up residence in its left flank. Opposite, the multi-tiered neo-Gothic spire of the red-brick Church of St Peter and St Paul towers above the surrounding roofs. Inside it, the frescoes, painted during the Second World War by the Croatian artist, Mirko Rački, might easily grace a Ladybird book. The shrunken head and curious angle of the risen Christ suggests that he is falling backwards in an act of surrender rather than ascending to heaven.

At the Gallery of Fine Arts, the theoretically impressive permanent collection was in storage while two less appealing temporary exhibitions had been staged. Sarah chatted to the museum's guardian about local artists, asking if he was one too. As it turned out, he was a structural engineer, "but a job's a job".

The main road leading to Tvrda was flanked by sizeable mansions from around 1900 in the Jugendstil (German Art Nouveau). They were highly visual, but their pastel shades were overwhelmed by the variety of decoration that their original owners had commissioned. They reminded me of Paddy Leigh Fermor's remark about "the fin-de-siecle stucco [that] might have come straight out of an icing gun"; white plaster floral borders, medallions with trails of swagging and classical heads with elaborate head-dresses competed with each other down the rows of houses. The windows peeping out from eye-shaped undulations in the red-tiled roofs seemed curious as to which of their number would find the greatest favour.

We walked down to the bank of the River Drava, the frontline in the late summer of 1991, when the Serb-Yugoslav forces sought to cement their control of Baranja, the north-east corner of Croatia. Osijek was badly shelled and many buildings in the town still bore evidence of scarring from shrapnel and bullets. At the end of the year, there was near panic here after the fall of Vukovar as the invading forces advanced towards the city, but by then Milošević had engaged in the UN peace process and the hammer blow never fell. Walking along the banks of the glassy river in the sunshine, the events of thirty years ago seemed impossibly close given the tranquillity around us. The onion domes on the butter-yellow towers of the Church of St Michael the Archangel glistened against the blue of the sky behind the immaculate green pitches of a local sports club, the colours so sharp that they could have been fixed in oil. Inside, its rococo flourishes were more effective for having been applied sparingly. Five elegant elderly ladies sat chanting their rosaries in a methodical drone.

The great square at the centre of Tvrda is dominated by the pale pink baroque headquarters of the Austro-Hungarian military command, now the agriculture faculty of the local university. Its clean classical lines are a welcome contrast to the empire's later building style. The architectural harmony in the ordered, if faded, streets of the old fort lifted our spirits. People stood in the street attending evening mass at the already full Church of the Holy Cross, built on the site of an old mosque. The many bars and restaurants that inhabit the area began to come to life. We sat in the main square enjoying the gentle human theatre being played out against this elegant backdrop, while deciding which doorway looked most welcoming. We chose well and ate a dark boar and venison stew with dumplings that echoed the vitality of its wild progenitors. Walking back to our lodgings, we marvelled at the tranquillity.

Vukovar

The road the next morning ran again through flat expanses of farmland, with fields of grain or early planted corn interrupted occasionally by vineyards. The villages that we passed through reminded me of their Saxon equivalents in Transylvania; there was extensive German settlement here in the mid-18th century as part of the Austro-Hungarian border policy under Empress Maria Theresa, and the common roots seemed to show. Simply decorated facades embellished the ends of otherwise plain, long farmhouses. Many were accessed by their own bridges over streams that ran alongside the road. Their modern neighbours were less appealing, some presumably rebuilt rapidly out of post-war necessity, often in the violent colours of penny sweets.

We walked into Vukovar through a wide, open promenade with modern, glass-fronted buildings on each side. People sat chatting over mid-morning coffees in the cafes around us. We crossed over the diminutive River Vuka, which flows into the Danube 100 yards or so downstream. On first sight, it looked as though there had never been a conflict here. The sturdy, low arcades that offer shelter down much of the old main street were newly painted, and everything looked orderly and well maintained. As we turned the corner down to the larger river, however, the past came into sight more clearly. The building on the corner was a ruin, although geraniums still cascaded out of the upper-floor window boxes below flapping black plastic agricultural bags that acted as makeshift blinds. Down the street, the pockmarked and graffitied remains of a wall sheltered a small, fully functioning children's funfair. Over one side of the main square that served as a basic car-park, a dingy ochre block of flats looked out to the Danube on the other. Next door, the Yugoslav-era Hotel Dunav, a symbol of modernity in its time, was gradually falling in on itself behind mesh barriers. On the riverbank was a poignant sight: a row of concrete gravestones collapsing back on each other like a row of dominoes. Each had an architectural detail embedded in it - a piece of wrought iron, a grille, a door fitting. It spoke of the devastation wreaked on the town and the murder of its people more eloquently than words. A large white cross not far upstream, where the Vuka joins the fast breadth of the Danube, re-emphasised the point.

Vukovar was one of the epicentres of the Croatian War in 1991. At the start of May, local Serbs ambushed and murdered a busload of policemen who had come to rescue two kidnapped colleagues from the Serb village of Borovo Selo, a few miles north of the town. The local police chief, probably the greatest force for peace in the area, was murdered by one of his own men. The Yugoslav army stepped in "to keep the peace", leaving the town stranded as a Croat island in a hostile sea. As fighting increased in the key border areas of Croatia, Vukovar came under siege for almost three months. The inhabitants of the town held out against intense shelling from the army that left almost no building undamaged. It became clear that no relief was coming from Zagreb, partly because of the difficulties in delivering it, but probably also because Croatian President Tudjman believed that any peace agreement would require him to surrender the town to the new Serb state of Krajina. In mid-November, the defenders were no longer able to continue. Yugoslav army tanks escorted the remaining inhabitants out of the town, primarily the elderly, women and children. Footage of them hobbling out dwarfed by the guns of their armoured "protectors" is heart-rending; some, unable to walk, were pushed in wheelbarrows or carried on makeshift stretchers. Many had been living underground in freezing cellars for weeks by then as winter hardened. The Serb paramilitary forces marched into town chanting: "There will be flesh, there will be flesh, we'll slaughter all the Croats."

We walked up the hill past a mixture of the well restored, the yet to be restored, the new and the non-existent. Occasional ruins were draped off by heavy curtains; it was unclear if this was to shield them from prying eyes or to protect passers-by from falling debris. The earlier elegance of the baroque town is still apparent in the remaining upper half of a pilaster or the head of a putto oddly isolated against a denuded brick wall. The Franciscan monastery that sits at the brow of the hill is gleaming white and beautifully reconstructed. As we rounded the corner to the entrance behind it, four young figures sat outside the school smoking in the sunshine. It was unclear if they were staff or pupils.

Entering the church, we were greeted by a display of before and after photographs highlighting how shocking the destruction had been and how remarkable the rebuild. The pictures from 1991 show it roofless, windowless and with only a splinter of tower remaining. The whole seems to be a melange of collapsed and blackened beams above the vacant gaze of former windows. Some memories have been left deliberately in the fabric of the restored space. A candle sits in a rough hole in a pillar, one of twenty-two drilled out for explosives by the Serbs. The surrounds of an altar are deliberately left in raw brick. A badly damaged wooden Christ hangs on the wall; it had been found on a pile of rubble. They prompt rather than jar in the newly restored white serenity; but looking at pictures of the immaculate frescoes that once covered every inch of the interior of the church, one bitterly regrets their loss.

On emerging, we were greeted by a monk who chatted to us about the past and the rebuilding work. The determination of the desecration had been incomprehensible. The Serbs had tried to tear large canvas paintings of Jesus into pieces and, when that failed, they machine-gunned them. They had disinterred the skull of a member of the Eltz family – the German principal local estate-owners over the centuries – and placed it on top of the family crypt with a cigarette between its teeth. The 70-year-old *paterfamilias*, Jakob Eltz, had returned to Vukovar in 1991 and taken up arms alongside the defenders of the town. We asked about the relationship between Serbs and Croats in the town now – "They coexist but they cannot trust." We were waved goodbye with the gift of a pottery Vukovar dove, the local symbol, a replica of a piece of Vučedol pottery, nearly 2,500 years old, that was found a few miles outside the town on the banks of the Danube at a site that must have been one of the largest settlements in Europe at the time.

Outside, the shattered main bell of the church stood in the centre of a grassy lawn. Looking up to the end of the street, we saw a ruined water tower commanding the otherwise empty space above the low houses; a giant triumphal torch through which one could see the sky wherever one of 600 shells had hit their mark. Prior to the war, it had housed a restaurant at the top. Now, it remains as another reminder of the town's suffering. Miniature versions are sold in souvenir shops.

Before returning to the car, we wandered through the modern market area, where life had the humdrum normality of a midsize town as people went about their daily errands. We bought scented cherries in the market. "Where are you from?" asked the girl serving us. "England." "I wish I was there," she said, and tried to refuse payment for the fruit. We had an all but identical conversation at a shoe shop in Karlovac a few days later. Away from the coast and the capital, the past hovers and life lacks glamour.

At the memorial cemetery outside town, 980 white crosses stand in ordered ranks below an eternal flame burning in the centre of a large, stylised metal cube that echoes their shape. School parties posed around it holding Croatian flags. Behind it, ranks of formal cypresses and tightly clipped conifer hedges frame the grey lines of graves that hold the remains of those who fell defending Vukovar. The severity is punctuated by large box balls and beds of ferns, along with the profusion of flowers that still decorate almost every tomb. The scale of the horror is driven home as one walks past row after row. A few empty rectangles await the now unlikely arrival of their missing occupants.

A larger cemetery surrounds it, containing both Serb and Croat graves, a reminder that this has always been a mixed town. It was roughly half-Croat and a third Serb before the most recent war, but at the beginning of the 20th century, it was 40% Croat and a third German, with Serbs and Hungarians making up the balance. After the Second World War, the Germans were expelled or interned by the communist administration. The aggression has not always been one way. The Croatian Second World War leader, Ante Pavelić, gave a speech in Vukovar in

1941, saying that Croatia "must be cleansed of Serbs and Jews. There is no room for any of them here. Not a stone upon a stone will remain of what once belonged to them". Fifty-year-old speeches and atrocities cannot remotely justify what happened more recently, but they may help explain how politicians in Belgrade and Zagreb could reignite the darker tribal forces that became manifest.

A few miles up the road is a final reminder of just how dark those forces were. On 20th November 1991, two days after resistance had ceased, 261 patients from the local hospital were brought to a local farm by the Yugoslav army, despite earlier assurances that they would be allowed safe passage in a Red Cross convoy. They were mostly Croat, but included ethnic Serbs and Hungarians, Muslims and both a French and a German national, all ranging in age from sixteen to seventy-two. They were beaten up all day by local Serbs and Serbian paramilitaries, who forced the Yugoslav military police to withdraw. Over the course of the evening, all of them were shot. The building was subsequently used as a Serb prison camp. In a large, darkened circular room, its concrete floor studded with bullet cases, the faces of the dead stare out. It is impossible to stand there for long.

Madeleine Albright visited the site during the course of the war, when it was guarded by Russian peacekeepers. The then Serb local authorities were quite prepared to acknowledge its existence but failed to understand why it was a concern to those who understood the history of the region.

We drove on to Ilok, Croatia's easternmost point, where we ate grilled zander on a terrace overlooking the Danube, hard on the Serbian border, which almost entirely encircles the hill town. The lido on the Serbian side of the river was a welcome change from the hostile troops that would have been there twenty-five years earlier. High above, the heart of the old town is still enclosed by its 15th-century walls. They were built by the Croatian-Hungarian nobleman Nikola Ilочки, a claimant to the thrones of many of the surrounding areas from Bosnia to Transylvania. He also rebuilt the church and monastery here, the former dedicated to St John of Capistrano, an Italian Franciscan, now the patron saint of jurists and military chaplains. John – "the Soldier Saint" – had joined John Hunyadi in the successful crusade against the Turks to raise the siege of Belgrade in 1456, but died of the plague in Ilok three months later. The town became part of the Ottoman Empire for most of the 16th and 17th centuries, but soon after its liberation in 1688, Emperor Leopold I gifted it to Livio Odescalchi, a nephew of Pope Innocent XI, as a reward for his efforts in helping to defeat the Turks. His descendants were largely responsible for the development of the local winemaking tradition. The town was little damaged in 1991 as it was surrounded so speedily by the Serbs. The army summoned the inhabitants of the town to a public meeting and ordered the Croats to leave; 8,000 refugees headed west, leaving only a few elderly women and the priest behind.

Djakovo

The order of Ilok suggested that harmony and even prosperity had returned there, but as we headed west, many of the unevenly picturesque villages through which we drove showed signs of the traumas of war. Old homes were collapsing in on themselves while churches had worn onion domes, gap-toothed roofs and partial plasterwork. Newer additions to the housing stock were strictly functional.

Our destination was Djakovo, the see of Bishop Strossmayer, probably the greatest early proponent of the Yugoslav ideal. The twin spires and great dome of his cathedral dominated the landscape long before we arrived at the town. We parked opposite it and resisted the entreaties of the town drunk to sit on a bench and pass the afternoon in his company. It was built in the second half of the 19th century and is filled with light. Delicately patterned pillars, bundled together in a Gothic style, soar to create high, elegant arches down either side of the nave. On the ceiling, gold stars adorn a pale blue sky. The high altar is lit from above by the windows in the cupola, and the figures around the apse and in frescoes high above the arches on each side are lifelike but not syrupy. Adam, clearly modelled on the Sistine Chapel, is overawed but also incredulous as God presents him with a voluptuous Eve, her maidenhead barely covered by tendrils of blonde hair, as if Botticelli's Venus has walked into the wrong scene. The cathedral reflects its patron in many ways – his deep religious beliefs, his love of (especially Italian) painting and his desire for unity among the south Slavs. South Slavic peoples appear in pastoral backgrounds; while an Orthodox woman and a Bosnian Muslim appear near St Peter's throne in the main set of paintings behind the altar.

Josip Juraj Strossmayer was born in Osijek in 1815, of German-Croatian heritage, and was educated by the Franciscans here in Djakovo. His ability was evident at an early age, to himself as well as to others, and he spent time in Vienna, where he became the Hapsburg palace chaplain. At an improbably young thirty-four, he was sent back to East Slavonia as Bishop of Djakovo with a glittering future ahead of him, but he remained in the post for fifty-five years, an idea that must have seemed inconceivable to him at the outset. His plain speaking undermined both his ecclesiastical and political advancement.

Politically, he was the effective leader of the National Party in Croatia from 1860 to 1873. He had been much influenced by the mid-19th-century Governor (*Ban*) of Croatia, Josip Jelačić, and like him sought to promote the greater independence of the south Slavs within the context of the Hapsburg Empire. Jelačić had led the Croatians to fight for the Hapsburgs to help suppress Hungarian dissent, only to find Croatia relegated by *realpolitik* to a subsidiary level again once its usefulness had passed. Strossmayer in turn sought to exploit the differences between the two halves of the empire, refusing to cooperate with the proposed new imperial assembly in Vienna until the nature of Croatia's relationship had been clarified. When Austria and Hungary reached the compromise of the dual monarchy in 1867, Dalmatia and Croatia were effectively split apart, with one in the Austrian sphere and the other under Hungarian rule. Strossmayer's demand that Franz Joseph should equally be crowned King of Croatia in Zagreb if he was being crowned in Budapest was viewed as presumptuous, despite its logic.

In his ambitions to gain greater independence for the south Slavs, he and his friend, Franjo Rački, popularised the use of the term *Jugoslavenstvo* to describe their common destiny, an extension of the earlier, not dissimilar Illyrian movement. He attempted to befriend Serbia but was distrusted, not least because of his Catholic background. In reality, Serbia's view of unity was highly Serbo-centric, with a strong faction believing that all Slav peoples in the relevant areas were really Serbs anyway. Strossmayer's belief in Slavic unity was also reflected in his desire for the reconciliation of Christian peoples, manifest notably in his brave stance against the doctrine of papal infallibility at the First Vatican Council in Rome in 1870; his speech had to be cut short as it could not be heard over the chanting of the doctrine's hard-line proponents.

He was a great benefactor, founding the Yugoslav Academy of Sciences and Arts in Zagreb, launching the upgrade of Zagreb's existing academy into a fully-fledged university, and establishing the Strossmayer Gallery of Old Masters there, to which he donated the 284 works of art that represented its initial collection, strongly tilted to works on religious themes, primarily Italian. They include a brooding diptych of St Augustine and St Benedict by Bellini and an exquisite St Sebastian by Carpaccio. A painting of the expulsion from Eden by Fra Bartolomeo's friend, Mariotto Albertinelli, shows a very different Adam and Eve to those at Djakovo: a guilt-filled Eve, numb with shock, marches from the Garden directed by God's index finger, while Adam looks back, imploring, but with a faint air of truculence.

Outside his foundation in Zagreb stands a fine sculpture of Strossmayer carved by the omnipresent Meštrović. It is more naturalistic than many of his works. West wondered if Meštrović had seen him in the flesh, as he was already twenty-one when the bishop had died in 1905. Strossmayer sits deep in thought; his raised right hand indicates that he may just have arrived at a realisation or that he wants to interrupt someone with whom he disagrees. Either would be in character. The one eccentricity is the way in which his hair forms cloud-like horns on either side of his remarkable brain; one might believe that he is receiving direct celestial input.

We lingered in the cool calm of the cathedral, resisting offers of a guided tour from our friend on the park bench, who had followed us in with an unconvincing air of authority, hoping to raise funds to accelerate his path to oblivion. As we made our escape at the end, he waved from the pavement with a loud exhortation, likely a last-ditch request for a contribution. We headed west across the Pannonian plain. After an hour or so, distant ridges began to emerge to the left and right; another hour on, we turned right towards the more distinct hill that forms the backdrop to Zagreb.

Zagreb

Croatia's capital is delightful but, as Brian Hall put it: "To the Serbs, Zagreb's prettiness is Zagreb's shame." Securely in the orbit of the German-speaking world, it suffered no meaningful damage in either World War, to the extent that it even allowed the Allies to overfly en route to bombing its patron Germany in the latter stages of the conflict on the condition that Croatia itself remained untouched. In earlier times, the Ottomans conquered most of Croatia but passed Zagreb by, their sights set on more important targets like Buda or Vienna; even in the late 18th century, the population was only 2,800. In the homeland war, well away from the border areas that the Serbs targeted, it was largely unscathed physically, if not psychologically, although two Serb rocket attacks on civilian areas in 1995 killed seven people and injured 200. The greatest historical damage to the city structure was caused by the great earthquake of 1880, which wreaked widespread destruction and spurred the mass development of the city in the following years.

In the spacious main square, an equestrian statue fulfils its traditional role of political commentary. In the centre of the plaza named after him, Ban Josip Jelačić, in full uniform with an eagle's plume proudly upright at the front of his headdress, points forward with his sword. When it was erected in 1866, the sword pointed towards Budapest, the city against which he had fought for the Hapsburgs, without achieving any noticeable improvement in Croatia's lot, although its positioning was primarily for aesthetic reasons. His statue was removed in the communist era as an unwelcome symbol of Croatian nationalism, its setting renamed Republic Square. With independence in 1991, the name of the square reverted and the statue was restored facing in the opposite direction, towards the heart of Croatia, and specifically at Knin, capital of the short-lived breakaway Serb state.

Around the corner is the statue of a genial, rotund figure, who could easily have a walk-on part in a Gilbert and Sullivan operetta. It is Stjepan Radić, the *de facto* leader of Croatia in the aftermath of the First World

War and vociferous defender of Croatia's right to a strong voice now that its allotted monarch was Serbian. It was his assassination in 1928 that triggered the move to absolutism.

Above the square are the original constituent parts of the city, Gradec (the old town) and Kaptol (the cathedral quarter). The two had a contentious relationship in medieval times, with regular fights over the narrow stream that divided them. The street on the site of the bridge that used to link the two settlements is still known as "Bloody Bridge".

The construction of the cathedral dates back to the late 15th century, and it was heavily fortified from an early stage to protect it from the Ottoman threat. The present facade is much more recent, part of the post-earthquake reconstruction, made from soft sandstone that has needed extensive renewal. An old clockface on the wall outside marks the time of impact. Around it is the archbishop's palace, still boasting the "squat round towers under their candle-extinguisher tops" that West observed. Inside, the cathedral's scale affords uncluttered space.

There has been one particularly notable and controversial addition since West visited. Behind the main altar, a silver-roofed glass casket contains a life-size effigy of Cardinal Alojzije Stepinac. His eyes are closed and he lies in full red and gold regalia, his right hand raised in a final and permanent act of benediction. On a wall near the sacristy is his tomb, memorialised by his friend Meštrović's stone tablet. It depicts Stepinac kneeling in prayer, clearly seeking guidance; his gaze is firmly fixed on Christ, who stands before him looking down tenderly, touching the supplicant's left brow with his right hand in a gesture that suggests the gift of both peace and knowledge. Both tomb and monument attract a steady stream of believers seeking the cardinal's intercession.

Blessed Alojzije Stepinac was born in 1898 in a village 30 miles to the west of Zagreb, the son of a winemaker, but he was educated from high school onwards in the city. He had fought for the Austro-Hungarian army in the First World War like his later nemesis Tito. Aged twenty-six, he went to Rome to train for the priesthood, becoming Archbishop of Zagreb before he was forty. He was a fervent believer in both the Catholic faith and Croatian nationalism, but in some ways it is easier to define him by what he disliked, a list that included Protestantism, the Orthodox Church, freemasonry and above all communism, alongside swearing, sunbathing and mixed swimming. The advent of the Second World War appeared to bring him what he wanted – a strong Croatian leader who would be highly supportive of the Catholic Church and even identify his regime with its advancement. Initially, fascism seemed an acceptable price to pay.

He was received by Ante Pavelić the day before Yugoslavia's surrender in 1941 and gave him his unequivocal support, "convinced ... that the Church in the resurrected state of Croatia will be able to proclaim in complete freedom the incontestable principles of eternal truth and justice". As reports of the scale of atrocities that were being perpetrated in Croatia grew, so did Stepinac's level of discomfort, but for too long he seemed willing to attribute the horrors to rogue elements in the country and to absolve Pavelić's regime of direct responsibility. In the spring of 1942, he began to speak out about the need to observe God's laws; a year later, he became more vociferous about racism and the resultant evil that was unfolding. He stayed in Croatia, despite threats of violence, when he could have left, and did help the lot of non-Catholics, which included issuing guidance that forced conversions of Serbs could be considered temporary if they saved lives. He also smuggled lists of Ustaše victims to Rome for safekeeping. However, as late as 1945, he was photographed shaking hands with Pavelić and celebrated the regime's fourth anniversary with a service. His uncertain stance against fascism sits uneasily with his more robust rejection of communism. Presumably, that was due to some combination of naivety, his realisation that it was impossible for him to sway Tito, the equivocal stance of elements of the Roman Church towards fascism, and the inflexibility of his internal beliefs.

The Catholic Church was firmly in Tito's sights when he came to power. Religion clashed with his worldview and the Church was closely identified with the wartime regime in Croatia. Undoubtedly, Catholic priests had been involved in atrocities; a Franciscan friar had been chief guard at the infamous Jasenovac concentration camp and the Archbishop of Sarajevo had publicly supported forced conversions. The backlash was savage. On 20th October 1945, a pastoral letter from Stepinac enumerated the number of clergymen who were dead, arrested or missing. Tito retaliated in print, attacking Stepinac as a fascist sympathiser. The following year, he was arrested, Tito's counterbalance to the execution of Mihailović, showing the Serbs that retribution was even-handed.

Djilas, on a visit to New York, acknowledged to Meštrović that the conviction was unjust. Stepinac served five years in jail and lived out his life under house arrest in his home village. He was made a cardinal in 1953, leading to a severing of diplomatic relations between the Vatican and Yugoslavia, and was beatified by the vigorously anti-communist Pope John Paul II in 1998, twenty-seven years after his death. He and Pope Benedict both prayed at Stepinac's tomb on visits to Zagreb. In 1992, the Croatian parliament had overturned the court decision against him as the country started its independent journey. He remains a divisive figure but a key element in the Croatian nationalist narrative.

I had read that there was a Dürer triptych in the sacristy, so I pushed the door open and entered tentatively, only to be shooed out by a studiedly busy nun. I pointed at the altar within to be told repeatedly: *"Zehn Minuten kommen"*. On re-presenting ourselves as instructed, we were allowed to study the masterpiece. To the left, a stoic, pink-robed Jesus carries his cross out of the medieval gate of Jerusalem towards Calvary, assisted by Joseph of Arimathea. To the right, he emerges whole from a sarcophagus whose lid has been removed by an angel. The central image is more unusual; it shows three figures suspended on their crosses some distance from the walls of the city. All three have their eyes closed, already peaceful in death. In front of them, a large crowd shows no interest in the scene at all; a man beats a boy with a baton, two athletic figures stride along bearing spears on their shoulders in an ostentatiously relaxed fashion while women engage in domestic conversation. A lone figure, scarcely visible at the rear, stares up in compassion. The commentary on disengagement from Christianity and disregard for the suffering of others is all too clear. I wondered if Stepinac had contemplated the image as he tried to decide the best course of action in appalling circumstances. We left surprised that so many visitors to the cathedral would have no idea of its existence.

Outside in the sunshine, the red umbrellas of the main market competed with the brightness of the fruit for sale on the tables that they sheltered. The narrow pedestrianised streets could have been at the heart of any central European town, painted and scrubbed as thoroughly as a film set. At the Stone Gate, on the boundary between the two old settlements, a black-painted grille protects another site of pilgrimage, an icon of Mary that was miraculously preserved from fire in 1731.

Figures knelt on the step in front of the street's side altar, which is barely visible behind the flowers arranged on and around it. Their eyes were locked on the sacred image of the mother and child, both now adorned with jewelled crowns since the fire's 200th anniversary. The walls around it are covered with plaques large and small giving thanks for favours granted over the centuries. I added my entreaties to the mix.

A couple of blocks away is the Church of St Mark. Its present structure is essentially 14th century, but its steeply pitched roof is an arresting sight. Polychrome tiles mark out the coats of arms of the Triune Kingdom of Croatia, Slavonia and Dalmatia and the city of Zagreb. The backdrop and borders are derived from Croatian folk patterns, largely in red, white and pale blue, including those from the patterned aprons made in the Djakovo area. It could be a nationalist billboard, and one wonders momentarily if it is not a publicity stunt. It dates back to 1878, when Croatia was trying to define its own culture in the context of the Austro-Hungarian Empire. Bishop Strossmayer campaigned to restore St Mark's and engaged Friedrich von Schmidt as the principal architect to work on it. Von Schmidt had led the restoration of St Stephen's Cathedral in Vienna, with its own famous decorative tiled roof, and had also completed the building of Strossmayer's cathedral in Djakovo. The garish outcome was not universally popular at the time, but suggestions that the pattern should be toned down or the coats of arms removed were rendered irrelevant by the immense rebuilding work needed after the earthquake. It has subsequently become a lurid totem of the city. Von Schmidt's pupil, Bollé, went on to restore Zagreb Cathedral with a significantly more muted tile roof than St Mark's, but the expense of maintenance led to its replacement with copper cladding in the 1970s.

St Mark's stands in the centre of its square, surrounded by Zagreb Town Hall, the pedimented front of the Parliament (*Sabor*) and the long, low buttermilk and white Ban's Palace. The shutters on the latter were closed against prying eyes on the ground floor but were thrown open above, giving it a surprisingly light and welcoming air, at odds with its function from 1941 to 1945 when it housed the office of Ante Pavelić, the self-styled *Poglavnik* ("Chief").

Pavelić was born near Jajce in Bosnia in 1889 to Croatian parents who had moved there for work. His early life was very humble and he interacted well with the majority Muslim community in his village, not least as the local imam was the only educated man there. His Croatian nationalism seems to have been sparked by a visit home with his parents when he realised that Croatians were not all peasants. He received a doctorate in law from Zagreb University aged twenty-six, but during his time as a student he had been arrested for a suspected part in an assassination attempt on the authoritarian Ban of Croatia, Slavko Cuvaj. In 1927, he was elected to the parliament in Belgrade as part of an extreme Croatian nationalist bloc opposed to Radić's more nuanced dealings with Belgrade. Earlier that year, he had reportedly visited Rome to seek Italian backing for some form of independent Croatia outside of Yugoslavia.

In the wake of Radić's assassination and the subsequent suspension of parliament in 1929, Pavelić fled the country, but not before he had established the Ustaša Croatian Revolutionary Movement (*ustati* being the Croatian verb for "to rise up"), widely shortened to the plural Ustaše. Its aim was to liberate Croatia by any means available and to establish a state that would only be ruled by Croats. It took an aggressive anti-Serb stance.

He spent the next twelve years in exile, visiting Sofia, where he formed an alliance with IMRO, before settling in Italy. He was sentenced to death *in absentia* in Belgrade for promulgating revolution. In Italy, he had informal support from Mussolini, who had designs on Dalmatia, and was allowed to operate training camps. The Ustaše committed a few, relatively minor terrorist acts in Yugoslavia, but following Pavelić's role in organising the assassination of King Alexander of Yugoslavia and the French foreign minister in 1934, Mussolini had him jailed under pressure from France. He was released seventeen months later but kept under house arrest in Siena for much of the time, while his cadre was interned on the volcanic island of Lipari off the coast of Sicily.

With the onset of the Second World War, Italian manoeuvres around the future of Croatia became more intense. They tried to encourage the leading Croatian politician, Vladko Maček, to lead an internal declaration of independence, but he opted to become deputy prime minister in Prince Paul's Yugoslavian government after negotiating significant independence for Croatia (and much of Bosnia). Mussolini's son-in-law and foreign minister, Count Galeazzo Ciano, was sent to engage with Pavelić. As Germany declared war on Yugoslavia in 1941, Mussolini summoned Pavelić, who must have been amazed by his sudden turn of fortune. He was announced as Poglavnik of the Independent State of

Croatia by his henchmen in Zagreb, and Mussolini rushed him over the Italian border to assume his role to forestall any alternative plans from his German allies. There was overwhelming enthusiasm in Croatia at the prospect of independence at last, but the paucity of broad support for the Ustaše would prove problematic for Pavelić over time.

His early actions signalled his intent: he banned the Cyrillic script used by the Orthodox Church in its daily practice and enacted a variety of anti-Semitic legislation. Forced conversions of the Orthodox faithful to Catholicism followed, along with the establishment of detention centres. His negotiations with Italy resulted in the deeply unpopular concession of the Dalmatian coast as far as Split, with the rest of Dalmatia as an Italian protectorate. Meanwhile, a cousin of the Italian king was installed as King of Croatia, although he never visited the country. On an early visit by Pavelić to Hitler, he was lectured about racial purity, although Pavelić's views on the subject were in many ways more extreme than the Führer's. Reportedly, Hitler warned Pavelić, on the subject of the Croatian Orthodox community, that it was "not so simple to annihilate such a minority, it is too large". Hitler would have been well advised to rein Pavelić in harder, as the horrors of the Poglavnik's regime were a significant factor in the growth of resistance movements within Yugoslavia; the following fifty years might have turned out very differently had he done so. A photograph shows Pavelić, beetle-browed, with unnaturally large earlobes, displaying an air of guarded concentration as he witnesses an exchange between Hitler and Goering at the Berghof, Obersalzberg. His manner suggests a desire to be part of the cabal of power while simultaneously fearful of saying the wrong thing and being excluded.

By the end of the war, most of the Gypsies and as much as 75% of the Jewish population of Croatia and Bosnia had been killed, the latter despite Mrs Pavelić's part-Jewish heritage. The Poglavnik's greater target was the population of close to two million Serbs; 300,000 had fled or been deported, in addition to the killing of probably two thirds of that number. The brutality of the Ustaše camps, mass killings, forced conversions and deportation transports appear to have been among the worst in Europe, with many of their war crimes carried out with glee and in a competitive, even exhibitionist spirit. The volume of bodies floating down the Sava from Croatia clogged the bridges of Belgrade in 1942, and then again in 1944 as the Ustaše tried to clear the evidence from their camps when defeat was looming. Even the local German military leader, long-time Nazi general, Edmund Glaise-Horstenau, protested both to Pavelić and to Berlin about the nature of the atrocities and their counter-productive nature, rather more vociferously, it could be argued, than Bishop Stepinac. He was ultimately removed from his post to allow the continued implementation of ethnic cleansing.

The complete alienation of the Serb community, along with the distaste felt by the majority of Croats, appalled by what they were witnessing, meant that Pavelić's government swiftly lost authority, while the resistance movements gained recruits. Eight months after he had assumed power, he could only really control about a third of his nominal territory. He claimed Dalmatia as Croatian after the fall of Mussolini, but the Partisans managed to gain control of the majority of the Italian army's weaponry; by 1944, Pavelić was in practice little more than Mayor of Zagreb. As Germany collapsed, Pavelić and his troops headed to Austria. Many of them were cornered by Partisan troops or sent back to Yugoslavia, where they faced summary retribution. Some 50,000 men, with another 30,000 women and children, were executed by the Partisans over a five-day period. Pavelić himself escaped to Italy and ultimately made his way to Perón's Argentina. There, he set up a construction company and tried to remain politically active. He was subject to a number of assassination attempts directed by the Belgrade government and was seriously wounded in a gun attack in 1957 by a former Chetnik. By then, Perón had lost power, and to avoid extradition to Yugoslavia, Pavelić moved to Spain, where he died of complications relating to his bullet wounds in 1959.

He is buried in surprising style in a private graveyard in Madrid. The grave was desecrated in 2019, and there have been suggestions in Spain that Pavelić should be moved to a less prominent site or sent back to his homeland – not that the now largely Serb population of his childhood home of Jezero would be likely to welcome him. The memory of the all but inconceivable brutality that he directed would be the touch paper to ignite the horrors that unfolded fifty years after his installation.

We wandered back down the hill, dropping in on the Museum of Broken Relationships, where a series of exhibits illustrates a detail of various failed pairings – a drawing of a couple made by a stranger when they were still together, the axe with which he chopped up her furniture, the boots that she hid when she discovered that he was cheating on her, alongside surprising corporeal remains. Each is accompanied by some description of the break-up. Most are poignant, some funny, and the whole presumably therapeutic for those dealing with the potential end of a relationship. In the shop, I bought a "bad memories eraser" for a daughter who I thought could use one.

A ten-minute cab ride up the hill brought us to the Mirogoj Cemetery, the resting place of the great and the good. It is a remarkable edifice designed by Hermann Bollé, who is also buried here. Work had started before the 1880 earthquake, although it was only completed some fifty years later. A great green copper dome rises behind a formal pedimented entrance, with creeper-covered arcades sweeping to each side. Smaller, more oriental versions sit atop the regular balustraded buttresses of the outer walls that stretch far into the distance. One might be entering the palace of an exotic potentate.

The geometric black and white marble floor of the arcades led us past simple tablets and ornate monuments, many set between unlit black wrought iron lamps. An austere white bust marked the tomb of Strossmayer's friend, the historian Franjo Rački. A black bust of Radić on a white column is centred beneath one of the subsidiary domes, surprisingly understated given his status in Croatia's history. It is flanked by the tablets of his two successors as leaders of the Croatian Peasant Party. On the left is Vladko Maček, who opted for independence within Yugoslavia rather than a deal with Mussolini, and spent months interned at Jasenovac before seeing out the war under house arrest. On the right is Maček's anointed successor, Juraj Krnjević, who spent the war in London as part of the royalist government-in-exile, in the difficult position of trying to protect Croatia's position in a Serbian-led enterprise that was fast losing relevance.

Beyond the formal structure, the trees and monuments stretch in every direction. A gold lion asleep on a massive black plinth commemorates early members of the Illyrian movement who were killed by the Austrian army when they demonstrated against vote fraud in 1845. A tablet remembers the victims of Bleiburg, the members of the Ustaše forces and their travelling companions who were slaughtered by the Partisans in Carinthia at the end of the Second World War.

A simple black grave contains the remains of the great Croatian soprano, Milka Ternina, who sang at the Moscow concert to celebrate the inauguration of Tsar Nicholas II and also premiered the role of Tosca at both the Royal Opera House and the Metropolitan Opera in New York, the latter alongside Enrico Caruso. She was a great Wagnerian but angered Cosima Wagner when she sang the role of Kundry in *Parsifal* in its first Metropolitan production in 1903, which the composer had stipulated should only be performed in his home theatre at Bayreuth. Fresh flowers and a photograph adorned her grave, and I noticed that the previous day had been the 75th anniversary of her death.

The grandest of all is the black marble slab right at the foot of the main church, angled up within its generous matching surround on a massive plinth of its own. The gold lettering told us that it was the tomb of Dr Franjo Tudjman, architect of Croatian independence and the country's first president, much revered inside his homeland but a divisive figure externally. The details differ, but the spirit is of a piece with Tito's grave in Belgrade – a monument not to an individual, but to an institution or concept.

Politics here continues to have echoes of the past. The most recent president until 2020, the conservative Kolinda Grabar-Kitarović, was perceived to be equivocal in her attitudes to the Ustaše, making supportive remarks about Croatian war criminals and talking of Argentina as a haven for Croats after the Second World War. She also expressed her liking for the work of ultra-nationalist musician "Thompson" Perković, who has sung songs glorifying the Ustaše regime. Her Social Democrat successor, Zoran Milanović, started his term in office more hopefully by removing the busts of famous Croatians from display in his office, including representations of Stepinac, Tudjman and Strossmayer; the first two went to storage, while the latter was returned to his Croatian Academy of Science and Arts, "where it belongs".

It was time to move on and I gathered my thoughts about Zagreb (and to a lesser extent, Croatia proper), which felt so different to the other parts of the peninsula that I had passed through, other than Vojvodina. Much must be due to its long connection to the powers further north; the Bishopric of Zagreb had been founded by the Hungarian king, Ladislaus, in 1094 and had remained in the Hungarian or Austro-Hungarian spheres of influence until the end of the First World War. Hapsburg rule may have been unpopular at times, but compared to what came after – the vicious thuggery of the Ustaše sandwiched between two spells of rule from Belgrade – it must have looked highly civilised. The citizens of Zagreb feel more at home in Vienna than south or east, something that can result in a condescending manner when dealing with their Balkan neighbours. Meanwhile, Zagreb's relative familiarity to Western visitors has lent itself to tourism, which at times gives it a pasteurised air. Nonetheless, during the course of our stay, we ate consistently well and were looked after with real charm.

West's take on Zagreb was similar:

> It has the warm and comfortable appearance of a town that has been well aired ... [The] past occupancy by the Austro-Hungarian Empire ... always means enthusiastic ingestion combined with lack of exercise in pleasant surroundings ... It has very few fine buildings except the Gothic Cathedral, and that has been forced to wear an ugly nineteenth-century overcoat. But Zagreb makes from its featureless handsomeness something that pleases like a Schubert song, a delight that begins quietly and never definitely ends.

It is truly very easy to spend time there.

Rijeka

We set forth for the Dalmatian coast, but wanted to visit the old Austro-Hungarian fort town of Karlovac (originally Karlstadt) en route. Its star-shaped fortress was built in 1579 on the instruction of Charles II of Austria, one-time suitor of both Elizabeth I of England and Mary, Queen of Scots, forming part of the Hapsburgs' southern defences against the Ottomans, against whom it withstood seven sieges. The main square was clearly handsome once, but two sides were now very run down. In its centre stands a squat granite cylinder with a scallop-shaped basin – the old well; the mournful looking figures on top represent the four rivers of the town. Nearby looms a plague pillar from 1691.

The largely empty baroque town retained a simple formality, with occasional flourishes and a muted palette, although much of the latter was due to neglect. There were still the marks of the most recent conflict on countless buildings, nowhere more shocking than on the local high school. We saw the students emerging happily for their lunch break into the green expanse of the park that occupies the former moat of the old fort, but the walls of the plain white block from which they had come sported an assortment of random pits that could only mean one thing. The southern side of Karlovac was right on the border with Krajina and suffered heavy bombardment in 1991.

The formal white front of the oldest baroque palace in Karlovac is enlivened by rows of sculpted windows. The central one on the first floor leads out to a wrought iron balcony, from which one imagines an address could be made. This was the residence of the 17th-century Karlovac fortress commander, General Vuk Krsto Frankopan, whose family were the ancient lords of the island of Krk. His daughter Katarina married Count Petar Zrinski here in 1641, uniting two of Croatia's greatest noble families. Katarina's husband and her brother, Fran Krsto Frankopan, plotted against Austro-Hungarian rule, angered by the relative independence afforded by the Hapsburgs to non-Croat settlers to encourage immigration into neighbouring Krajina, and also by their reluctance to push back the boundaries of the clearly weakening Ottoman Empire. The two brothers-in-law hawked the poisoned chalice of the Croatian crown to France, Poland and then to Istanbul. As news leaked out, they launched a failed rebellion in March 1671. Both were executed in Vienna at the end of the following month and Katarina sent to a convent. Their estates were forfeit. The Curia Frankopan is now the town museum.

Crossing the River Kupa, we left the charm of Karlovac and turned towards the coast. The landscape changed almost at once. The plains of Slavonia gave way to wooded green hills, much gentler than those of Bosnia or Montenegro, but still home to bears, wolves and lynx, and a welcome variation after a week of endless horizons. As we descended into Rijeka, I remembered West's comment that "no weather can make the Northern Dalmatian coast look anything but drear", but she was there in winter, and by May her grey hills were green.

Rijeka (or "Fiume" in Italian) is also full of faded Austro-Hungarian grandeur. West did not write about the town proper as it was part of

Italy when she visited, one of the earliest victims of Mussolini's expansionism. She had stayed at Sušak, traditionally the Slavic quarter, on the other side of the river that divided the city in the interwar period and after which the town is named (both *fiume* and *rijeka* mean "river"). She complained about the "imbecile" border that she had to cross to catch a ferry on departure: "at places where no frontiers could possibly be, in the middle of a square, or on a bridge linking the parts of a quay, men in uniform step forward and demand passports".

Fiume was traditionally the Italian area, and we found an authentic pizzeria in a pale green covered alleyway, where we savoured the sense of holiday brought on by the Mediterranean atmosphere. Large groups of young people had pulled tables together around us and seemed to be entering and reappearing at random from doors along the passage, as if playing a human equivalent of "Find the Lady". The only door to escape their attention was that opposite us, the entrance to a doctor's surgery, an unpromising spot for a confidential consultation.

After coffee and an ice cream, we walked along the Korzo, the main shopping drag, a kilometre or so long. The shoreline is home to Croatia's biggest port, which served Vienna from the mid-15th century when it was bought by the then Hapsburg emperor. For a period, it was ruled by a Budapest-appointed governor to satisfy Hungarian demands for their own access to the sea. When a young and excitable Meštrović passed through at the turn of the 20th century, he was incensed to find that the officials at the post office refused to speak Croat, offering the alternatives of German or Hungarian alone.

The buildings that face the commercial area have massive ornamental facades. Grandest of all is the ferry company's Adriatic Palace, an excessively high baroque building of the late 19th century; at the top of the pillars above its grandiose butterscotch and white exterior stand four life-size seafaring action figures. Nearby, the early 20th-century Capuchin Church of Our Lady of Lourdes is a successful blend of palazzo and Tuscan cathedral, whose double staircase ascends from the piazza to meet an imposing main archway set in horizontal bands of brick and white stone. Much of the money seems to have been raised for it by a tame fraudster of the friars, "St Johanca", who would sweat blood on demand until his arrest in 1913.

Over the river in Sušak are the ship repair yards, which give its waterfront a much more industrial air, although looking up the hill, the faded, grand 19th-century buildings retained "a brown matter-of-fact handsomeness". We retraced our steps and climbed on the Rijeka side. The old city gate was converted into a clocktower in the late 18th century as part of the rebuild that followed an earthquake in 1750. Hapsburg Emperors Charles VI and Leopold I preen themselves above the archway that leads to the heart of the old town. A few blocks above, we found the Maritime and History Museum, described by Osbert Sitwell as being "built in the well-known Renaissance-elephantoid style that is the dream of every Municipal Council the world over – for it had formerly been the Town Hall". He was visiting it while it fulfilled another function, that of the palace of Gabriele D'Annunzio, in his short-lived role as Comandante of Carnaro and the successive Free State of Fiume, which he ruled for fifteen months from 1919 to 1920.

D'Annunzio was so multi-faceted that he is impossible to define clearly; primary labels include self-publicist, poet, war hero, philanderer and extreme aesthete. The voluptuous and often violent style of his literary works had made him a towering and much-translated figure across Europe by the end of the 19th century. He turned to drama and wrote a number of successful plays, one for Sarah Bernhardt, another – *Francesca da Rimini* (based on an episode from Dante's *Inferno*) – for his lover, the actress Eleonora Duse. Its tale of the tragic and differing desires of three ill-matched brothers for the deceived Francesca, referencing Tristan, Isolde, Lancelot and Guinevere, was later turned into an opera by Zandonai and is still performed fairly regularly. D'Annunzio also worked with both Puccini and Mascagni.

His earnings were considerable, but his love of luxury even more so, necessitating a move to France to evade his creditors. There, he co-wrote a musical play with Debussy for Ida Rubinstein, *Le Martyre de Saint Sébastien*, a play that so outraged the Church authorities that they blacklisted all D'Annunzio's works. Despite his short stature, he appeared to have a magnetic attraction for women, a reputation that he promoted keenly, even reportedly dressing as a woman himself to visit his residence on a white horse at night to suggest the existence of a mysterious love in a lull between affairs.

He had agitated for Italy to join the Triple Entente at the start of the First World War and had raised his profile further by becoming an active fighter pilot at the age of fifty-two. At the end of the war, he was outraged that the majority-Italian Fiume looked likely to be ceded to Yugoslavia under the terms of the Treaty of Paris rather than joining Trieste as part of Italy. Claiming that Fiume was "Italian by right of landscape", he led a liberating force of irregulars to take control of the city. Flowers were strewn in their path as their pilgrimage advanced. With an array of medals and wearing a full black and silver uniform of his own design, he faced down the Italian general who had been ordered to stop him with the words: "All you have to do is order the troops to shoot me."

The substantial stone balcony that projects from the "palace" over the arches of the drive-through entrance hosted regular interactions between D'Annunzio and the crowds outside, where he would make emotional speeches and try to discern the peoples' will in what he claimed was the first example of true dialogue between leader and people since the Greek era. His magnetism was such that he had to dissuade new recruits from coming as it became impossible for the city to cater for them. Sitwell described him as having "a face of rather Arab cast" and bearing a strong resemblance to Igor Stravinsky. By then, he was completely bald and had lost his left eye in a flying accident. Sitwell found the new principality to be "full of paradox and of hope, as well as of a certain menace". D'Annunzio seems to have relished the role but, "surrounded solely by peasants and soldiers", was prone to boredom.

The end came swiftly. The Italian government had denounced D'Annunzio's escapade but sought to use it to their own ends. Having signed the Treaty of Rapallo, which gave Istria to Italy and independent status to Fiume, they needed to be seen to stand by its terms. Shortly before Christmas 1920, the Italian navy threatened the city with bombardment and D'Annunzio slipped away to save it. He returned to his home at Lake Garda, where he wrote and tried to maintain a political presence. An unexplained accident in 1922 restricted him, but he was clearly an influence on Mussolini and tried unsuccessfully to dissuade him from allying with Hitler. Il Duce was generous to him, probably to dissuade him from any thoughts of rivalry. In later life, D'Annunzio affected a monk-like habit as a sign of newfound spirituality, somewhat undermined by his custom of wearing a mauve silk shirt beneath it. When he died in 1938, Mussolini gave him a state funeral. Fiume's flirtation with fascism, featuring D'Annunzio's love of uniform, straight-armed salutes, balcony speeches and his aura of macho Italian nationalism had been almost a dress rehearsal for the darker performance of the succeeding decades.

Following D'Annunzio's departure, Fiume remained an independent state for three years, but was increasingly plagued by Italian nationalist attempts to take power. After Mussolini took office in 1922, the writing was on the wall, and in January 1924 Italy and Yugoslavia agreed to divide the Free State of Fiume between them. Sitting right at the Italian border and having lost its links to its previous principal trading partners, its importance dwindled. At the end of the Second World War, it was restored to Yugoslavia, along with Istria and various other Italian-ruled territories in Dalmatia. Tito, whether from political expediency or genuine belief, seemed to identify all Italians (and Germans) as fascists. A series of executions and relentless discrimination over the first decade of communist rule led to the departure from Rijeka and Istria of the great majority of native Italian speakers (known as the *esuli* or "exiled ones"). They now represent only 2% of the city's population, though Rijeka resolved to reintroduce bilingual signs from 2018 in a gesture of rapprochement.

That evening, we visited Trsat, a small village a couple of miles away in West's day, now a tasteful suburb on the hill. The earliest record of more than just its then name of Tarsatica seems to be reports of the destruction of the town by Charlemagne's forces in 800 in revenge for the murder of one of his lords here. It boasts two particular points of interest – a Frankopan castle and the Church of Our Lady of Trsat. The former sits high above Rijeka, with expansive views over the port to the misty outline of Istria in the distance. The key buildings have been thoroughly restored, although they had been substantially overrun by a cocktail bar. Young lovers sat around the castle walls admiring each other, and occasionally the view, but showing no interest in the empty tables and chairs spread across the main terraces of the fort. The main attraction for us was the mausoleum, restored by an Irish army officer, Graf Laval Nugent von Westmeath, who had risen to the rank of field marshal in the Austrian army fighting against Napoleon. His portrait shows a thoughtful figure with a cluster of impressive decorations and a fittingly Wellingtonian nose. He had bought the castle above Rijeka, which he had played a key role in liberating. It was one of several that he acquired, though Trsat was conceived not as a home but as a museum to show off his collections and as a final resting place for him and his offspring.

West had seen the "neat nineteenth-century neo-classical temple, built with the fidelity to antique classicism that does not deceive the eye for an instant, so obvious is it that the builders belonged to a later civilization that had learned to listen to orchestral music and to drink tea from fine cups". The inscription on the frieze reads "MIR JUNAKA" (peace for heroes) and one of the two "well-bosomed matrons" that recline on the pediment is still "decapitated by an idiot bomb dropped by one of D'Annunzio's planes". It is flanked by two cockerel-headed dragons, the shield bearers on the Nugent crest.

West had commented on the unusual practice of the Nugents' being buried upright in niches in the wall so that they were ready to meet their enemies or their maker; and also of the surprising presence of a Jane Shaw among the assembled Nugents, an aunt of George Bernard Shaw (more likely a great aunt from a perusal of his family tree). Sadly, there is no sign of the sarcophagi now other than a pile of marble and stone slabs in a lower courtyard, some engraved with crosses, one with a chalice, but none with visible inscriptions.

Nugent's son Albert was an ardent supporter of the Illyrian movement, as was his brother Artur, although the latter was described as prodigal and had to sell off his father's collection of sculptures and Greek vases to the National Museum in Zagreb. Albert's daughter Ana inherited the castle from her uncle; at the castle, we were told that "the people of Trsat remember her as an evil, bad and eccentric woman", although in early photographs she looks beguiling. She seems to have inherited massive debts and rejected help from the local government to help repair her dilapidated property. The castle had contained the column erected at Marengo to commemorate Napoleon's victory in 1800 and removed by the Austrians in 1814. Ana sold it back to the Italians in 1922, who replaced it on its original site in Piedmont. She died in her nineties in a castle whose crumbling nature must have reflected the world outside it in 1941. Twenty years later, the government started restoration work.

Not far away is the Church of Our Lady of Trsat, which has been venerated since it provided a temporary home for the house of the Virgin Mary in the late 13th century on the journey to its ultimate destination at Loreto on the other side of the Adriatic. The journey is said to have been effected by four angels, who sought to rescue the sacred dwelling from likely Muslim destruction in the wake of the fall of Acre, the last crusader state. It is more likely that it was the result of the close relationship between the Frankopans and the Angevin rulers of Naples, who had married off a son to the daughter of the Despot of Epirus with a dowry listing "the holy stones from the house of Our Lady". It is claimed that it had been in use as a church in the Holy Land since shortly after the Crucifixion, subsequently protected within a basilica built by the Empress Helena, which superstructure accounts for its Roman appearance. Its arrival had been foreshadowed by a vision of St Francis of Assisi, who had been shipwrecked here en route to Syria in 1212. After its departure, Pope Urban V gave the Trsat church a miraculous icon of the Virgin Mary, possibly painted by St Luke, to ameliorate the loss.

The exterior of the church is unremarkable, although it has been lavished with ornate altars and chapels within. The icon is in the treasury of the monastery, but a steady stream of supplicants prays in front of the copy that occupies the main altar. Its romantic richness looks quite unlike the image of the naive original in the guidebook. A deep groove in the floor leads behind the altar screen and back again, the path to the icon and the "stone from the house of the Annunciation" on show there. Below in the crypt lie the 15th-century Frankopan founders of the Franciscan monastery. Off a cloister beside the church is the chapel of votive gifts, where neat lines of chairs occupy a room that at first sight looks like a school arts and crafts display. Every inch of the walls is filled with artefacts that have been presented over the years, paintings, framed pieces of lace, carved ships and more, gestures of gratitude for prayers heard. To my jaundiced eye, the joy of the givers would clearly have been greater than that of the receivers.

Up the hill, we found a restaurant that specialised in truffles and gorged ourselves on ravioli and veal infused with their earthy scent. The menu rather charmingly advertised "first-rate saltwater fish" and, less appetisingly, a variety of foal dishes. When we finally decided to head down the hill, our taxi driver bemoaned the state of the local economy. The only boats now built in Rijeka are ferries, and many of the big local employers went out of business in the years after independence. Like much of Dalmatia, the best hope for recovery is tourism.

Breakfast in the Grand Hotel the next morning suffered from the habitual curse of out-of-season large hotels, a buffet of considerable variety and indifferent quality. The orange juice was a faintly flavoured clear liquid, one of six otherwise tooth-clenching alternatives on offer. Two varieties of filming sausage, limp bacon and a choice of solidifying scrambled or fried eggs looked unlikely to be consumed by any fellow guests at the very few occupied tables in the extensive dining room. It was unclear if the brown liquid from the coffee urn was intended to revive the consumer or scour the container.

Senj

We drove south out of Rijeka and along the coast road. Throughout our travels in Croatia, there was a preponderance of billboards advertising Italian bikinis and underwear. May must be peak season for the former. The pictures revealed an alarming complexity of design but, as my wife observed, the Italians tend to dress from the inside out while the British dress from the outside in. As with architecture, they favour the rococo while we prefer baroque.

Round corner after corner, terracotta clusters nestled in bays. Handlebar-moustached Slovenian bikers seemed to be the principal road users, but they showed a surer and better-mannered sense of the road than the locals that I had encountered at many points on my travels. Out to sea, islands were often denuded on the land side where the Venetians had stripped sheltered coasts of trees to construct their fleets. The resultant erosion of topsoil makes the prospect of reforestation look all but impossible.

Senj was once the home of the fearsome Uskoks, and crossing from the harbour carpark into the town, the first sight that greets one is three life-size piratical figures in bronze. It is sheltered from the Adriatic proper by an archipelago of islands and relatively shallow channels, and thus provided a base once upon a time for a cadre of refugees who had helped to defend the Austrian border against the Ottomans near Split. They were reinforced over time by a variety of freebooters and collectively honed their seafaring skills in small boats, allowing them to raid passing Ottoman vessels from Senj, which was impenetrable to the fleets of the great powers and well protected from the land by mountains. Initially, they were encouraged in this by the Venetians and the Hapsburgs, although the situation changed once Venice started to guarantee the safety of Ottoman trading ships in the mid-16th century. With the Venetians taking the Ottoman side, they too became legitimate targets in Uskok eyes, resulting in both their ships and Dalmatian territories suffering Uskok raids. The Hapsburgs remained discreetly supportive, not least as a portion of the Uskoks' substantial booty found its way to Austria. There was considerable savagery on both sides; the Uskoks reportedly fixed turbans to their Turkish prisoners' heads with nails and would drink the blood of their enemies or flavour their bread with it; meanwhile, the Turks would cover naked Uskok prisoners with sweetmeats, tie them to a tree and leave them to the local wildlife. All parties practised head-collecting, the Venetians displaying a substantial collection in St Mark's Square in 1613. For almost 100 years, the Uskoks continued their way of life until 1618, when the Hapsburgs and Venetians agreed that the scale of their piracy had become intolerable. They were dispersed, many to Slovenia, and some to the area around Karlovac.

The town itself was full of architectural interest, the handsome harbourfront mansions showing what a thriving port it must have been after the Uskoks had gone. A saint in a loincloth looked down from the top of a pillar on a corner, his frame too full to be a natural stylite. Many houses have key features in stone, arched entrances and solid window frames with ancient grilles. Some of the original co-cathedral from 1169 was still visible, but it had been much rebuilt of necessity after the Second World War. The Partisans used Senj as a supply port after the Italian surrender, and it was bombed heavily by the Luftwaffe, who destroyed half the town's buildings. It is surprising that it still feels so timeless.

A monumental gate with a crowned medallion bore the legend "JOSEPHINAE FINIS". It marked the end of the Josephina, the 18th-century road that linked Senj to Karlovac. It was built on the instruction of the Hapsburg Emperor Joseph II, who is said to have realised how bad the access had become after he fell from his horse near the Vratnik mountain pass linking the coast to the plains ten miles to the east. Distances are given for all points to Vienna, which on my reading was 63 hours distant by horse via Zagreb at the 21-hour mark. Sadly, the coming of the railway from Rijeka to Karlovac in 1873 turned Senj into a backwater.

Through the gate, one can glimpse the well-restored Uskok fortress that looks down on the town from the top of a wooded hill, but Senj was a thriving town even before its most infamous era. A plaque commemorates the Senj Statute that granted the town a privileged position in 1388. A bust remembers Blaž Baromić, who set up Croatia's second printing press here a century later, printing one of the earliest Glagolitic missals. Another bust is of Senj's most eminent son, Nikola Jurišić, the Hapsburg general who stalled the advance of Suleiman's army towards Vienna at Kőszeg Fort on the Hungarian border in 1532 with fewer than 1,000 soldiers against an Ottoman force more than 100 times larger.

We found lunch in a courtyard, the tables set under the arches of a colonnade carved with delicate ropes of vegetation. Here, eating fresh squid and risotto marinara, breathing in their freshness, we admired the 19th-century sketches of the town, by which point the castle was a ruin, but the tall houses glowed with prosperity and carts laden with goods awaited instructions by the substantial fountain in the main square. The front of the restaurant sported a picture of a distinguished elderly man with a glass of wine. Expecting to discover another famous native of Senj, we were told that he was simply an old town resident who liked a drink.

Rab

Thirty miles south, we caught a ferry to the island of Rab, having passed the bleak white menace of Tito's infamous prison island, Goli Otok, out in the dark blue water. The Rab coast on arrival is harsh too, a jagged surface of rough, bleached stone that looks as though nothing could ever live on it again, but as we drove over the ridge to the seaward side, the palette was transformed in an instant, with all that was white now green.

The harbour of Rab must still look very much as it did when West proclaimed it

> ... one of the most beautiful cities of the world. It is very little. One can see it all at once, as if it were a single building; and that sight gives a unique pleasure ... The city covers a ridge overlooking the harbour. It is built of stone which is sometimes silver, sometimes at high noon and sunset, rose and golden, and in the shadow sometimes blue and lilac, but it is always fixed in restraint by its underlying whiteness. It is dominated by four campaniles, set at irregular intervals along the crest of the ridge. From whatever point one sees it these campaniles fall into a perfect relationship with each other and the city.

We walked through the near deserted town past a series of white stone churches with their delicate towers. The view out to sea was vivid turquoise studded with other islands, in legend the limbs of Medea's brother, Absyrtus, whom Jason slew as he pursued the fleeing Argo. At the end of an alley, children played grandmother's footsteps, retreating to the start point with remarkable obedience on command. We descended to the main square by walls carpeted with the purple stars of Dalmatian bellflowers. The town abounds in carvings: a lion dances on a wall or sits on a balustrade; worn medallions signal the heraldry of ancient owners; ropes of pineapples adorn a pair of window arches; the head of a man sits above a door scrutinising all entrants, his sumptuous locks complementing his centuries-old foppish hat. From all angles, the campaniles reappear, soaring singly above an alleyway or punctuating the low slope of the old town harmoniously from across the harbour. We ate dinner in the garden of our hotel, savouring the warm stillness, interrupted only by the chime of halyards on masts from the nearby waterfront.

The next morning, I went to mass in the cathedral, a church that was consecrated by Pope Alexander III in 1177 on a site where Christian worship has taken place since the 4th century. Above its main door is an early 15th-century stone sculpture of the Pietà, which West much admired for its refusal to sugarcoat the tragedy: "With a stiff spine, with her chin high, she sits and holds a Christ that is dead, truly dead". There is a desperate emptiness in her stare that conveys the horror of having to live with the loss of her son for the rest of her life. It is heart-rending.

Inside were more carvings; angels and austere saints at the top of pilasters near the entrance guard the font and stand at the ends of the altar rails. A bishop lay vertically (in Nugent style) with arms crossed as he waited for the second coming. The light-filled nave became more crowded. Conversation got ever louder as elderly figures climbed into what seemed to be their accustomed groupings, beckoned in by neighbours or friends. Other than their more modern Sunday clothing, it must have been very similar eighty years earlier. In the front row, a young nun with a gentle smile supervised twenty or so children, most of the girls in deep shades of pink. A row of older girls sat behind the choir stalls, one wearing a grey sweatshirt with the slogan "True Love Forever", a subject that she seemed to spend most of the service discussing with her neighbour. Behind the baldachin, a small choir sang in solemn and moving harmony. The priest made his entrance and processed to the aisle, followed by six pairs of small boys in white robes and yellow sashes being shepherded sympathetically by a burly youth. The priest was greeted by three families, who presented infants to him for baptism that day. After an initial application of ointment, received for the most part with good grace, the enlarged party advanced to the front of the church to the purring of camera shutters.

The mass proceeded much as I had expected, other than the slow pace and monumental harmonies of the set pieces. The word "Hosanna" alone lasted as long as the entire Sanctus in a brisk northern mass, and in so doing seemed to embody the joy of its meaning, entirely lost in a speedier recital. Within these walls, there seemed to be an ecstasy and an elemental quality that predated the colonial formalities of the last few centuries and even reached back to a time when all Christian churches were one. On exiting, I faced the Campanile of St Mary, whose Euclidean perfection West's husband had remarked on, although wrongly ascribing it to a different church. The ascending pairs of windows evolve from single slotted arches on the second storey to double arches above and then to triple, with the topmost a larger four-arched whole, giving a progression of increasing openness as the eye travels up to the delicate balustrade around a spire that points on to the blue sky. "This geometric revelation of a universe in which there is not an angle."

Much of the rest of the island is given over to tourism now, its beaches the destination for a primarily Germanic audience, evidenced by the fellow travellers on our ferry. We spent a happy afternoon wandering along a coast path. On the other side of the island, Kandarola Beach is popular with naturists, popularised by Edward VIII skinny-dipping there with his married lover, Wallis Simpson, while on holiday together, not long before he was forced to renounce the throne. Rab's newfound prosperity must be welcome after centuries of deprivation. It was under brutally exploitative Venetian rule for a century from 1699. Its principal export was salt, which had to be exported to Venice at a price of their masters' choosing, leaving little income and difficulties for the local fishing industry in preserving their catch. Meanwhile, almost all imports had to come from Venice and were likely to be well priced. By the time the Hapsburgs had acquired control of Dalmatia a century later (in a land swap with Napoleon, who had defeated Venice and claimed her territories), the poverty was ingrained enough that it would persist throughout their rule as well.

Knin

We left Rab with reluctance but before following West's path down the coast, I wanted to make one last trip inland. As we climbed from the Dalmatian coast, we looked back at the bleached skeletal outline of the island of Pag, appearing to emanate white heat in its azure setting. Its inhospitable climate produces a cheese from the sheep who graze on its marsh grass, like a slightly creamier manchego with an edge from the brisk air of its wild birthplace. No green could be discerned on the island from our vantage.

We were moving back into hill country, utterly different in feel from the languid coast below. Dalmatian girls were wont to say: "I'd rather marry a Turk than have to go around in black and wear a kerchief." A road sign warned of a school ahead with stick figures running in a red triangle, the foremost engulfed in a bright yellow flash that burst out of its confines. We passed through the town of Gospić, which had been close to the frontline in the war of independence. In 1991, two men were sent from Zagreb to take charge of the defence of the town against the Serbs. They led a brutal pogrom against the town's Serb population, which was followed by widespread looting of the abandoned homes of those who had been murdered or fled. Complaints from locals to Zagreb were ignored as all atrocities could be seen to be committed by the Serb side only. The principal complainant was blown up by a car bomb. Charges were finally brought against five men in 2001, and both the ringleaders were found guilty and jailed. It looked prosperous and clean now, although the now familiar marks of bullet rounds were still visible on some buildings, while on the outskirts one or two collapsing buildings contrasted with their otherwise tidy neighbours.

A statue of Nikola Tesla used to stand in the town. The Serb-American inventor was born in a village nearby and his father had been parish priest here. He is arguably the pre-eminent figure to have emerged from the Balkans in modern times, effectively responsible among other things for the worldwide use of alternating current; as a Serb, however, he does not fit easily into a Croatian nationalist narrative. The statue was torn down in 1992, and the town mayor refused to erect a replica in 2013, insisting that it should be replaced with one of the deceased Franjo Tudjman. Reinstatement finally occurred eight years later. Across the border, meanwhile, Belgrade boasts a Nikola Tesla Airport and the Nikola Tesla Museum, where his ashes are housed in a gold-plated sphere. After his death, his nephew had his personal property and writings shipped over to create a permanent legacy. Having received his further education in Graz and Prague, and spent most of his working life in the US, Tesla had only visited the city once, on a flying 31-hour trip to receive the Order of St Sava from King Alexander Obrenović. Nonetheless, his legacy remains a source of great pride to Serbia.

An hour on, we came to Knin, twice a capital. The great castle on the hill above the existing town guarded the route from Dalmatia to northern Croatia. For almost 500 years, it was the capital of Croatia in a variety of guises until it fell to the Ottomans in 1522 after several decades of failed attempts. Migration, initially from Bosnia and latterly from the surrounding rural area, changed the population mix radically over time. During the Second World War, it was a centre of Chetnik activity, and as Yugoslavia started its fragmentation, the great majority of its population was Serb. In 1989, a local lawyer was arrested for agitation in the over-vigorous celebrations of the 600th anniversary of the Battle of Kosovo that featured Milošević's rabble-rousing some 500 miles distant. The sight of royalist flags in the streets was especially galling to most Croats, who equated the monarchy with Serbian domination.

Knin became the centre of the movement to oppose Croatian secession from Yugoslavia, which was unsurprisingly feared. It evolved into a local government for the Serb parts of Croatia, led by a local dentist-turned-politician, Milan Babić. Broadcasts from Belgrade equating Tudjman's government with the Ustaše regime of the Second World War were relentless and highly polarising. In mid-1990, the Knin government set up roadblocks to physically separate their Serb majority area from the coastal regions, and at the end of the year the new administration proclaimed the Serbian Autonomous Oblast of Krajina, even though Knin had never been part of the historic border area. By April 1991, the new state declared itself part of Serbia, no longer within Croatia. After Croatia's declaration of independence in June, local Serb forces, bolstered significantly by the Yugoslav army under the command of Ratko Mladić (then based locally), expanded their territory almost to the coast, linking up Serb pockets while seeking to rid their enlarged territory of its non-Serb population. Following the Vance peace plan in November, Knin declared that the entity was now the Republic of Serbian Krajina, which had grown into a U-shape around the Bosnian border along with the part of eastern Slavonia around Vukovar that abutted Serbia. In total, it represented over 25% of Croatia's landmass, which was all but divided in two, an almost insuperable problem for Franjo Tudjman as president of the newly independent state of Croatia, albeit partly of his own making.

Tudjman had been born in a village north of Zagreb in 1922, 15 miles from the birthplace of Tito. He had fought with the Partisans in the Second World War and worked in the defence ministry in Belgrade afterwards, ultimately becoming a general, unusual both for his youth and being a Croat in a Serb-dominated institution. He retired and returned to Zagreb aged thirty-nine, disenchanted with the superior attitudes of the Serb officer corps and with the tendency in Belgrade to identify Croatia with the Ustaše, which, as a Partisan veteran himself, must have seemed particularly offensive. He felt the slur was often used for ulterior motives to disadvantage Croats. Back at home, he got a job at Zagreb University and focused on developing a Croatian narrative of the country's history. This included questioning whether the numbers commonly used for the victims of the Ustaše death camps were accurate or had been exaggerated for political purposes. In the late 1960s, he became deeply involved in the Croatian Spring, a movement that sought to gain greater autonomy for Croatia within Yugoslavia, calling for fairer representation of all nations in the key Yugoslav institutions, and for more of Croatia's earnings to be recycled at home rather than redistributed to poorer parts of the federation. He was expelled from the Communist Party and jailed as part of the ensuing clampdown. He was jailed again in 1981 for public remarks about both the "brutal suppression" of the Croatian Spring and the persistent linkage of Croatian nationalism with the Ustaše. His view, as expressed in his first election manifesto, was that the Ustaše had indeed been a fascist crime but that there was a sense in which its emergence had been a manifestation of Croatia's desire for independence. This seems accurate, but it was a subtle message and all too easy for Milošević to militarise when the time came. Warren Zimmermann described Tudjman as resembling "an inflexible schoolteacher. Prim steel-rimmed eyeglasses hang on a square face whose natural expression is a scowl". He was not a man to placate those who might fear his policies.

As Yugoslavia entered its final phase, Tudjman launched a new political party (HDZ, the Croatian Democratic Union) ahead of elections in 1990. Its aims had evolved from those of the Croatian Spring to a much fuller form of independence (but still at this stage within a loose Yugoslav federation). The principal focus was on establishing Croatian institutions that would balance the Serb-dominated structures of Yugoslavia. He achieved an absolute majority in parliament, but his assertive positioning on Croatian history caused alarm among the Serb part of the population. This alarm was fanned by insensitivity on his part and attacks on local Serbs by extremist members of his party. Some of his early actions were clearly designed to make a point, such as removing the "Socialist" prefix from the Republic of Croatia. Others, notably the statement in the new constitution that Croatia was the homeland of the Croatian nation and the dropping of the official use of Cyrillic script, may have seemed of a piece with the broader manifesto to the new government, but they engendered considerable fear in the Serb minority, not least in the echoes of the early policies of Pavelić. In addition, the process of starting to rebalance the ethnic mix of public sector entities caused resentment in the Serb community where the job losses inevitably fell. Serbian media broadcast a stream of programmes about Croat atrocities in the Second World War; Croatian television responded in kind with footage of Chetnik equivalents. The instinctive reaction of the Krajina Serbs is all too understandable, even if their subsequent actions were indefensible.

Tudjman appeared not to have foreseen the dangers of creating an alliance between the Croatian Serbs and Serbia itself. The Yugoslav army had started to distribute weapons to the Serbs in anticipation of the potential disintegration of the Stalinist system to which it was wedded. Croatia's police force were not remotely equipped to take on the federal forces, and Tudjman was reluctant to strengthen Croatia's military capacity, in contrast to Slovenia and despite the efforts of his defence minister, Martin Špegelj, to convince him otherwise. As an ex-general, he may have been too respectful of his alma mater. Up until September 1991, Tudjman seemed to be entirely reactive, disbelieving that a substantial part of the country would not obey a democratically elected government or that the federal institutions would wage war on one of their own, albeit in the guise of peacekeeping. It was two months after the real aggression had started before Tudjman finally authorised Croatian forces to surround Yugoslav army bases in territory that he controlled, a policy for which he had effectively sacked Špegelj for promoting only nine months earlier. The shocking upsurge in violence that resulted brought intensity to the peace process, and by the end of the year a deal had been agreed. Serbia and the Croatian Serbs had almost everything that they had fought for, although UN peacekeepers occupied Krajina, against the wishes of the local leadership, who were overruled by Milošević. Croatia had to be content with international recognition of its independence, in large part courtesy of German Foreign Minister Hans-Dietrich Genscher, who was appalled by the bloodshed that the Serbs had unleashed but paid insufficient attention to their rights within the country. Tudjman had achieved his aim, but he also seemed to realise around this time that, if he was to deal with an amoral animal like Milošević, then he would need to adopt some of his tactics.

When the war rolled into a newly independent Bosnia, Tudjman had to make a choice between supporting the preservation of the state as a whole or working with the Croat-dominated parts of the country to join it to Croatia proper. He had long believed that Bosnia's pre-Ottoman status as Catholic rather than Orthodox meant that it sat more naturally with Croatia than Serbia, and that the majority of Bosnian Muslims were of Croat descent. Paddy Ashdown believed that Tudjman had discussed the possible partition of Bosnia with Milošević at a summit at Tito's old hunting lodge of Karadjordjevo back in March 1991, which he had illustrated by drawing a map on the menu for Ashdown at a dinner some years later. Tudjman sponsored a change of leadership among the Bosnian Croats in response to the early wave of Serb aggression, resulting in the establishment of their own autonomous state within Bosnia, relating to Zagreb in much the same way that Knin and Pale did to Belgrade. As the situation inside Bosnia degenerated into a confusing three-way brawl, the Croats became responsible for a number of well-documented atrocities and set up their own concentration camps for enemy captives, where starvation, random beatings and killings were widespread. Tudjman by now felt that if others had camps, the Croats could too. He also used the headlines about the scale of Serb atrocities to begin to test the boundaries of his own manoeuvrability at home. In January 1993, the Croatian army recaptured a key bridge, airport and dam near the isolated coastal city of Zadar. Despite the deaths of two French peacekeepers and resultant UN protests, there was no attempt to reverse the acquisitions. When, post-Mostar, Tudjman was finally forced by his international supporters to accept the preservation of Bosnia in its existing boundaries and an alliance with the Muslims against the Serbs, he appears to have done so on the tacit understanding that he would be allowed to repair his own borders.

On 1st May 1995, in response to incidents in Western Slavonia, Croatia asked UN troops to withdraw from positions in that part of the state of Krajina; by the following day, they had gained control over a 215-square-mile wedge that controlled a key east-west road. In response, the Krajina Serbs fired rockets at Zagreb, killing seven civilians and wounding 200, to universal condemnation. Thousands of Serb refugees fled into northern Bosnia. In July, as the Croats came to the relief of the Bosniak forces in the north-western city of Bihać, just over the Croatian border, and together pushed on with surprising ease into other Serb-held areas, Tudjman saw his opportunity. The barely discernible US disapproval of the Croatian military build-up had heartened him, and a multi-point attack was launched on Krajina on the morning of 4th August. By mid-morning the following day, the Croatian flag was flying again over Knin Castle. Despite Tudjman's assurances to the Krajina Serbs that their property and rights would be protected, they fled en masse into Bosnia; the resultant looting and village-burning by Croats suggests that they were wise to have done so. At the Dayton agreement in November, Tudjman negotiated the return of the last part of Croatia under Serb control, the area around Vukovar. He agreed to a two-year interlude under UN administration; Milošević scarcely demurred. General Rose believed that they had pre-agreed a deal over Krajina in return for limiting the extent of the Muslim victory in Bosnia.

As we neared Knin, the number of abandoned and ruined houses became considerably greater. Buildings had terracotta rims but no roofs, and trees sprouted from within. Windows and doors were of plywood, sacking or corrugated iron. Nowhere was this more obvious than on the high street, where the vacant, unloved runs of houses offered a dismal echo of its former prosperity. Windows were shuttered or opaque with grime, and much-faded paintwork provided only sporadic covering. It was a scene of abandon rather than past fighting and more depressing than shocking as such. The Orthodox church sported new facings, suggesting extensive restoration; its rust-coloured dome, while scenic, suggested that work had not yet been completed. It was tightly secured and had no signage to indicate regular use. A hundred yards away, the Catholic church looked comparatively well loved. The industrial zone contained broken-windowed hulks and no discernible activity. A brand-new church stood nearby, its gleaming white stone and clean angles standing out in the otherwise lifeless shades of the town.

On the hill above is the fortress. The tricolour of the Croatian flag flew proudly over its mass, the banner ostentatiously long. The walls guard a long hill with separate battlements encircling each rocky outcrop. As we climbed the fortified approach to the main gate, the curved walls contained such a density of arrow slits that any more would have called its structural integrity into question. The delicate purple of bellflowers growing in gaps between the old stones offered a homely contrast to its great grey bulk. From the top, one surveys the valleys and hills around with such authority that it must have felt impregnable to each occupier over the years.

An exhibition in one of the buildings gave a Croatian angle on the war years. Posters of the ruins of refugees and the dead of Vukovar were captioned "A shame for Europe and the World on the brink of the 21st century. The Aggressors are Serbia and the Yugo Communist Army". A photograph of the Serbian nationalist politician and war criminal, Vojislav Šešelj, showed him with a mulish group of Croatian Serbs in 1990 waving a flag emblazoned with the skull and crossbones. An "army" beret, banknotes, passports and independence posters from the short-lived state of Krajina sat alongside pictures of the destruction of Catholic churches, including the charred timbers and rubble that was all that had remained of the nave in Knin. Photographs of dead bodies after the rocket attacks in Zagreb felt especially immediate; in one, a passer-by checks the pulse of a figure lying beside a pool of his own blood; in another, a woman lays face down on the pavement in a smart raincoat, her bag still over her shoulder, detailing the instant catastrophic interruption of normal life. Inevitably, there were several pictures of Tudjman. When we climbed to the peak of the castle, there he stood in bronze, his head turned and gesturing with his right hand as if to signal that the territory all around him has been reunited with its homeland. The inscription beneath reads "IMAMO HRVATSKU" (We have Croatia). There is a hint of weariness about him, as if to acknowledge that the road to this point had been harder than he could ever have imagined.

He had come here the day after his army had taken the fortress in 1995 and kissed the Croatian flag on the spot where this statue was later erected on the 20th anniversary of that day. By then, there was a party atmosphere in the town, wreaths were laid to commemorate the dead, and people drank and sang. Among the songs that the band played was the old Ustaše favourite, *Here Comes the Dawn, Here Comes the Day*. Meanwhile, on the border with Bosnia, the Prime Minister of Serbia and the President of Republika Srpska threw wreaths into the River Sava from the bridge that the refugees had escaped over.

After Dayton, Tudjman became less sure-footed. His privatisation programme was perceived to be politically driven and delivered no clear benefits. He reinforced the worst isolationist instincts of the Bosnian Croats, which ultimately backfired on them. The global banking crisis of 1998 led to a severe recession in Croatia, but by then Tudjman knew that he was near the end. He had been diagnosed with cancer back in 1993 and his condition had worsened considerably over the preceding year. He died on 10th December 1999. Large numbers of his countrymen stood to pay tribute along the funeral procession, but the turnout from the international community was muted. His legacy in Croatia is secure: "the father of independence", after whom Zagreb Airport is now named.

Outside views are more nuanced. His death meant that he was never indicted by The Hague, although the prosecutor, Carla del Ponte, said that she would have done so. In trials of Herzegovinian Croats, it was ultimately concluded that the war crimes at the centre of the trial could not be attributed to Tudjman, although it found that he had sought to create "a Croatian entity that reconstituted earlier borders". It is impossible to believe that he had not been aware of some of the horrors that were being unleashed by his men on the ground; the best that one can say is that he was willing to turn a blind eye to the detail, though his continued support for the perpetrators beyond the end of the war suggests more than that. It could be argued that he was so traumatised by the first two years of his presidency and the Serbian tactics in first Croatia and then Bosnia that he was not prepared to stand up against the same sorts of excesses on his own side. If forced to make odious comparisons, Tudjman was only an aggressor in one war, whereas Milošević started three. Most people would conclude that Tudjman was trying to look after his people, a case that is all but impossible to make for Milošević. In the final balance, Tudjman left Croatia with a reasonably clear path towards a brighter future, while Milošević left Serbia in need of intensive care, and the Serb satellite states that he had envisioned all but terminal. Throughout my travels, from Knin to Vukovar, from Banja Luka to Višegrad, in Mitrovica or in Peć, the life of the Serbs that Milošević had sought to bind to the motherland remained wretched.

We had a surprisingly good meal at the cafe above the main gate, although we had to retreat indoors as the wind grew ever stronger. Before long, the cushions of the chairs outside were flying through the air, some over the castle walls into the scrubland far below. We helped our waiter gather up those that were more easily retrievable before he started off on his long trudge downhill. After lunch, we visited the small chapel opposite, which was whitewashed with a plain altar and cross and equipped with a couple of dozen directors' chairs in neat rows. On the wall, in place of the stations of the cross, were war photographs. A plaque outside commemorated "Croatian defenders of Knin" who were "detained, tortured and killed at this place in 1991". A large abstract sculpture nearby had an over-cheery trim of red and white begonias. We both felt that it was time to return to the sea.

Split

Šibenik, an hour short of Split, is unusual on this coast for having been founded by Croats in the 11th century rather than having a deeper Illyrian, Greek or Roman history. Its cathedral shows the continued links between the Dalmatian coast and Italy. The construction was started in 1431 under guidance provided by Bonino da Milano, who had already delivered impressive works in Korčula and Dubrovnik. Two Venetian-trained masons followed, one likely to have been a pupil of Donatello. The skill of the stoneworkers enabled them to build a barrel-vaulted nave that reflects the shape of the exterior. Standing in the main aisle, the height of the arched ceiling far above is disconcerting; it appears out of proportion with the narrowness of the main structure, but that height allows for the rosette windows above the western portal and arched windows the length of the main body of the church that flood it with natural light. The simplicity of the structure highlights the quality of the carvings along the border above the arches, on the benches, in the entire upper part of the baptistery and on its three main external faces. On either side of the northern portal, naive figures of Adam and Eve stand on pillars guarded by jovial and maybe even lascivious lions at their base. Both hold a protective fig leaf in place with their left hands. Eve, whose navel suggests that she may not have been the product of Adam's rib after all, looks impassive. Adam, right hand clasping his breast, looks distraught. The carvings here were the first brush with art for Meštrović and an evident influence. His father walked him to market here as a small boy. Late in life, in America, he completed a statue of the local executing sculptor, Juraj Dalmatinac, who now stands in the square surveying his creation.

We seemed to circle the old city of Split interminably in our attempts to manoeuvre through its labyrinthine one-way system with advice from various passers-by. Finally, we pulled up somewhere near where our hotel seemed to be. I asked for help again from the proprietor of a coffee stall, who grinned, marched me down the hill, through the "Silver Gate" and delivered me behind an ancient wall to a welcoming reception. Minutes later, our car was parked and our bags heading up to our room – "The oldest you will ever stay in," said the proprietor, "1,700 years." A partition wall provided some separation between the sleeping area and a small table and chair behind it. The light that illuminated the whole came through a semi-circular window formed by the top of one of Diocletian's massive stone arches.

Over breakfast in a little courtyard in front of the hotel the next morning, we were sheltered from the bustle of the world by another 4th-century wall. Through an archway, steps led down to a small square of ancient stone where we could see tall 18th-century houses with faded shutters and sheets hanging out to dry that would have been at home in one of Thomas Jones' Neapolitan sketches. Beyond it, multi-storeyed Roman arches bisected a small alley, a banner hanging from the lower level. In front, the outline of a bell stood out in its medieval tower, the sun at the heart of its clockface resembling an exotic sea anemone. Behind it was a sturdier and slightly more modern pillared campanile. In the foreground, cafes and neat shopfronts beamed out between ancient pilasters, while above them stone residences stretched up several storeys to garret windows. Nowhere could you easily tell where old finished and newer began.

The heart of Split is the colossal palace of Diocletian, completed in 305 CE for the emperor's retirement on the south side of the peninsula that separates it from the remains of Salona, the old Roman capital of Dalmatia and his birthplace. After Salona's destruction by nomadic invaders in the 7th century, the survivors found their way to the ruins of Diocletian's villa and made a home within. Over the centuries, the city evolved. Some parts of the structure were adapted in their entirety for other tasks, like the Baptistery of St John, repurposed from its original function as a temple of Jupiter, Diocletian's deemed father. Others were co-opted into entirely new forms.

From a distance, the central Split skyline is dominated by the tower of the Cathedral of St Domnius, which occupies the emperor's former mausoleum, although his porphyry sarcophagus is lost somewhere in the mists of time and the tower is a medieval addition. The octagonal structure is encircled by pillars that he looted from Greek and Egyptian temples and its inner darkness is lined with more trophies. The gold-panelled archway above the ornate main altarpiece looks to be celebrating the return of a great warrior. The exposed brickwork of the cathedral's dome is framed by a frieze of hunting scenes and staring faces, which seem out of place in a sacred space; but then Diocletian would no doubt be surprised to find that his mausoleum is now a place of worship for a religion that he persecuted with such intent. Two of his many victims are interred here: St Domnius, the Bishop of Salona beheaded there in 304; and St Anastasius, who is depicted lying on the altar that contains his remains with a millstone around his neck to symbolise his martyrdom by drowning. The altar was executed by Juraj Dalmatinac, who went on to build the cathedral at Šibenik. Its central panel shows the scourging of Christ, held by a figure who has raised his right leg to gain extra purchase while gripping Jesus' side with such force that it is indented. His companion grasps his victim by the forelock with his left hand as he raises his right to deliver another blow. Christ himself looks over his shoulder at his wounded back, hidden from us, with an expression of melancholy fortitude. It has remarkable dramatic force.

West would never have seen the cavernous barrel-shaped chambers that stretched under the original Roman structure. They were only cleaned out after the Second World War, having been protected over the centuries by the waste deposited there. At one end, the detritus is still visible, a solidified mass of ash, stone and crockery bound together by calcified excrement. The scale of the vaults is extraordinary, needed to compensate for the severe slope of the rock on which the palace was built and to satisfy the emperor's desire to raise the main living area to catch sea breezes. A bust of Diocletian greets visitors to this underworld, although his implacable gaze and jutting chin are far from welcoming. Wandering through its vast emptiness conveys a far clearer sense of the scale of his great palace than the chaotic and crowded town that it has now become above ground.

Split's palm-lined seafront boasts a contemporary arcade of shops below the "great Corinthian columns in the outer gallery of Diocletian's palace". The windows of elegant houses are "squeezed between" them and peer over, as if the Roman remains are a temporary stage set for the genteel day-to-day world behind. From the top floor of a handsome shuttered house was a sign advertising "Tattoo & Piercing". It is an invigorating millennial mash-up. Nonetheless, it retains the spirit of the sight that greeted West, who remarked that "[i]t would be as frivolous to object to the adaptations the children of the palace have made to live as it would be to regret that a woman who had raised a large and glorious family had lost her girlish appearance".

Robert Adam had visited almost two centuries earlier, expecting to find preserved Roman remains and amazed to find that it had metamorphosed into a contemporary settlement. Despite the suspicion of the town's Venetian governor, he completed detailed studies of the palace, which were published in London in 1764. They were the inspiration for the Adam brothers' Adelphi development between the Strand and the River Thames at the end of that decade. A street in the heart of Split is named after him. His tour was rather more successful than West's, who was irritated that her guide seemed to focus largely on sights relating to his own career.

A 15-minute walk brought us to the house that Ivan Meštrović had built for himself in Split in the 1930s, palatial, if not quite on the scale of Diocletian. A broad and surprisingly steep flight of steps leads up to a generous terrace, across which another run carries one higher again to a pillared portico flanked by two simple but elegant wings. It is light-filled and handsome, although it has the slight fascist air that lingers around much architecture of that period. It had been built as his family home with workshops, storage space and room to display his work. It looks out to the sea over trees and vegetable allotments.

Meštrović had spent his childhood in the family village 40 miles or so inland, where his father was a farmer and stonemason. In 1900, he had moved to Split, aged seventeen, to study stone carving, funded by a group of dignitaries from a nearby town who had become aware of the talent of the local boy. The workshop to which he was apprenticed was working at the time on the restoration of the tower of St Domnius' Cathedral, and he would have come into contact with a number of Italian sculptors and masons. Within a year, he had moved to Vienna, where he received his formal training and stayed for seven years. He became involved with the Secessionists, but ultimately found the art of the movement too cold and removed from the classical ideals that he admired.

He spent the following ten years based in each of Paris, London, Rome, Belgrade, Geneva and Cannes, before deciding to settle in Zagreb in 1919. During the First World War, he had been deeply involved in exile in the Yugoslav Committee, in which context he sought to shape a south Slav state that balanced the interests of Serbia, Croatia and Slovenia. He had sculpted King Alexander in London, and Rodin twice while in Rome, the latter praising him as the greatest phenomenon among sculptors of his day, who worked so quickly that he "makes sculptures grow like mushrooms after the rain". Meštrović was a plain-speaking chain-smoker, who would often have three separate cigarettes on the go as he worked in his studio.

Back in Croatia, as a highly regarded international artist, he enjoyed considerable prestige, a leading figure in the Yugoslav movement, which informed much of his work. He was friends with Tesla, King Alexander and later Archbishop Stepinac, although he was more clear-sighted about Pavelić than the churchman and was incensed by the cession of Dalmatia to Italy. He was imprisoned by the Ustaše for several months, coming close to execution, before being allowed to leave the country in 1942. After the war, he resisted the blandishments of Tito to return and settled in America, where he lived out his life. He returned briefly to Croatia for a visit in 1959, during the course of which he met up with Stepinac and Tito and visited his gallery in Split. He died in 1962, aged seventy-eight, in South Bend, Indiana, but his body was brought back to be buried in the mausoleum that he had created in his Dalmatian hometown. The authorities refused to allow a service in Zagreb, fearing a repeat of the emotional nationalist sentiment seen at Stepinac's funeral.

The museum here holds the finest collection of his work in the world. Walking around, I was struck by his strengths and weaknesses. He speaks with great power when he addresses the Balkan soul, which obviously resonated deeply within him, whether it is the passion of the Slav peoples' greatest sons or the stoicism with which their womenfolk bear the endless cycle of disaster. The caryatids that support the tomb of the unknown soldier on Mount Avala reappear here, supporting the lintel above his fireplace. A careworn bust of his mother suggests that she was the model on which they were based.

He is a master of anguish and character, but when he drifts towards sentimentality, as he is inclined to do with the female form, he can become lost. He has a love of awkward head angles and oversized hands and feet, which makes his work intensely expressive as long as there is a clear narrative but can look unnatural when not. A Pietà is absorbing, the contorted dead weight of Christ cradled by the two heavily shrouded Marys, whose eyes gaze imploringly at the solemn face of Joseph of Arimathea as he lowers him gently towards them. A bronze Job sits naked on a mound of earth – feet, hands and body clenched, calling out to God in desperation, physically as well as vocally. You can all but hear him, and I felt my own fingers and toes tighten in sympathy. But then a white marble relief shows a sturdy mythological woman climbing out from her bath with her head angled so unnaturally to her left shoulder that you question whether she can still be living. Another stylised recumbent figure could be a three-dimensional version of a Tamara de Lempicka nude, wholly pneumatic and not remotely human. His best work tears at you, but it is far from uniform.

Just down the road is the converted fortified residence of the Capogrosso family. Originally built to guard against seaborne attacks by the Turks, it had later functioned as a tannery and dyeworks, as well as an asylum for those with infectious diseases. Meštrović bought it in 1939, restoring the main courtyard and building a plain chapel to house a Crucifixion and a cycle of twenty-eight carved wooden reliefs on the life of Christ that he had started during the First World War and finally completed in exile in America over thirty years later. The emaciated Christ, who dwarfs the tiny altar over which it hangs, is the oldest piece. In its gaunt form, with bulbous joints and massively long hands that still plead after death, one senses the horrors of the world that Meštrović was observing in 1916. Eleven years later, the sensuality of *Christ and the Woman of Samaria* seems to reflect his contentment in the hopeful early years of the royal delivery of the Yugoslav ideal. The later scenes, many of them depicting the events of Holy Week, seem to have a more personal humanity, as if life in exile has led him to focus on human interactions at an individual level.

In the heart of Split outside the "Golden Gate" stands Meštrović's massive statue of Bishop Grgur Ninski (Gregory of Nin), which he had gifted to the city on the condition that it was erected in the centre of the Royal Palace. Grgur was a 10th-century bishop who had unsuccessfully championed the use of the Slavonic language and Glagolitic script by the Church. It is almost eight metres tall, and West could not conceive why he "wanted this statue to be put here, or why the authorities humoured him". She described it as "an ungodly misfit", which reduced "the architectural proportions of the palace to chaos". The Italian authorities removed the statue from its original location during the Second World War as it was a symbol of nationalism, and it was re-erected at its new location in 1954, to Meštrović's distress – "the peasant is not allowed inside the city". Photographs of its pre-war positioning allow one to see both points of view; the temple provided a magnificent setting for the sculpture, which must have pleased its creator, yet the harmony of the peristyle was quite lost in the process. The bishop now stands out by a small park that leads to the original main entrance from Salona, where one can admire the vigour of the message that he delivers in isolation, the cross atop his conical mitre echoing that on the belltower behind him. His outstretched finger signals to Rome the rejection of Latin universality and to Italy that Dalmatia is Croatian. His gleaming big toe indicates that he is seen to bring good fortune; the evident patchwork to the sculpture suggests that he may need some of his own.

Just inside the gate is the tiny Church of St Martin, squeezed into the city wall itself, originally a narrow Roman guardhouse. West had visited it, complaining of its now vanished "hideous *bondieuseries*", but inspired by the carvings on the "slender stone screen ... which write in shapes as fresh as dew the faith of a people that ... have found a beneficent magic to banish the horrors of life". A tree grows out of the floor, one branch possibly in the form of a dragon's head; it shields an ancient cross. An eagle and a mythological creature guard another cross above the central arch, while stylised waves or tongues of fire lick up to its summit above them. I remarked to the elderly nun who had greeted us that it had been written about by a well-known English author nearly eighty years earlier when it had been more extravagantly decorated. She knew nothing of it, having only arrived a couple of years before, but she told us that the small convent that cares for the church contained six or seven nuns, which was very full. That seemed to be a hopeful advance from the situation at the time of the historic visit, when West seemed to think that the order was in danger of extinction. The nun told us that all who come here find it a place of peace; we sat in contemplation as if to prove her point.

Over dinner on our last night, we were the only customers in a health-oriented restaurant not far from the city walls. We quizzed our waiter about various items on the menu, including "chicken in a sack" and "tenderloin step by step". We opted for other dishes, ordering a starter and main course each, which we consumed to an early '60s soundtrack that might have come from the Tito era, when Dalmatia was the holiday destination for the affluent from across the peninsula. We asked for the bill, only to be asked in turn: "What about your third meal?" It became clear that the waiter, thinking we had ordered two main courses each, was about to produce the dishes that we had discussed with him earlier. An embarrassed discussion resulted in a two-course bill, a large tip and a civilised exit.

Trogir

Trogir, 20 miles to the west, had a holiday feel, full of hidden passages, inviting shops and restaurants, and devoid of traffic. The main square was filled with tables and umbrellas, although at the back of the loggia on the main square, a display of black and white faces looked out beside a tablet listing the names of those who had died between 1991 and 1995 in the homeland war.

The Cathedral of St Lovro (Lawrence), a local 3rd-century martyr, dominates the square. Its greatest jewel is evident immediately – the magnificent portal from 1240. Densely carved twin arches surround the doorway and lunette above it. A red-robed St Lovro adds a dash of colour in a niche high up. The whole is framed by the outline of a stone canopy supported by a bewildered Adam and Eve standing on lions. The complexity and character of the carvings is bewitching, a blend of Italian, Byzantine and folk art. Two and a half centuries later, Donatello's pupil, Nikola Firentinac, came on here from his work at Šibenik to build a new chapel to house the tomb of Trogir's other great saint, the 11th-century bishop, Ivan. He constructed a barrel-vaulted chapel that clearly references his work up the coast. Each of its panels contain the serene head of an angel conducting a benign stewardship of the elaborate Renaissance altar that contains the bishop's remains. From a wreath in the centre, God the Father leans down, his right hand in an act of benediction, so lifelike that you question the positioning of the lower half of his torso that stops him from tumbling into the earthly space. As we left, I revisited Firentinac's Italianate baptism of Christ above the door to the baptistery. Jesus stands utterly still while John pours a stream of water over his head with an air of intense concentration. God the Father and the Holy Spirit sit directly above, each channelling their blessing to the earthbound member of the Trinity through the flow of liquid, and by extension to all who walk through the gate below.

We had walked in over the bridge that joins the island town to the mainland. Small pleasure boats were tied up along the quays on each side of the narrow channel that it spanned. From here, in 1241, the Mongols had issued their demand to the town to hand over the Hungarian king, Béla IV, who was holed up inside. The town offered no response in obedience to the king and feared the worst, but it never materialised. Before any action could be initiated, the Mongol forces turned and rode off, having received the unexpected news of the death of Ögedei Khan, son of Genghis, which required an immediate return home to elect his successor. The death provided a remarkable respite for the beleaguered European powers, and a turning point in the Mongols' westward ambitions.

At the end of the Riva stands the dusty Kamerlengo Fortress, built by the Venetians as a naval base and once connected to the walls that enclosed the town. They had been torn down by Marshal Marmont, Duke of Ragusa, who had governed Dalmatia for Napoleon for five years. The French had taken control from Austria after their decisive victory at Austerlitz in 1805. The arrival of a revolutionary government after the long, sapping rule of Venice must have been a considerable relief to many Croatians. Marmont fell in love with Dalmatia, describing Ragusa (Dubrovnik) as an oasis of civilisation in the middle of barbarity. He introduced progressive policies in education and agriculture and built new hospitals and roads. He pulled down the walls of

Trogir, hoping that the sea winds would help counter the prevalence of malaria, leaving the town's appearance in West's eyes as "like a plant grown in a flower-pot when the pot is broken but the earth and roots still hang together". It made little difference; malaria was only stamped out with the draining of the swamps at this end of the island a century later.

The Napoleonic flowering was short-lived. Marmont was summoned to take charge of the French army in Portugal in 1811 and was badly wounded in his defeat by Wellington at Salamanca the following year. Two years later, after Napoleon's calamitous campaign in Russia, the Austrians took back control of Dalmatia, other than the islands of Vis and Korčula, which were claimed by Britain.

Beyond the fort, a small six-pillared pavilion sits on a stone platform by a football pitch. It is Marmont's Gloriette, now roofless and somewhat graffitied, where the marshal would sit and play cards with his officers, catching the sea breezes in the stifling heat of mid-summer. The view has been rendered less lovely by the shipyard on the island of Čiovo opposite, but one can still picture Marmont here as he whiled away his evenings, arguably the most benign of Croatia's many foreign rulers. It is tempting to think that, through him, the influence of the French Revolution, in contrast to the heavy hand of the Hapsburgs, led to the emergence of a Slav and ultimately Croatian nationalism.

Korčula

From our gleaming little hotel on the island of Korčula, we looked out over the sparkling blue bay to the pale outline of the Pelješac peninsula. It was in these straits that the Battle of Korčula was fought in 1298, where the Genoese navy won a crushing victory over the Venetians, during which Marco Polo is said to have been captured and imprisoned, giving him the time to write about his travels. He is claimed as Korčulan, but it is more likely that he was Venice-born with island antecedents. His name is certainly well used here, blessing each of a museum, a hotel, a shop, a pizzeria and his "Birth House".

A short walk around the harbourfront brought us to the low, balustraded steps that swept up to the entrance tower of the old town. On it was a playful Venetian lion and a plaque celebrating the thousandth anniversary of the coronation of King Tomislav of Croatia in 925. Below, a line of stalls pitched along the protective walls of the old town displayed summerwear and trinkets, while the stallholders sat patiently in patches of shade on fold-up chairs making desultory conversation with their neighbours. Inside the gate, a steep, narrow street led us further upwards through honey-tinged buildings. At each corner, an architectural detail, a flash of colour or tantalising scent tempted us to divert before proceeding.

The town was planned in a fishbone shape to best protect its inhabitants from wind and sun. At the top, the main spine opens out into the small central square, which was still "smoothly paved and therefore had that air of being within the confines of some noble household". It serves the 15th-century St Mark's Cathedral, whose main entrance is almost wilfully bizarre. The mitred patron saint sits above the doors, extending a blessing with his right hand, although he glowers as if to question the motive of any would-be visitor. On either side, Adam and Eve appear to be squatting in the act of relieving themselves, almost crushed by the weight of the plinths above them, on which fearsome lions toy with terrified rams. Elsewhere in Croatia, the figures had been regretful; here, they were abject.

At the doorway, a flirtatious schoolgirl issued tickets; she had a penetrating giggle that must have hampered attempts at peaceful contemplation within. We wandered around the interior, admiring its innate serenity and simplicity while trying to find an angle from which to see the Tintoretto altarpiece of St Mark clearly. An elderly lady approached and asked if we were looking for anything in particular. She showed us a Meštrović relief of an etiolated St Blaise and another "Tintoretto" of the Annunciation, though more likely by his son or a follower. She also pointed out a 14th-century icon belonging to the Franciscan monastery at Badija, of which West had spoken so highly and which we intended to visit. She told us that the monastery had been taken over by the communist government after the Second World War and used as a health camp for fifty years or so. It was now back in the hands of the Franciscans, but its restoration was clearly a slow process, and the icon looked likely to be staying in the cathedral for some time yet.

On the same wall hung a selection of weaponry from the Battle of Una, at which the Croatians defeated an invading Ottoman army in 1483, as well as a cannonball from the Battle of Lepanto nearly a century later. The Korčulans fought the Turks for centuries and were great shipbuilders. The interior of the church reflects it; the oddly angled wooden ceiling fitted to the slightly skewed nave might easily be the underside of a deck. It is suspended between walls of pale golden stone from the neighbouring islets that also supplied stone for the building of Diocletian's palace and parts of Dubrovnik. The Chapel of St Roc, the patron saint of plagues, commemorates a serious outbreak in the 16th century. His weary representation in wood stood on the altar flanked by two other medical saints; it is known locally as "the clinic".

Our new friend asked us where we were from; on hearing that we were English, she gave us an excited recitation of the links between the town and Fitzroy Maclean, who had spent a happy interlude here during the Second World War, in the gap between its difficult occupation by the Italians and its retaking by the Germans. Korčula had been designated as a suitable place to land supply drops, which had become too hazardous inland. He had been shown around the island by the local Partisan commander, a Franciscan friar, whose focus on Croatian freedom must have blinded him to the likely damage that Tito would unleash on his church and many of his parishioners. Maclean had been given a tour to inspect local detachments. It was only at the third stop that he realised that the heroic-looking leader at the head of each group, presented anew to him each time, was a single man who had galloped on ahead to take up his fresh position. He also recounts a bleary memory of a village dance being "dramatically interrupted by the explosion of a small red Italian hand grenade which became detached from one of the girls' belts as she whirled round the barn in which it was being held".

Maclean had returned after the war, drawn by his memory of "the old churches, houses and palaces golden in the morning sunlight". Tito had given him the unique honour as a foreigner of being allowed to own a house in Yugoslavia on the strength of his wartime record and friendship. His home had been beside the cathedral, where his wife regularly attended mass, and where one of their sons had been married some decades earlier.

In the town museum across the square, a display of photographs of the Partisan struggle on Korčula shows Maclean, with his field service cap at a rakish angle, staring out quizzically with a gummy island companion in Soviet-style headwear clasping a submachine gun. Others show Partisan life in the hills, radiating innocent enthusiasm in the surprising way that off-duty war photographs tend to. Particularly joyous was the display put on by the pioneers for a Partisan conference in October 1943, in the brief period that they controlled the island; a ring of smiling girls in local costume danced in the sun for a watching crowd. A month later, the first German bombardment would start.

That evening, we sat on the terrace of our hotel in the late May warmth, enjoying a soup made with the head of a John Dory, its fillets serving as the main course, all accompanied by the local white wine, Pošip, an experience so heady that I felt I was inhaling incense. The following night, I drank another local wine, Grk (a name, per Maclean, of "admirable succinctness"), which also boasted a wonderfully complex taste. It was hard to reconcile the different circumstances in which each of us had enjoyed it for the first time. He, just arrived from a perilous journey after months in the mountains to be greeted with a glass; I, savouring it over a languorous dinner. I relished it, but to him it must have tasted like liquid sunshine.

The next morning, we walked into town again and followed the town wall to the right in search of the icon museum. Pine trees shaded the restaurant tables that looked out over the bay. Up an alleyway, we found the simple room hung with fewer icons than one might have expected, but our real quest lay beyond it. Up a few steps, in the corner and through a small chamber that doubled as a bridge over the alleyway, we climbed down into a little church owned by a confraternity who still keep their treasures and records in the museum, as they had in West's day. The church boasted a stone 16th-century baldachin hung with silver lamps that shielded a large wooden Pietà. Both ceiling and balcony were painted, the latter with Jesus and his apostles, Judas' place having been taken by an angel. From the balcony, an open bridge led back across the alleyway, where we found a representative of the fellowship. He showed us the robes in which they parade around town each year at the end of

July, although he was oddly uncertain of the date. The members all come from old Korčulan families; one proudly showed us a photo of a boyish version of himself from a gathering twenty-five years earlier. In an older picture, he identified his father and grandfather. His brother was also a member but had been away at sea for twenty-five years, currently as first officer on a Disney cruise ship in America, so could only attend sporadically. It was clear that the "mystical, uplifting version of the pleasures of brotherhood" that West had witnessed was still alive. Her local guide's remark that Korčula would someday not "need the tourist traffic though the money will come in welcome" felt less than prophetic.

After lunch, we took a water taxi to Badija, hoping to see the Franciscan monastery that we had discussed the previous day. The old town looked surprisingly compact as we sped away from it, its roofs forming a geometrical mosaic of white and pale orange spreading out from the sugar shaker of the cathedral's cupola, all contained in a necklace of light stone and dark pine. On arrival, the formal rectangular front of the monastery seemed unnaturally spruce, built of the customary pale golden local stone and sitting in solitary splendour on the quay, with low wooded hills behind and tantalising turquoise water in front. It was clear that a significant building programme had taken place, but there was little evidence of its continuing other than for a looming crane at one end (admittedly, it was a Saturday). The bare bones of a large concrete-beamed gathering hall could be freely inspected, but all other doors were secured and handle-less, and our knocking elicited no response. In the hall we found a ladder, which we propped against an inner wall and climbed up to look through a high window into the monastery compound, within which we could see a jeaned figure at work in a cultivated area in its centre. We walked around to the rear where a gate opened. Inside, we could appreciate its scale. The tower indicated a substantial church, and the regimented blocks that stretched back from the main waterfront building could house a substantial community, whether vocational or vacationing. The gardener inside spoke no English but conveyed clearly that it was impossible to see the church and cloisters that West had admired. We agreed with her conclusion that it "lies as comfortably and unspiritually among its gardens as a Sussex manor-house", albeit with a severity that was not apparent from her description.

We wandered off around the coast, picking our way past the remains of the communist-era resort, a deserted basketball court, discoloured climbing frames and the disintegrating yellow and green runways of a clock golf course. Following a track through the trees for a while, we eventually settled under some pine trees by the shore, where I read and Sarah sketched a view of the green islet just offshore. The scent of salt-tinged resin lulled us. Before long, the water – "clean as ice, but gentle" – beckoned me in.

Back on the main island that evening, we had dinner at a hilltop restaurant a few miles out of the town. Sitting in the open air within a cluster of old stone buildings, we ate startlingly fresh food prepared only feet away from us. We got into conversation with a stocky son of the family, who asked about our travels in Croatia. When it became clear that we had visited Vukovar, he became agitated and struggled to enunciate his thoughts. "It was the most beautiful city ... It is one of the darkest moments in our history ... They did terrible things ... They used gas ..." Even here, where the world holidays in an ostensibly untroubled paradise, the memories and potential enmities lie deep.

Before we left Korčula, we walked along the waterfront to see the English Piazzetta, "a very pretty semicircle of stone seats, conceived in the neo-classical tradition", the steps to its low, paved platform guarded by a pair of obelisks. It is one of the main relics of the brief two-year period of British rule here, between the end of the Napoleonic era and the conclusion of the Congress of Vienna, which handed Dalmatia in its entirety to Austria. During that period, the British oversaw the writing of a local constitution that enshrined freedom of religion. The diaries of the presiding admiral express disappointment at his sailors' drunken behaviour and his affection for the local inhabitants. Engraved on one of the obelisks are the thanks of Korčula for the favourable administration.

We took the ferry over to the Pelješac peninsula and began the final leg of our journey. We passed through Ston, famous for its oysters, the beds marked out like a chess board in the blue waters of the vast sheltered inlet between it and the mainland proper. Old stone walls ran vertically up the forbidding hills, built to protect the town's famous salt pans.

As we met the coastal highway, we found ourselves only ten miles from the Bosnian border, where the country intrudes bizarrely through Croatia to the sea. It is a hangover from the Treaty of Karlowitz in

1699, when Ragusa agreed to create a buffer zone between its land and that of their potential aggressor, Venice, by giving two strips of land to the Ottoman Empire, effecting their access to the sea in the process. The southern strip was reassigned to Montenegro by Tito after the Second World War, but the northern one persists, a source of irritation to Croatia, which secured EU funds to build an as yet unopened bridge over to the peninsula, circumventing Bosnian territory and the border checks that it entails. This in turn has aggravated Bosnia, which fears adverse economic effects. The distant rumbles of the centuries take many forms.

Dubrovnik

In less than an hour, we had reached Dubrovnik. From where we were staying across the bay, it looked like a grandiose version of Korčula, its famous walls rising out of the deep blue sea and the roofscape a similar patchwork of terracotta and faintest gold; but the distinct outlines of the cathedral dome and baroque facade of St Ignatius' Church added gravitas. Dubrovnik was the most important city on the Balkan peninsula for more than a millennium, growing rich by channelling the output of the mines of the interior to the markets of Western Europe. Somehow, it retained an effective independence from the 7th century until the arrival of the French in 1806. It had at different points recognised the overlordship of each of Byzantium, Venice, the Normans, Hungary and the Ottoman Empire, but remained self-governing throughout. It was staunchly Catholic, disallowing any Orthodox place of worship in the city until the 18th century and sending ships to fight as part of the Spanish Armada against Protestant England, an action which drew a complaint from Elizabeth I to their nominal ruler, and her ally, the Turkish sultan. Dubrovnik was also liberal, allowing Jews to settle from 1407 and abolishing slavery in 1416. The greatest historical damage that it suffered came not from attack but from a massive earthquake in 1667, which killed 5,000 people and destroyed most of the city. The rebuilding in its wake accounts for its remarkable architectural harmony.

Its beauty is in some ways a curse. As we walked down the main street of the town, "a paved fairway ... lined with comely seventeenth-century houses that have shops on their ground floor", it must have looked very little different structurally to the sight that greeted West, but it suffers from the fate of a number of highly photogenic and accessible historic sites. It is a tourist scalp, and for much of the year in prime daylight hours, its principal public areas are filled to a point where one's ability to appreciate their beauty is gravely tested. In the early morning or in the evening, it reveals its considerable charms more naturally.

Above the door of the Franciscan monastery sits what West described as "a most definite and sensible Pietà", clearly "noble". She looks as though it would be an unforgivable breach of etiquette to show any emotion, despite her dead son's wooden form across her legs. Neither figure's dignity is improved by their halos, which resemble inverted frisbees. Inside, the exquisite cloisters provided some relief from the hubbub outside, a welcome coolness emanating from the trees and box hedging in the middle while we marvelled at the variety of the carved capitals on the pairs of octagonal pillars whose high arches formed the boundary.

We made for the rather plain cathedral, an earlier version of which was constructed with the help of a donation from Richard the Lionheart, who had been shipwrecked on the nearby island of Lokrum on his way back from the Third Crusade. Well shielded behind a roped-off wall, we found a lady who grudgingly sold us a ticket to visit the treasury, indicating a door tucked in on the far side of the main altar. Gilded shelves on three walls displayed an astonishing range of reliquaries; the array of golden limbs suggested a shop selling prostheses for the ultra-wealthy. In the foreground was a case containing the greatest treasures. The skull, right arm and left leg of the patron of Dubrovnik, St Blaise, purchased from Byzantium in 1026, took pride of place. They are encased in ornate goldwork decorated with jewels and enamel images. Beside them lay a 15th-century dish depicting Dubrovnik flora and fauna, thought to have been made as a gift for a Hungarian king who died before being presented with it. West memorably described seeing it when the substantial stomach of her ecclesiastical guide skewered her hand onto a spike, creating a painful if inadvertent wound. She loathed the natural realisation of the vegetation, lizards, snakes and fish, describing it as having "the infinite elaborateness of eczema", imitating nature while failing to understand it. It was hard to disagree with her - had I not known otherwise, I would have taken it for Victorian tat.

Emerging from the cathedral, we were greeted by a shopfront advertising a full range of *Game of Thrones* merchandise. We entered to find a poster emblazoned with the familiar faces of the key characters and the legend: "Do you know in front of this store were filmed the most important scenes of *Game of Thrones*?" As we walked through the aisles of teacups and T-shirts, I heard a Frenchman remark to his wife, "*Mais Jon Snow est mort.*" I forbore from updating him on the miraculous reincarnation that we had witnessed in the most recent couple of episodes. We walked out, now recognising that we were in King's Landing, the capital of the Baratheons and Lannisters, and amused ourselves by spotting scene settings as we walked around. We recognised the Dominican monastery steps from which a naked Queen Cersei had been paraded through the streets as punishment for adultery. In its treasury, I was surprised to find a reliquary cross of the decidedly less fictional Serbian king, Uroš II Milutin, the founder of Gračanica who had fought hard against the imposition of Catholicism in the Balkans. The majority of his remains are in St Nedelya Church in Sofia; a saint in Orthodox but not Catholic eyes, though I suppose this mortal fragment was still a treasure in monetary or historical terms to the resident monks.

In the main square, Dubrovnik's Meštrović statue is a bronze of the Renaissance writer Marin Držić sitting in contemplation, his prominent nose even shinier than Gregory of Nin's big toe in Split. Beyond it, we entered the Sponza Palace, whose two-storied arcades offered further shelter from the crowds. Inside, an exhibition commemorated those who died in 1991. A scrap of charred red, white and blue cloth hung on the wall. It was the tattered remnant of a Croatian flag that had flown above the Napoleonic fort on Mount Srdj, the small hill that rises behind Dubrovnik, which saw some of the fiercest fighting during the most recent wars.

It was not the first time that Dubrovnik had been attacked from the hills. Two years after the Napoleonic takeover of the city in 1806, the Montenegrins and Russians had besieged it, looting and causing significant damage outside the city walls before they retreated, having failed to seize their hoped-for prize.

In 1991, the Montenegrins were again at the forefront of the Yugoslav army's move on Dubrovnik, justifying the aggression in the interests of their territorial integrity and the preservation of federal Yugoslavia. On 1ˢᵗ October, the army attacked Mount Srdj and the eastern outskirts of Dubrovnik, while the Yugoslav air force destroyed the city's water and electricity supply; much of the former came from Herzegovina anyway. By the end of the month, the inhabitants were suffering from relentless shelling and the army was closing in on all sides. 15,000 refugees took shelter in the city from the surrounding areas, about half of whom were evacuated by sea.

Ultimately, Dubrovnik was rescued by its photogenicity; the sight of one of the great architectural jewels of southern Europe under artillery bombardment focused attention on the horror of the Yugoslav break-up in a way that the human tragedy of Vukovar had failed to do. Television footage showed shells landing in the old city as clouds of smoke billowed out through windows and above the battlements of its great walls. Flames leapt up from historic buildings and tourist hotels, while pleasure boats alight in the marina emitted clouds of black, evidencing the mindless destruction of a familiar holiday destination and the warped thinking behind it. Many of the residents of the city looked more bemused than angry, although over eighty civilians died in the siege, as well as around 360 members of the military forces of both sides. Warships out at sea emphasised the thuggish nature of the destruction, an impression reinforced by the navy's attempts to prevent humanitarian aid from reaching the city. International intervention brokered a number of ceasefires, and by early December the guns had fallen silent. By June the following year, as the situation in Bosnia deteriorated, the Croatians had regained control over all the territory in the Dubrovnik area that had been taken. One wonders why the Bosnian Croats had not learned from the outcome here when they targeted the Mostar bridge two years later.

Today, the lure of the Dalmatian coast and membership of the European Union give an optimism and clarity about Croatia's future (along with Slovenia) of a different order to that of other former Yugoslav states. Montenegro can envision similar tourist potential for itself, but it will be hard for the rest to follow suit. No wonder so many middle-class Serbs reminisce about the good old days when summers by the Adriatic were an annual highlight. It must also rankle, somewhat understandably, to see Croatia's future look so bright when it stood on the wrong side of history for much of the first half of the 20th century. In the interim, one hopes that the lustre of coast and capital might at least spread to the country's less prosperous interior. Karlovac, full of history and sited conveniently between Zagreb and Rijeka, would seem a logical early beneficiary.

Together, Sarah and I walked around Dubrovnik's walls. Odd pockets of damage were still visible well away from the main tourist areas – a shell of a house, some early-stage rebuilding work in a mess of ruined walls – but no one seemed to know or care about it that much now. Meanwhile, in the harbour below, the small boats bobbed in tidy white lines, evidence of the city's carefree rebirth. We had dinner that night in the grandest old restaurant within the walls, sitting out on the terrace in the warmth of a late May evening, eating scallops in truffle sauce and gratinated bream with olives. The service was as discreet as it must have been for the restaurant's famous patrons, Edward VIII and Mrs Simpson, who dined here as part of their Adriatic cruise during his brief reign, shortly before West's own visit. One could quite understand why West had thought it the perfect place for a second honeymoon, "should anything happen to my husband and should some suitor with a taste for maturity present himself". Dubrovnik's capacity to preserve and reinvent itself was still intact over 1,300 years after its foundation.

Epilogue

The spring after my travels around Serbia, I went walking on Mount Athos with three friends. We were all men – women are not allowed to set foot on the holy mountain – and we hiked between monasteries carrying all our needs on our backs for three days. On the last night, we stayed at the great foundation of Vatopedi, which was established in the 10th century. Its extensive, roughly paved courtyard was surrounded by stone-arched arcades and neat white windows set in deep red walls, the epitome of a community of learning and worship for over a millennium, with something of the air of an Oxbridge college, yet still more venerable. We ate simply in the communal dining hall and chatted with a monk for a while afterwards in the still warm evening about the peaceful rhythm of his life. We bought small wooden crosses, which were then blessed over the girdle of the Blessed Virgin Mary in the chapel. The sacred relic has a reputation for great healing powers, which would not be diminished by the onward travels that my little clutch embarked on. We fell into our beds early, exhausted by our long day's walking, and awoke before dawn to stumble across the yard to join in morning prayers. In a semi-hypnotic state, I listened to the monks chanting in the candlelit gloom. As the grey of the early light outside crept into the sacred space, the mesmerising strand of sound meandered and the candles were extinguished one by one. My mind and body retained only the faintest interconnection as I glimpsed an unknowable eternity. With time, the voices faded to silence, I returned to the world, and we shuffled out into the early morning sun.

We had to catch a ferry from a jetty up the coast, a leisurely walk of a few hours, but two miles beyond the departure point was a place of particular interest to me, the great Serbian Orthodox Monastery of Hilandar (*Chilandari* in Greek). Before long, it became clear that without setting an uncomfortably fast pace, we would fail to see Hilandar and still catch the boat back to the mainland. I explained and strode out, assuring my companions that if all else failed, I would see them at our departure point. Behind me, Vatopedi looked like a small fortified village spreading back from the silvery bay; it had needed such defences for much of its history as a target of seaborne predators out to loot monastic treasures. The scree banks along the path sparkled with pink and white rock roses in the early sun. Far below me, a small, red-capped building sat alone on a promontory in a sea of turquoise washed silk. I passed by the well-worn tiered entrance gate of another monastery but barely gave it a glance in my haste to accomplish my mission. At last, a great defensive tower rose up to my right, startlingly geometric in the wooded expanse. This had to be the Milutin Tower, built by the Serbian king as part of the same programme that had also restored the great church of Hilandar in the early 14th century.

I turned inland along a track that was soon lined with gravely noble cypress trees. A roadside shrine displayed a painted Orthodox cross alongside an emblem of the double-headed eagle and the legend: "Cross of Tsar Dušan". Dušan had quarantined from the plague at Hilandar, bringing with him his wife, who in legend had had to be carried for the length of her stay so as not to touch the strictly masculine soil. I quickened my pace, and there came into view the surprisingly homely sight of two storeys of sky-blue windows set high in great defensive stone walls. A crane in the background and scaffolding over the square main entrance signalled the ongoing work to repair the damage from the fire that had destroyed much of the monastery in 2004, although mercifully not its library.

I was shown into the main compound, apologising for my overheated appearance, while the welcoming monk in turn excused the condition of many of the buildings. The main church was pale and lovely, still with a mantle of metalwork, but its many-windowed main cupola was instantly reminiscent of Studenica, with an added calmness from the absence of brick detailing. The rippling arches of the front elevation gave the faint suggestion of an old-fashioned carriage. Another great tower loomed alongside together with the propped-up ruins of a large burnt-out section of building. The church interior was surprisingly bright; light flooded in from above where much-restored biblical figures gazed down from a blue background. Above a doorway, a wine-coloured banner sporting a crown commemorated the visit of King Alexander I Obrenović in 1896.

Epilogue

Outside in the sun, the shell of a stone sarcophagus marked the original resting place of Stefan Nemanja before he was moved to Studenica. Now, it has acquired a covering of deep red ornamental ironwork, which protects the vine that grows out of the gravesite and spreads over a wooden terrace above. The grapes that it produces are believed to help childless couples.

One of my travelling companions had caught up with me, and my cheerful escort showed us both to the guesthouse beside the main compound, where he pressed on us glasses of water and the inevitable *šljivovica* before we dashed to catch our boat. The quarters were clearly well set up for visiting groups. To come on a retreat here must be truly revivifying, praying where men have done for so long and walking in the surrounding wilderness; but even in this remote corner, there are echoes of more recent history.

Milošević flew in by helicopter for a fleeting (and possibly not entirely welcome) visit in 1991, despite having skipped the service at Gračanica that had accompanied his high-profile performance at the Kosovo anniversary celebration two years earlier. The motive is unclear. Presumably, in part, to align himself more clearly in the eyes of the public with the line of the monastery's supporters, which stretches from the founders, Stefan Nemanja and St Sava, through their direct successors, including Milutin and Dušan, and later both Skanderbeg and Lazar. Milošević's companion, the minister of religious affairs, felt that it had marked a conversion from the hard-line communism espoused by his wife towards a more spiritual path. Looking at his subsequent record, I believe that the strictly practical president had viewed the Church as a vital endorsement to secure along the path that he had embarked on.

The Orthodox Church had been tightly entwined with the state since the earliest days of Byzantium. The gospels used to sit on an empty throne in the imperial palace to symbolise the presence of Christ. There was no practical division between church and state in Nemanjić times, and all the kings were considered saints, other than Dušan, who was disqualified for his patricide. As nationalism came to a fore in the 19th century, the religious divisions coincided with many of the emerging political entities. The longing for self-determination as empires withered was often defined in part by spiritual allegiance. At several points, the Churches in the Balkans, in their enthusiasm to fulfil their evangelical aims, have blessed and even identified with regimes whose nationalism was manifestly ugly. The most obvious beneficiaries were Pavelić and Milošević, but there were also reports that Hilandar had offered Karadžić refuge from justice as he sought to avoid extradition to The Hague.

As I walked down to the harbour, I thought how appalled West would have been by the horrors in the sixty years after the publication of her book. At the time, she was warning in part against the threat of a particular war; she could hardly have conceived of the amplified reverberations half a century on. She had admired many of the warrior-like qualities, even bloodthirstiness, that could be seen as heroic in the 19th century but are viewed as barbaric today. In the Second World War, most deaths in Yugoslavia were the killings of Yugoslavs by Yugoslavs, while more than two thirds of the victims in the more recent conflicts were civilians or unarmed. To this day, there are meant to be unmarked yet known burial pits in the mountains dating back seventy-five years or so, where families have for decades gone to mourn their dead. More troublingly still, there are reportedly stores of weapons buried in readiness to avenge those deaths. Too often has the Black Lamb, the earthly sacrifice of religion, been elevated over the spiritual quest embodied by the Falcon.

It is not clear that it needed to be that way. Bosnia was a multi-cultural society for centuries under the Ottomans, where the different religions cohabited in reasonable harmony. When the Croatian Ban Josip Jelačić was invested in 1848, he was accompanied by the Orthodox Patriarch of Sremski Karlovci, and subsequently attended both a Catholic and an Orthodox service to signify the twin strands of religion in his domain. Even under the royal family, there was an evolution towards a more balanced structure from their Greater Serbian starting point. Alexander Karadjordjević, in the early days, and the Regent Paul even more so, had sought to balance Croatian and Serbian interests, albeit dealing less constructively with their Albanian and Bulgar subjects. In some ways, the unwilling regent marked the one point at which the Yugoslav ideal had achieved a moment of reality, before being swept away by Hitler. A successful Yugoslavia could only have worked as a federation rather than a central state, and the coercions of both Alexander Karadjordjević and Tito simply masked rifts rather than healed them. The former US national security advisor, Brent Scowcroft, remarked of his time as an air force attaché in Belgrade between 1959 and 1961: "I don't remember ever hearing people call themselves Yugoslavs, they always called themselves Serbs, Croats, Slovenians."

When the Berlin Wall fell, the situation for unoccupied Yugoslavia was quite different to that of the Soviet-dominated remainder of Eastern Europe. Tito had created an unwieldy structure to try to balance the interests of the constituent parts as he sought to respond to the unrest that his centralist control had created. There were definite positives to a federation, most notably in achieving a critical mass in internal trade and thereby improving both competitiveness and political recognition in the world outside. With goodwill, a post-Tito Yugoslavia might just have evolved into a more workable structure, but it was frail enough that it could never have survived the naked power grab that Milošević unleashed. As Zimmermann observed: "The conflagrations didn't break out through spontaneous combustion. Pyromaniacs were required."

The situation was considerably complicated by minorities and their historical experience. Time and again over the centuries, discrimination against a minority group had turned into outright persecution in times of war. Once the dissolution of Yugoslavia had become a nationalist power game, the double standards that came into play were extraordinary, and the ability for unprincipled leaders to manipulate fear all too easy. Milošević sought to deny the Kosovo Albanians the same rights that he encouraged the Bosnian and Croatian Serbs to pursue. Tudjman urged self-determination for Croatia, while denying it to the Serbs of Krajina. Both sought to deny the Bosnian Muslims any historical rights at all. Both dredged back through the centuries to twist strands of history to suit their own narratives. Meanwhile, the instrument of conflict was the federal army, a symbol of unity bent to the ends of one member alone. Reworking history was nothing new in Yugoslavia: the anti-clerical Tito had laid claim to the values of Bishop Strossmayer; while the prevalence of Meštrović's statues across the public spaces of its former states attests not just to his skill as a sculptor, but also to his ability to recruit prominent historical figures to different purposes.

Twenty years on from the last major conflict, there are some hopeful signs of a new *modus vivendi*: cross-border responses to national disasters; halting steps towards a regional economic area of the non-EU former states of Yugoslavia; the progress made by the multi-ethnic *Naša stranka* party in Sarajevo. But these are still limited, and other strands remain cause for concern. Chief among these is the continued apparent links between governments and organised crime in much of the non-EU parts of the region; but the widespread revisionism, apparent most conspicuously in Republika Srpska, also hampers healing. On the 25th anniversary of the massacre at Srebrenica, ceremonies were held at the cemetery to commemorate the 8,000 victims, while three miles away a group of Serbs celebrated the "liberation day of Srebrenica", denying the genocide for which Mladić had been convicted. Without recognition of the past, it is hard to see a harmonious future.

It is worth recalling the words of Biljana Plavšić, former President of Republika Srpska, at The Hague in 2002. She attributed her acts, and her inability to recognise the acts of herself and others, to:

> a blinding fear that led to an obsession, especially for those of us for whom the Second World War was a living memory, that Serbs would never again allow themselves to be victims ... The knowledge that I am responsible for such human suffering and for soiling the character of my people will always be with me.

She went on to talk of the long history of the construction of St Sava's Church in Belgrade, "a monument to a man who more than any other formed the character of the Serbian people ... The path he followed was marked by self-restraint and respect for all others". However genuine these remarks may have been in the context of her trial is debatable, yet her late clarity of vison is a quality not widespread enough. The Serb leadership in Belgrade and Bosnia in the 1990s may have acted in the name of Lazar, but they chose the path that he had rejected. They opted for victory on earth at the expense of their souls.

In the haste of the former Yugoslav states to establish their own identities and cast off their imperial and federal histories, they have tended to discard the good along with the bad, prime among these being multi-culturalism. Ironically, they have done so just as the majority of Europe – of which they would like to and should be a part – has been moving in the opposite direction. The Ottoman era has left its mark, and not just in beautiful bridges and mosques; it is also identifiable when one eats *ćevapčići* (kebabs) and (dare I say it) when one listens to a Serbian folk song accompanied by a *gusle*. Openness to one's history in all its forms and dialogue with one's neighbours must be the key to a happier future.

Despite the intervening horrors, West would no doubt still recognise much of what she saw. The astonishing beauty of the legacies of empires, both local and foreign, is visible throughout the region. The mountain scenery is as magnificent as any I have seen. Despite their turbulent history, the people of the Balkans are endlessly hospitable. I will always want to return.

I learned something else on my journey about the duality of time: that it is both a commodity and a space. Through much of my life, I had measured out my hours on the basis that they were, by definition, limited, and had thus sought to achieve the maximum possible in any allotted day. Travelling though the Balkan lands, I repeatedly allowed myself to occupy the space afforded by time when one stops parcelling it out and surrenders to the joy of a particular experience. Whether marvelling at the humanity in the detail of ancient frescoes, contemplating alternative belief systems or being transported by the elemental beauty of sacred song, I found myself glimpsing another dimension. I needed to go further.

> "Music is entirely independent of the phenomenal world, ignores it altogether, could to a certain extent exist if there was no world at all ... This is why the effect of music is so much more powerful and penetrating than that of the other arts, for they speak only of shadows, but music speaks of the thing itself."
>
> **Arthur Schopenhauer**

Acknowledgements

Thanks above all should go to Rebecca West, my continued inspiration as I travelled. I may have disagreed with her at times, but she was unfailingly good company. I hope that this book will lead others to read *Black Lamb and Grey Falcon*. I also highly recommend the authoritative histories of the constituent countries of the region by Tim Judah, Noel Malcolm, Elizabeth Roberts and Marcus Tanner, as well as Misha Glenny's magnificent take on the last two centuries of the broader Balkan area. Balkan Investigative Reporting Network (birn.eu.com) has been an invaluable and objective source for current news from the region.

I especially want to thank Philip Kerr for the beautiful illustrations inside and out, which add so much to the book's appeal. Lyn Davies' skilful cover artwork has presented the latter to considerable advantage.

Various friends have encouraged me, read early versions and made invaluable suggestions, notably Nicholas Coleridge, Edward Stourton, Daniel Sunter and Kate Weil. Bill Colegrave added real impetus to my quest for a publisher.

Others who have helped me in different ways, and always with enthusiasm, include Jules Alexander, Tim Bouverie, Johnny Boyer, Andrew Duncan, Melanie Gibson, John Gimlette, James Heneage, Siniša-Jakov Marušić, Dragana Nikolić-Solomon, Jane Pleydell-Bouverie, Barnaby Rogerson, Lazar Šećerović, Simon Vandeleur and Barney White-Spunner. Ultimately, all opinions are my own.

John Ridgley gave great assistance in identifying plants.

I would also like to note my debt to David Evans, who taught me both history and the appreciation of art as a teenage schoolboy, inspiring me with a lifelong love of both.

I am particularly grateful to Anthony Weldon, who was prepared to take on a novice writer when I was close to giving up hope.

Meanwhile, my editor, Dominic Horsfall, has helped shape, streamline and enhance this book with an attitude of such positivity, but also sensitivity, that each change has felt like a triumph. I have hugely enjoyed working with him.

Above all, I would like to thank Sarah, Helena, Jonny, Lexi, Matilda and Ada, who allowed me, throughout the great COVID lockdown of 2020, to lock myself away writing and ignore my more mundane duties.

List of Key Events

335 BCE	Battle of Pellion, Alexander the Great defeats Illyrian tribes
305 CE	Diocletian retires to Split
886	St Clement is sent to Ohrid
1014	Battle of Kleidion, defeat of Tsar Samoil of Bulgaria by Byzantium
1102	*Pacta Conventa*, great Croat families recognise King of Hungary
1166	Accession of Stefan Nemanja to throne of Serbia
1331-55	Reign of Stefan Dušan, marking high point of Nemanjić dynasty
1377	Tvrtko I becomes first King of Bosnia
1389	First Battle of Kosovo, death of Lazar and Sultan Murad I
1440	Skanderbeg becomes Sanjak (Governor) of Dibra
1448	Second Battle of Kosovo, Ottomans defeat Hungarians
1463	Bosnia falls to Ottoman Empire
1493-1592	Croatia and Dalmatia come steadily under Ottoman control
1565-79	Tenure of Sokollu Mehmed Pasha as Grand Vizier of Ottoman Empire
1697	Election of Danilo as Vladika of Montenegro, first of the Petrović dynasty
1699	Treaty of Karlowitz, Hapsburgs take control of Croatia and Slavonia, Venice takes Dalmatia
1804-13	First Serbian Uprising under Karadjordje
1805-10	Tenure of Marshal Marmont as Governor of Dalmatia
1815-7	Second Serbian Uprising under Miloš Obrenović
1830	Accession of Petar II (Njegoš) as Vladika of Montenegro
1848	Croatian army under Jelačić helps Hapsburgs suppress Hungarian revolt
1860	Accession of Prince (later King) Nikola of Montenegro
1867	Withdrawal of Ottomans from Belgrade
1878	Congress of Berlin, Bosnia occupied by Austria-Hungary, first meeting of League of Prizren, Niš liberated by Serbia
1903	Assassination of King Alexander I of Serbia (Obrenović), accession of King Peter I (Karadjordjević), Ilinden uprising in Macedonia
1908	Austria-Hungary annexes Bosnia, Young Turk revolution
1912-3	First Balkan War, Balkan League vs. Ottomans

1913	Second Balkan War, Bulgaria vs. Serbia and Greece
1914	Assassination of Franz Ferdinand in Sarajevo, outbreak of First World War
1915	Serbian army retreat over the mountains
1918	Advance from the Salonika front, end of First World War
1919-20	Brief rule of Gabriele D'Annunzio over Free State of Fiume
1928	Assassination of Stjepan Radić
1929	King Alexander I of Yugoslavia (Karadjordjević) introduces personal dictatorship
1934	Assassination of Alexander I, Prince Paul becomes regent
1941	German invasion of Yugoslavia
1945	End of Second World War, abolition of Yugoslav monarchy, Tito comes to power in reunified Yugoslavia
1948	Tito breaks with Stalin
1966	Dismissal of Aleksandar Ranković, easing of political repression in Yugoslavia
1980	Death of Tito
1989	Slobodan Milošević becomes President of Serbia, Gazimestan speech at Battle of Kosovo site
1991	Slovenia leaves Yugoslavia, Croatian War, Macedonia declares independence
1992	Vance Plan achieves ceasefire in Croatia, Bosnian Serbs declare autonomy, Siege of Sarajevo begins
1995	Dayton peace agreement, end of Bosnian War, collapse of autonomous State of Krajina
1996	Siege of Sarajevo lifted
1999	Kosovo War, NATO bombing and administration of Kosovo, death of Franjo Tudjman
2000	Milošević loses presidential election to Vojislav Koštunica
2001	Milošević extradited to The Hague
2004	Slovenia joins EU
2006	Death of Milošević in custody
2008	Kosovo declares independence
2013	Croatia joins EU
2018	Former Yugoslav Republic of Macedonia changes name to North Macedonia

List of Selected Rulers

SERBIA *Period of rule*

Stefan Nemanja (St Simeon)	1166-96
Stefan Nemanjić (the First-Crowned)	1196-1228
Stefan Radoslav	1228-34
Stefan Vladislav	1234-43
Stefan Uroš I (the Great)	1243-76
Stefan Dragutin	1276-82
Stefan Uroš II Milutin	1282-1321
Stefan Konstantin	1321-2
Stefan Uroš III Dečanski	1322-31
Stefan Uroš IV Dušan	1331-46 (as King of Serbia)
	1346-55 (as Emperor of Serbia)
Stefan Uroš V (the Weak)	1346-55 (as King of Serbia)
	1355-71 (as Emperor of Serbia)
Lazar Hrebeljanović	1371-89
Miloš Obrenović I	1815-39 (first reign)
Milan Obrenović II	1839
Mihailo Obrenović III	1839-42 (first reign)
Alexander Karadjordjević	1842-58
Miloš Obrenović I	1858-60 (second reign)
Mihailo Obrenović III	1860-68 (second reign)
Milan Obrenović IV	1868-82 (as Prince of Serbia)
	1882-9 (as Milan I, King of Serbia)
Alexander I Obrenović	1889-1903
Peter I Karadjordjević	1903-18 (as King of Serbia)

YUGOSLAVIA

	Period of rule
Peter I Karadjordjević	1918-21 (as King of Serbs, Croats and Slovenes)
Alexander I Karadjordjević	1921-34
Paul Karadjordjević (Prince Paul)	1934-41 (as Regent)
Peter II Karadjordjević	1934-45

MONTENEGRO

	Period of rule
Petar I Petrović-Njegoš (St Petar of Cetinje)	1784-1830
Petar II Petrović-Njegoš (Njegoš)	1830-1851
Danilo II Petrović-Njegoš	1851-52 (as Prince-Bishop of Montenegro)
	1852-60 (as Danilo I, Prince of Montenegro)
Nikola I Petrović-Njegoš	1860-1910 (as Prince of Montenegro)
	1910-8 (as King of Montenegro)

Nemanjić Dynasty

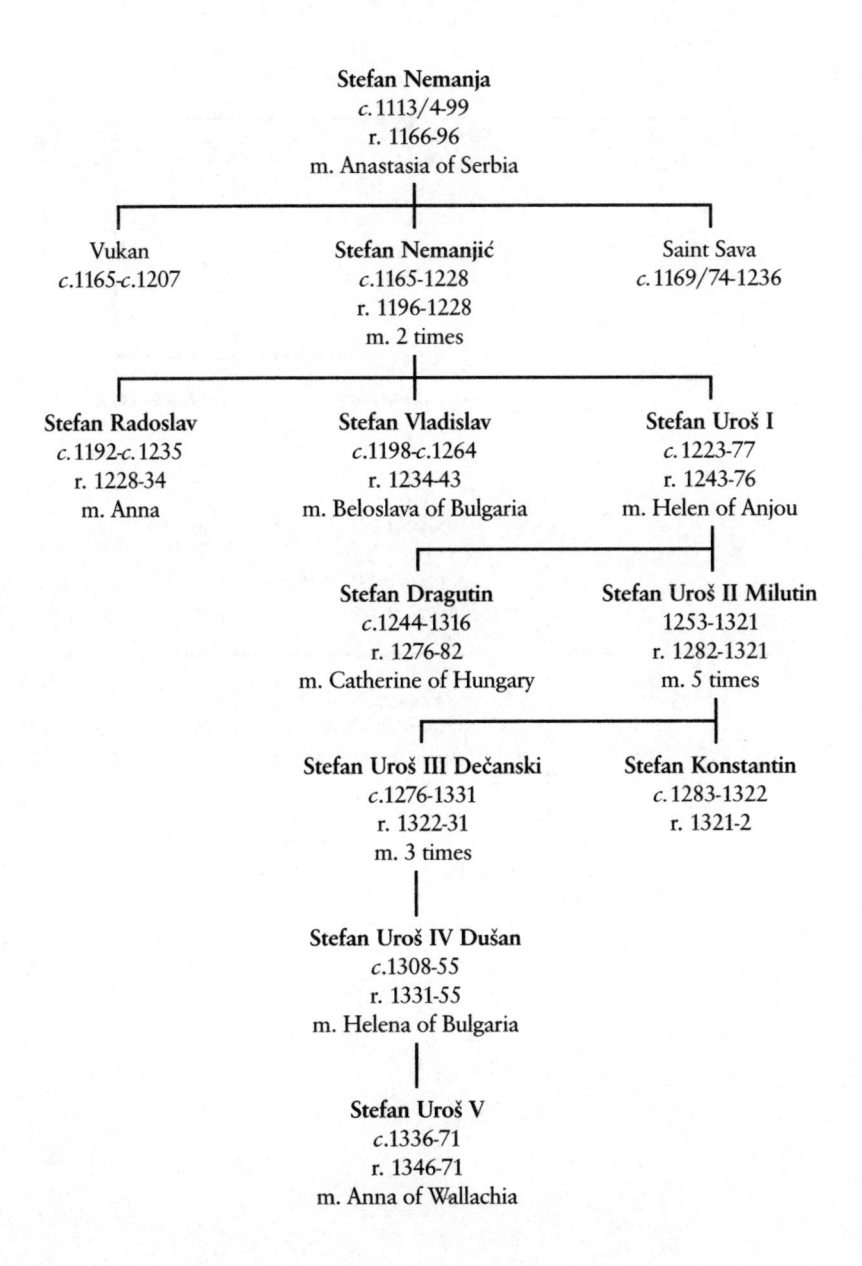

Stefan Nemanja
c. 1113/4-99
r. 1166-96
m. Anastasia of Serbia

- **Vukan**
  *c.*1165-*c.*1207

- **Stefan Nemanjić**
  *c.*1165-1228
  r. 1196-1228
  m. 2 times

- **Saint Sava**
  *c.*1169/74-1236

  - **Stefan Radoslav**
    *c.*1192-*c.*1235
    r. 1228-34
    m. Anna

  - **Stefan Vladislav**
    *c.*1198-*c.*1264
    r. 1234-43
    m. Beloslava of Bulgaria

  - **Stefan Uroš I**
    *c.*1223-77
    r. 1243-76
    m. Helen of Anjou

    - **Stefan Dragutin**
      *c.*1244-1316
      r. 1276-82
      m. Catherine of Hungary

    - **Stefan Uroš II Milutin**
      1253-1321
      r. 1282-1321
      m. 5 times

      - **Stefan Uroš III Dečanski**
        *c.*1276-1331
        r. 1322-31
        m. 3 times

      - **Stefan Konstantin**
        *c.*1283-1322
        r. 1321-2

        Stefan Uroš IV Dušan
        *c.*1308-55
        r. 1331-55
        m. Helena of Bulgaria

        Stefan Uroš V
        *c.*1336-71
        r. 1346-71
        m. Anna of Wallachia

Petrović-Njegoš Dynasty

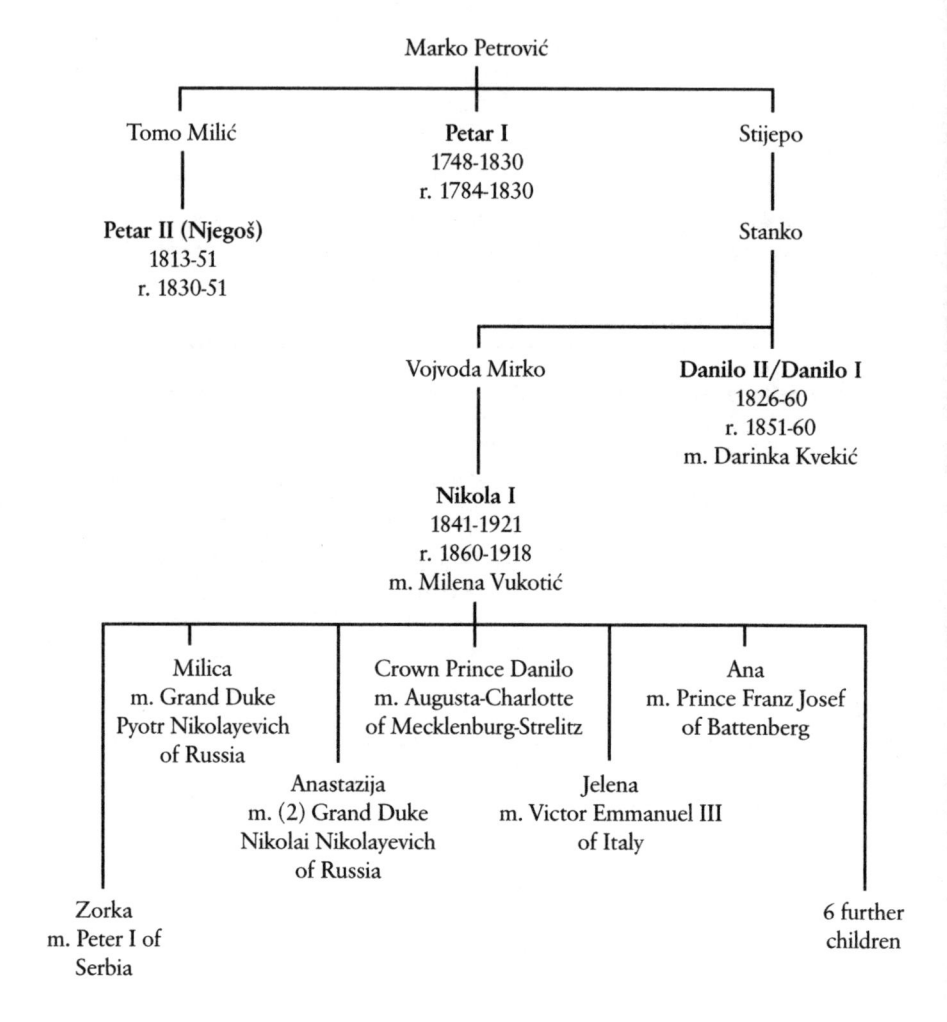

```
                              Marko Petrović
          ┌──────────────────────┼──────────────────────┐
     Tomo Milić              Petar I                 Stijepo
                             1748-1830
     Petar II (Njegoš)       r. 1784-1830            Stanko
     1813-51
     r. 1830-51
                                         ┌──────────────┴──────────────┐
                                   Vojvoda Mirko              Danilo II/Danilo I
                                                                  1826-60
                                                                  r. 1851-60
                                                                  m. Darinka Kvekić
                                      Nikola I
                                      1841-1921
                                      r. 1860-1918
                                      m. Milena Vukotić
  ┌──────────────────┬──────────────────┼──────────────────┬──────────────────┐
  Milica              Crown Prince Danilo                   Ana
  m. Grand Duke       m. Augusta-Charlotte                  m. Prince Franz Josef
  Pyotr Nikolayevich  of Mecklenburg-Strelitz               of Battenberg
  of Russia
                          Anastazija                 Jelena
                          m. (2) Grand Duke          m. Victor Emmanuel III
                          Nikolai Nikolayevich       of Italy
                          of Russia
  Zorka                                                                6 further
  m. Peter I of                                                        children
  Serbia
```

Karadjordjević Dynasty

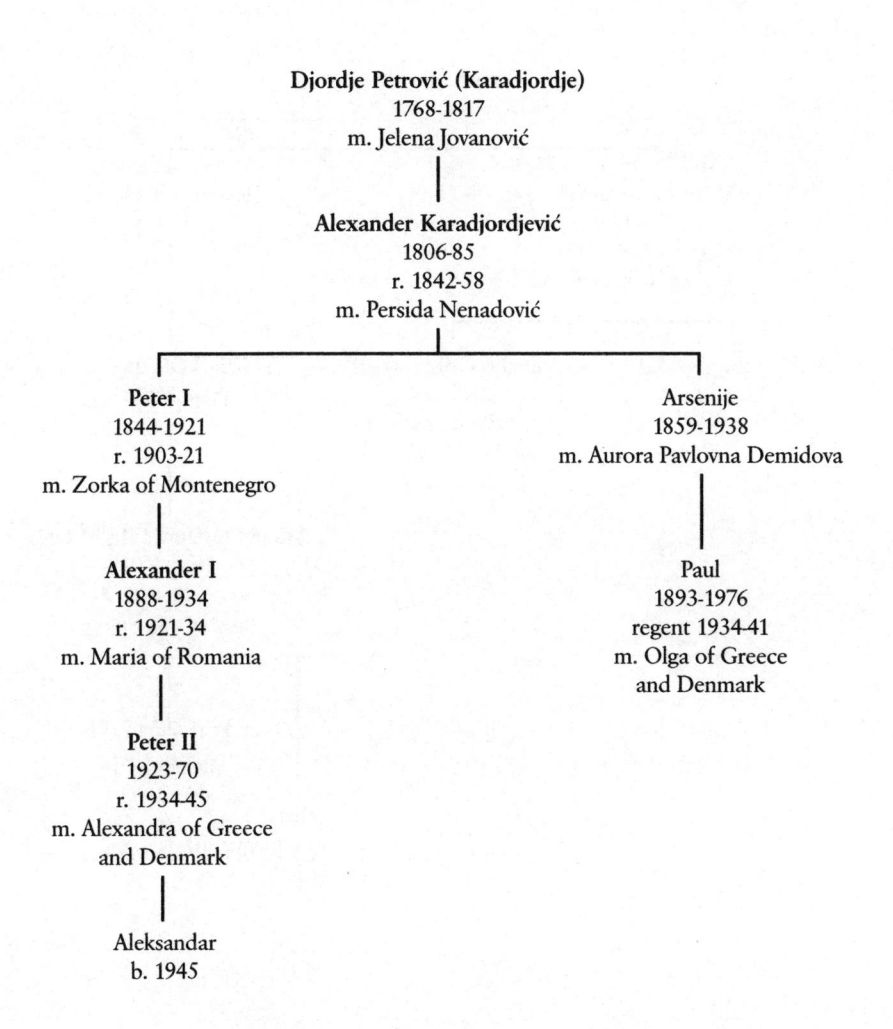

```
                    Djordje Petrović (Karadjordje)
                              1768-1817
                          m. Jelena Jovanović
                                  │
                       Alexander Karadjordjević
                              1806-85
                             r. 1842-58
                         m. Persida Nenadović
          ┌───────────────────────┴───────────────────────┐
        Peter I                                        Arsenije
       1844-1921                                       1859-1938
       r. 1903-21                              m. Aurora Pavlovna Demidova
    m. Zorka of Montenegro                               │
          │                                            Paul
      Alexander I                                     1893-1976
       1888-1934                                    regent 1934-41
       r. 1921-34                                 m. Olga of Greece
    m. Maria of Romania                             and Denmark
          │
        Peter II
        1923-70
       r. 1934-45
   m. Alexandra of Greece
       and Denmark
          │
       Aleksandar
        b. 1945
```

Obrenović Dynasty

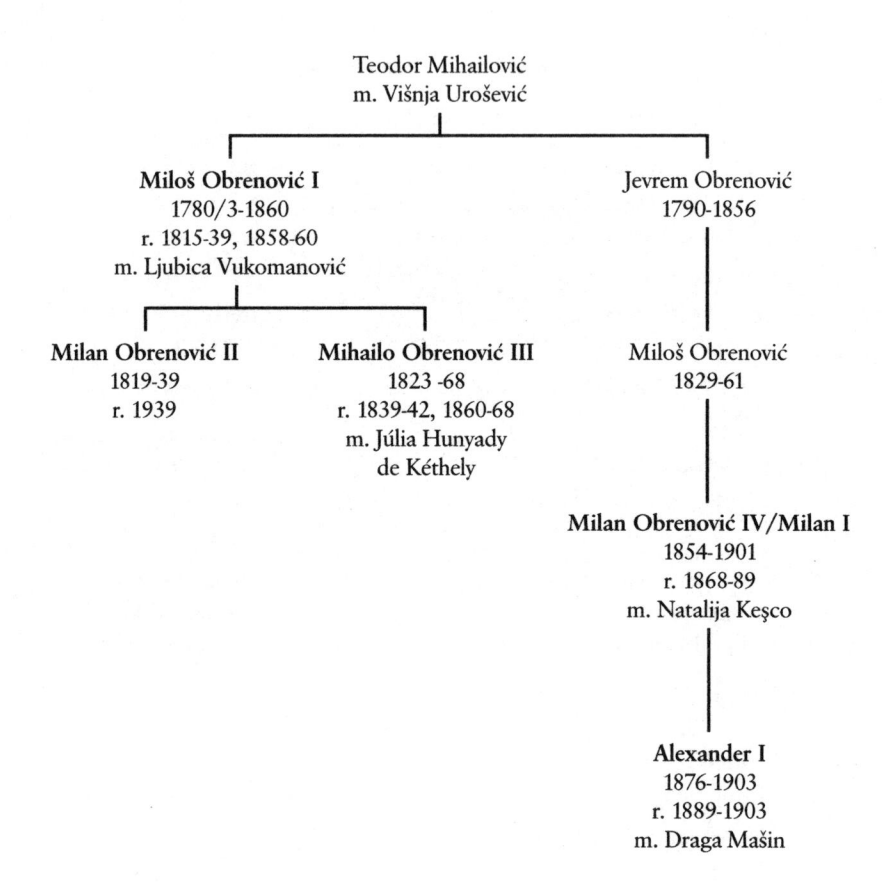

Teodor Mihailović
m. Višnja Urošević

Miloš Obrenović I
1780/3-1860
r. 1815-39, 1858-60
m. Ljubica Vukomanović

Jevrem Obrenović
1790-1856

Milan Obrenović II
1819-39
r. 1939

Mihailo Obrenović III
1823 -68
r. 1839-42, 1860-68
m. Júlia Hunyady
de Kéthely

Miloš Obrenović
1829-61

Milan Obrenović IV/Milan I
1854-1901
r. 1868-89
m. Natalija Keşco

Alexander I
1876-1903
r. 1889-1903
m. Draga Mašin

Bibliography

Albright, Madeleine, *Madam Secretary: A Memoir*, Miramax, 2003
Andrić, Ivo, *The Bridge over the Drina*, 1945, tr. Lovett F. Edwards, George Allen & Unwin Ltd, 1959
Andrić, Ivo, *Bosnian Chronicle*, 1945, tr. Joseph Hitrec, Alfred Knopf, 1963
Andrić, Ivo, *The Woman from Sarajevo*, 1945, tr. Joseph Hitrec, Calder & Boyars, 1966
Andrić, Ivo, *The Damned Yard and Other Stories*, 1954, tr. Celia Hawksworth, Dereta, 2000
Ashdown, Paddy, *Swords and Ploughshares*, Weidenfeld & Nicolson, 2007
Henry Baerlein, *The Birth of Yugoslavia, Volume 1*, Leonard Parsons, 1922
Balfour, Sir John, *Not Too Correct an Aureole*, Michael Russell, 1983
Balfour, Neil and Sally Mackay, *Paul of Yugoslavia: Britain's Maligned Friend*, Hamish Hamilton, 1980
Butcher, Tim, *The Trigger*, Chatto & Windus, 2014
Chang, Jung and Jon Halliday, *Mao, The Unknown Story*, Jonathan Cape, 2005
Channon, Henry "Chips", *The Diaries 1918-38* and *1938-43*, ed. Simon Heffer, Hutchinson, 2021
Churchill, Winston, *The World Crisis: 1911-1918*, Thornton Butterworth, 1923-31
Clancy, Tim, *Bosnia & Herzegovina*, Bradt Travel Guides Ltd, 2004
Clark, Christopher, *The Sleepwalkers: How Europe Went to War in 1914*, Allen Lane, 2012
Clark, Victoria, *Why Angels Fall*, Macmillan, 2000
Colville, John, *The Fringes of Power: Downing Street Diaries 1939-55*, Hodder & Stoughton, 1985
Cooper, Duff, *The Duff Cooper Diaries*, ed. John Julius Norwich, Orion, 2005
Ćosić, Dobrica, *A Time of Death*, 1978, tr. Muriel Heppell, Harcourt Brace Jovanovich, 1983
Dalrymple, William, *From the Holy Mountain*, HarperCollins, 1997

Damjanović, Dragan, "Polychrome Roof Tiles and National Style in Nineteenth-Century Croatia", *Journal of the Society of Architectural Historians*, 2011
Dayot, Armand, *La Serbie Glorieuse*, L'Art et les Artistes, 1917
Demick, Barbara, *Besieged. Life Under Fire on a Sarajevo Street*, Granta, 2012
Djilas, Milovan, *Conversations with Stalin*, Harcourt Brace Jovanovich, 1962
Djilas, Milovan, *Land without Justice*, Harcourt Brace Jovanovich, 1958
Djilas, Milovan, *Tito: The Story from the Inside*, 1980, tr. Vasilije Kojic and Richard Hayes, Weidenfeld & Nicolson, London, 1981
Drakulić, Slavenka, *They Would Never Hurt a Fly*, Abacus, 2004
Drašković, Vuk, *Knife*, 1982, tr. Milo Yelesiyevich, The Serbian Classics Press, 2000
Durham, M. E., *Albania and the Albanians: Selected Articles and Letters, 1903-1944*, ed. Bejtullah Destani, Centre for Albanian Studies, 2001
Durham, M. E., *Some Tribal Origins, Laws and Customs of the Balkans*, Allen & Unwin, 1928
Durham, M. E., *Through the Land of the Serb*, Edward Arnold, 1904
Durrell, Lawrence, *White Eagles over Serbia*, Faber & Faber, 1957
Elsie, Robert (ed.), *Gathering Clouds: The Roots of Ethnic Cleansing in Kosovo and Macedonia - Early Twentieth-Century Documents*, Dukagjini Publishing House, 2002
Evans, Thammy, *Macedonia*, Bradt Travel Guides Ltd, 2004
Fortier Jones, Paul, *With Serbia into Exile*, W. Briggs, 1916
Frankopan, Peter, *Croatia Through Writers' Eyes*, eds. Francis Gooding and Stephen Lavington, Eland, 2006
Galloway, Steven, *The Cellist of Sarajevo*, Atlantic Books, 2008
Gilbert, Martin, *The First World War: A Complete History*, Weidenfeld & Nicholson, 1994
Glendinning, Victoria, *Rebecca West: A Life*, Weidenfeld & Nicholson, 1987
Glenny, Misha, *The Balkans, 1804-1999: Nationalism, War and the Great Powers*, Granta, 1999 (2012 ed. with new epilogue)
Gowing, Elizabeth, *Travels in Blood and Honey: Becoming a Beekeeper in Kosovo*, Signal Books, 2011
Gunther, John, *Inside Europe*, Hamish Hamilton, 1936
Hall, Brian, *The Impossible Country*, Martin Secker & Warburg, 1994
Hall, Brian, *Rebecca West's War*, The New Yorker, 1996
Hammond, Andrew (ed.), *Through Another Europe: An Anthology of Travel Writing on the Balkans*, Signal Books, 2009

Hawton, Nick, *Europe's Most Wanted Man: The Quest for Radovan Karadzic*, Hutchinson, 2009
Hegarty, Neil, *Frost: That Was the Life That Was*, WH Allen, 2015
Holbrooke, Richard, *To End a War*, Random House, 1998
Hussain, Tharik, Minarets in the Mountains, Bradt, 2021
İçduygu, Ahmet and Deniz Sert, *The Changing Waves of Migration from the Balkans to Turkey: A Historical Account*, Springer, 2015
Jennings, Christian, *Bosnia's Million Bones*, Palgrave Macmillan, 2013
Jergović, Miljenko, *Sarajevo Marlboro*, 1994, tr. Stela Tomasević, Penguin, 1997
Jezernik, Božidar, *Wild Europe, The Balkans in the Gaze of Western Travellers*, Saqi Books, 2004, in association with the Bosnian Institute
Judah, Tim, *Kosovo: What Everyone Needs to Know*, Oxford University Press, 2008
Judah, Tim, *The Serbs*, Yale University Press, 1997
Kadare, Ismail, *Chronicle in Stone*, 1971, tr. Arshi Pipa, Canongate, 2007
Kadare, Ismail, *The Traitor's Niche*, 1984, tr. John Hodgson, Penguin Random House, 2017
Kadare, Ismail, *Three Elegies for Kosovo*, 1998, tr. Peter Constantine, Harvill Secker, 2000
Kaplan, Robert, *Balkan Ghosts*, St Martin's Press, 1993
Kapor, Momo, *A Guide to the Serbian Mentality*, Dereta, 2008
Kennan, George F., *The Other Balkan Wars: A 1913 Carnegie Endowment Inquiry in Retrospect with a New Introduction and Reflections on the Present Conflict*, Carnegie Endowment for International Peace, 1993
Knaus, Verena and Gail Warrander, *Kosovo*, Bradt Travel Guides Ltd, 2007
Krleža, Miroslav, *On the Edge of Reason*, 1938, tr. Zora Depolo, Quartet Books, 1987
Lampe, John, *Yugoslavia as History: Twice There was a Country*, Cambridge University Press, 2000
Lane Fox, Robin, *Alexander the Great*, Penguin, 1986
Adam LeBor, *Milosevic: A Biography*, Bloomsbury, 2002
Leigh Fermor, Patrick, *Mani: Travels in the Southern Peloponnese*, John Murray, 1958
Letcher, Piers, and Rudolf Abraham, *Croatia*, Bradt Travel Guides Ltd, 2007
Anthony Loyd, *My War Gone By, I Miss It So*, September Publishing, 2015
Maclean, Fitzroy, *Eastern Approaches*, Jonathan Cape, 1949

Major, John, *The Autobiography*, HarperCollins, 1999
Malcolm, Noel, *Bosnia: A Short History*, Macmillan, 1994
Malcolm, Noel, *Kosovo: A Short History*, Macmillan, 1998
Marriott, J. A. R., *The Eastern Question*, Oxford: Clarendon Press, 1917
Martis, Nikolaos K., *The Falsification of Macedonian History*, 1984, tr. John Philip Smith, Alexander S. Onassis Public Benefit Foundation, 1989
Mazower, Mark, *The Balkans: From the End of Byzantium to the Present Day*, Weidenfeld & Nicholson, 2000
Mazower, Mark, *Salonica: City of Ghosts*, HarperCollins, 2004
Meštrović, Maria, *Ivan Meštrović, The Making of a Master*, Stacey International, 2008
Michalski, Sergiusz, *Public Monuments: Art in Political Bondage 1870-1997*, Reaktion Books, 1998
Mironski, Jasmina, *Mother Teresa: The Light is Still Burning*, 2003
Mitchell, Laurence, Serbia, Bradt Travel Guides Ltd, 2005
Morrison, Kenneth and Elizabeth Roberts, *The Sandžak: A History*, Hurst, 2013
Murphy, Dervla, *Through the Embers of Chaos*, John Murray, 2002
Orga, Irfan and Margarete, *Atatürk*, Michael Joseph, 1962
Petrović Njegoš, Petar II, *The Mountain Wreath*, 1847, tr. Vasa D. Mihailovich, unabridged internet edition, 1997
Perica, Vjekoslav, *Balkan Idols: Religion and Nationalism in Yugoslav States*, Oxford University Press, 2002
Pettifer, James (ed.), *The New Macedonian Question*, Palgrave Macmillan, 2001
Phillips, John, *Macedonia: Warlords and Rebels in the Balkans*, Yale University Press, 2004
Plazibat, Danica, *Ivan Meštrović: Imprints in Time and Space*, Muzeji Ivana Meštrovića, 2015
Rellie, Annalisa, *Montenegro*, Bradt Travel Guides Ltd, 2008
Rhodes James, Robert (ed.), *"Chips": The Diaries of Sir Henry Channon*, Weidenfeld & Nicolson, 1993
Riley, John Erik, *Ignoble: On the Trail of Peter Handke's Bosnian Illusions*, Literary Hub, 2019
Roberts, Elizabeth, *Realm of the Black Mountain: A History of Montenegro*, Hurst, 2007
Rose, General Sir Michael, *Fighting for Peace*, The Harvill Press, 1998

Seierstad, Åsne, *With Their Backs to the World*, 2004, tr. Sindre Kardtvedt, Virago, 2005

Sherman, Laura Beth, *Fires on the Mountain: The Macedonian Revolutionary Movement and the Kidnapping of Ellen Stone*, Boulder: East European Monographs, dist. Columbia University Press, 1980

Sitwell, Sir Osbert, *Noble Essences: A Book of Characters*, Little Brown, 1950

Sullivan, Stacy, *Be Not Afraid, for You Have Sons in America*, St Martin's Press, 2004

Swain, Geoffrey, *Tito: A Biography*, I. B. Tauris, 2011

Tanner, Marcus, *Croatia: A Nation Forged in War*, Yale University Press, 1997

Tokić, Mate Nikola, *Croatian Radical Separatism and Diaspora Terrorism During the Cold War*, Purdue University Press, 2020

Tolstoy, Leo, *Anna Karenina*, 1878, tr. Kyrill Zinovieff and Jenny Hughes, Alma Books Ltd, 2008

Wakefield, Alan and Simon Moody, *Under the Devil's Eye: The British Military Experience in Macedonia 1915-18*, Sutton Publishing, 2004

West, Rebecca, *A Train of Powder*, Viking Press, 1955

West, Rebecca, *Black Lamb and Grey Falcon*, Macmillan, 1942

West, Rebecca, *Selected Letters*, ed. Bonny Kime Scott, Yale University Press, 2000

West, Rebecca, *The Meaning of Treason*, Macmillan, 1949

White, Tony, *Another Fool in the Balkans*, Cadogan Guides, 2006

Winchester, Simon, *The Fracture Zone: A Return to the Balkans*, Viking, 1999

Wood, William and A. J. Mann, *The Salonika Front*, A. & C. Black, 1920

Zimmerman, Warren, *Origins of a Catastrophe*, Random House, 1996

Index

Abdul Hamid II, Sultan, 180
Adam, Robert, in Split, 305
Albania, independence movements, 64–5
Albanians, 18
   in Kosovo, 47, 52, 54–5, 61–2, 66, 68
   in North Macedonia, 169, 184, 193
Albright, Madeleine, 75–6
   in Sarajevo, 230–1
   at Vukovar, 266
Aleksandar Karadjordjević, Crown Prince of Serbia, 121
Alexander Karadjordjević, Prince of Serbia, 103–4
   tomb, 87
Alexander the Great, Macedonia and, 163
Alexander I Karadjordjević, King of Yugoslavia, 36, 87–90
   assassination (1934), 89, 168, 275
   and Bulgaria, 89–90
   and Meštrović, 134, 306
Alexander I Obrenović, King of Serbia, 104, 132
   assassination (1903), 104–5, 219
   at Hilandar, 324
Alexander III, Pope, 291
Alexandra, Princess of Greece and Denmark, 93
Alfred, Prince of Montenuovo, 221
Amanpour, Christiane, CNN, 110
Anastasia, wife of Nemanja, 130
Andrić, Ivo, 88, 95, 217, 239
   Bridge over the Drina, 236–8, 241

Travnik Chronicle, 248
Andrijevica, Montenegro, 39–40
   massacre (1944), 40
Angelina, St, 114–15
Apis (Dragutin Dimitrijević), leader of Black Hand, 104–5
Arkan (Željko Ražnatović), leader of Serb Tigers, 95–6, 233
Arsenius, Patriarch, 114
Ashdown, Paddy, High Representative in Bosnia, 232, 298
Atatürk, Mustafa Kemal, 180–1
Athos, Mount, Greece, 323
Auschwitz, 16
Austria-Hungary,
   and Bosnia, 218–19
   and Croatia, 268, 279–80
   First World War, 71, 221–2
   and Serbia, 113–14, 211–12
   victory over Ottomans (1717), 82
Avala, Mount, Monument to the Unknown Hero, 93–4

Babić, Milan, 295
Bader, General Paul, 142
Badija, Croatia, monastery, 312–13, 315
Bajramović, Šaban, musician, 139
Baker, James, US Secretary of State, 230
Balfour, John, 174
Balkan League, against Ottoman Empire, 81
Banja Luka, Bosnia-Herzegovina, 232,

254–7
    Ferhat Pasha Mosque, 255
    Museum of Republika Srpska, 254–5
    twinning, 254
Bansko, North Macedonia, 190–1
Bardylis, Illyrian king, 164
Basil, Byzantine Emperor, 163, 177
Basil, St, 42
Bayezid II, Sultan, 30
Bektashi, Sufi Muslims, 170–1
Belgrade, 46–7, 80–3, 94–110, 157–8
    Church of St Sava, 107–8, 328
    German bombing (1941), 92
    Hotel Moskva, 80
    Kalemegdan park, 81
    Knez Mihailova street, 81
    Meštrović statues, 81
    Museum of Yugoslavia, 97
    Nemanjina street, 46
    New Belgrade, 105
    "New Cemetery", 94–6
    Republic Square, 80–1
    St Mark's Church, 96
    siege of (1456), 266
    Tašmajdan Park, 96
    Tito's mausoleum in Dedinje, 102–3
    Topčider Park, 103
    Waterfront project, 158
    Zemun, 105–6
Beljanica, Mount, 144
Bellucci, Monica, 205
Berenson, Bernard, 90, 133
Berlin, Congress of (1878), 64
    Bosnia and, 218
    Serbia and, 86
Bibesco, Prince Antoine, 175
Bihać, Bosnia-Herzegovina, Muslim enclave, 231
Birčanin, Ilija, *knez*, 118, 119

Birkenau, 16
Bischofhausen, Captain von, 147
Bistrica, River, 56, 63
Bitola (Manastir), North Macedonia, 180–7
    and First Balkan War (1912), 183
    German cemetery, 185–6
    Jewish community, 183
    museum, 180–1
    old bazaar, 185
    Širok Sokak ("Wide Street"), 183
    Yeni Mosque, 183–4
    and Young Turk movement, 180–1
Black Hand movement, 105, 219
Bobovac, Bosnia, 243
Böhme, General, and Kragujevac massacre, 146–8
Bollé, Hermann, architect, 274, 278
Boris, King of Bulgaria, 89–90
Boškoski, Ljube, Lions paramilitary group, 184
Bosna, River, 242
Bosnia,
    Croat Serbs in, 298–9
    Islamisation of, 245
    under Ottomans, 326
Bosnia and Herzegovina, 204–57
    1990 election, 225–6
    1992 independence referendum, 226
    annexation by Austria, 86
    border with Croatia, 255–6
    coastal strip, 316–17
    constitution, 255–6
    and Croat and Serb identities, 223–4
    and disintegration of Yugoslavia, 152–3
    Muslim population, 121, 152–4, 206, 224, 231, 245
    recognition as independent state (1992), 228

Second World War, 224
Slavic nationalism, 219
Bosnian Serbs,
and Serb Autonomous Regions in Bosnia, 226–8
see also Milošević, Slobodan; Mladić; Srebrenica
Bosnian War, 215, 226–34
casualties, 232, 234
Mostar, 211
peace negotiations, 229–33
Višegrad, 238
Boutros-Ghali, Boutros, UN Secretary-General, 231–2
Brailsford, H. N., 162
Bridge over the Drina (Andrić), 236–8, 241
Brijuni Islands, 101
Budva, Montenegro, 37–9
Bulgaria,
First World War, 71
and Macedonia, 163, 181, 186
Bulgars, in Macedonia, 163
Buneva, Mara, IMRO, 198

Cadmus, founder of Thebes, 37
Catherine of Hungary, Princess, 126
Ceca, wife of Arkan, 96
Cetinje, old capital of Montenegro, 25–37
Biljarda residence, 32
Eagle's Crag, 32–3
Hotel Grand, 28–9
monastery, 29–31, 33–4
museum, 32
Channon, Sir Henry "Chips", 90
Charles II, of Austria, 280
Chekalarov, Vasil, IMRO, 162
Chernopeev, Hristo, IMRO, 190–2

Chernyaev, General, 135
Chetniks,
atrocities against Bosnian Muslims, 121
and Battle of the Neretva, 214–15
Croatia, 294–5
resistance to German occupation, 119–21, 147
resistance to Tito, 61–2
China, and Serbia, 158
Churchill, Winston, 252
on Balkan national ambitions, 83
and Prince Paul of Yugoslavia, 92, 148
and Tito's Partisans, 93, 98–9, 121
Ciano, Count Galeazzo, 275
Ciganović, Milan, Black Hand movement, 219
Clark, Kenneth, 90
Cleitus, Illyrian king, 164
Clinton, Bill, US President, 230, 234
Colville, John, 98–9
Constantine, Emperor, birthplace at Niš, 139
Crna Gora mountain, Montenegro, 36–7, 55
Croatia,
atrocities against Serbs, 276–7, 297
and Austria-Hungary, 268, 279–80
declaration of independence (1941), 275–6
independence (1991), 151–2
legacy of Tudjman, 301
modern tourism, 320
Serb population, 295, 320–1
Serbian uprisings, 151–2
within Yugoslavia, 88, 91, 295
see also Krajina; Ustaše movement
Croatian Spring movement, 296
Croatian War, 297–9, 300–1

Vukovar, 263–4, 299, 300
Croats,
  Bosnian, 152
  and Bosnian War, 211
  relations with Serbs, 264, 265
Čubrilović, Vaso, 111
Cuvaj, Slavko, Ban of Croatia, 275
Cyrillic script, 175
Częstochowa, Poland, 17

Dalmatia,
  and Croatia, 277
  Italy and, 275, 302
  Napoleonic era, 310–11
Dalmatinac, Juraj, sculptor, 303
Dandolo, Anna, wife of Stefan the First-Crowned, 126
Danilo I, Petrović-Njegoš, Prince-Bishop of Montenegro, 32–3, 35
Danilo, Crown Prince of Montenegro, 28
Danilo, Prince of Montenegro, 26
D'Annunzio, Gabriele,
  Comandante of Carnaro, 283–5
  as playwright, 283
Danube, River, 110
Dayton peace agreement, Bosnia (1995), 75–6, 153, 232–3, 255
  Croatia and, 299
Deakin, William, 252
Debar, North Macedonia, 172–3
decapitation,
  and display of heads, 163
  Montenegrin custom of, 33
"Declaration of the Bishops of the Serbian Orthodox Church against the Genocide...by the Albanians...on the Serbian Population" (1988), 57–8
del Ponte, Carla, ICT prosecutor, 300
Delčev, Goce, IMRO, 165

Democratic League of Kosovo (LDK), 75, 76
dervishes, Kosovo, 62–3
Dickinson, Charles, US consul in Constantinople, 191
Dimitrijević, Dragutin "Apis", 104–5
Diocletian, Emperor, 303
Djakovo, Croatia, 267–9
  cathedral, 267–8, 269
Djilas, Milovan, 27, 34, 102, 273
  and Tito, 99–100
Djindjić, Zoran, 95, 106
Djoković, Novak, tennis player, 158–9, 240
Djukanović, Milo, 43
Dobro Polje, Battle of (1918), 187
Dobrun Monastery, Bosnia-Herzegovina, 236
Dodik, Milorad, Republika Srpska, 240, 256
Doiran, First Battle of (1917), 186
Doiran, Second Battle of (1918), 187
Drašković, Vuk, 121
Drava, River, 261
Drina, River, 236
  Bridge over, 236–9
Držić, Marin, 319
Dubrovnik, 18, 24, 317–21
  cathedral, 318–19
  Franciscan monastery, 318
  and *Game of Thrones* scenes, 319
  history of, 317–18
  Mount Srdj Napoleonic fort, 319–20
  St Ignatius's Church, 317
  shelling of (1990s), 32, 152
  siege (1806), 319
  Sponza Palace, 319
Duff Cooper, Alfred, 71
Durham, Edith,

on Alexander Obrenović, 104
on Gjakova, 60
on Kruševac, 133
on Monastery of Žiča, 132
on Niš, 138, 139
on Old Servia, 39
on Podgorica, 42
on Serbian retreat (1916), 72
Durmitor, Mount, 214
Duse, Eleonora, 283

eagle, double-headed, 84
earthquakes,
   1667 (Dubrovnik), 317
   1880 (Zagreb), 270
   1963 (Skopje), 169, 198
   1979 (Montenegro), 29, 37
Edward VIII, Duke of Windsor, 181, 293, 321
Einstein, Albert, 112
Einstein, Mileva, 112
Eltz family, Vukovar, 264
Erdoğan, Recep Tayyip, President of Turkey, 235
Eugene of Savoy, Prince, 82, 223
European Union, and Serbia, 158

Falcon Society, 251–2
Fehmiu, Bekim, actor, 157
Ferdinand, Tsar of Bulgaria, 187
Firentinac, Nikola, architect, 309–10
First Balkan War (1912), 28, 65–6, 86–7, 183
First World War, 71–2
   Macedonia, 71, 186–7
   Montenegro, 28, 39–40
   opening of, 221–2
   Serbia, 71–2, 87, 95, 106
Fitzgerald, F. Scott, *The Great Gatsby*, 27

Fiume, 284–5
   see also Rijeka
Fočić, Mehmed-aga, *dahi* (janissary leader), 118, 119
folk music, Albanian, 166
Fonteyn, Margot, 109
food,
   Bosnia-Herzegovina, 209, 213, 242, 249
   Croatia, 262, 287–8, 290, 314
   Kosovo, 48, 60, 76–7
   Montenegro, 29
   North Macedonia, 172, 193
   Poland, 17
   Serbia, 81–2, 109, 117
football, 38–9
Ford, Ford Madox, 175
Franciscan order in Kraljeva Sutjeska, 242–3, 244–5
Frankopan, General Vuk Krsto, 281
Frankopan, Katarina, m. Count Petar Zrinski, 281
Franz Ferdinand, Archduke, assassination, 71, 105, 215, 219–23
Franz Joseph, Austrian Emperor, 36, 219, 222, 268
Franz Joseph of Battenberg, 27
Frashëri brothers, Albanian dervish adherents, 62
Frost, David, interview with Karadžić, 227
Fruška Gora ("Frankish Hills"), Serbia, 113–17
   monasteries, 114

Galičica Mountains, 178
Garašanin, Ilija, 34
Gavrilo, Serbian Patriarch, 43
Genscher, Hans-Dietrich, German Foreign Minister, 297

George VI, King, 93
    and Prince Paul, 90, 91
Georgiev, Vlada, assassin of Alexander of Serbia, 198
Germany,
    Second World War atrocities in Serbia, 92, 116, 117, 141, 143
    Kragujevac massacre, 146–8
    Yugoslav migration to, 100
    and Yugoslavia, 89, 91–2, 141, 214–15, 275
Giesl, General, 222
Gjakova, Kosovo, 60–3
    Bektashi Tekke (dervish lodge), 62
    Catholic cathedral, 63
    clock tower, 60
    Hadum Mosque, 62
    Hotel Çarshia e Jupave, 60
    Taliqi Bridge, 63
Glagolithic alphabet, 175
Glaise-Horstenau, General Edmund, 277
Glenny, Misha, 152
    on First World War, 222
    The Balkans, 82
Goering, Hermann, 89, 91
Goli Otok prison, 100, 139, 290
Gorna Dzhumaya, North Macedonia, 190–1
Gospić, Croatia, 293–4
Grabar-Kitarović, Kolinda, Croatian President, 279
Gračanica Monastery, 50–2
    frescoes, 51–2
Great Britain, First World War, 186–7
Greater Albania, 62, 199
Greater Serbia, 34, 85, 105
    Chetniks and, 121
    Milošević and, 145
Greece, ancient, and Macedonia, 163–4

Greece, modern,
    and Macedonia, 181–2, 198
    and North Macedonia, 164
    Second World War, 198–9
Greek Civil War, 198
Gruevski, Nikola, Macedonian Prime Minister, 184
Gunther, John, 85–6, 100, 175
    on Belgrade, 82

The Hague, War Crimes Tribunal, 154–5, 233
Hall, Brian, 270
HDZ (Croatian Democratic Union), 296
Helen of Anjou, 51
Helena, Princess, of Bulgaria, 236
Helena, St, mother of Emperor Constantine, 139–40
Hellenic Macedonian Committee, 167
Herzegovina, 204
    tobacco, 208–9
    uprisings against Ottomans, 207
    see also Bosnia-Herzegovina; Republika Srpska
Hilandar monastery, Mount Athos, 107, 131, 323–6
Hitler, Adolf,
    Pavelić and, 276
    and Prince Paul of Yugoslavia, 91–2
    and reprisals against Yugoslavia, 120, 142, 214
    waxwork, 168
Holbrooke, Richard, 153
    and Banja Luka, 255
    and Bosnia, 231–2
    and Kosovo, 75
Hoxha, Enver, Albanian leader, 62
Hungarian Revolution (1848-9), 111
Hunyadi, John, 266
Hurshid Pasha, 140

Ilidža, Bosnia-Herzegovina, old spa, 215–16
Ilinden uprising, Macedonia (1903), 165, 168, 182–3, 192
Illyria, 20
Illyrian movement, uprising (1845), 278
Iločki, Nikola, 266
Ilok, Croatia, 266–7
IMRO (Internal Macedonian Revolutionary Organisation), 65, 88, 89, 162, 182
    kidnappings to fund fight, 190–2
    slogan, 168
    and VRMO, 184
Innocent XI, Pope, 267
International Commission on Missing Persons (ICMP), Bosnia, 234
International Criminal Tribunal, The Hague, 154–5, 233
Irig, Serbia, 115
Irinej, Patriarch of Serbian Orthodox Church, 93
Islam,
    in Serbia, 127–8
    and Sufism, 170–1
Istria, Italy and, 284–5
Italy,
    and Croatia (Second World War), 275–6
    Dalmatia and, 275, 302
    and Fiume (Rijeka), 284–5
    invasion of Libya, 86
Ivan, St and Bishop, of Trogir, 310
Ivankovac, Battle of (1804), 84
Izetbegović, Alija, Bosnian President, 211, 226, 233
Izetbegović, Bakir, Bosnian President, 235

Jablanica, Bosnia-Herzegovina, 213–15
    museum, 214
Jajce, Bosnia-Herzegovina, 249–54
    besieged, 250
    catacombs, 251
    Falcon Society building, Museum of the Second AVNOJ Session, 251–2
    fortress, 250
    Franciscan monastery, 251
    St Luke belltower, 251
    St Mary's Church, 251
    temple of Mithras, 251–2
Jasenovac concentration camp, 100
Jashari, Adem, Kosovo Liberation Army, 49–50
Jazak, Serbia, church, 116
Jelačić, Josip, Ban of Croatia, 268, 270, 326
Jevrem Obrenović, 82, 104
Joanikije, Serbian Orthodox Metropolitan, 31
John the Baptist, St, mummified hand of, 29, 30
John of Capistrano, St, 266
John Paul II, Pope, 273
Jones, Paul Fortier, 71–2
Joseph II, Emperor, 289–90
Jurišić, Nikola, General, 290

Kaplan, Robert, 48, 131
Kara Mahmud Pasha, death mask, 32
Karadjordje (Djordje Petrović), 103
    First Serbian Uprising (1804), 84–5, 119
Karadžić, Ljiljana, 227
Karadžić, Radovan, 43, 58, 226–8
    indictment and trial for war crimes, 232, 233–4
Karadžić, Vuk, 227
    The Beginning of the Revolt against

the Dahis (1815), 118–19
Karlovac (Karlstadt), Croatia, 280–1
　palace, 281
Karlowitz, Treaty of (1699), 113, 260, 316–17
Karpoš, King of Kumanovo, 163
Kiril (Cyril), St, 170, 175
Kleidion, Battle of, 177
Kliment (Clement), St, 175
Klimt, Gustav, 80, 134
Knin, Croatia, 293, 294–5, 299–302
　castle, 294, 299
　chapel, 302
　evidence of war, 299, 300
Kolubara, Battle of (1914), 187
Korčula island, Croatia, 311–17
　Chapel of St Roc, 313
　English Piazzetta, 316
　museums, 314–15
　St Mark's Cathedral, 312
Korčula, Battle of (1298), 311
Kordić, Dario, Bosnian Croat commander, 233, 250
Kosovo, 46–77
　and Albanian independence movements, 65–6, 88
　Albanian–Serb population split, 47, 52, 54–5, 66, 68
　autonomous region in Serbia, 62, 101
　declaration of independence (2008), 76
　Monastery of the Holy Archangels, 66–7
　Muslim refugees (1877-8), 65
　Serbian ethnic cleansing in, 154
　UN administration, 76, 154
Kosovo, First Battle of (1389), 53, 72–3, 81
　model of planned Meštrović monument, 134–5

Kosovo Liberation Army, 49–50, 75–6
　graveyard, Prishtina, 74
Kosovo Polje, battlefield, 53, 65, 71–4
　Gazimestan Monument, 72–3
　mausoleum of Sultan Murad, 73–4
　rally on 600th anniversary, 73
Kosovo, Second Battle of (1448), 53
Kosovo War (1990s), 54–5, 57–8, 75–6
　and North Macedonia, 184
Kostajnica, Bosnia-Herzegovina/Croatia border, 256–7
Koštunica, Vojislav, President of Serbia, 154
Kotor, 25
Kotor, Bay of, 24
Kragujevac, Serbia, 146–8
　memorial to German massacre (1941), 146–8
Krajina, 281
　and Croatian War, 298–9
　Serb Republic of, 255, 263, 295
Krakow, Poland, 16
Kraljeva Sutjeska, Bosnia-Herzegovina, 242–6
　Bosnian royal palace, 245
　Franciscans in, 242–3, 244–5
　mausoleum of Bosnian kings, 244
　monastery, 244–5
　oldest house in Bosnia, 245–6
　walled city, 243–4
Kraljevo, Serbia, 132–3
Krasniqi, Adrian, KLA, 56
Krnjević, Juraj, 278
Krušedol monastery, Serbia, 114–15
Kruševac, Serbia, 47, 133–8
　heroes of Kosovo monument (1904), 134
　Russian Church, 135–7
Kruševo, North Macedonia, 182

Krusi, Battle of (1796), 32
Kusturica, Emir, 205
   and Andrićgrad development, 240–1
   Underground (film), 240

Ladislaus, King of Hungary, 279
Lamartine, Alphonse de, 140, 141
Lazar, contact in Belgrade, 108–10
Lazar Hrebeljanović, Prince, Serbian lord, 47, 52–3, 133–4
   First Battle of Kosovo, 53, 65, 73, 81, 151
   remains, 115–16
   sarcophagus, 144–5
lead mines, Mitrovica, 69–70
Lehár, Franz, *The Merry Widow*, 27
Leigh Fermor, Patrick, 119, 261
Leopold I, Emperor, 267
Lim, River, 39, 123
Ljubibratić, Mićo, 207
Lovćen, Mount, Montenegro, 34–7
Loyd, Antony,
   on siege of Sarajevo, 229
   on Tito, 102
Lukić, Milan, Bosnian Serb leader, 238
Lukić, Sreten, 238

Macarius, Archbishop of Peć, 57
Macedonia, 90
   Albanian resistance groups (Second World War), 172
   ancient, 163–4
   Bulgarian independence forces, 162
   Bulgarian occupation, 169
   concept of, 198
   First World War, 71, 186–7
   League of Prizren and, 64–5
   Muslim refugees (1877-8), 65
   regional tensions, 198–200
   uprisings against Ottomans, 181–3
   see also IMRO; North Macedonia
Macedonian language, 163, 167
Maček, Vladko, 275, 278
Maclean, Fitzroy, 99, 121, 172, 215, 252
   in Jajce, 249–50
   in Korčula, 313–14
Maglič, Nemanjić fortress, 132
Malcolm, Noel, 245
Manastir *see* Bitola
Maria Feodorovna, Dowager Empress of Russia, 30
Maria Theresa, Empress, 262
Marina, Princess of Greece, 90
Marko, King, of Serbia, 188–9
   and talking horse Šarac, 189
Marmont, Marshal Auguste de, 33
   and walls of Trogir, 310–11
Mašin, Draga, wife of Alexander Obrenović, 104, 105
Matka, Lake, 193
Mediana, near Niš, birthplace of Constantine, 139–40
Mehmed Ali Pasha, Ottoman official, 64
Mehmed II, Sultan, 243
Mehmed III, Sultan, 48
Meštrović, Elizabeth, 92
Meštrović, Ivan, sculptor, 36, 89, 327
   Monument to the Unknown Hero, 93
   and Prince Paul, 92
   in Split, 302–3, 305–8
   statues, 81, 111, 269, 319
Metodi (Methodius), St, 175
Mihailo Obrenović III, Prince of Serbia, 80–1, 103–4
Mihailov, Ivan, IMRO, 198
Mihailović, Dragoljub "Draža", 272
   and Chetnik resistance (1941), 119, 120, 121, 123, 147–8

statue, 122
Milan, Edict of (313 AD), 139
Milan Obrenović, King of Serbia, 104, 140
   tomb of, 114–15
Milano, Bonino da, 302
Milanović, Zoran, Croatian President, 279
Milena, Queen of Montenegro, 28
Mileševa Monastery, Serbia, 123–5
   frescoes, 124–5
Miletić, Svetozar, 111–12
Milica, wife of Prince Lazar, 133
Miljacka River, 217
Miloš Obrenović I, Prince, founder of dynasty, 82, 103, 149
   ban on nationalist songs, 118
   Second Serbian Uprising (1815), 85, 103
Milošević, Marko (son of Slobodan), 156–7
Milošević, Mira (Mirjana Marković) (wife of Slobodan), 149, 155
Milošević, Slobodan, President of Serbia, 21, 149–56, 327
   and 600th anniversary of Battle of Kosovo, 73, 145, 151
   and Bosnian Serbs, 232, 233
   character, 155–6
   death in prison, 155
   and disintegration of Yugoslavia, 150–2
   at Hilandar, 325
   indictment for war crimes, 154–5
   and Kosovan Serbs, 58
   and Kosovo, 154
   rise to power, 150–1
   Special Operations Unit, 106
   and Tudjman, 296, 299
Milutin *see* Stefan Uroš II Milutin
Milvian Bridge, Battle of (312 AD), 140
Mišić, Field Marshal Živojin, 187
Mitević, Dušan, on Miloševiću, 149–50
Mithras, temple at Jajce, 251–2
Mitrovica, Kosovo, 67–71
   concentration camp, 69
   lead mines, 69–70
   North Mitrovica (Serb), 67–8, 69
   Sokolica Monastery, 68–9
   Zvečan Castle, 68, 69–70
Mladić, Ratko, Bosnian Serb commander, 153, 158, 226, 233
   and Srebrenica, 231
Montenegro, 18, 19, 24–43
   attacks on Dubrovnik, 319–20
   blood feuds, 27
   fêted in Europe, 26–7
   incorporated into Serbia (1918), 40
   relations with Serbia, 151
   reputation as fighters, 26–7, 28
   and secession of part of Kosovo, 64
   severing of noses, 60
Morača Monastery, 40–1
   frescoes, 40–1
Morača, River, 39, 42
Morava River, 47
Mostar, Bosnia-Herzegovina, 209–13
   evidence of war, 209–10
   Koski Mehmed Pasha Mosque, 212
   restoration, 211, 212
   Stari most bridge, 210–12
   Vidoški fortress, 209
Murad I, Sultan, 52–3, 189
   mausoleum, 73–4
Muslims,
   in Bosnia, 121, 153–4, 206, 224, 231, 245
   mass expulsions (1877 and 1878), 65
   in Serbia, 127–8

Mussolini, Benito,
  and Pavelić, 275
  waxwork, 168
Musulin, Baron Alexander von, 222

NATO,
  air attacks on Bosnian Serbs, 153, 231
  bombing of Serbia, Kosovo and Montenegro (1999), 76, 153–4
  KFOR in Kosovo, 68, 76
  and siege of Sarajevo, 230
Naum, St, 175, 178
Nemanjić dynasty,
  Serbia, 40–1, 51, 52, 116, 126
  see also Stefan Nemanja
Nenadović, Aleksa, *knez*, 118, 119
Neretva, Battle of the (1943), 213–14
  film (1969), 213–14
Neretva, River, 212
Nicolson, Harold, 92
Nikola I, Petrović-Njegoš, King of Montenegro, 25–6, 28, 40, 86
  dynastic connections, 27, 86
  statue, 43
Nikšić, 26
Ninski, Bishop Grgur (Gregory of Nin), 307–8
Niš, Serbia, 135, 138–43
  Bubanj Hill, 141, 143
  Ćele kula ("Tower of Skulls"), 140–1
  fort, 138
  Logor Crveni Krst (Red Cross Camp) concentration camp, 141–2
  monument to King Milan Obrenović, 139
  mosques, 138
Nišava, River, 138
Niyazi Bey, Young Turk leader, 181
Njegoš, Prince-Bishop of Montenegro
  see Petar II

Njeguši, Montenegro, 25
Non-Aligned Movement, 97, 224
North Macedonia, 162–200
  Albanian minority in, 169, 199
  demography, 187, 199
  and EU accession, 164, 200
  independence referendum (1991), 193
  internal tensions, 198, 199–200
  name of, 164, 193
  Slav population, 163
noses, severing of, 60
Novi Pazar, Serbia, 125, 127–8
  Altun Alem mosque, 127
  Church of the Holy Apostles Peter and Paul, 128–9
Novi Sad, Serbia, 110–13
  Catholic cathedral, 111
  Franz Joseph Bridge, 113
  Hungarian massacre (1942) memorials, 112–13
  Orthodox Bishop's Palace, 112
  Petrovaradin Fort, 113
  synagogue, 112
Novo Brdo,
  castle ruins, 52, 53
  mines, 52, 53–4
Novo Hopovo Monastery, Serbia, 115
Nugent, Albert, 286
Nugent, Ana, 286
Nugent, Artur, 286
Nugent von Westmeath, Graf Laval, 285–6
Nureyev, Rudolf, 109

Obrenović dynasty, mansion, 103
Odescalchi, Livio, 267
Ohrid Agreement (2001), 184, 199
Ohrid, Lake, 173, 175
Ohrid, North Macedonia, 174–8

Archbishopric of, 175–6
as centre of learning, 175
Church of St Bogoroditsa Perybleptos, 177
Church of St John, 177
Fortress of Tsar Samoil, 177
St Sophia church, 176–7
Olga, Princess of Greece, 90
On the Milky Road (film), 205
Orthodox Church, 19
and forced conversion to Catholicism (Croatia), 276
Macedonian, 199
Montenegrin, 31
and politics, 325–6
Serbian, 31, 57, 107, 113–14, 116
Osijek, Croatia, 260–2
Church of St Michael the Archangel, 261–2
Church of St Peter and St Paul, 260–1
Gallery of Fine Arts, 261
Ostrog Monastery, 30, 42–3
Ottoman Empire, 18, 24
and 1718 Treaty of Požarevac, 149
attack on Serbia (1813), 85
cedes part of Kosovo to Montenegro, 64
and First Balkan War, 183
and Ilinden uprising, 168
legacy of, 328–9
and Macedonia, 181–2
Montenegrin and Serbian attack on (1876), 26
Serbian agreement with (1815), 85
Our Lady of Philermos, at Cetinje, 32
Owen, David, and Vance Plan, 229–30
Oxenberg, Catherine, 92
OZNA, Yugoslav secret police, 99

Pag island, Croatia, 293
Paget, Lady, 108
Pale, Bosnia-Herzegovina, Karadžić's headquarters, 227, 231, 233–4
Paris, Serbian statues (Place de Colombie), 81
Paris, Treaty of, 284
Partisans, Communist resistance group, Second World War, 93, 98–9, 120–1, 148
and Battle of the Neretva (1943), 213–15
in Macedonia, 172
Pašić, Nikola, Serbian Prime Minister, 222
Paul Karadjordjević, Prince, Regent of Yugoslavia, 90–2, 148, 326
Pavelić, Ante, Ustaše leader, 89, 91, 224, 274–7
and Cardinal Stepinac, 272
and Mussolini, 275–6
in Vukovar, 265–6
Pawlikowski, Pawel, *Serbian Epics* (documentary), 227–8
Peć, Patriarchate of, 56–7
frescoes, 56–7
Peja, League of, 65
Peja (Peć), Kosovo, 55–60
Bajrakli Mosque, 55
street names, 56
Pellion, Battle of (335 BC), 164
Perković, "Thompson", 279
Perón, Juan, President of Argentina, 91
Petar I Petrović-Njegoš (St Petar of Cetinje), 30, 33
Petar II, Petrović-Njegoš, Prince-Bishop of Montenegro, 31, 32, 33, 34–7
statues, 36–7, 239
The Mountain Wreath (poem), 32–3, 34, 35–6
Peter I, King of Serbia (Peter

Karadjordjević), 27, 28, 65–6, 86–7, 104, 132
Peter II (Karadjordjević), King of Yugoslavia, 30, 42–3, 92–3, 99
Petrović, Djordje *see* Karadjordje
Petrović dynasty, 25
Philip II of Macedon, 175
Plavšić, Biljana, former President of Republika Srpska, 328
Pliva, River, 251
Podgorica, Montenegro, 26, 40–3
    Crna Gora Hotel, 41–2
Poland, 15–17
    food, 17
Polish-Lithuania Commonwealth, 16–17
Polo, Marco, 311
Požarevac, Serbia, 148–59
    1718 treaty with Austria, Venice and Ottoman Empire, 149
    Bambipark, 156–7
    home of Slobodan Milošević, Nemanjina street, 149
    recreation area, 156
Poznan, Poland, 15
Prespa, Lake, 178
Prilep, North Macedonia, 188–92
    King Marko's fortress, 188–9
    Monastery of St Michael the Archangel, 188–9
    Monastery of Treskavec, 189–90
Princip, Gavrilo,
    assassin of Archduke Franz Ferdinand, 103, 105, 218, 219–23
    statue, 223
Prishtina, Kosovo, 47–55, 74–7
    ethnographic museum, 49
    Fatih Mosque, 48
    Jewish cemetery, 74
    Martyrs' Hill, 74
    National Library, 50
    Pirinaz Mosque, 48
Prizren, Kosovo, 63–7
    League of Prizren Museum, 64
    Monastery of the Holy Archangels, 66–7
    Orthodox Church of St Saviour, 66
    Sinan Pasha mosque, 66
Prizren, League of, 62, 64–5

Rab island, Croatia, 290–3
    Campanile of St Mary, 292
    cathedral, 291–2
    harbour, 291
    Kandarola Beach, 293
Rački, Franjo, 268, 278
Radić, Stjepan, 89, 98, 278
    assassination, 275
    statue, 270–1
Radoslav, grandson of Nemanja, 130
Raffael, monk at Cetinje, 29–31, 33–4
Ranković, Aleksander, 62, 100–1
    and OZNA, 99
Rapallo, Treaty of (1920), 284
Ras, Serbia, ancient capital of Nemanjas, 126
Raška region, Serbia, 82, 125
Raška, River, 126
Ravanica Monastery, Serbia, 144–5
    sarcophagus of Lazar, 144–5
Rayevski, Colonel Nikolai (model for Tolstoy's Count Vronsky), 135–7, 138
Ražnatović, Anastasija (daughter of Arkan), 158
Republika Srpska (part of Bosnia), 153, 157, 204, 254, 256
    declaration of, 226
    organised crime, 328
Richard I, King, the Lionheart, 318
Rijeka, Croatia (Fiume), 280, 281–8

Adriatic Palace, 282
  Capuchin Church of Our Lady of Lourdes, 282
  Maritime History Museum, 283
  palace of Gabriele D'Annunzio, 283, 284
  Sušak, 282–3
Roma population,
  Croatia, 276
  Skopje, 196
Roman Empire, 20
Roman International Exhibition (1911), 134
Rose, General Sir Michael,
  on Izetbegović, 226
  on Karadžić, 227
  on Mladić, 226
Rugova, Ibrahim,
  statue, 77
  tomb, 74–5
Rumelia, Ottoman region, 164
Russia,
  assassination of imperial family (1918), 88
  Azov region, 15
  and Serbia, 222

Šabac, Serbia, German atrocity (1941), 116
St Mark, winged lion of, 25, 37
St Naum Monastery, North Macedonia, 178–80
  Church of the Holy Archangels, 179
  frescoes, 179
  iconostasis, 179
Salonika (Thessaloniki), 92
Samoil, Tsar, Bulgarian Emperor, 177
Sandanski, Yane, IMRO leader, 190–2
Šar Mountains, 169
Sarajevo, Bosnia-Herzegovina, 215–35

Ali Pasha Mosque, 235
assassination of Archduke Franz Ferdinand, 219–23
Austrian-Ottoman division, 217, 223
Begova Mosque, 225
Bosnia Hotel, 216–17
evidence of war, 225
Grbavica suburb, 233
Latin Bridge, 218
liberation (1945), 224
mortar strikes on Markale market, 230, 231
museum, 222
non-ethnic *Naša stranka* party, 235, 327–8
Ottoman bridges, 217–18
St Mark's Cemetery, 222–3
Serbian Orthodox church, 224
shelling of, 227–8
siege of (1992-96), 153, 228–31, 235
Vrbanja Bridge, 234
Winter Olympics (1984), 217
Sava, Father, abbot of Visoki Dečani Monastery, 59
Sava, St, 41, 56, 107, 124, 130
Schmidt, Friedrich von, architect, 274
Schopenhauer, Arthur, 329
Scowcroft, Brent, US national security adviser, 326–7
Second Balkan War, 186
Second World War,
  Bosnia and Herzegovina, 224
  Croatia, 275–6
  German reprisals, 92, 116, 117, 141, 143
    Kragujevac massacre, 146–8
  Greece, 198–9
  Kosovo Albanians, 61–2
  in Macedonia, 172
  Montenegro, 40

Serbia, 91–3
  Yugoslavia, 95, 141, 326
  see also Chetniks; Partisans
Senj, Croatia, 288–90
  Josephine gate, 289–90
Serbia, 18, 91–3
  atrocities in Yugoslav wars, 152–3, 298
  and Austria-Hungary, 219
  and European Union, 158
  First Balkan War, 86–7
  First World War, 71–2, 87, 95, 106
  and Kosovo, 65–6, 73, 75–6
  and Macedonia, 181, 186, 199
  Muslims in, 127–8
  National Museum, 90
  Russian influence, 158, 159
  secessionist regions, 82
  under Milošević, 157–8
Serbian army, retreat to Albania (1915-16), 40, 42, 71–2, 87, 213
Serbian Uprising, First (1804), 84–5, 117, 118–19, 140–1
Serbian Uprising, Second (1815), 85
Shaw, Jane, 286
Šibenik, Croatia, 302–3
  cathedral, 302
silver mines, Novo Brdo, Kosovo, 52, 53–4
Simeon, St (Stefan Nemanja), 41, 130, 131
Simpson, Wallis, Duchess of Windsor, 293, 321
Sindjelić, Stevan, Serbian commander, 140, 141
Sitwell, Osbert, 283, 284
Skadar, Lake, 36, 38
Skanderbeg, Albanian national hero, 48, 77
  statue, 172

Skanderbeg Division, SS unit, 40, 61–2
Skopje, North Macedonia, 162–9, 193–200
  1963 earthquake, 169, 198
  birthplace of Mother Theresa, 196–7
  bridge, 163
  Čaršija Turkish area, 164–5
  Church of St Andrew, 193
  Kale Fortress, 166–7
  Makedonia street, 197–8
  Monastery of St Panteleimon, 194–6
  Museum of the Macedonian Struggle, 167–8
  Mustafa Pasha Mosque, 165–6
  old bridge site, 168–9
  St Dimitri church, 167
  Šuto Orizari area, 196
  Sveti Spas church, 165
Slav migrations, 18
Slovenia,
  independence, 151
  within Yugoslavia, 88
Sokolica Monastery, Kosovo, 68–9
Sokollu Mehmed Pasha, grand vizier, 57, 205–6, 237
Sophie (Chotek), Archduchess, assassination, 215, 220–1
Sopoćani Monastery, 125–6
Špegelj, Martin, Croat Defence Minister, 297
Split, Croatia, 302–9
  Baptistery of St John, 303
  Capogrosso fortified residence, 307
  Cathedral of St Domnius, 304
  Church of St Martin, 308–9
  museum of Meštrović's work, 306–7
  palace of Diocletian, 303
  seafront, 305
Srebrenica, Serb massacre of Bosnian Muslims, 153, 231

Sredska, Church of St George, 67
Sremska Ravanica-Vrdnik monastery, 115–16
Sremski Karlovci, Serbia, 113
  Patriarch of, 326
Stalin, Joseph, and Tito, 99, 100, 101
Stambolić, Ivan, later President of Serbia, 106, 149–50, 154
Stanko, Blessed Martyr, 42
Stari Trg, Kosovo, 70
statues,
  equestrian, 48, 80–1
  King Marko, 189
  Skopje, 162–3, 199
Stefan Dragutin, Prince, 126
Stefan Lazarević, Prince, 81
Stefan Nemanja (later St Simeon), founder of dynasty, 40–1, 68, 130, 131, 325
  re-christening, 128
Stefan Nemanjić, the First Crowned, King of Serbia, 42, 130
Stefan Radoslav, King of Serbia, 130
Stefan Uroš I the Great, King of Serbia 125–6
Stefan Uroš II Milutin, King of Serbia, 51, 58, 319
Stefan Uroš III Dečanski, King of Serbia, 58, 59, 60
Stefan Uroš IV Dušan, Emperor of Serbia, 58, 66, 96, 166, 189, 236
  at Hilandar, 324
Stefan Uroš V, St, the Weak, Emperor of Serbia, 52, 116, 188
Stefan Vladislav, King of Serbia, 124
Stepinac, Cardinal Alojzije, 271–3, 306
Stjepan Kotromanić, Ban of Bosnia, 243, 244
Stjepan Tomašević, last King of Bosnia, 243, 251
Stojadinović, Milan, Prime Minister of Yugoslavia, 90–1
Stone, Ellen, kidnapping by IMRO, 190–2
Strossmayer, Bishop Josip Juraj, 267, 268–9, 274
  statue, 269
Struga, North Macedonia, 173
Studenica Monastery, Serbia, 130–1
  carvings, 130
  frescoes, 131
Sufism, 170–1
Sulzberger, C. L., 168
Šumadija region, Serbia, 146
Sutjeska River, 46
Swain, Geoffrey, 100

Tatiana, Grand Duchess of Russia, 88
Tennyson, Alfred, Lord, 26
Ternina, Milka, 279
Tesla, Nikola, 306
  statue, 294
Tetovo, North Macedonia, 169–73
  Bektashi Tekke, Sufi monastery, 170–1
  mosque, 169–70
  under Serb control (1913), 169
Thaçi, Hashim, President of Kosovo, 76
Theodora Komnene, Byzantine princess, 196
Theresa, Mother, 196–7
Tigers, Serb paramilitary force, 95–6
Tischler, Robert, 186
Tito (Josip Broz), 20, 62, 97–102, 326, 327
  break with Stalin, 99, 100, 101
  and Catholic Church, 272–3
  cult of, 102
  election as marshal, 252
  and film of *Battle of the Neretva*, 214

Fitzroy Maclean and, 249–50, 313–14
and Fiume, 285
funeral, 102
as leader of Communist Party, 98
and Partisans (Second World War), 98–9, 120–1, 148
political skills, 100–1
tobacco, crop, 188, 208–9
Tolstoy, Leo, and model for Count Vronsky, 135–7, 138
Tomislav, King of Croatia, 312
Topola, Serbia, 84–94
    Church of St George, 85–6
    Karadjordje's "palace", 85
Travnik, Bosnia-Herzegovina, 246–9
    coffeehouses, 247
    fortress, 246–7
    Holocaust monument, 248
    Ivo Andrić Museum, 248–9
    Jeni Mosque, 247
    Jewish cemetery, 247–8
Trebević, Mount, 235
Trebinje, Bosnia-Herzegovina, 204–9
    Arslanagić Bridge, 205–6
    Duži Monastery, 207–8
    memorials, 207
    museum, 206–7
    Muslim population, 206
Trebišnjica, River, 205
Trepča, mining company, 69–70
Treskavec, Monastery of, 189–90
Trogir, Croatia, 309–11
    Cathedral of St Lovro, 309–10
    Kamerlengo Fortress, 310
Trotsky, Leon, 65
Trsat, Croatia, 285–7
    castle, 285–6
    Church of Our Lady of Trsat, 286–7
    Franciscan monastery, 287

Tsilka, Katerina, kidnapped by IMRO, 191, 192
Tudjman, Franjo, president of Croatia, 151, 152, 233, 295–9, 327
    and attack on Mostar, 211
    at Banja Luka, 232
    and Bosnia, 298–9
    legacy, 300–1
    and Milošević, 296, 299
    statue, 300
    tomb, 279
    and Vukovar, 263
Turkey *see* Ottoman Empire
Tvrda, Croatia, 262
    Church of the Holy Cross, 262
    fortress, 260, 261
Tvrtko, King of Bosnia, 228, 243

Ukraine, Russian invasion (2022), 159
Una, Battle of (1483), 313
United Nations,
    arms embargo on Yugoslavia, 228–9
    and Bosnian War peace negotiations, 229–32
    peacekeepers
        in Bosnia, 230, 231–2, 234
        in Krajina, 297, 298
    Vance Plan (1992), 152
United States,
    and Bosnian War, 230, 231, 233
    and Greece, 198–9
    and Yugoslav wars, 153
Urban V, Pope, 287
Uroš the Great *see* Stefan Uroš I
Uskoks, pirates, 288–9
Ustaše movement (Ustaša Croatian Revolutionary Movement), 89, 272, 275
    atrocities against Serbs, 91, 100, 120, 276–7

Užice, Serbia, 123

Valjevo, Serbia, 117–23
  Hotel Grand, 117
  Muselim's House, 118
Vance, Cyrus, 229
Vance Plan (1992),
  Bosnia, 229–30
  Croatia, 152
Vasojevići clan, Montenegro, 39–40
Vatopedi Monastery, Greece, 323
Venice,
  and 1718 Treaty of Požarevac, 149
  and Senj, 289
Victor Emmanuel, King of Italy, 27
Victoria and Albert Museum, Great War Exhibition (1915), 134
Vinaver, Stanislas, Yugoslav press bureau, 174
Vis, island, Croatia, 99, 311
Višegrad, Bosnia-Herzegovina, 235–42
  Andrićgrad development, 239–41
  ethnic cleansing, 238
  ethnic communities, 237
  Muslim graveyard, 241–2
  Serbian military cemetery, 241
Visoki Dečani Monastery, 58–60
Vitaz, Bosnia-Herzegovina, 246
Vladislav *see* Stefan Vladislav
VMRO party, North Macedonia, 184
Vojvodina region, Serbia, 82, 101, 110–11
  German population, 111
  Hungarian minority in, 111
Vrbas valley, Bosnia-Herzegovina, 249
Vučedol pottery, Iron Age, 265
Vučić, Aleksander, President of Serbia, 96, 158, 159
Vuk Branković, 51

Vuka, River, 262
Vukovar, Croatia, 262–7
  evidence of war, 262–3
  Franciscan monastery, 264–5
  Serbian attacks on, 152
  siege of, 263–4
  site of massacre (1991), 266

West, Rebecca, 19–20, 326, 329
  on Alexander I of Serbia, 88
  on Andrijevica, 39–40
  on Belgrade, 82
  on Bitola, 183, 185–6
  Black Lamb and Grey Falcon, 17–18, 20, 37, 92
  on Cetinje, 25
  dislike of Tolstoy, 136
  in Dubrovnik, 318–19
  on Gračanica Monastery, 50–1, 52
  on Ilidža, 216
  on monastery of St Naum, 178, 179–80
  on Monastery of St Panteleimon, 195–6
  and Monument to the Unknown Hero, 93–4
  on Mostar bridge, 210
  in Ohrid, 174
  on Prince Paul of Yugoslavia, 92
  on Prishtina, 47
  romantic attachments, 175
  on sarcophagus of Lazar, 144–5
  in Skopje, 164–5
  in Split, 305
  on Sremski Karlovci, 114
  on Stari Trg, Kosovo, 70
  in Struga, 173
  support for Mihailović, 121
  at Sušak, 282

in Travnik, 247–8
on Zagreb, 280
Wilkinson, Sir John Gardner, 33
Winter Olympics (1984), 217, 235
Woollcott, Alexander, 21
Wrocław, Poland, 16, 17

Young Turk movement, 65, 181
    uprising (1908), 181
Yugoslav Academy of Sciences and Arts, Zagreb, 269
Yugoslav Wars, 54–5, 57–8, 75–6, 151–4, 212, 261
    legacy of, 327–8
    and scale of corruption, 157–8
    see also Bosnian War; Croatian War
Yugoslavia,
    anti-German coup (1941), 92
    creation of state, 88–9
    disintegration, 20, 150–2, 327
    federal state (from 1945), 99
    and Germany, 89, 91–2
    multi-culturalism in, 327, 328
    nostalgia for, 199–200
    Second World War, 95, 141, 326
    under Tito, 54, 100–2, 109

269
    Yugoslav Academy of Sciences and Arts, 269
Zemun, Belgrade, concentration camp, 106
Žerajić, Bogdan, 223
Žiča, Monastery of, 132
Zimmermann, Warren, US ambassador to Yugoslavia, 77
    on Izetbegović, 226
    on Milošević, 155
    on Tudjman, 296
    on Yugoslav Wars, 327
Živković, Lieutenant Petar, 104
Zlatar, Mount, 123
Zrinski, Count Petar, 281
Zvečan Castle, Mitrovica, 68, 69–70
Zvečan, Mitrovica, lead mines, 68, 69–70

Zadar, Croatia, 298
Zagreb, Croatia, 270–80, 298
    cathedral, 271, 273
    Church of St Mark, 274
    Gradec (old town), 271
    Kaptol (cathedral quarter), 271
    Mirogoj Cemetery, 278–9
    Museum of Broken Relationships, 277–8
    statues, 270–1
    Stone Gate, 273–4
    Strossmayer Gallery of Old Masters,

Nine Elms is an independent specialist imprint that is dedicated to bringing you the most creative and interesting minds in contemporary writing today.

From crime fiction and history to biography, **Nine Elms** features a diverse list of titles, showcasing both well established and exciting new authors.

※※※

NINE ELMS BOOKS
Unit 6B, Clapham North Arts Centre,
26-32 Voltaire Road, London SW4 6DH

TEL + 44 (0)20 7720 6767
EMAIL info@nineelmsbooks.co.uk
WEB nineelmsbooks.co.uk

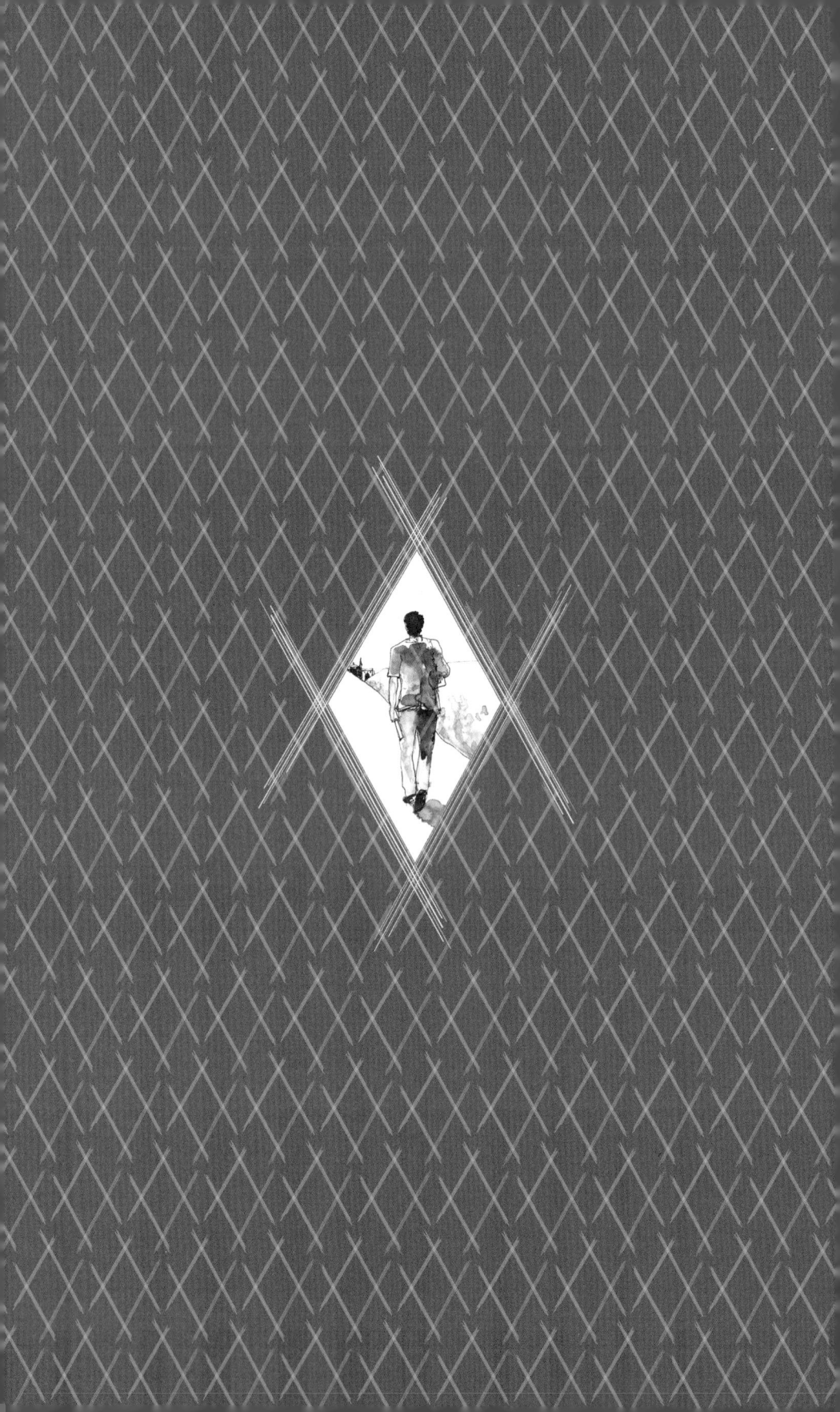